THE ROAD TO POVERTY

Although urban poverty in America commands a great deal of attention in the media, the rate of poverty in rural America is fifty percent higher: one out of four children in rural America lives in destitution. This is particularly true in Central Appalachia, which has become a symbol of intractable poverty and the failure of public policy. Sadly, the problem of chronic low income is as persistent there today as it was in 1964, when President Lyndon Johnson visited and announced his famous War on Poverty. How poverty develops and why it remains are the broader topics of this provocative social historical analysis of poverty in a rural Appalachian county.

Dwight Billings and Kathleen Blee examine the making of wealth and inequality in persistently poor rural communities through the history of Clay County, an especially poor section of the Eastern Kentucky mountains in Appalachia. Though this area has been the target of repeated antipoverty and economic development programs, few of these have had a lasting impact. The authors uncover the systemic problems and patterns of low income by tracing the economic, sociocultural, and political development of Clay County from early agricultural and industrial development in the midnineteenth century to the advent of the timber and coal industry in the twentieth century.

In the process, they take to task the overly simplistic "culture of poverty" and "internal colonialism" explanations for poverty, providing a much more compelling and complex picture that will upset many people's long-held perceptions. Appalachia, the authors remind us, has always been multiracial. Eastern Kentucky, rather than being isolated from the world capitalist system (commonly cited as the reason for its retarded development), was very much a part of it. Billings and Blee analyze economic inequality as the interaction over time of markets, culture, and the local state.

This study of the long-term institutional basis of rural poverty contains fascinating, new historical detail based on the authors' meticulous archival research. This book makes an important contribution to basic research on inequality – pointing to the shortcomings of treating symptomatic problems of low income while failing to address systemic ones – at a time when American policymakers are struggling to design and implement effective programs to overcome poverty.

Dwight B. Billings is Professor of Sociology and Associate Director of the Appalachian Center at the University of Kentucky. He is the author of *Planters and the Making of a "New South": Class, Politics and Development in North Carolina, 1865–1900* (1979) and co-editor of *Appalachia in the Making: The Mountain South in the Nineteenth Century* (1995) and *Confronting Appalachian Stereotypes: Back Talk from an American Region* (1999).

Kathleen M. Blee is Professor of Sociology and Director of the Women's Studies Program at the University of Pittsburgh. She is the author of *Women of the Klan: Racism and Gender in the 1920s* (1991) and editor of *No Middle Ground: Women and Radical Protest* (1998).

THE ROAD TO POVERTY

The Making of Wealth and Hardship in Appalachia

DWIGHT B. BILLINGS
University of Kentucky

KATHLEEN M. BLEE
University of Pittsburgh

PUBLISHED BY THE PRESS SYNDICATE OF THE UNIVERSITY OF CAMBRIDGE
The Pitt Building, Trumpington Street, Cambridge, United Kingdom

CAMBRIDGE UNIVERSITY PRESS
The Edinburgh Building, Cambridge CB2 2RU, UK   http://www.cup.cam.ac.uk
40 West 20th Street, New York, NY 10011-4211, USA   http://www.cup.org
10 Stamford Road, Oakleigh, Melbourne 3166, Australia
Ruiz de Alarcón 13, 28014 Madrid, Spain

First published 2000

Printed in the United States of America

Typeface Garamond 3 11/13 pt.   *System* QuarkXPress [BTS]

A catalog record for this book is available from the British Library.

Library of Congress Cataloging in Publication data
Billings, Dwight B., 1948–
The road to poverty : the making of wealth and hardship in
Appalachia / Dwight B. Billings, Kathleen M. Blee.
p. cm.
ISBN 0-521-65229-4 (hardbound)
1. Poverty – Appalachian Region.   2. Appalachian Region – Economic
policy.   3. Income distribution – Appalachian Region.   I. Blee,
Kathleen M.   II. Title.   III. Title: Making of wealth and hardship
in Appalachia.
HC107.A127B55   1999
330.974′044 – dc21   98-51561
                                                              CIP

ISBN   0 521 65229 4   hardback
ISBN   0 521 65546 3   paperback

To James S. Brown
and the people of Beech Creek

CONTENTS

LIST OF ILLUSTRATIONS

TABLES

PREFACE AND ACKNOWLEDGMENTS

When we began this study, two very different ways of explaining Appalachian poverty had been advanced. An older approach, which attributed the region's persistent poverty to an antiquated system of cultural values, conceived alternatively as a traditionalistic folk culture or a culture of poverty, was giving way to a newer model that conceptualized Appalachia as an exploited internal colony. By documenting the history of railroad building, timbering, and coal mining around the turn of this century, social scientists and historians had shown that the mountain region's poverty needed to be understood in terms of Appalachia's intimate connection to the wider national economy, not its supposed isolation from it. However, it also seemed clear to us that depictions of Appalachia's economic exploitation by absentee corporations begged the question of why such dependency characterized Appalachia's road to rural poverty in the first place. We thus became interested in studying the contours of Appalachian social life before, in the vernacular, "Coal became King," or, to paraphrase a lyric by Kentucky songwriter John Prine, before "Mr. Peabody's coal train done hauled the region away."

We chose a longitudinal case-study approach in order to see why and when Appalachian individuals and households began to experience and cope with impoverishment, and we chose Appalachian Kentucky as a window on the wider Central Appalachian experience. The brilliant ethnographic and survey research of James S. Brown, conducted in the three rural neighborhoods of "Beech Creek" (a pseudonym) in Clay County, Kentucky, beginning in the early 1940s, and on their outmigrants to the urban and industrial Midwest in the 1960s, provided us with an indispensable starting point for the present study.

By first studying the historical trajectories from 1850 to 1910 of the ancestors and their neighbors of the people of Beech Creek, about which Brown taught American social science so much, we began to understand in human terms that profound changes had taken place throughout Appalachian history well before the era of the modern coal industry. And, by comparing the experiences of these Beech Creekers with those of others in the wider but not so distant environment – farmers and merchants, men and women, wealthy people and poor, African Americans and whites – we began to develop a complex picture of Appalachian social change that, we hope, challenges conventional wisdom and stereotypes of the region. At the same time, we hope to have contributed to the broader understandings of regional development, social inequalities, and the efficacy or limits of particular public efforts aimed at social betterment.

When Brown first began studying the already impoverished inhabitants of Beech Creek, he meticulously documented the rapidly vanishing way of life of Appalachian subsistence farming households. What began as a dissertation project directed by Talcott Parsons at Harvard University became a life-long work of science, art, and love for Brown who, to this day, has maintained a relationship of friendship and respect with the people he lived among and visited for almost sixty years. Because our work would not have been possible without his prior labors, direct assistance, and constant encouragement, this book is dedicated to James S. Brown and the people of Beech Creek whom he respected so much.

Many other people have also helped us in this undertaking. Data collection was greatly facilitated, and often made fun, by archivists such as Terry Birdwhistle, Kate Black, Lisa Carter, and Bill Marshall at Special Collections and Archives of the Margaret I. King Library of the University of Kentucky; Shannon Wilson at the Berea College Library; and Mark Wetherington, director of the Filson Club. Laura E. Johnson of the Clay County (Kentucky) Historical Society was also remarkably helpful and generous with her time. We are grateful as well to the staffs of the Baker Library of the Harvard University School of Business, the Clay County (Kentucky) Clerk's Office, the Kentucky Historical Society, the Kentucky State Library and Archives, the Louisville and Nashville Railroad Archives, and the University of Louisville Photographic Archives.

Besides our countless debts to intellectuals whom we know only through their writings, we are grateful to so many scholar/friends for their insights, advice, and encouragement – in some cases over many years, in others at crucial moments. Included are Richard Angelo, Mary Anglin, Tom Arcury, Alan Banks, Fred Bateman, David Brown, Francie Chasen-Lopez, Tim Collins, Wilma Dunaway, Cynthia Duncan, Ronald Eller, Dick Gilbreath, Linda Gordon, Thomas Hakansson, David L. Harvey, James Hougland, John Inscoe, Robert Ireland, Ronald Lewis, Sally Ward Maggard, Clyde McCoy, Virginia McCoy, Mary Beth Pudup, Paul Salstrom, Harry Schwarzweller, Susan Silbey, Gene Summers, Louis Swanson, Ann Tickamyer, Altina Waller, and Halliman Winsborough. The mere listing of their names does so little to convey our deep appreciation and indebtedness. Two special scholar/friends deserve particular thanks. We will be forever grateful to Pam Goldman and Karen Tice for their many years of critique, encouragement, and patience. They heard more about salt and hogs than they might ever have imagined.

In addition to numerous Clay Countians who generously contributed their time and good will for interviews, special thanks, in particular, are due to Jess Wilson, local historian extraordinaire who opened many doors to us onto the past and into the present in Clay County, Kentucky; to James Klotter, State Historian of Kentucky, who pointed us on promising paths many years ago and critiqued a draft of the present volume; to Bart and Kaye Smith and John Colson who provided us with important Clay County oral history and manuscript evidence; to Nancy Blazer who gave us important historical materials; to Beverly White and Evelyn Garrard Strode who provided helpful information on their families; and to Anne Shelby who helped us interview descendants of the Beech Creek neighborhoods. Above all, we are indebted to the painstaking efforts and historical and legal acumen of attorneys Pam Goldman, Sharon Hardesty, and Lee Hardesty who assembled and interpreted over a thousand legal records for us, and to Pam Goldman who pointed us to the history of Clay County's feud.

Further, we are especially grateful to numerous research assistants who carefully coded historical records, especially Roberta Campbell, Gaye Holman, Gloria Lester, Betsy Neale, Jack Thigpen, and Paul Weingartner, and to Cathy Schnegel-Smith who helped proofread the manuscript. Cecil Tickaymer, Louis Swanson, and Jane Eller provided crucial technical expertise at early stages of sampling and data management. Marlene Pettit and Nancy Collins provided much needed clerical support. Such good assistance would not have been possible without generous financial support from the following organizations: the Rural Economic Policy Program of the Aspen Institute for Humanistic Studies; the Berea College Appalachian Center; the Ford Foundation; the Fund for Research on Dispute Resolution of the National Institute for Dispute Resolution; the U.S. Department of Agriculture (Economic Research Service); the U.S. Department of Health and Human Services; the University of Kentucky's Appalachian Center, College of Arts and Sciences, and Division of Research and Graduate Studies; the University of Pittsburgh Faculty of Arts and Sciences; and the University of Wisconsin Institute for Research on Poverty.

Finally, we wish to acknowledge each other. The alphabetical listing of our names does little to convey the extent to which our efforts in this research and writing have been truly equal as well as the mutual satisfaction and joy of collaboration that this project has meant for both of us.

xiii

Grateful acknowledgment is made to the following publishers for permission to reprint sections of the authors' previously published works: Duke University Press for work from *Social Science History*, vol. 20 no. 3 (fall 1996) pp. 345–73, "Race Differences in the Origins and Consequences of Chronic Poverty in Rural Appalachia"; University of North Carolina Press for works from *Southern Cultures*, vol. 2, nos. 3–4 (1996) pp. 329–52, "Where the Sun Set Crimson and the Moon Rose Red" and from *Appalachia in the Making* (UNC, 1995) "Agriculture in the Kentucky Mountains," and "Taking Exception with Exceptionalism"; JAI Press for work from *Sociological Perspectives*, vol. 33, no. 1 (1990), "Family Strategies in a Subsistence Economy"; Law and Society Association for work from *Law and Society Review*, vol. 30 no. 4 (1994), "Violence and Local State Formation: A Longitudinal Case Study of Appalachian Feuding."

I
PUBLIC POLICY AND HISTORICAL SOCIOLOGY

1

INTRODUCTION

Almost a generation ago, the National Advisory Commission on Rural Poverty called attention to the plight of millions of impoverished rural Americans whom it called "the people left behind."[1] Now, after several decades of economic restructuring and political indifference, Americans once again are beginning to recognize rural poverty as a persistent and escalating phenomenon of social life in the United States. Although urban poverty currently commands more attention in the popular media, several recent surveys document the deepening of poverty in rural areas throughout the United States.[2] The rural poverty rate is 50% higher than in urban areas and it is estimated that one out of every four children in rural America is living in poverty.[3]

Just as earlier – when President Lyndon Johnson launched his widely heralded War on Poverty in 1964 from the home of an impoverished family in Appalachian Kentucky – no region of the United States remains more deeply mired in poverty and economic distress than Appalachia.[4] Central Appalachia in particular, as a region of chronic and persistent low income, is virtually synonymous both with rural poverty and with difficulty of implementing effective policies of social betterment.[5] Despite decades of sympathetic attention to the economic distress of Appalachia, however, the *social origins* of its rural poverty, that is, its long-term institutional basis, remain obscure.[6]

Today, there is a pressing need for public policy aimed at eradicating poverty in persistently poor rural areas like Central Appalachia, especially in light of policy demands to move people from welfare to work, but the ability to design effective programs for such areas is hampered by the paucity of basic research on persistently poor communities and populations.[7] The overwhelming emphasis of today's so-called "welfare reform" on changing the behavior of poor individuals diverts attention from the question of how *places* grow poor. The absence of a long-term view on the social dynamics of poor rural areas means that relief measures in Appalachia, however essential, confront symptomatic but not necessarily systemic problems. Contextual and historical patterns have not been adequately investigated.

The severity of Appalachia's seemingly insuperable economic problems and the relative lack of success in efforts to combat its endemic poverty represent important challenges for those committed to a new round of struggle in the twenty-first century against persistent rural poverty. Our goal is to contribute to basic research on the historical roots of chronic rural poverty by investigating cultural, economic, and political development in an especially impoverished section of the eastern Kentucky mountains in rural Appalachia. We hope that a better understanding of the nature of chronic rural poverty will contribute to more fruitful policy initiatives in Central Appalachia and in other persistently poor rural areas in the United States.

Mapping Persistent Poverty

Chronic rural poverty is concentrated in several regions. Figure 1.1 displays the most persistently poor rural counties in the United States. Each of these 540 nonmetropolitan counties is characterized by having had 20% or more of its population living in poverty for each of the past four decennial census years from 1960 through 1990. A cursory glance reveals easily recognizable regions of economic distress – the coastal and delta regions of the Deep South, predominantly Hispanic regions such as the Lower Rio Grande Valley of Texas and New Mexico, Native American territories in Alaska and the West, and, of course, Appalachia.

Defined officially as the 406 counties served by the federal government's Appalachian Regional Commission (ARC), Appalachia is a highly diverse regional entity that includes counties in thirteen states, ranging from New York in the North to Mississippi and Alabama in the South. Although each of its three officially defined subregions (Figure 1.2) is characterized by significantly higher rates of poverty than average for the United States as a whole, the total region – like other poor regions – is highly varied.[8] Northern Appalachia, like other northeastern areas, is currently experiencing economic distress associated with deindustrialization whereas portions of Southern Appalachia benefit from economic growth. Central Appalachia, however, continues to suffer from persistent poverty and underdevelopment. In 1990, for instance, roughly 25% of its population was impoverished, a rate almost double that of the United States as a whole.[9]

A closer examination of Figure 1.1 reveals not only that the most persistently poor Appalachian counties are in Central Appalachia, but that they are mostly in Kentucky. Sixteen of the twenty poorest ARC counties, including nine of the top ten, are there. Indeed, 10% of the poorest counties in the United States are in Kentucky; almost all of these are in the Kentucky mountains. Of the twenty-five counties with the lowest per capita income in the

4

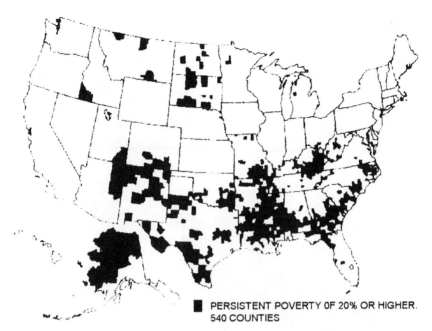

PERSISTENT POVERTY OF 20% OR HIGHER.
540 COUNTIES

Figure 1.1 Nonmetro counties with persistent high poverty, 1960–90. (Courtesy of Calvin Beale, Economic Research Service, U.S. Department of Agriculture).

United States in 1990, six were in Appalachian Kentucky.[10] In this book, we explore the roots of entrenched poverty in Central Appalachia by probing the history of impoverishment and its opposite – the making of wealth – in Appalachian Kentucky. (See Figure 1.3.)

Perhaps it should not be surprising that Appalachian Kentucky would manifest an extreme version of Appalachian poverty. John Fox, Jr., the Kentucky novelist who did much to popularize negative images of Appalachia at the turn of the century, once claimed that "any trait common to the Southern mountaineer seems to be intensified in the mountaineers of Kentucky." The geographer Ellen Churchill Semple argued in 1901 that the "conditions of the Southern Appalachians" could be found "nowhere in such purity or covering so large an area as in the mountain region of Kentucky."[11] Unfortunately, poverty has not been Appalachian Kentucky's only reason for notoriety.

Late nineteenth- and early twentieth-century Appalachian Kentucky was nearly synonymous with violence and social conflict in popular image. Twenty

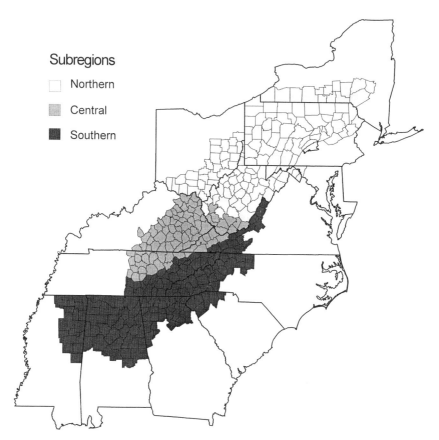

Figure 1.2 ARC designated Appalachian subregions. (Courtesy of the University of Kentucky Appalachian Center).

so-called "family feuds" involving hundreds of casualties and repeated inter-ventions by the state militia earned the Kentucky mountains a reputation as "the Corsica of America" and contributed to enduring stereotypes of Appalachia as a "community of lawlessness."[12] Sensationalistic travelers' accounts exploited images of feuds to depict Appalachian Kentucky as a primitive and untamed place:

> We swept deeper and deeper into the mountains, and traces of civi-lization became scarcer. . . . We were getting into the feudists' country, where the sun set crimson and the moon rose red.[13]

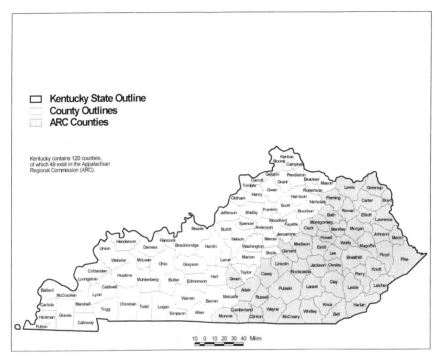

Figure 1.3 Kentucky counties and Appalachian Kentucky. (Courtesy of the University of Kentucky Appalachian Center).

Together with images of poverty and backwardness, stereotypes about feuds seemed to set the Kentucky mountains apart from national norms and suggested that they comprised a culturally distinct region.

In the course of our analysis, we will challenge many stereotypes about Appalachia, including the nature of its feuds, but we will nevertheless explore the historical relationship between feuds and poverty in order to understand how a history of protracted violent conflict has contributed to the inability to address chronic poverty in Appalachian Kentucky.

While we were working on this book, one of Kentucky's two statewide newspapers ran a nine-part series of articles entitled "Little Kingdoms: Local Government at Your Expense" that described widespread corruption, abuses of patronage and nepotism, fiscal irresponsibility, and misgovernance among Kentucky's counties.[14] To the surprise of few in Kentucky, a disproportionate number of the newspaper's examples came from Appalachian Kentucky.

Although the mountain region has been the target of repeated antipoverty and economic development programs, many of these have not lived up to their promise. Economic stagnation in the Kentucky mountains has been reproduced by severe political inertia. Just as contemporary poverty cannot be fully understood without an investigation of its social origins, we cannot comprehend the contemporary corruption, political stagnation, and governmental incapacity that mark so many counties in Appalachian Kentucky today without attention to that history. As we examine the social history of Appalachian poverty, we analyze also the lasting consequences of early political conflicts that deformed public life, helped to define local government as an instrument for private gain, and blunted the capacity of local government to confront poverty and envision alternative futures.[15]

Conventional Models of Appalachian Poverty and Politics

Appalachia's rural poor have been discovered and rediscovered many times throughout the twentieth century.[16] Two principal explanations have been offered for their poverty. Culture-of-poverty theory directs attention to how families and individuals in Appalachia, for better or worse, cope with poverty. The theory of internal colonialism, on the other hand, attempts to focus attention on the structural causes of poverty in Appalachia. Both yield insights, yet each is seriously deficient.

Culture-of-poverty theory gained popularity during the 1960s, but its application to Appalachia was dependent on discursive traditions of Appalachianography that emerged during the late nineteenth century. Conceptualized as a distinct region and people, Appalachia first came into American consciousness in the decades that immediately followed the Civil War. Writers such as James Lane Allen and John Fox, Jr., contributed to a distinct genre of local color fiction that simultaneously created, exploited, and tried to explain images of the mountain South as a place that was vastly out of step, culturally and economically, with the progressive trends of industrializing and urbanizing late nineteenth-century America.[17]

By the turn of the century, William Goddell Frost, president of Berea College in Kentucky and one of the most influential creators of the discourse on Appalachia, had named the people of the southern mountains "Appalachian Americans" and reconciled their presumptive backwardness to the social dynamics of fin de siècle America by pointing to the region's geographical, sociocultural, and economic isolation. Mountain people, Frost said, were "our contemporary ancestors," a surviving remnant of the white pioneer culture that had first settled the eastern seaboard and contributed to the building of early American institutional life.[18] Frost's writings influenced

George Vincent's description of Appalachia in a 1908 article in the *American Journal of Sociology* as a "retarded frontier."[19]

Frost portrayed the people of Appalachia as impoverished yet morally upright and therefore deserving of the charitable and educational uplift efforts that institutions such as Berea College were prepared to offer, with the help of northern philanthropy. Many accounts, however, called attention to seemingly darker aspects of southern mountain culture such as moonshining and feuding. The cover of a 1913 issue of *The Berea {College} Quarterly* focused on "Men Proud of Being Dangerous" (see Photo Essay). This publication, like many others of the period, included articles on "The College and the Feud" and "How to Make Something out of This Fighting Stock" that linked Appalachian poverty and violence to cultural isolation and, at the same time, promoted the efforts of educational institutions like Berea College to modernize the Appalachian region.

As Henry Shapiro's intellectual history of the idea of "Appalachia," *Appalachia on our Mind: The Southern Mountains and Mountaineers in the American Consciousness, 1870-1920*, has ably shown, such early writings about life in the mountain South contributed to the social construction of Appalachia as "a coherent region inhabited by an homogeneous population possessing a uniform culture."[20] Regardless of how people in the mountains defined or identified themselves, the popular representations that created "Appalachia" stressed sameness and identity to the neglect of locality differences and population diversities. Early documentary accounts of the region such as John C. Campbell's *The Southern Highlander and His Homeland* (1921), James Watt Raine's *The Land of the Saddle-bags* (1924), and Samuel Wilson's *The Southern Mountaineers* (1914) contributed to highly selective interpretations of preindustrial Appalachian life that shaped a discourse about the mountains that continues to influence current thinking. They helped to create the enduring image of Appalachia as a region apart, an *other* in the heart of America.

The early social construction of Appalachia as a distinct sociocultural world was reinforced by reform efforts that adapted settlement house programs and other urban-based strategies of benevolence and education to the task of bringing the rural Appalachian poor into the majority culture.[21] Reformers' vision of the region was likewise reinforced by efforts to document and preserve preferred versions of the folk culture of the southern mountains by enthusiasts, for example, of highland crafts and music.[22] Their accounts of the cultural isolation and separateness of the region were augmented by the writings of social scientists and even more importantly by journalists and popular writers. Between 1904 and 1927, at least 476 silent films depicted life in the Southern Appalachians to American moviegoers; 145 of these films featured moonshining and 92 featured feuds along with countless assaults and homicides.[23]

Positively, the early construction of preindustrial Appalachia as an isolated folk culture inspired a later tradition of ethnographic studies of rural Appalachia that continues to provide an indispensable viewpoint on social change in the mountains because of its close attention to daily life, especially family and community institutions.[24] Our study builds on this rich ethnographic legacy in ways we describe in what follows and elsewhere.[25] Negatively, however, the cultural approach reinforced the image of Appalachians as a "people without history" by defining the study of the region as belonging largely to the professional domain of anthropology rather than historiography. Appalachia, it seemed, offered good material for ethnographers, as well as novelists and story writers, but little to warrant the serious attention of historians. Symptomatically in 1922, William Connelley and E. M. Coulter concluded an influential two-volume *History of Kentucky* whose 1,211 pages almost never mentioned Appalachian Kentucky with a brief ethnographic addendum on the "Cumberland Gap Region."[26] As a result of this discursive tradition, a popular writer in the 1960s described the whole of early Appalachia as a place where "time was standing still."[27]

When Appalachian poverty was rediscovered in the 1960s, it was but a short conceptual step from viewing Appalachia as a traditional folk culture to viewing Appalachia as a regionwide culture of poverty. More than any other popular work of that era, Jack Weller's *Yesterday's People: Life in Contemporary Appalachia* made explicit the link between folk society and the culture of poverty in Appalachia.[28] Weller claimed that "independence-turned-individualism" had become a great "stumbling block for [the mountaineers'] finding a place in our complex and cooperative society." Mountaineers' "traditionalism," he argued (quoting Horace Kephart), was "stubborn, sullen, and perverse" and where "fatalism" had become a way of life in Appalachia, "there [was] no rebellion, little questioning, little complaining." In Weller's bleakly pessimistic view, "The greatest challenge of Appalachia, and the most difficult, [was] its people."[29] Such people simply did not want to change in order to improve their lives.

With poor families totaling more than half the population in many Central Appalachian counties during the late 1960s,[30] the depiction of Appalachian culture as approximating a regionwide subculture of poverty made sense to many social scientists, policymakers, and popular writers.[31] Rupert Vance, a distinguished expert in the sociology of the South, wrote:

> Thus mountain isolation, which began as physical isolation enforced
> by rugged topography, became mental and cultural isolation, holding

people in disadvantaged areas, resisting those changes that would bring them into contact with the outside world. The effect of conditions thus becomes a new cause of conditions, but the cause is now an attitude, not a mountain.[32]

The practical implications of this approach were clear: "to change the mountains," Vance asserted, "[was] to change the mountain personality."[33]

Efforts to transform Appalachian personalities by modernizing Appalachian culture went hand in hand with regional economic development efforts. These efforts were based on the assumption that Appalachia suffered economically because, in the language of the President's Appalachian Regional Commission, Appalachia was a "region apart," a place insufficiently integrated into the national "free enterprise orbit."[34] Thus, culture-of-poverty theory, with its stress on cultural isolation, was bolstered conceptually by the combination of neoclassical economic theory and central place theory that guided the development strategies of the Appalachian Regional Commission, which aimed at overcoming economic isolation. "The resulting regional development model," according to one of its critics, was "concerned with providing social overhead capital, training people for skills for new industrial and service jobs, facilitating migration, and promoting the establishment or relocation of privately-owned industries through a growth center strategy."[35] Local projects designed to encourage "maximal feasible participation" of the poor in community development during the War on Poverty thus complemented federal investments by ARC in transportation, education, and health care that were designed to overcome isolation and stimulate economic development, especially in federally designated "growth centers."[36]

VISTA (Volunteers in Service to America) workers and Appalachian Volunteers, like their Peace Corps counterparts in the Third World, initially devoted themselves passionately to cultural modernization in the mountains.[37] Soon, however, many antipoverty workers began to develop a more radical approach. By enlisting the poor in projects designed to overcome fatalism and alienation, they came up against major obstacles to participation – the political and economic powerlessness of those who had been trapped in poverty for generations and the reality of entrenched local power structures that served the interests of absentee corporate owners who monopolized land, mineral resources, and politics. Influenced by the writings of Third World scholars, they began to describe Appalachia as an "internal colony."[38]

Analyzing the causes of Appalachian poverty in 1968, Bob Tanner, a VISTA worker in West Virginia, wrote:

> In West Virginia . . . as throughout Appalachia, we live in a system of
> absentee control by large financial and industrial corporations pursuing
> their economic ends without respect for the lives of the people in the
> state or region. The responsibility for the damage – political, economic,
> and social – can be attributed to these colonial exploiters. . . . West
> Virginia is a rich state. Yet it is obvious that West Virginia is a poor
> state. Much wealth has been extracted from West Virginia's natural
> resources, but little of that wealth has remained in the hands of West
> Virginians.[39]

Appalachia was poor, according to the internal colonialism model, because
of the nature of its integration with – not isolation from – the U.S.
corporate economy. Some contributors to the colonialism model explored
how the denigration of Appalachian culture in culture-of-poverty theory
helped to legitimate the exploitation of the region's land, resources, and
people whereas others interpreted indigenous cultural patterns as forms of
resistance to colonization rather than simply the remnants of an "arrested
frontier."[40] A few activists and scholars romanticized early mountain folkways
to dramatize the effects of exploitation, but most radical scholars shied away
from discussions of Appalachian culture altogether, viewing the latter as
either conducive to victim blaming or as diverting attention from hard-core
economic realities.

   In a widely influential article, Helen Lewis contrasted the Appalachian
subculture and colonialism models by stating that "In simple terms it [the
cause of poverty] is either fatalism or the coal industry."[41] Thus, by the use
of metaphor and metonomy, Lewis and others reshaped the discourse on
Appalachia. The metaphor of colonialism soon largely displaced the metaphor
of folk society in discussions of regional poverty and coal came to symbolize
the whole of Appalachia as an impoverished and exploited region. More than
any other work of the period, however, Harry Caudill's history of Appalachian
Kentucky, *Night Comes to the Cumberlands: Biography of a Depressed Area*,
although marred by cultural stereotypes, forcefully advanced the internal
colonialism model and set the stage for the contributions of a younger generation of scholars and activists in the 1970s and 1980s who documented the
economic exploitation of Appalachia and its impact on the region's culture
and politics.[42]

   Looking back on the culture-of-poverty and internal colonialism models
today, the limits of both are readily apparent. Although still frequently
applied today,[43] culture-of-poverty theory hinges on a faulty view of culture
that leads one to think of Appalachian culture as a collection of traits that
are settled, nonnegotiatory, and fixed. More recent "postmodern" approaches

to Appalachian culture, such as Shapiro's account of the discourses that constructed a "mythic system" about the mountain people and region, enable us to see that essentialistic and universalizing statements about Appalachian people, in fact, derive from assumptions about a complex, intertextual reality, "Appalachia," rather than about the diverse populations actually living there. Images of fatalism, for instance, constitute Appalachians as victims and obscure the possibilities for agency and empowerment, but are refuted by the rich history of struggle and resistance in the region.[44]

Although the culture-of-poverty theory was justly criticized in the 1970s for blatant stereotyping and victim blaming,[45] the model did grasp the fact that remarkably high levels of poverty in rural Appalachian communities represented a systemic problem for those trapped in impoverished conditions and it underlined the extent to which intergenerational experiences of living in poverty are likely to blunt people's faith in personal efficacy.[46] The culture-of-poverty theory erred terribly by attempting to explain chronic poverty in terms of individual behaviors and family patterns, but its emphasis on the consequences of entrenched poverty was potentially suggestive nonetheless.

In the chapters that follow, we recast the culture-of-poverty model in order to examine the means by which impoverished families in Appalachian Kentucky have maintained themselves over time and across generations. Further, we attempt to reread accounts of daily life in Appalachia that were influenced by the culture-of-poverty theory for insights they can be made to disclose about what we will describe as Appalachia's patriarchal moral economy, an agricultural system that featured subsistence farming, kinship cooperation, and various strategies of survival.[47]

The theoretical model that understood Appalachia as an internal colony of the U.S. economy underlined the great extent to which land and mineral resources in Appalachia are owned by nonlocal corporate investors and the adverse effects of this ownership pattern on local taxation, political dependency, and alternative forms of economic development.[48] Despite such important contributions, adherents to the internal colonialism model erred by isolating absentee ownership *per se* as the principal cause of regional poverty.[49] They overlooked the fact that several Central Appalachian states – most notably Kentucky – contained significant sectors of indigenous coal ownership and extraction that were notorious for low wages, job insecurity, and the lack of health and safety benefits for employees in comparison with larger, absentee-owned firms.[50] These theorists also ignored the fact that other coal mining regions – notably Illinois – were even more absentee-owned than Appalachia yet had significantly more equitable tax policies and better diversified local economies.[51] Totalistic arguments about absenteeism failed to probe temporal and spatial variations in how corporate capitalism influences the uneven economic and political development of local and regional society.

Positively, however, the colonial model improved on the culture-of-poverty theory by placing Appalachian history squarely at the center of attention for the first time. Harry Caudill embraced many pejorative views about mountain people commonly associated with the culture-of-poverty theory, but he also tried, at least in part, to account for what he called the "biography of a depressed area" by writing about the history of resource monopolization, railroad penetration, and timbering; the building of coal towns and the boom-and-bust cycles that have endlessly plagued the coal industry; and more generally the economic exploitation of Appalachian Kentucky.[52] His pioneering work was followed up on a regional level some years later by Ronald Eller whose *Miners, Millhands, and Mountaineers* remains the definitive saga of Appalachian colonization and early corporate capitalist industrialization.[53]

Negatively, however, Caudill and subsequent scholars minimized the impact of the local state and political development on poverty and economic development by reducing political domination to a corollary of economic exploitation. Their view reinforced the assumption that Appalachian history really only began with the history of corporate capitalist industrialization in the late nineteenth century. Also, the thinness of scholarly accounts of agriculture and early industry in Appalachia in particular did little to challenge the fallacious assumption that, to borrow an image from a popular John Prine song, Appalachia was a stable and idyllic society before Mr. Peabody's coal train began to haul it away.[54]

In retrospect, then, the internal colonialist interpretation of Appalachian poverty was no less essentialistic than the culture-of-poverty model in how it conceptualized the mountain South. This essentialism explains why as insightful an economist as Ann Markusen would suggest that the structural forces shaping Appalachia "can be reasonably encompassed by beginning with an inquiry into the coal industry" that she described as "the most obvious force in the history of Appalachia."[55] As obvious as the diverse impacts of the coal industry have been on the region, there is nevertheless more to Appalachia than just coal mining.

Even though historically coal mining has exerted a unique and profound influence on many communities in the region, it is important to note that most of Eastern Kentucky's poorest counties are only marginal coal producers and some produce no coal at all. An understanding of Appalachian poverty must explain how corporate capitalist industrialization has fed on, rather than created, Appalachian poverty. It must show how the Appalachian road to persistent poverty was blazed in part by early conditions that proved vulnerable to exploitation yet also provided resources for opposition to exploitation and oppression. Such social capital resources, though hardly a guarantee for victory, continue to encourage "fighting back in Appalachia," as the title of a recent collection of essays on grassroots struggles acknowledges.[56]

Toward A New Approach

In the present study, we examine poverty in Appalachian Kentucky by investigating its history of economic, political, and cultural development. By viewing Appalachian Kentucky's rural poverty in relation to Appalachia's incorporation into and peripheralization in the world capitalist system, we affirm the fundamental insight of the internal colonialism model that Appalachia cannot be studied in isolation.[57] Like prior scholars, we analyze cultural strategies such as reciprocity among kin by which rural Appalachians have maintained themselves across generations. Unlike researchers in the internal colonialist and culture-of-poverty traditions, we also investigate the history of state development and political coercion. In searching for clues about the social origins of the region's poverty before, as they say in Kentucky, coal became king, we give equal attention to the historical impacts of capitalist markets, state coercion, and cultural strategies.

In focusing attention on the early history of Appalachian Kentucky before the building of railroads and coal towns, our approach follows from Barrington Moore's brilliant demonstration that social relations of the past have long-lasting impacts on the processes of economic, political, and cultural development in divergent national economies.[58] Moore showed that social dynamics in the rural sectors of Europe, Asia, and the United States profoundly influenced the motivation and capacity of agrarian classes to sponsor or resist industrialization during the nineteenth and early twentieth centuries as well as whether economic development contributed to authoritarianism or democracy in the places where it flourished.

Moore focused primarily on the "First World" societies that had successfully industrialized, but sociologists who study social change among late developers today follow Moore's lead in concluding that "[i]n general those interested in development focus on industrialization at the expense of agrarian class relations only at their peril."[59] Now, as earlier among developing nations, rural class relations, especially when viewed in a global context, provide a significant key to questions about power and poverty, democracy and development. Thus, just as we have criticized the theory of Appalachian internal colonialism for its exclusive focus on coal, Peter Evans and John Stephens sum up an important lesson from studies of contemporary development in the Third World by concluding succinctly that "those working within the dependency traditions should have paid more attention to agriculture."[60]

In applying this approach to Appalachia, we join a number of other social scientists who have effectively used Moore's model to investigate how specific systems of agriculture have contributed to regionally distinct paths of capitalist development in the United States.[61] It would be extreme to say that if plantation agriculture gives you the deep South, subsistence agriculture gives you Appalachia. We contend, nonetheless, that one cannot fully understand why Appalachia is impoverished today without taking into account the agricultural history of the region. Just as scholars have shown that the history of slavery, debt peonage, and the cotton plantation economy is crucial for understanding the roots of African American poverty and, more generally, social problems in the contemporary South,[62] we contend that the social dynamics of agrarian Appalachia left a lasting imprint on the southern mountains today.

The effects of early agriculture and industry, however, have largely been neglected in the study of Central Appalachia's persistent poverty. An examination of the historical impacts of subsistence agriculture – and what we describe as the cultural strategies of the patriarchal moral economy it sustained – along with the effects of antebellum capitalist industry and commerce will contribute to basic research on the historical roots of chronic poverty. Likewise, analysis of the historical development of the local state in Appalachian Kentucky offers insights into how politics and governance influence the making of poverty and wealth. *Capitalist markets, state coercion*, and *cultural strategies* worked together to set and keep Appalachian Kentucky on a distinct pathway that might be called Appalachia's road to rural poverty.

Finally, as we analyze the economic, political, and cultural history of Appalachian Kentucky, we also critique past discursive efforts to describe these processes. Because such writing has rarely identified actual historical actors in the region, portraying them stereotypically as the faceless victims of history and exploitation, we identify by name and describe many actual persons who struggled to shape and/or resist the changes that were occurring there. We attempt to depict both the wealthy and powerful who left many documentary traces of themselves behind and the common folk about whom written records are more sparse and we make special efforts to identify and discuss individual women and African American Appalachians because they, especially, are absent in much of the past writing about the region. In attempting to convey a sense of Appalachians' agency, we thus rely on the methodological insight of C. Wright Mills that the sociological imagination consists of understanding how history and social structure intersect in biography.

The Beech Creek Studies: A Window on Appalachian Kentucky

Because so much that is assumed about Appalachia is mythical and so little of the region's early history has been properly explored, our approach in this study has both critical and positive components. Throughout each of the chapters that follow, we attempt to challenge critically and deconstruct mythical representations and stereotypes about Appalachia that blunt a clear vision of the region, its past, and its current social problems. Positively, we investigate the historical origins, socioeconomic causes, and political ramifications of poverty in a chronically depressed community in rural Appalachian Kentucky.

Our study is based on a longitudinal historical analysis of Clay County, Kentucky, with particular attention to "Beech Creek," a set of well-studied rural neighborhoods within the county. Clay County and its Beech Creek neighborhoods provide excellent vantage points on persistent poverty in Appalachian Kentucky for several reasons. First, this area is representative of the depth and duration of poverty in the Kentucky mountains as well as the cultural, economic, and political conditions that surround it. As a recent report documents, Clay County lies within a cluster of ten eastern Kentucky counties that are among the most economically distressed communities in Appalachia and in the United States.[63] With an average per capita income of only $6,472 and poverty rates averaging 42% in 1990, each of these ten counties presently has poverty rates at least three times higher than the nation as a whole. Ironically, however, they have received proportionately little of the federal aid allocated by the Appalachian Regional Commission because they fall outside the so-called "growth centers" of Appalachia. Without special attention, such communities can be expected continually to fall economically farther behind the rest of the nation.[64]

Clay County's median income of $8,693 in 1990 ranked it as the twenty-third poorest county in the United States and the seventh poorest in Kentucky,[65] but being identified among the poorest U.S. counties is nothing new for Clay County since it has ranked there for decades. Near the end of the War on Poverty in 1970, it was Kentucky's second most impoverished county when an astonishing 65% of its population lived in poverty, and as late as 1986, it remained the second poorest county in the state.[66] In 1990,

49% of the population in the census tract containing Beech Creek was officially defined as poor as was 40.2% of Clay County's population. An official unemployment rate of 9.4% in 1989 failed to capture the extent of economic distress in the county when the "real" level of unemployment was estimated at a rate of 54.3%. With 43.5% of Clay County's population having less than a ninth-grade education, only three other Kentucky Appalachian counties have lower levels of educational attainment; 28% of its people receive public assistance.[67]

A second reason for selecting Clay County for study is its relationship to coal. Appalachian Kentucky's ten most highly distressed communities are economically varied; five are coal-producing counties and five produce little or no coal. Clay County is not a major coal producer, yet 19% of its paid workforce is employed in the coal industry. Coal mining is an important element in Clay County's struggling economy, but coal alone does not explain the area's long-term poverty.

The very last county in Kentucky to be reached by railroad lines, Clay County was already poor when railroads finally reached there in 1920 and when coal mining became locally important. Once a densely populated subsistence farming community, Beech Creek is located well outside the county's most important mining districts and its history has been shaped largely by forces independent of the vicissitudes of the coal industry. Thus, because of the relatively late date when both were incorporated into the modern corporate capitalist nexus of extractive industry, the socioeconomic development of Beech Creek and Clay County provides a sort of natural experiment that permits us to examine how significant portions of rural Central Appalachia might have developed had they, too, been relatively independent of the effects of the coal industry. By "holding coal constant," so to speak, we are able first to probe the internal logic of Appalachian Kentucky's indigenous agrarian development and then to ask how that social logic influenced historically the nature and consequences of subsequent economic development including coal mining.

Our most important reason for choosing this area for longitudinal study, however, is that so much is already known about Clay County's poor population because of the pioneering sociological research on Beech Creek begun in 1942 by James S. Brown and continued into the 1970s in collaboration with his associates, Harry Schwarzweller and J. J. Mangalam. Carried out independently of the conceptual battles between the culture-of-poverty and internal colonialism theories, this body of work provides a unique observation of rural Appalachians as well as those who chose – or were forced – to leave the Kentucky mountains for hope of opportunity elsewhere.

Introduction

The Ethnographic Baseline

On the eve of World War II, James Brown identified three remote, rural neighborhoods for study in Clay County that were representative of the rapidly vanishing subsistence farming communities of Central Appalachia outside the coal mining districts. The "Laurel" (pseudonym) neighborhood lay along both sides of a principal river and included wide expanses of fertile bottom lands. Much more hilly, yet within easy access of country roads, was "Flat Rock," a small creek-bed community with almost no level land. Most isolated was the "Beech Creek" basin neighborhood where Brown lived while conducting his fieldwork. He described this vicinity as looking like "from the air . . . a great gully with subsidiary ditches branching off in vine-line fashion."[68] Emptying into the river near the Laurel neighborhood, the Beech Creek drainage system had carved a steep and narrow valley that ran about five miles along the stream but was never more than 200 yards wide. Numerous families lived and farmed in the basin area despite its rugged terrain. Although separated by high ridges, the three neighborhoods were closely interconnected by kinship and social interaction. Brown referred to all three simply as "Beech Creek," as do we throughout this book.

Brown's original report on Beech Creek described a system of small, self-sufficient family farms; almost every head of a household[69] in Beech Creek was a farmer when Brown first visited there. His comprehensive analysis of family budgets found that 89% of all farm production was still consumed at home in 1942, and only a small surplus (principally tobacco) was marketed commercially. Despite some part-time wage labor and the influx of government monies through pensions and farm subsidies, cash levels in the poor community were exceedingly low. Annual expenditures averaged only $84 per capita and fully one-third of these expenditures went for farm supplies, one-fourth for food items not produced locally, and one-fifth for clothing. The economics of Beech Creek were thus still insulated in large degree from the market structure of the larger national economy.

In Beech Creek, Brown found a system of interdependent households based on simple (nuclear) families. Internally, they were stratified by age and gender. These households were quite large compared with other rural U.S. families, averaging 5.4 members in 1942. Nonetheless, Brown found that nonnuclear family households were uncommon. Only 23% of all Beech Creek families were extended or multiple units in 1942; 74% were nuclear. Virtually everyone in Beech Creek married, and almost no one lived alone.

Despite stress on the residential independence of nuclear families, however,

Brown documented the centrality of the wider kinship network to the way of life in Beech Creek. Among the 38 families that lived there, three-fourths were linked through kinship. Ethnographic observation revealed the presence of eighteen distinctive "family groups." These groups, as Brown described them, were "composed of two, three, or more family-households that were particularly solidary and bonded together by strong ties of mutual aid, friendship, and frequent visiting exchanges, as well as by ties of kinship."[70] Along with nuclear households, family groups were the most important unit of local society.

Kinship solidarity in Beech Creek was strong, but not independent of other social forces. Among the greatest threats to the kinship network in the 1940s were antagonisms centering around social inequality. As if mirroring the wider, feud-torn society of earlier times, endemic local conflict caused local residents, only half jokingly, to refer to Beech Creek as "Squabble Creek." Virtually all households were impoverished by national standards, yet Brown discerned a complex system of social stratification in the community. The fundamental basis for stratification among families was landownership; approximately 25 of the 67 households in Beech Creek for which data were available in 1942 (37%) were landless. Families Brown classified as "high class" were descended from original Beech Creek settlers who were "large landowners who had settled on the best bottom land." The ancestors of "low-class" families, on the other hand, "had been poorer, had owned less land, and had been less successful economically."[71]

Class differences based on access to land profoundly influenced family survival strategies, including the decision to stay in Beech Creek or to leave for waged employment elsewhere. Members of landowning families were the first to leave Appalachia and establish stable, working-class careers in industrial cities of the Midwest after World War II. Members of landless families followed later, typically ending up in urban slums and casual labor markets. For both groups, membership in family groups aided the processes of migration and urban adjustment.

Thus, in the 1940s, before the community was absorbed into the national capitalist economy and the vast majority of its population had departed for jobs and opportunities elsewhere, Beech Creekers survived through a system of subsistence agriculture carried out among nuclear families bound together in wider kin networks of cooperation and reciprocity. Stratification, ranked by ownership of land, continued to mark social life and economic opportunities in Beech Creek, even as elsewhere the basis of stratification was shifting toward rankings of occupation, income, and education.[72]

Introduction

A New Phase of the Beech Creek Studies

We initiated a new phase of the Beech Creek studies, initially focusing on the history of Beech Creek from the time of its settlement in the early nineteenth century until Brown's ethnographic survey with our primary attention devoted to the years from 1850 to 1910. Our study began with a longitudinal historical analysis of individuals and families in the Beech Creek neighborhoods, using linked individual, relationship, and household files created from the manuscript federal decennial censuses of population from 1850 to 1910 and the manuscript federal censuses of agriculture for 1850, 1860, 1870, and 1880, the only available years. (These and other data are described more fully in Appendix 1.) Genealogical information collected by Brown made it possible to create unusually reliable longitudinal files since we could trace women through marital name changes; establish the precise relationships among brothers, sisters, uncles, aunts, and cousins; and distinguish between household members who were extended kin and those who were unrelated coresidents. These data were supplemented with information from tax rolls, deeds, wills, and court records. (Clay County did not have a newspaper until well into the twentieth century.) Our files thus link people, family groups, households, and farms across decades and generations and permit household-level and individual-level analysis of data on demographic patterns, family structures, agricultural practices, wealth accumulation and inequality, as well as outmigration from the Beech Creek area. With these data, we are able to examine the persistence of poverty across generations and the strategies that households and families used to cope with and/or escape poverty.

In order to understand how poverty in Beech Creek fit into a wider pattern of social change and development, we also collected extensive data on the social, demographic, political, and economic development of Clay County as a whole. These include census data over time for all slaves and slave owners, merchants, and manufacturers; county wide data from local tax rolls in 1850 and 1892 and from population and agricultural censuses for 1860; data on land and personal property acquisition and dispersal from deeds, wills, mortgages, and land surveys; merchant log books; contemporary accounts from nonlocal newspapers, visiting preachers, and state accounting boards; records of apprenticeship and employment; and official data collected at the county and state levels.

Nineteenth-century Clay County was the site of one of the most significant of all Appalachian feuds, the bloody Garrard-White or Baker-Howard feud. To probe the impact of this long-enduring conflict, we also analyzed nearly 6o years of civil and criminal litigation and political activity among these families and their allies. Although infrequently used by sociologists, local court records proved to be an unusually rich source of data on Appalachian economic, social, and political practices and relations. Clay County's Circuit Court docket contains not only records of official litigation, but also information on sureties, bonds, wages, prices, and slave transactions, providing data on networks of indebtedness and patronage, alliances among the county's elites, early industry, and the antebellum economic structure of slavery. Along with standard sociohistorical sources such as censuses, tax rolls, and property records, local court records allow us to glimpse everyday life in Appalachian Kentucky for periods of time long before other sources of information such as ethnography are available.

Finally, because Beech Creek's population was almost entirely white, we compare the living conditions and life course trajectories of its families with those of African Americans throughout the county in order to see the effects of race on poverty in Appalachian Kentucky. This comparison is especially important since Appalachia has been assumed, wrongly, to be a singularly "white" province of poverty, even though its racial composition is an historically changeable facet of socioeconomic and political development. Altogether, the data we have assembled on Beech Creek and Clay County are, we believe, the longest running sets of longitudinal data currently available on a U.S. rural population as well as the most extensive body of data available for a persistently poor rural Appalachian community.

Overview of the Book

This book is both a social history of the creation of chronic poverty in an Appalachian county and an explication of how capitalist markets, state coercion, and cultural strategies interact to shape local society. As such, it has both policy and theoretical implications. By linking a longitudinal study of a single place to broader understandings of the historical development of the capitalist world system, this book contributes to policy discussions of the underlying causes of persistent regional poverty and reasons for the chronic failure of governmental programs to alleviate such poverty. On a theoretical level, the close focus on social relations in a small area over a long period of time suggests how attention to the historical interrelationships among capitalist markets, state coercion, and cultural strategies can explain the developmental trajectories of local places.

The findings of this study challenge a number of conventional understandings of Appalachia life and history that have underpinned much public policy and regional theory. Traditionally, Appalachia's chronic poverty has been assumed to be the outcome of an *isolated and backward mountain economy*. In fact, as Chapter 2 demonstrates, Appalachia was never isolated from the world market system. Even in the frontier period, mountain life was integrated into regional development paths and shaped by interdependent systems of subsistence production and market exchange. We use historical analysis to show how the modern underdevelopment of mountain economic systems stemmed not from its separation from commercial markets, but from the manner in which it was integrated into larger economic systems.

Conventionally, preindustrial mountain society also is pictured as *egalitarian and homogeneous*, at least before the onslaught of postbellum industrialization and railroads. Our examination of industry and commerce in antebellum Clay County in Chapter 3, however, presents a much different image. Antebellum Clay County society was vastly unequal. Large numbers of slaves were brought into Clay County to provide labor for its salt industry and farms and even among the free population, disparities of wealth and landholding were dramatic. We explore how such market inequities endured over time as cooperative economic strategies among kin bolstered profit making among the wealthy and sustained subsistence economic production among the poor.

Few stereotypes of Appalachia are as entrenched as the notion that the ineffectiveness and corruption of modern mountain politics are rooted in *frontier lawlessness and individualism*. In Chapter 4, we examine the interconnections of commerce and state making in early Clay County and find that stunted civic culture and corrupt local governance were the product of historical manipulation of Clay County's government by local elites seeking political and economic advantage. We examine a famous local murder case in the 1840s to understand the clientelist relationships that bound ordinary Clay Countians to competing elite families and set the stage for corrupt local governance.

The subsistence agriculture practiced in much of rural Appalachia in the nineteenth century could easily be blamed for the *economic stagnation* of the region. In Chapter 5, we use census data and ethnographic records to scrutinize agricultural production in Clay County and Beech Creek. We find that culture and market forces were highly interdependent: Self-sufficient production required landownership, but sales of land were influenced by cultural norms and kinship strategies. Moreover, on the eve of the Civil War, Clay County's agriculture was highly productive, comparing favorably to northern farms. It was only in the postbellum years, as mountain societies faced the imbalance of land and population that northeastern U.S. locales had confronted a century earlier, that Clay County's agriculture experienced a decline.

Modern Appalachian communities are *largely white*; the common assumption is that this has always been the case. But, as Chapter 6 shows, the racial homogeneity of Kentucky mountain society – like its chronic poverty – was created over time. A significant number of African Americans lived in ante-bellum Clay County, but faced with few economic opportunities in the post-bellum period, most left the region. We examine racial differences in economic access, familial resources, and political power to explain the dramatic exodus of African Americans from Appalachian Kentucky in the late nineteenth century.

Since the late nineteenth century, Appalachians have been depicted as *historically insular and passive*, remote from mainstream society and without the determination to change their fate. Our investigation of postbellum economic life in Chapter 7, however, belies this image. Clay County's elites – including some of its women – were major actors in regional industrial development and were prime beneficiaries of the plundering of local resources by outside corporations at the turn of the century. Our examination of court records and deeds further indicates that even poor Clay Countians used lawsuits and exacting contract negotiations against outside corporate speculators to resist exploitation.

Appalachia has long been stereotyped as an incubator of violent *feuding, born of ignorance and poverty*. In fact, the violence that brought turn-of-the-century Clay County national notoriety as a land of feudists was a conflict between two families of highly educated, wealthy elites and their supporters. In Chapter 8, we explore the nature and long-term consequences of this period of violence for Appalachian political and economic life.

Finally, in the Epilogue, we suggest four lessons of this historical examination of Clay County's road to persistent poverty for public policymakers today. We argue that the longitudinal case study of Clay County demonstrates the limits of market-driven development for poor places; the need to preserve cultural strategies that sustain social capital in impoverished regions; the importance of the local state in shaping local development; and the need for a long-term viewpoint to understand the challenges of chronic regional poverty.

II

ANTEBELLUM CAPITALIST MARKETS

2

FRONTIER KENTUCKY IN THE CAPITALIST WORLD SYSTEM

In 1785, ten years after the first settlements had been established in what was soon to be Kentucky, Judge Harry Innes published a letter in the *Boston Magazine* that described a trip he had taken during the previous year across the desolate Appalachian mountains from Virginia to his home in the Bluegrass region of central Kentucky in the trading town of Danville, at that time a village consisting of only fifteen "quite sociable" families. "The howling of wolves and croaking of ravens," throughout the vast expanse of uninhabited mountains that he crossed, along with "apprehension of the danger from Indians," caused Innes, perhaps understating his emotions, to feel "somewhat gloomy." He described the mountainous terrain that ran 200 miles between the last settlements in Virginia and the first ones in what would soon be the state of Kentucky as simply "the wilderness."[1]

Only fifteen families lived in Danville in 1785, but enough people already populated central Kentucky that a number of them convened that year in Danville to register a series of demands on their distant state government in Richmond, Virginia that would eventuate, seven years later, in the formation of Kentucky as a separate state. But when they complained about the physical distance between them and the Virginia capital, these Kentuckians, like Inness, described the Appalachians that lay between their Bluegrass homes and Richmond as "a mountainous desert."[2] At that time, there still were no permanent settlements to their east in Appalachian Kentucky where the Cumberland Plateau posed a formidable barrier to migration and settlement.[3]

Two years after the Danville Convention, Herman Harman, a German pioneer, established one of the first settlements in eastern Kentucky near the Big Sandy River in 1787. A slow but steady movement of population into the mountains began to follow soon thereafter. Especially when land values rose dramatically in central Kentucky and slave-based plantations began to dominate much of the best lands of the Bluegrass, yeomen farmers began to be attracted into Appalachian Kentucky by "good land in the lower valleys

27

of the streams, plenty of forage for stock, excellent springs of fresh water, numerous salt springs, and abundant game." But the representatives of wealthy slave-owning families were drawn there as well by hopes of enterprise and profits.[4] Early market opportunities thus began to shape the contours of wealth and poverty that would define Clay County for centuries.

The first settlers probably reached present-day Clay County in the late 1790s and by 1804, several entrepreneurs including Hugh White were employing slave labor to manufacture salt on Goose Creek, a tributary of the Kentucky River, where they operated thriving mercantile businesses as well. According to his carefully kept ledger, Hugh White extended credit to ninety-five accounts for goods worth more than £2,922 (the equivalent of nearly $10,000) in 1806, an indication of the small but potentially viable market economy that was beginning to emerge in the "wilderness" of the Kentucky hills.[5] Salt manufacturing, as we shall see more fully in the following chapter, fueled the local Clay County economy and helped to hook it into interregional markets at an early date.

Longstanding traditions about how we think about Appalachia make it difficult to conceive of industry and commerce flourishing in eastern Kentucky as early as 1806, as well as that industry there would depend heavily on slave labor. Images of Appalachia as an isolated folk society, such as in ARC's representation of the region even in the 1960s as "a region apart," stand in the way of understanding Appalachian Kentucky's actual historical development and the road it followed to today's economic hardship. As we will explore in more detail in later chapters, such images also make it difficult to design effective policies to counteract the region's impoverishment. Antipoverty initiatives and economic development strategies need to take into account the complex and enduring political, cultural, and economic legacies of Appalachia's historically varied economic activities.[6]

One particular intellectual tradition that has functioned like blinders to divert attention from early economic life in Appalachian Kentucky is the commonplace notion that the settlement and social development of eastern and central Kentucky had little to do with one another, an idea that reinforces stereotypes of Appalachian essentialism and otherness. In 1886, at a crucial time when the modern discourse on Appalachia was taking form, the Kentucky novelist James Lane Allen published a travelogue in *Harper's Magazine* entitled "Through the Cumberland Gap on Horseback." Here Allen argued that the "blue-grass country" of Kentucky, which he referred to as "civilization," and the "primitive society" of "the eastern mountains" were "two worlds," separate and apart. By arguing against speaking singularly of "the Kentuckians," and by introducing the trope of the "two Kentuckies" to distinguish the highland and lowland sections of the state, a theme John Fox,

Jr., echoed in 1901 in *Blue-Grass and Rhododendron*, Allen set in motion a way of thinking about the Kentucky mountains that still influences popular and academic thought.[7]

The notion that the Bluegrass and mountain sections of the state were as distinct as "two Kentuckies" wrongly encouraged writers to imagine, as James Lane Allen did, that "two entirely distinct elements of population" had settled the two areas and, further, that the people of the mountains had made less of the opportunities and challenges they encountered than did their Bluegrass counterparts. According to Allen, on entering the Cumberland Gap country in the late nineteenth century, one encountered an "abjectly poor" population, "living today as their forefathers lived a hundred years ago; hearing little of the world, caring nothing for it; responding feebly to the influence of civilization . . . [and] lacking the spirit of development within."[8]

Horace Kephart picked up on Allen's theme but generalized it beyond Kentucky to all mountaineers throughout the highland South, claiming that "while the transmontane settlers grew rapidly in wealth and culture, their kinsfolk back in the mountains either stood still or retrograded." Besides the natural effects of isolation, Kephart claimed that "the mountains were cursed with a considerable incubus of naturally weak or depraved characters."[9]

By the 1920s, the idea that a separate and inferior people had settled Appalachia was in vogue among social scientists. Reversing the actual geographical direction of settlement in Kentucky, which was from west to east, the sociologist Ellsworth Huntington, for instance, reasoned that "a sort of natural selection" among population groups must have occurred in Kentucky "whereby one type stayed in the mountains" but "the more energetic, adventurous, well-informed, and competent" went on to settle in the Bluegrass. Later, Arnold Toynbee imagined that because the challenge of mountain life had been so great for the sad people who settled there, they had become "no better than barbarians," representing "the melancholy spectacle of a people who have acquired civilization and then lost it."[10]

Despite the existence of research in the 1930s showing that "the Mountains and the Bluegrass were settled by people of the same racial stock . . . many of whom were members of the same families and migrated to Kentucky at the same time," the assumption of Appalachian otherness was carried over during the 1960s into the culture-of-poverty theory. In *Yesterday's People*, Jack Weller asserted that "those who came to the tight [Appalachian] valleys were generally not the ones interested in settling down to a stable way of life and accumulating wealth and comfort and the benefits of a regulated society." Never to be outdone when it came to denigrating Appalachians, Harry Caudill went even further in *Night Comes to the Cumberlands* to claim that it was mainly "social outcasts" – "as cynical, hardened, and bitter a lot as can be imagined outside prison walls" – who settled in Appalachian Kentucky because they were "unable or unwilling to compete effectively in the society of the Old Dominion." Claiming elsewhere that an "essential difference in fundamental psychology" distinguished this "ragtagle of humanity" from other pioneer Kentuckians, Caudill speculated that the mentality of Appalachian settlers "projected through a half-dozen intervening generations, accounts in part, at least, for the singular 'apartness' of the Southern high-lander from the rest of the nation to this day."[11]

Because of the power of such a dreary discourse to shape, even today, how we think about Appalachia and how we design social policies for the region, the best way to begin understanding early social life in Appalachian Kentucky is to put aside momentarily the entire idea of "Appalachia" and think instead about the socioeconomic development of frontier Kentucky as a whole.[12] Especially before 1850, two principal arteries of commerce and population movement, the Kentucky River and the Wilderness Road, closely linked the fate of the Bluegrass and mountain sections of Kentucky. (See Figure 2.1.) To grasp the intimate relationship between economic growth in these two places, it is important not to look at them separately but to see each as involved in an uneven but interconnected process of socioeconomic development that was unfolding throughout the whole geographical area that lay within the watershed of the Kentucky River.

Draining 7,870 square miles in Kentucky, roughly half in the mountains and half in the Bluegrass, the Kentucky River originates in the hills of Eastern Kentucky where three forks – the North, Middle, and South – form its head-waters and converge. After helping to carve out the nearly 4,000 square miles of the Cumberland Plateau that defines Appalachian Kentucky, the river winds through central Kentucky before emptying into the Ohio River. In early times, the principal overland route through the Kentucky River country was the Wilderness Road. First blazed by Daniel Boone who followed buffalo traces and Indian trails known as the Warriors' Path from the Cumberland Gap into the drainage basin of the Kentucky River, one branch of the Wilderness Road led to Lexington and another to Danville and Louisville. In early times, population and commerce primarily entered Kentucky via the Wilderness Road and both settled first in the central basin area of the Kentucky River, the Bluegrass zone, before spreading up into the hills of Appalachia and down to the Ohio River.[13]

Since river traffic and the Wilderness Road both linked the people and commerce of the upper Kentucky River to its middle section in the Blue-grass, Immanuel Wallerstein's concept of nested hierarchies of economic exchange, whereby the processes of uneven development that characterize the

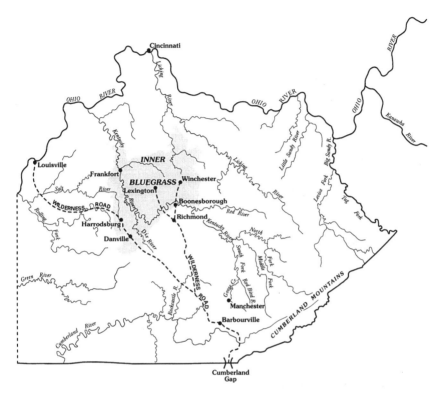

Figure 2.1 Wilderness Road and the Kentucky River Country. (Map by Dick Gilbreath, Director of Cartography, University of Kentucky, Department of Geography).

world economy as a whole also occur within its zones, helps us to represent the connection between both regions. That is, if all of frontier Kentucky were being incorporated into the world system as a peripheral region in the early nineteenth century, then the Bluegrass counties functioned as the zone's center and Appalachian Kentucky as its periphery, not as its opposite or unconnected other.[14]

Before sketching the historical development of these zones of economic activity, however, it is worth noting that in a curious way, the old imaginary opposition of the populations in these two regions – the acquisitive and enterprising spirit attributed to Bluegrass settlers and the complacency and fatalism attributed to mountaineers – helps us to connect the early discourse on Appalachia with recent debates about the formation of early America.

For more than a decade, scholars have hotly debated the relative contributions of commercial entrepreneurism and a cultural orientation to self-subsistence to American social, economic, and political development. Initially argued most furiously over the development of New England, "market historians" contend that New England's farmers were entrepreneurial and acquisitive from the region's earliest period, capitalist commercial and industrial development representing no more than the gradual deepening of market participation. But "social historians" contend that many of New England's farmers subordinated economic gain to yearly subsistence and the long-run security of the family unit, their way of life revolving around subsistence-oriented farms and local barter where production was geared more to *use* than to *exchange* and where primarily the desire for security, that is, a "competency," not capitalist profits, motivated economic action.[15] In a study of western Massachusetts, Christopher Clark contends that "cultural attachment to kinship and neighborhood ties and to a spirit of mutual cooperation" persisted even into the nineteenth century, so that even local businesses there "were enmeshed also in a web of social relationships and cultural expectations that inhibited the free-play of market forces."[16]

The debate about the role of markets versus subsistence agriculture in early U.S. history has expanded to other regions including the West and the South. John Mack Faragher, for instance, has argued that subsistence farming predominated on the Illinois prairie in the early 1840s. "The existing state of the means of production limited capitalist agriculture but allowed most families to achieve a minimum of modest sufficiency, so farmers directed their energies to production for domestic use, placing the security of their families first." Likewise, Steven Hahn contends that subsistence activities predominated among antebellum yeomen farmers in the Georgia Upcountry where the household stood "at the center of economic life" and where "the relations of production were mediated primarily by ties of kinship rather than the marketplace."[17]

In the most sweeping examination of the tensions between commerce and subsistence in the early United States to date, Charles Sellers has interpreted the Jacksonian Era as a nationwide struggle between competing cultures of "land" and "market." "The market fostered individualism and competitive pursuit of wealth by open-ended production of commodity values that could be accumulated as money. But rural production of use values stopped once bodies were sheltered and clothed and bellies provided for. . . . Therefore the subsistence culture fostered family obligation, communal cooperation, and reproduction over generations of a modest comfort." According to Sellers, industrial capitalism based on commodified wage labor eventually came to dominate social life in the United States by pushing "a market revolution across the countryside to transform economy, culture, and politics by commodifying the family labor of subsistence producers" but not before subsistence culture left enduring effects on U.S. ideals and institutions.[18]

Eventually, by linking the understanding of Appalachian development to these wider debates about early U.S. regional development, we can begin to discern the Appalachian road to capitalist development and rural poverty more clearly. First, however, by unthinking the notion of "Appalachia" during the earliest years of eastern Kentucky's development, we can avoid the assumptions of exceptionalism that have plagued most renditions of its past.

In due time, we will argue that the pejorative discourse about Appalachia captures as well as conceals traces of the region's subsistence culture. In calling attention to attributions of enterprise to the Bluegrass and complacency or fatalism to the mountains, we will not, however, argue that such characterizations can be reread to suggest simply that a capitalist economy thrived in one place and a "moral economy" in the other. In Kentucky, no less than elsewhere in the South, as historians Bode and Ginter note, a "model that presents no more than a dichotomy between regions integrated into a market network and those on the periphery of commercial exchange is clearly inadequate." Too often, commerce and subsistence have been opposed as either/ors, leading one historian to suggest that "a judicious synthesis" of the views of "market historians" and "social historians" more accurately "describes American reality than either of the two alone."[19] Better than synthesis, however, is the strategy of avoiding the dualism of economy and society altogether by recalling the central insight from economic sociology that economic action is always embedded in social structure.[20]

Although in the remainder of this chapter and the next, we will stress the role of market forces in the incorporation of frontier Kentucky as a peripheral region of the world capitalist system, it is important to avoid the common mistake – an ideology on the rise in Western democracies during the past decade and tragically becoming hegemonic in former communist societies – of thinking of economic markets as separate and autonomous from social structure and social control. Critics of the myth of self-regulating market societies from Karl Polanyi to Jürgen Habermas argue that three modes of societal integration – culture, political power, and markets – are present to variable degrees in every society to regulate socioeconomic life.[21] "Market interaction," as Enzo Mingione makes clear, "does not take place within the abstract model of an atomized society." "On the contrary," Mingione argues, "it occurs within historically established conditions of social organization, shaped by complex mixes of reciprocity [norms] and redistribution [political power]."[22] Thus, throughout these first chapters, we explore the mutual effects of capitalist markets, state coercion, and cultural strategies on the development of one local society on the Appalachian frontier, Clay County, Kentucky.

Frontier Kentucky in the Capitalist World System

Only thirty-one years spanned the time between 1775 when Daniel Boone, legendary symbol of the Appalachian backwoods, led the first party of settlers through the Cumberland Gap into Kentucky and 1806 when Henry Clay was first sent to Washington, D.C., to represent "the Bluegrass establishment, and those hemp and tobacco planters, land speculators, merchants, distillers, and lawyers [who] chose him to defend their interests" in the U.S. Senate.[23] In only the brief span of a generation, between the era of the backwoodsman Boone and that of the Bluegrass aristocrat Clay, the Kentucky wilderness was transformed from what Wallerstein calls an "external arena" of the European capitalist world system to one of its incorporated peripheries. What is more, the thriving town of Lexington, the commercial and industrial center of the Bluegrass, had become the premier city of the western United States by 1815. Seymour Martin Lipset was wrong to claim that the whole of early America was born modern, but the political and economic structures of world capitalism nonetheless cradled the Kentucky frontier from its birth. Together, the ambitions of "enterprise" and the virtues of "competency" served as the midwives to Appalachian Kentucky, no less than to the Bluegrass. Coercion stood in waiting.[24]

Even prior to white settlement, the European capitalist world system had already inscribed, at least indirectly, the imprint of its domination in the early eighteenth century on the territory that was to become Kentucky, a territory claimed by England and bordered on the north by French possessions. Spanish lands lay farther south. Though uninhabited, this territory was also claimed as a hunting ground by two nonresident Indian tribes whose economic and political lives had already been profoundly reshaped by their incorporation into the world system through fur trading, not to mention their exposure to European disease. These were the Shawnee, who lived north of the Ohio River and were affiliated with the Iroquois, and the Cherokee, who lived in the Southern Appalachians southeast of Kentucky. Even the most naturalistic aspects of this "wilderness" landscape, the intricate network of buffalo traces and warrior paths that traversed the mountain and Bluegrass regions and is faithfully retraced today by modern highways, reflects the imprint of European fur trading and its territorial ramifications.[25]

Following prior French explorations, Anglo-American explorers Christopher Gist and Thomas Walker penetrated the Kentucky wilderness for the first time in 1750, working separately on behalf of two Virginia land companies representing, in part, the financial interests of London investors. Settlement in Kentucky was made unsafe, however, by violence spawned by the Europeans' Seven Years' War (known in the English colonies as the "French and Indian Wars") and it was legally prohibited at the end of that war by the English Proclamation of 1763, a momentary concession to the Indian population that restricted white settlement to the eastern side of the crest of the Allegheny Mountains. The defeat of the Shawnee and their cession of Kentucky to the English at the close of Lord Dunsmore's War in 1774, however, opened the way for the first English settlements in Kentucky beginning in 1775. Warfare with the British and their Indian allies during the Revolutionary War slowed Kentucky's initial settlement, especially along the Ohio River, but soon the pace of migration into Kentucky, the nation's first western state, accelerated dramatically, amounting to what has been called "the first mass movement by colonists in America." Kentucky's population rose from less than 1,000 in 1780 to more than 100,000 by the early 1790s.[26]

If European merchant capitalism influenced Kentucky territory even before permanent settlements were established there, the further incorporation of early Kentucky into the world system can be gauged by three interdependent political-economic processes: the *commodification of labor*, the *commodification of land*, and the integration of local economic actors as producers and consumers into the *commodity chains* that Wallerstein has described as linking the far-flung zones of the capitalist system as a whole.[27] The commodification of labor is the simplest of these three processes to demonstrate.

Labor

Karl Marx identified the advent of capitalism with the commodification of free wage labor, but Wallerstein has shown that in peripheral zones of the world system, functionally equivalent forms of labor control were achieved by combining commodification with political coercion. One result was modern slavery. Family labor can be applied to production for either use (subsistence) or exchange (profit), but the ownership of slaves, according to Wallerstein, can best be interpreted as an index both of incorporation and peripheralization in early modern world capitalism. "Simply put," as one historian writes, "slavery *required* production for the market."[28] Slaves accompanied Daniel Boone on his first effort to bring settlers to Kentucky and they comprised one-fifth of Kentucky's total population fifteen years later in 1790. Growing at a faster rate than the state's white population, slaves were 25% of Kentucky's population in 1830. They comprised 11% of Clay County's population in 1840.

Land

Because the historical processes by which land was commodified are harder to describe than labor but no less important for the social, political, and economic development of frontier Kentucky, a lengthier discussion is necessary.[29] In an important examination of the commodification of land on the Appalachian frontier, Wilma Dunaway argues persuasively against "the pervasive myth that capitalism expanded into the region [no sooner than] after the Civil War, with the coming of extractive industry" by showing that in the eighteenth century, "global capitalism was [already] entrenched in the region with the westward advance of speculators, settlers, and squatters." Claiming that these economic agents engrossed more than four and a half million acres from Indian populations on the Appalachian frontier between 1763 and 1773, Dunaway's analysis reveals how rapidly they transformed the land there from a common resource, as defined by indigenous peoples, to a privately possessed commodity.[30]

Along with the commodification of labor, the commodification of land is a primary source of inequality wherever it takes place. Beyond this fact, however, the historically unique process by which Virginia's ancient land system was modernized in the eighteenth century had especially detrimental and long-lasting consequences for the subsequent economic and social development of its former territory, Kentucky. As we shall show in later chapters, some effects of this process persisted even until the early twentieth century in Appalachian Kentucky, where they influenced both the violent disputes ("feuds") that took place there as well as the methods used by corporate land, timber, and mining companies to acquire Appalachian land and resources.

Colonial Virginia's contradictory land policies, including the provision of several means by which land could be acquired, encouraged both settlement and speculation, resulting in both the distribution and concentration of landholding in early Kentucky. In 1776, Virginia reaffirmed the validity of an earlier 1705 law that granted headright of 400 acres with conditional rights to preempt additional acreage to settlers who built cabins, raised a corn crop, surveyed their land, and registered their deeds with the appropriate county courts. This law and others like it encouraged many farmers and livestock grazers living in increasingly populated backcountry sections of Virginia and the Carolinas to venture beyond the mountains to Kentucky to acquire new land there.[31]

In addition to granting headright, Virginia's policy of paying soldiers for military service in the French and Indian and Revolutionary Wars with warrants to obtain specific quantities of western land depending on rank and service also contributed to the land's commodification. So did Virginia's policy of selling treasury warrants, redeemable in land shares, to pay off the colony's war-incurred debts. Since both types of warrants were transferable, they encouraged speculation more than settlement and set the stage for later conflicts in Kentucky between actual settlers who made preemption claims on the lands they had taken up and absentee holders of military and treasury warrants who claimed the same properties.[32]

Land companies, benefiting from royal grants, also played a key role in the commodification of Appalachian and transmontane territories and their incorporation into the world economy. Well before actual attempts were made to settle Kentucky, various land companies had already petitioned for, and sometimes been granted, vast amounts of western lands in, and beyond, the Appalachians. Seventy years before the settlement of Kentucky, for instance, London speculators who formed the Vandalia Company petitioned in 1705 for one-third of what is now Kentucky. The Virginia Company, organized in 1747 by another group of London and Virginia investors, also laid claims to unoccupied lands there and sponsored one of the first English explorations of Kentucky in 1750.[33]

When the actual establishment of permanent settlements began in 1775, this process was led not by independent homesteaders, but by the agents of land companies and other groups of speculators in competition with one another for the first fruits of possession.[34] Thus, with official support from Virginia officials, James Harrod led a party of surveyors and settlers down from the Ohio River to establish a settlement near the Kentucky River at the present town of Harrodsburg at the same time that another group, led by Daniel Boone, hurried north through the Cumberland Gap to a lower site on the Kentucky River where they erected Fort Boonesborough. Despite the popular image of Daniel Boone as the quintessential independent frontiersman, his early attempt at Kentucky settlement was made on behalf of the Transylvania Company, a land company formed by a syndicate of North Carolina investors whose purchase of rights to millions of acres of land in the Kentucky River basin from the Cherokee nation was invalidated by Virginia courts the following year, to the lasting benefit of Virginia landlords and investors.[35]

Greed and inefficiency, fueled by colonial Virginia's need for revenue, thus meant that "by 1784, when the Kentucky country had only a few thousand widely scattered settlers, more rights to land had been granted there than land was available." Additionally, all forms of land dispersal were fatally flawed by "the failure on the part of the Crown and then Virginia to devise a systematic scheme of western land survey before settlers crossed the Cumberland mountains." According to Paul Gates, "prodigal conveyances that greatly exceeded the area of land available, looseness of entry procedure, and absence of the rectangular system of survey permitted extensive frauds, duplicating and overlapping boundaries, huge and multiple grants to the same persons, concentration of holdings and a large amount of absentee ownership" in Kentucky. Thus, besides its contribution to Kentucky's incorporation on the periphery of world capitalism, the legacy of colonial Virginia's land laws was a nightmarish pattern of hopelessly overlapping land claims that caused early Kentucky to become a "hothouse of litigation" and frustrated the hopes of many thousands of homesteaders of acquiring property there.[36]

Many white Kentuckians had hoped that statehood, achieved in 1792, would allow them greater control over land distribution, but it is said that the new government "displayed equally lavish generosity in dispensing its public lands, and when the granting process came to an end sufficient land had been promised to cover the state four times over." Between 1797 and 1820, Kentucky legislators did, however, pass a series of "occupying claimants" bills to protect the property improvements and rights of actual settlers who held some form of title to the lands they claimed, but most of these laws were invalidated by the U.S. Supreme Court as violations of the compact with Virginia that had effected Kentucky's separation from the Old Dominion and had made the honoring of all prior Virginia land laws a condition of statehood.[37]

Henry Clay denounced Kentucky's land laws in 1829 as "a vicious system, a calamitous system," but as an attorney who moved to the new state of Kentucky in 1797 to take advantage of the opportunities provided there by the huge volume of litigation arising from conflicting land claims, Clay also understood the state to be "a lawyers' paradise." Countless thousands of ordinary settlers who lacked the benefit of expensive legal representation lost the lands they thought were theirs whereas "men of wealth, gentry speculators, sons of planters and the like possessed the tools to manipulate the legal tangle to their advantage. The best lands fell into their hands and the hands of absentee owners." Even Daniel Boone left the state propertyless despite numerous litigations to defend his claims. According to Gates, by the beginning of the nineteenth century, one-quarter of the entire state was claimed by twenty-one speculators, including such "Barons of the Bluegrass" as George May and Humphrey Marshall (cousin of U.S. Supreme Court jurist John Marshall) whose holdings exceeded 1,100,000 and 405,000 acres, respectively.[38]

Similar patterns, if not more extreme, held for Appalachian Kentucky where, in the Big Sandy River district for instance, 43% of the area's 1,356,000 acres was already claimed by a small number of absentees by 1791 when few actual settlers had arrived there to make their preemption claims. Dunaway estimates that in the settled areas of Appalachian Kentucky between 1790 and 1810, 57% of all non-enslaved households were landless, the top 25% of owners possessed three-fourths of all the land, and more than half (56%) of all owners were absentee.[39] Because of all these factors relating to the commodification and distribution of land in Kentucky, many early migrants to the state found it to be a bad "poor man's country." As one historian puts it, "At an incredibly early stage of its development, Kentucky became a place of landlords and tenants, of rich estates for the few and second- or third-rate smaller farms for the many."[40]

Commodity Chains

The third indicator of regional incorporation in the world capitalist system is the participation of local producers and consumers in the global commodity chains that link distant places around the world through economic exchange. When and to what extent such participation occurred in early America, as we have already noted, is controversial. On the one hand, historians as dissimilar as Douglas North and Charles Sellers contend that, despite the rapid growth of population in Kentucky and other western areas of the United States between 1810 and 1820, the bulk of the free frontier population was devoted to "a self-sufficient way of life geared to local exchange" and was "still either outside the market or peripheral to it." But historians who have examined merchant accounts and probate records from frontier Kentucky to gauge the extent of commerce and markets there argue on the other hand that "a remarkably sophisticated, international pattern of consumption" existed "even on the rude frontier of eighteenth-century Kentucky."[41]

Scholars are similarly divided over the relative importance of self-sufficiency and commercialization in the socioeconomic development of early Appalachia. Mary Beth Pudup contends that the counties of Harlan, Perry, and Floyd in eastern Kentucky were primarily "oriented toward simple household subsistence" between 1850 and 1880, and Altina Waller has described economic life in the geographically isolated communities of the Tug River that forms a border between Kentucky and West Virginia as largely subsistence-oriented until almost the very end of the nineteenth century. On the other hand, Durwood Dunn describes the Tennessee mountain village of Cades Cove as having been "oriented to the larger regional market economy" since well before the Civil War. Located only forty miles from Knoxville, eastern Tennessee's most important commercial city, the people of Cades Cove, according to Dunn, were "tied . . . closely to regional markets, and through these markets, to the broad mainstream of American political and social culture throughout the [nineteenth] century." Similarly, John Inscoe has described the mountain section of western North Carolina before the Civil War as "a thriving, productive, and even progressive society" where slave holding and commercial agriculture were widespread. Other scholars have emphasized the importance of commercialism in the settlement and early development of the Blue Ridge Mountain section of Appalachian Virginia. Even scholars surveying the entire region disagree on the relative mix of commercial and subsistence agriculture. Using very restrictive criteria to estimate subsistence farming, Dunaway argues that as few as 10% of the entire region's farm owners were subsistence or near-subsistence producers before the Civil War, but Paul Salstrom, paying closer attention to subregional variations, argues that subsistence farming predominated in the Allegheny-Cumberland platteau country of today's Central Appalachia throughout the late antebellum and early postbellum eras.[42]

The discrepancies among accounts of early Appalachia that contrastingly depict the region as an isolated, subsistence-oriented local economy or as a commercially oriented regional economy that was well integrated from an early date into wider market networks suggest at least two implications. First, scholars and policy analysts should be wary of broad generalizations that are made across diverse geographical areas in Appalachia. Indeed, one of the most pernicious effects of the popular discourse on Appalachia has been the disregard for differences and diversities throughout the mountains, whether these be in regard to populations, geographical areas, or historical periods. Second, the discrepancies among accounts also suggest that subsistence and marketing activities should not be polarized as incompatible processes of economic life. Since capitalist development occurs unevenly across geographical space and historical time, the local mixes of capitalist and noncapitalist production should be expected to have varied across the vast area defined by the Appalachian Mountain range and to have contributed to potentially distinct local trajectories of social change.

Especially in the early years of Kentucky, before markets and the means of transportation had been improved and consumer goods made more widely available, many frontier households undoubtedly found it necessary, and were probably content, to reproduce themselves by farming for home consumption and only limited market sales, supplemented by hunting, fishing, and other more casual subsistence activities. But for other classes of Kentuckians with significant amounts of capital invested in land and slaves, the production of profitable commodities, along with the development and expansion of opportunities to market them, was a matter of considerable urgency. The seeds of class division and cultural distinction among white Kentuckians were thus sown in the state's soil at the time of its first settlement as were the already hardy roots of racial oppression. Along with the appropriation of Native American hunting lands, the enslavement of African Americans ensured the establishment of a racial hierarchy in early Kentucky as well.

Pressure to integrate Kentucky into the wider economy thus came from several directions. Speculators interested in finding profitable uses for their lands, slave owners needing to employ their laborers in productive activities, and east coast merchants readily extending goods on credit to local merchants in order to create new market opportunities in the west each fueled the growth of frontier enterprise. Elizabeth Perkins was thus correct to argue that "stores, traders, and consumer goods accompanied the first settlers to Kentucky."[43] Richard Henderson, director of the Transylvania Company, established a store at Boonesborough in 1775 during the fort's first year of existence, an indicator that from its earliest moments Kentucky was – in the words of a recent governor's public relations slogan – "open for business."

The international fur trade provided the earliest economic opportunity for pioneer Kentucky, especially in the Cumberland Mountains since prior French trading for pelts had already depleted much of the wildlife in the central region of the state. As early as 1770, English hunters had begun taking furs from Kentucky downriver to Natchez and, in 1776, the Philadelphia firm of Baynton and Morgan sent a cargo of goods down the Ohio River from Fort Pitt to French traders and trappers at Fort Chartres (St. Louis) on the Mississippi in an attempt to divert the fur trade toward the east. Four years later, merchants in the river town of Louisville created the beginnings of a banking system in Kentucky by issuing transferable certificates for furs that circulated widely as a form of money.[44]

In the decade of the 1780s, as the population began to spread out into the countryside from the fortified "stations" around which it had first clustered, commercially oriented farmers and planters began to search for farm products and other commodities that would prove valuable enough to bear the onerous costs of transport over the great distances that separated Kentucky from established markets. Living in the first western state, they turned naturally to the Ohio and Mississippi Rivers as possible outlets for whatever commodities that they had to trade, but prior to the invention of the steamboat, the slow upstream return on these rivers encouraged only one-way ventures.

One of the first entrepreneurs to delve into the river trade was General James Wilkinson, later commander of the U.S. Army. From his base on the Kentucky River at Frankfort, Wilkinson sent several boats loaded with salt, one of the state's most important commodities, from central Kentucky to Nashville in 1786 in exchange for cash or furs. A year later, he departed on a flatboat loaded with tobacco and other farm products on a ten-month trip to the Spanish city of New Orleans where he won a brief monopoly on imports in a market otherwise closed to U.S. trade. By the time Spain opened New Orleans fully to U.S. commerce in 1789, Kentucky merchants were ready to engage in a long-distance triangular pattern of trade in which they sent farm products down river to be sold for cash in New Orleans. From there, they traveled up the Atlantic coast to mercantile centers at Baltimore and Philadelphia to purchase manufactured goods that could then be shipped overland, or down the Ohio River, to the newly emerging local markets of rural Kentucky. Thus, from an early date, at least some Kentuckians consumed goods from the West Indies, France, and India that were purchased in New Orleans and an even greater quantity of British goods purchased from U.S. coastal cities.[45]

According to Douglas North's characterization of economic life in the first years of the new republic, the period from 1793 to 1808 were "years of unparalleled prosperity" when rising income from international exports and restrictions on imports induced the rapid expansion of the domestic U.S. economy. Kentucky speculators, planters, merchants, and lawyers benefited greatly from this period of national economic growth. Throughout the period, they experimented with the export of various commodities including salt, flour, salted meats, whiskey, tobacco, and hemp as commercialization increased rapidly. This was especially true in the enormously fertile Bluegrass region of the Kentucky River country that surrounded the rapidly growing town of Lexington, a thriving inland city that emerged as the "the agricultural, commercial, and manufacturing center of the trans-Appalachian west" by 1800, when it surpassed in size and importance the Ohio River towns of Pittsburgh, Cincinnati, and Louisville.[46]

As the dispatching center for country produce and the distributing center for eastern and British manufactured goods, Lexington "throve on trade," its merchants mediating between mercantile firms in Baltimore and Philadelphia and rural producers and consumers throughout rural Kentucky and much of Tennessee as well. By 1792, twenty stores were doing business in Lexington, and in 1794, a knowledgeable observer from Pennsylvania called the town "the greatest place for dealing" he had ever seen. Probably a later account was apocryphal, but the French traveler François Michaux described the spectacular expansion of frontier commerce, as well as the customary flow of value from periphery to center that characterizes world capitalism, by claiming to have witnessed convoys of fifteen to twenty horses hauling specie back to Philadelphia and Baltimore from Lexington in 1802, Kentucky's payment for eastern goods.[47]

Though undoubtedly fueling urban growth in the eastern seaboard as well as Great Britain, the drain of capital from the periphery to core of the ascendent U.S. economy was not so complete that it left no opportunities for local merchant capital to accumulate in Kentucky. At the height of the national boom period that ended in 1808, it is estimated that sales from several Lexington mercantile firms each surpassed one million dollars per year and contributed to merchant incomes reaching as high as $60,000 annually.[48]

Mindful, however, that geography and the high costs of transportation put them at a disadvantage in selling unfinished products to outside buyers, Lexington merchants, planters, and other investors initiated a program of slave-based industrialization that made Lexington, along with Pittsburgh, a premier western industrial center.[49] Markets for rope and sails in the shipping industry and even greater demand from cotton growers in the South for bagging materials provided both Bluegrass planters and manufacturers after 1800 with a huge market for hemp products that were both grown and manufactured locally.[50] A dozen hemp yarn and bagging establishments were among the most important of sixty factories that operated in Lexington in 1817, representing a total investment of two million dollars, but a dozen cotton mills, three woolen mills, three paper mills, and three grist mills, along with several hat factories, coach manufacturers, soap and candle makers, gunpowder mills, iron and brass foundries, cabinet makers, tobacco manufacturers, tanners, a lead factory, and a silver plating firm also contributed to the city's industrial success.[51] Together, industry and commerce earned Lexington the reputation early in the nineteenth century as the "Philadelphia of the West." Boasting two newspapers, a public library, musical and drama societies, a coffee house that subscribed to forty-two national and international newspapers, and the first university to be established across the mountains, "Lexington was not only the mercantile center of the West but its social and cultural leader as well." The city served as "home of the West's leading medical and law schools" as well as to "one of the most distinguished professional classes in the nation, and disproportionately the largest."[52]

Such cultural accomplishments, however, were achieved at the high price of extreme inequality. It has been said that "no where in the West ... did the wealthy live in more opulence than in Lexington." The real and personal property of Lexington's sixteen wealthiest slave-owning merchants and manufacturers amounted to more than one-third of the city's taxable property near the end of the first decade of the nineteenth century and the top 10% of landowners held an astonishing 99% of the taxable land in town. Fully 81% of the town's population was landless in 1805 and one-third of its population was enslaved in 1816.[53]

In addition to coming at the price of a highly stratified social formation,

Lexington's preeminence in the West also proved to be short-lived. Economic growth slowed down momentarily throughout the United States once warfare among the European powers and the British-American War of 1812 was concluded, wars that had created both highly profitable markets for U.S. exports and protection for locally significant domestic industries. The national economy experienced "expansive surges" of growth in 1815–18 and 1832–9 and although growth was slow in the 1820s, the whole period from 1815 to 1860, was an "era of tremendous expansion" in the entire Atlantic economy, according to Douglas North.[54] During much of this period, international demand for cotton played a decisive role in American economic growth as it did indirectly in Kentucky. By 1820, however, "the industrial preeminence of [Lexington and] the central Kentucky [River] basin [had] become a thing of the past."[55]

Long-term postwar declines in the value of Kentucky's principal staple crops, tobacco and hemp, forced Bluegrass farmers to readjust to changing market conditions by restructuring their local economy around animal husbandry. Increasing world demand for cotton, and the specialization it evoked among southeastern planters, created expanding markets for Kentucky livestock including horses and mules for work and conveyance, and pork and cattle for meat and dairy products. So did the opening of new markets in the thriving cotton, rice, and sugar districts of the Southwest.

Utilizing the same "badly made roads and trails" that earlier had conveyed population into Kentucky, drovers began to lead huge quantities of livestock out from Kentucky via the Wilderness Road and the Cumberland Gap where connecting routes led to Richmond, Baltimore, and Philadelphia in the East; southeastern markets in Georgia, the Carolinas, and eastern Tennessee via Knoxville; and the Mississippi delta region via Nashville and the old Natchez Trail.[56] Turnpike records on the Wilderness Road indicate that farmers sent more than $600,000 worth of livestock through the Cumberland Gap in 1821 and one million dollars worth in 1828. In 1838, 4,039 horses, 4,540 beef cattle, 68,764 hogs, and 3,250 sheep worth $1,780,426 were driven through the gap on their way to southern markets in 1838, a level maintained until nearly 1850.[57] By then, however, the railroad-induced geographical shift of the meatpacking industry to cities further west, and the rise of the grain industry there as well, drastically diminished the comparative advantage in livestock raising that Kentucky farmers, especially in the Bluegrass region, had enjoyed for several decades.[58]

The fact that livestock could, as the saying goes, "walk themselves to market," helped Kentucky farmers deliver commodities to markets that could bear the expense of overland transportation. Located sixty miles from the Ohio River on an unnavigable tributary of the Kentucky River, however, Lexington faced a tremendous disadvantage once steamboats began to travel both up and down the Mississippi and Ohio Rivers. According to Wade, "The coming of the steamer in 1815 wrought such basic changes that it might be said to have ended the first era in the urban history of the West." Nowhere throughout the Ohio Valley was this felt more negatively than in Lexington. Rapidly, the river towns of Cincinnati and Louisville began to surpass Lexington in size and importance as the principal entrepôts for the commerce of the Kentucky hinterlands. Consequently, by 1830, the city and the surrounding central basin area of the Kentucky River "had lost its important manufacturing and commercial position in the West and even its primacy in Kentucky."[59]

Bluegrass entrepreneurs and their political allies scrambled to harness whatever meager state resources were available for the improvement of roads and waterways in Kentucky to the hegemonic project of restoring the economic advantages of the Bluegrass region. Despite their efforts, however, to improve the navigability of the Kentucky River, build the first macadamized highway in the United States to connect Lexington to its outlet on the Ohio River at Maysville, and initiate railroads that eventually would connect Lexington to Louisville in the West and to the Big Sandy River in the East, such measures failed ultimately to overcome the locational disadvantages and restore the economic significance of Lexington and the Bluegrass slaveocracy. Hard times and the commitment to restore the preeminence of central Kentucky, as we shall see, also undermined the common interests in internal improvements that previously had benefited both the mountain and Bluegrass sections of the state simultaneously.[60]

Clay County's Role in Early Kentucky Development

We have taken a considerable amount of time to sketch, at least in broad strokes, how the commodification of land, labor, and farm products hooked the frontier society of the Kentucky River country, and especially its Bluegrass section, into the capitalist world economy in the late eighteenth and early nineteenth centuries. Normally, however, the story of the growth of Lexington and the planter-merchant economy of central Kentucky is not linked to narratives about the development of Appalachian Kentucky. The latter, as we have seen, is most often assumed to have followed an altogether separate trajectory of development. Our research, however, suggests that frontier society in the mountains of eastern Kentucky was brought into the orbit of capitalist markets by the operation of many of the same historical forces that were at work in the rest of the state.

We have already noted that speculators engrossed lands and transformed them into potentially valuable commodities in Appalachian Kentucky well prior to settlement in many sections and that slavery was established in the mountain region from an early date. The particular commodity that played the most important role in hooking Clay County into extra-local trade networks was salt, although livestock exports were also significant.[61] The sale of salt manufactured from brine on the Goose Creek headwaters of the South Fork of the Kentucky River anchored Clay County's early place in the unified development of the social order that we have described as coming into being both upstream and down in the mountain and Bluegrass sections of the Kentucky River.

According to Thomas Clark, "When the first adventurer stood on the crest of the westernmost range of the Appalachian Highlands and peered over into the land of Kentucky, he, doubtless, speculated upon the presence of at least two minerals. These were salt and saltpeter, both of which were necessary to successful settlement." Much as cotton growing served as what Douglas North calls a "carrier industry" to generate growth throughout the entire antebellum U.S. economy, salt manufacturing and the commerce it stimulated influenced patterns of settlement and development throughout the whole trans-Appalachian frontier including Clay County. Across this huge territory, "salt was the one commodity readily converted into cash and the one commodity readily accepted in barter." As John Jakle shows in his analysis of its impact on the Ohio Valley frontier from 1770 to 1820, the manufacture of salt contributed directly to urbanization, the improvement of roads and riverways, commercialization of the livestock industry, and, when business cycles curtailed trade, it "kept trade routes open and the region's early commercial structure intact."[62]

During the Revolutionary War, settlers in Kentucky had petitioned the Virginia legislature to complain that they were "destitute" of salt – a crucial commodity for human and livestock consumption as well as meat preservation among rural households – because Indian attacks prevented their travel to salt licks to obtain salt. Daniel Boone was captured by Indians during one such attempt to boil brine for the settlers at Boonesboro. In response, the colonial government in Virginia gave a big impetus to the Kentucky salt industry by providing for the expansion of saltworks at Bullet's Lick near Louisville and building a garrison there to protect them.

Besides being an item constantly demanded by farm households, salt was also an essential curing agent in Kentucky's nascent meatpacking industry. A May 1801 article in the Lexington *Kentucky Gazette* reported a list of commodities being shipped down the Ohio and Mississippi Rivers from Louisville that included 92,300 pounds of pork and 91,300 pounds of bacon along with smaller quantities of dried beef, butter, and hardtack, each of which required large amounts of salt in its preparation. Thus, the increasing population of subsistence-oriented farmers and export-oriented planters alike stimulated the demand for salt. "When the pork trade was well developed, and the population had increased in Kentucky, there was a greatly increased demand for salt."[63]

Although the earliest saltworks in Kentucky were near the Ohio River, the saltworks on the waters of Goose Creek in Clay County soon became Kentucky's most important domestic producer of salt. As early as 1810, four manufacturers produced 70,000 bushels of salt annually on Goose Creek, a quantity amounting to one-fourth of Kentucky's entire output at the time.[64] The saltmaking industry in Clay County reached its peak before 1850 when fifteen manufacturers produced nearly a quarter of a million bushels annually.[65] Goose Creek salt circulated throughout Kentucky and other southern states, and in their dual role as manufacturers and merchants, saltmakers linked Clay County economically to the Bluegrass region and beyond.

According to the Kentucky River's foremost historian, Mary Verhoeff, for twenty-five years after Kentucky separated from Virginia (i.e., until about 1818), the Kentucky River was an important trade route throughout the state, taking its share in "the unprecedented commercial activity induced by the Napoleonic Wars."[66] During this time, Clay County salt manufacturers shipped significant quantities of salt down the Kentucky River on flatboats to markets in the Bluegrass region. But when steamboat commerce on the Ohio River denied Lexington and central Kentucky its former centrality in Kentucky trade and brought cheap sources of salt into the state as well, Clay County saltmakers shipped much of its product overland via the Wilderness Road and Cumberland Gap routes to better protected markets in eastern Tennessee and Virginia.

The heavy use of the Wilderness Road by Clay County saltmakers during the 1830s and 1840s corresponded to the road's era of maximum importance in interstate commerce as Kentucky's primarily route for livestock drives to southern markets. After this date, however, the Clay County salt industry began to decline as salt manufacturing elsewhere, in regions with better locational advantages, prospered. Furthermore, by 1850, as the meatpacking industry moved west and southern markets declined, the "Wilderness Road . . . lost practically all significance as a transmontane route and was of mere local importance." Whereas mountain roads had been "not much inferior to those of central Kentucky prior to 1830," the macadamization of roads in central Kentucky from 1830 to 1850 created "a magnificent system of highways" in the Bluegrass region. According to Verhoeff, "it was in this period that the rugged mountain region, left henceforth to shift for itself in the matters of highways, became isolated to such a marked degree."[67]

Conclusion

By describing the unified growth of capitalist enterprise in early Kentucky, instead of assuming the separate and unrelated development of Kentucky's mountain and Bluegrass subregions, we have tried to unthink the stereotype of Appalachian Kentucky as an isolated frontier. Saltmaking helped to hook antebellum Clay County and southeastern Kentucky into distant economic markets, led to the importation of an enslaved working class, and permitted the rise of a local elite that, as we shall see, exercised hegemonic power over local society. Nor was this industry an isolated case of capitalist development in Appalachian Kentucky. Iron manufacturing played a similar role in integrating northeastern Kentucky into the national economy. Here, in the Appalachian counties of Kentucky and Ohio, the Hanging Rock region was the leading iron-producing area in the United States in the 1830s.[68]

Although generally poorly capitalized and spread unevenly across the region, such industries were not uncommon throughout antebellum Appalachia. In a comprehensive survey, Wilma Dunaway has identified 6,019 industrial enterprises in Appalachia in 1860 that manufactured household goods ("baskets, brooms, carpets, furniture, cabinets, glassware, mattresses, pottery, soap, candles, and metalware"), paper, rifles, railroad cars, millstones, industrial bellows, farm implements, machinery, steam engines, textiles, and building materials to name but some of the manufactured goods she enumerates. Most important were the export-oriented, extractive industries of the antebellum era – timber, iron, salt, coal and other minerals, copper mining and smelting, and petroleum and natural gas production – that linked the region's economy to global capitalist markets but also resulted in dependency and ecological devastation.[69]

While speaking of antebellum Appalachia in a new way, as an integral part of the national economy, it is important to see Appalachian Kentucky, nonetheless, as the periphery of a periphery, an integrated but underdeveloped component of frontier Kentucky's early capitalist economy. Thus, although it is correct to speak of unified economic development throughout the countryside drained by the Kentucky River, it is also important to note that this economy was unevenly developed in both spatial and temporal terms.

Table 2.1 reports the total property valuation in each of the counties drained by the Kentucky River in 1839.[70] Although the absolute amount of wealth that had been accumulated by then in Clay County was third greatest among mountain counties because of the vitality of its salt industry, absolute levels of wealth were far less in mountain counties than in those of the Bluegrass region along the river. In 1815, when the Kentucky River and

Table 2.1. *Total Valuation of Property in Kentucky River Counties, 1839*

Appalachian Counties	Total Valuation ($)
Breathitt	239,818
Clay	677,361
Estill	1,117,027
Harlen	253,871
Knox	796,371
Laurel	352,780
Perry	231,324
	Subtotal: 3,668,552

Bluegrass Counties	Total Valuation ($)
Anderson	1,133,138
Carroll	1,384,278
Clark	6,067,637
Fayette (Lexington)	18,399,621
Franklin	4,090,912
Gallatin	1,171,293
Garrard	3,931,093
Henry	5,347,058
Jessamine	5,409,478
Lincoln	5,013,188
Montgomery (half)	2,489,472
Madison	8,289,785
Mercer	7,503,039
Owen	3,022,739
Shelby	10,326,438
Scott	6,704,968
Woodford	7,662,559
City of Louisville	26,730,587
	Total: 129,245,936

Source: Kentucky House of Representatives *Journal* (1839), Appendix, p. 207.

the Wilderness Road both played key roles in the Kentucky economy, total property in Clay County averaged $97.50 per capita, or roughly 54% of Kentucky's average per capita wealth of $179.41. A generation later, however, when both the Kentucky River and the Wilderness Road had declined in economic significance, Clay County had lost ground relative to the rest of the state when its per capita wealth of $133.63 had fallen to only 44% of the state average of $304.74.[71] Thus, by the midpoint of the nineteenth century, Clay County had already begun to travel along its historical path to poverty.

The underdevelopment of Clay County's antebellum capitalist economy meant that much of its population existed to large degree outside the orbit of capitalism. In Chapter 5, we will examine what we describe as the "patri- archal moral economy" of the Beech Creek neighborhoods in order to under- stand the noncapitalist economy of subsistence farming that sustained a significant portion of Appalachian Kentucky's population. But before that, we next take a closer look at the early growth of Clay County's capitalist economy in Chapter 3 and the role of its dominant class in the making of the local state and political order in Chapter 4.

3

INDUSTRY, COMMERCE, AND SLAVEHOLDING

A conceptual stumbling block for scholars and policymakers who want to understand the chronic poverty of regions like Appalachia is the assumption that such places have always been poor. As the case of Clay County demonstrates, however, places that are impoverished today were not necessarily poor in earlier times. Without understanding the historical dynamics that create poor places and poor people, it is impossible to develop effective policies to alleviate contemporary regional poverty. In this chapter, we take a closer look at the social relations of markets and coercion in antebellum Clay County that shaped its long slide into poverty in the twentieth century.

Contrary to stereotypes about the homogeneity of early Appalachia, an economically diverse population began to settle in Clay County at the start of the nineteenth century. Although the vast majority of white settlers in the county practiced general, subsistence-oriented farming and livestock raising with family labor only, a few owned slaves. The federal census of 1810, taken four years after the county's formation, counted a total of 141 slaves distributed among 39 of Clay County's 330 households (only 12%), yet slaveholders dominated local economic and political life throughout the antebellum era.[1]

Even by the "surprisingly unequal" standards of early Kentucky between 1800 and 1820,[2] the economic inequality of early Clay County was remarkably great. A decade after the county was formed, in presumably ample time for its earliest settlers to have surveyed, improved, and registered their land claims, three-fourths of all free households (73.5%) were still landless in 1816.[3] (Landlessness in Kentucky as a whole was 50% in 1820.[4]) Intense inequality existed among the county's small number of landowners as well. Six residents in 1816 (the top 5% of owners) possessed 41% of all the locally held land; thirteen (the top 10%) owned 56%, and thirty-two (the top 25%) owned 76%. Significant quantities of land were also claimed by absentee owners and distant speculators.

Thus, despite the stereotype of Appalachia as having been relatively egalitarian before the modern era of railroad building and coal industrialization, Clay County was a highly unequal – but not atypical – Appalachian community from the earliest years of its settlement.[5] Many ordinary white farmers undoubtedly hoped to acquire enough land there to secure a decent living, that is, "a competency" as it was called, and to leave a legacy for their offspring, but other white settlers, especially slave owners, were far more acquisitive and commercially involved, speculating in land and industrial endeavors in order to add to the wealth, power, and status that they brought with them into the Kentucky hills. As these alternative trajectories were played out over the ensuing decades of the antebellum period, a higher proportion of the white population would eventually become landowners, but the gap in wealth between rich and poor widened dramatically in Clay County. Landlessness decreased by 16.5% from 1816 to 1840 when 43% of the county's taxpayers owned land, but in 1860, the ten richest individuals – all slaveholders – averaged personal estates worth $45,890 in a county where the average estate was worth only $859, or fifty-three times less. In fact, the wealthiest individual in 1860, salt manufacturer Francis Clark, was 200 times richer than the mean, with an estate worth $175,000.[6]

Scholars have shown that short-range migrations across the trans-Appalachian frontier were often "financially and politically remunerative" for settler-capitalists and for the many ordinary farmers as well who sold land or bartered shares in family estates to purchase cheaper land in newly opened territories.[7] The earliest deeds recorded in the Clay County courthouse support this finding, preserving not only the transactions of early speculators, slave owners, and industrialists but also those of ordinary farmers like James Lewis who sold 100 acres of land back in the New River country of North Carolina in 1816 where he had formerly resided, or the several intermarried members of the landless Hollingsworth and Reid households in Clay County who appointed a brother still living in North Carolina that same year to act as their legate in an estate settlement also in the New River valley.[8]

As we noted in the previous chapter, writers in the 1960s such as Harry Caudill were unable to imagine that enterprising individuals had ever ventured onto the Appalachian frontier, leaving that zone for the renegades from civilization who wished to escape the demands of law and ordered society.[9] To move to the wilds of Clay County must have made sense, however, to pioneers like Egbert Fort who moved there before acquiring $2,100 from the sale of land and eight slaves in South Carolina in 1812.[10] The historical record is mute about the wisdom of Fort's wager on finding prosperity in Appalachian Kentucky. However, it is clear that settlement in Clay County greatly benefited Abner Baker, Sr., patriarch of one of the large family groups that figured so centrally in Clay County's violent nineteenth-century political history.

Abner Baker served as clerk of the Clay County Court from its formation in 1807 until the 1830s. Associated in salt manufacturing with some of the county's most prominent leaders and brother-in-law of a future Kentucky governor (Robert Letcher), Baker owned twenty-five slaves and more than 1,500 acres of land in Clay County worth $21,382 in 1825, the year before he wrote "a brief narrative" of his life "for the perusement and encouragement of his children."[11] Although Baker attributed what he called his "moderate gain" to an "aspiring spirit," "common sense," and "a kind providence," class-based resources and privileges available from family connections both east and west of the Appalachian Mountains facilitated his achievement of wealth in Appalachia.

Baker was born in Prince Edward, Virginia, in 1775, a younger son in a large family. His father's estate was sizeable, consisting of "about forty slaves and land and other property of not less value that $40,000," but Baker wisely recognized that the division of such wealth among ten children would "leave but little to each." Having "no doubt of success," yet stubbornly declining his father's offer of the education at Hampton and Sydney College that his older brothers had enjoyed, Baker vowed instead that he "would by industry procure a competency." To his father's dismay, he apprenticed himself at age fifteen to learn the art of cabinetmaking. After three years in apprenticeship and "[h]aving heard much in favor of Kentucky and believing that a new country would better suit [his] condition than one that was already in the grasp of the wealthy," Baker set out for the Kentucky frontier in 1793.

After a few difficult months in Kentucky, Baker's discovery there of a man who owed his father money afforded him enough money to return to Virginia. This prodigal son soon won his father's forgiveness in 1794 as well as "a piece of land" and "a negro man," modest wealth that enabled him to earn a small amount of money in agriculture. Viewing this Virginia land "as an indenture to poverty," however, Baker "could not after having seen Kentucky think of remaining there" and thus made plans to return to the new state.

In 1795, Baker and one slave went to live with an older brother who was already established in the Bluegrass region of Kentucky. By his own account, Baker worked hard each day and tried to improve his education by studying for three hours every night in the "good library" of this brother who "had received a liberal education at Hamden Sydney." Soon he married well, bought land, and trained himself in the art of surveying. His rapid rise in Bluegrass society is reflected in the fact that by 1802, at age 27, he was elected to the Garrard County Court and in 1804 to the Kentucky legislature.

Baker's most important opportunity for advancement, however, came in 1807 when he was appointed clerk of the county and circuit courts of newly formed Clay County where a kinsman, Robert Baker, served as the county's first sheriff and another cousin, Francis Clark, was soon to become a salt-maker. Baker's ambition, by his own account, was "limited only to procure such a competency as would enable [him] to raise, educate, and qualify [his] children in a way to be useful to themselves and society" and never "to toil for a fortune." To achieve this goal, Baker "surrendered" the "fruits of [Blue-grass] society" in order "to unclench the hard hand of fortune" on the rough Appalachian frontier, the conditions of which, he wrote, "prudence [forbade] a remark."

Not all migrants to Appalachian Kentucky and Clay County were descended from Virginia slave owners like Baker and few achieved his level of success near the top of that hierarchical society. Most Clay Countians during the antebellum period lived lives in far less plenty. The earliest settlers of the Beech Creek neighborhoods, the Andrews and the Johnsons, were representative of the majority of the population who owned no slaves in Appalachian Kentucky but even here, in remote Beech Creek – outside the zone of the county's most intense commercialization that grew up along the brine-producing waters of Goose Creek – early settlement witnessed the establishment of considerable inequalities as well.

Beech Creek's most prominent pioneer settler, Adoniram Andrews,[12] was born in New Hampshire in 1734, the same year that saw the birth of Daniel Boone and two years after that of George Washington. Dying in Beech Creek in 1838 at the age of 104, Andrews outlived both Boone and Washington by many years, his life spanning the entire compass of time that witnessed the vast movement of population down the Great Valley of Virginia, into the Carolinas, and up through the Cumberland Gap into Kentucky. A mechanic, ironworker, and shipbuilder by trade, Andrews moved from New Hampshire to North Carolina, Georgia, and possibly South Carolina before settling permanently in Clay County. Sometime near the end of the first decade of the nineteenth century, he built one of the first sawmills in the county.[13]

A descendant of New Englanders who had first settled in Massachusetts in the 1630s, and believed to have been a first cousin of a famous patriot from that region, Andrews served as a captain in the Battle of Kings Mountain during the American Revolution. It was probably this military service that allowed him to claim the 400 acres of land in Clay County he reported for taxes in 1808. Never an owner of slaves nor supremely wealthy by Clay County standards, Adoniram Andrews stood out, nonetheless, among the first generation of Beech Creek settlers, not only for being that neighborhood's wealthiest patriarch but – as the owner of a sawmill – certainly its most commercially involved resident as well.

More typical of the largely subsistence-oriented, general farmers of Beech Creek was Samuel Johnson, Sr., the original ancestor of the Preston Johnson household with whom James Brown lived in 1942, during the latter's first ethnographic study of Beech Creek. Probably an emigrant from North Carolina, Samuel Johnson and an adult son were identified as landless when the first Clay County tax roll was drawn up in 1807; but by 1811, Samuel had acquired a modest fifty acres on the stream from which the surrounding Beech Creek community took its name.

Although the Andrews and the Johnsons soon intermarried and became the two most prominent families in the Beech Creek neighborhood, the initial, though modest, wealth and status differences between them persisted across generations – testimony to the enduring legacy of inequality.[14] In 1850, Adoniram Andrews III was the wealthiest farmer in Beech Creek with 5,603 acres in fifteen tracts that were worth about $6,000. In comparison, the wealthiest member of the Johnson family, Elisha Johnson, accumulated, at most, 2,000 acres a few years later. Neither owned slaves. Although the descendants of both families were poor by national standards when James Brown lived among them in the 1940s, the descendants of Adoniram Andrews still ranked as the most highly respected members of the Beech Creek community in the 1940s and the ones that eventually achieved the greatest educational and occupational success in the urban United States after leaving Appalachia.

In later chapters, we will observe more closely the way of life in the Beech Creek neighborhoods of the nineteenth century and the socioeconomic trajectory of its population that eventuated, for many, in poverty and outmigration from Appalachia in the twentieth century. But the people of Beech Creek, like the yeomen farmers in other neighborhoods who constituted a majority of Clay County's nineteenth-century population, were neither architects nor primary beneficiaries of the area's foremost wealth-producing institutions, slavery and industry. Although eventually a couple of Beech Creek residents acquired slaves and many of the region's white "plain folk" benefited from the presence of a slave-based industry that created jobs and markets for farm goods, opportunities in manufacturing were reserved primarily for members of the South's backcountry elite.

Historians such as Gail Terry have already described the "frontier elite" that dominated social, economic, and political life in early Kentucky. Consisting of families like the Prestons, Breckinridges, and McDowells, to name but a few of those who moved into the Great Valley of Virginia during the late 1730s and 1740s and into Kentucky territory after the American Revolution, this group viewed land speculation on the southern frontier as its "avenue to wealth and power." Descendants of immigrants who had "consciously used the opportunities of empire to improve their own status" by crossing the Atlantic, they brought to Kentucky "a commercial outlook which prized the acquisition of wealth, power and social position." According to Terry, this elite "demonstrated little comprehension of a distinction between their own private interest and public good" in the pursuit of their ambitions.[15] Although Terry fails to recognize that hegemony is won by identifying the interests of subalterns with those of their superiors – not by being mindless of the former's interests altogether – her observation suggests, nevertheless, how extensively the backcountry elite exercised both political leadership and economic power in frontier Kentucky.[16]

Throughout the entire history of Clay County during the nineteenth century, the two most important local representatives of this backcountry elite were the Whites and the Garrards (Appendix 2). Both well-to-do families were drawn into Appalachian Kentucky by the prospect of earning further wealth there by the manufacture and sale of salt.

James White, "the wealthiest man in Washington County, Virginia," when he died in 1838, was born in Carlyle, Pennsylvania, in 1770.[17] White went to work at an early age as a clerk for the Baltimore firm of Talbot, Jones, and Company. At about the age of twenty, he took a stock of goods on credit from Baltimore to begin his career as a merchant on Virginia's southwestern frontier. Although White's commercial interests and landholding eventually spanned a huge portion of the southern backcountry from Virginia to Alabama, he maintained his primary residence on the eastern edge of the Appalachians in Abingdon, Virginia, where he began to manufacture salt around 1798. According to an unpublished family biography, all of White's

> enterprises seemed to prosper, and his control of the [Abingdon] salt works and its market enabled him to establish a great number of mercantile concerns (it is said that he had forty-five at one time), in the states of Virginia, Tennessee, Kentucky, Alabama, and Georgia. From the profits of these and the sale of salt, large revenues were realized. These profits were invested in Lead Mines in Wythe County [Virginia]; in Cotton Plantations; Slaves and other property, which at the time of his death were valued at more than two million dollars. His land alone, valued at two dollars an acre, amounted to more than seven hundred and fifty thousand dollars.[18]

According to traditional accounts, White first learned about the salt-producing waters of Goose Creek in soon-to-be Kentucky while serving as colonel in an army raised to protect white settlers on the western frontier. About 1803, he purchased an interest in land and salt furnaces on Goose Creek that he soon operated with slave labor, first in partnership with his younger brother, Hugh White (1777–1857), and later with Hugh's son, Alexander.

Although James White never lived in Clay County himself, Hugh White moved there in 1804 and eventually became one of the county's richest and most powerful citizens. Not yet wealthy when he went to Goose Creek at age twenty-seven to manage his brother's business, but already experienced in commerce from having operated a country store at the Cumberland Gap, White soon became an independent salt manufacturer and entrepreneur. By 1840, he had acquired an immense amount of property and was the richest individual on the Clay County tax roll when he valued his property at $105,400, including lands worth $88,000 and thirty-eight slaves.[19]

When Clay County was established in 1807, Governor Christopher Greenup commissioned Hugh White as an assistant judge for the county and circuit of Clay. In 1810, he was made a brigadier general in the Kentucky Militia.[20] That appointment signaled and solidified White's growing wealth, power, and status whereas the former was merely the first in a number of political appointments and offices by which members of the White family influenced the local government and political society of Clay County. As the father of thirteen children including eight males, Hugh White established a political as well an economic dynasty in Clay County, his sons, grandsons, and greatgrandsons holding local political offices as justices of the peace, county clerks, sheriffs, and later – when Kentucky's county governments were restructured – as county judge executives, assessors, magistrates, and school board heads. White's descendants represented Clay County in the state legislature and Appalachian Kentucky counties in the U.S. Congress. Hugh White's son John (1802–45), a Bluegrass lawyer, served in the U.S. House of Representatives from 1835 until 1845 and as Speaker of the House during the Twenty-Seventh Congress.[21] A grandson, John D. (Daugherty) White, represented Clay and surrounding counties in the U.S. House in 1875–7 and 1881–5. Another descendant was Clay County Judge-Executive in the 1960s during the War on Poverty. As recently as the early 1990s, a direct descendant of Hugh White had served as mayor of Manchester for twenty-four years.

As prominent as were the Whites in Clay County throughout the nineteenth century and much of the twentieth century as well, their power and influence was checked – indeed, challenged for decades – by Clay County representatives of the rich and powerful Garrard family, described by historians as "one of the first great political families of Kentucky."[22] In 1798, while serving as Kentucky's second governor, James Garrard (1749–1822) patented 500 acres of land surrounding the Buffalo Salt Lick on Goose Creek in order to engage in the manufacture of salt there. His last major land acquisition, this investment in Appalachian Kentucky was a final link in Governor Garrard's vast agricultural and commercial empire.

The son of a "moderately wealthy farmer," Garrard was born in Stafford County, Virginia, whose courthouse was erected on Garrard family land. Both Garrard and his father served as colonels in the Revolutionary War and the younger Garrard's "distinguished military service" is said to have earned him a seat in the Virginia House of Delegates.[23] Skilled as a surveyor, Garrard explored the territory of Kentucky soon after the Revolution and there he surveyed and patented thousands of acres of choice central Kentucky land for family and friends before Kentucky became a state in 1792, including 40,000 acres he reserved for himself.[24]

James Garrard's career illustrates clearly how kinship networks and the maintenance of political and economic connections in the seaboard states helped to consolidate the power and position of the southern backcountry elite as it engrossed lands in Kentucky and brought that zone, including Appalachia, into the orbit of the capitalist world economy. According to a biographer, Garrard's "father's influence in the militia and his own reputation as a soldier were generously rewarded by his efforts in Kentucky as he surveyed thousands of acres of land" while Garrard's "links or connections in the Virginia Legislature and land office further aided his acquisitive powers."[25]

Garrard settled permanently in the Bluegrass region of Kentucky in the early 1780s, along with his wife's kinfolk, the Mountjoys, and his family's long-term friends and allies, the Edwardses, both from Stafford County, Virginia. Together, these three families forged a long-lasting power bloc in supremely wealthy Bourbon County that proved strong enough to help elect Garrard as governor of Kentucky and to send his friend, neighbor, and daughter's father-in-law, John Edwards, to the U.S. Senate.[26]

As a representative of the Bluegrass region in the Virginia Legislature, Garrard played a central role in writing the enabling legislation that granted statehood to Kentucky and ensured that the Virginia land laws and land titles benefiting the members of the Old Dominion's transplanted aristocracy such as the Garrards and Mountjoys would be upheld. Later, serving as Kentucky's second governor from 1796 to 1804, Garrard was an effective advocate for the role of state government in making internal improvements and promoting commerce and industry.

Although a defender of conservative land laws, Garrard was a liberal Jeffersonian Republican who championed the expansion of popular sovereignty in the Second Constitution of Kentucky, which was partially implemented during his first term as governor. Still regarded as one of Kentucky's most effective governors, he is also remembered for his cooperation with Thomas Jefferson in sponsoring the so-called "Kentucky Resolutions" against the Federalists' Alien and Sedition Acts. Although a slave owner, he was one of those southern aristocrats who, in the eighteenth century before Cotton became King, advocated the elimination of slavery. As one of the most highly respected Baptist ministers and denominational leaders in Kentucky, he argued against the institution of slavery on moral grounds and, as governor, led an unsuccessful movement in the 1790s to make it illegal in Kentucky.

"[O]ne of the great planters of the West" and "a man of immense property and wealth,"[27] James Garrard retired from public life to his Bourbon County farm where he was known as both a great agriculturalist who imported fine livestock into Kentucky and pioneered in the thoroughbred horse and cattle raising that came to symbolize the Kentucky Bluegrass region and as a businessman who invested in commercial enterprises such as gristmills and – most importantly here – salt furnaces.[28]

Two of Garrard's sons in particular inherited their father's economic and – to a lesser extent – political ambitions. William Garrard represented Bourbon County for a number of years in the Kentucky legislature, but gained most recognition for his leadership in scientific agriculture and livestock breeding as did his own son, Charles.[29] Colonel Daniel Garrard (1780–1866) was only three years old when his father left Virginia to help settle the trans-Appalachian frontier. He married Lucinda Toulman of Mobile, Alabama, the daughter of Harry Toulman, a learned Frenchman who had migrated to the United States from England and served as the president of Transylvania College in Lexington before becoming James Garrard's Secretary of State. Daniel Garrard moved to Clay County in 1806 to establish his father's salt-works there and helped to build that industry in Clay County. He represented the county numerous times in the Kentucky legislature and – along with his sons, James H. Garrard and Theophilus Toulman ("T. T.") Garrard – indelibly shaped Clay County's political life and culture.

Whatever moral qualms James Garrard may have entertained about the ownership of slaves were apparently not passed down to Daniel Garrard and his sons whose way of life in Clay County was predicated on slave labor. Indeed, T. T. Garrard, a heroic brigadier general in the Union Army during the Civil War and later the aged, patriarchal head of the Clay County Democratic Party in the late 1890s when the Garrard-White feud was front-page news in the *New York Times*, is reported to have said that he would not have heeded Lincoln's call to arms had he known it would mean the abolition of slavery in Kentucky.[30] Slavery and salt were indissolubly combined for elite families like the Garrards and the Whites during the first phase of the capitalist development of Appalachian Kentucky, even though many Clay Countians, including the early settlers on Beech Creek, were able to forge a way of life based on family labor and general farming that was largely – but not wholly – independent of both slave ownership and industry.

Thus, we see that the early history of Appalachian Kentucky differed little from the history of frontier Kentucky as a whole when slaveholding and gentry rule constrained the egalitarianism of backcountry yeoman democracy as two strands of an emerging social order. From the mountain hollow carved out by the waters of Beech Creek where Samuel Johnson and his sons labored on their fifty-acre farm in 1811, to the brine wells and furnaces of Hugh White and Daniel Garrard on Goose Creek where African American slaves toiled to make salt the same year, wealth and egalitarianism confronted one another as contradictory principles in the formation of antebellum Appalachian Kentucky.

By suggesting that the engrossment and settlement of Kentucky land evinced a blend of traditionalism and modernism, it has been observed both that in "every Kentucky county, local family clusters linked by blood and marriage sorted out and organized society in the traditional, intimate, particularistic way" and yet that frontier Kentucky was profoundly influenced by "fiercely acquisitive agrarian capitalism."[31] These two only apparently contradictory statements by the same author suggest that traditional social relations and modern tenets of possessive individualism were interwoven in the formation of Kentucky, just as we have seen they both were put into play when James Garrard aggressively acquired land there for his family and friends. The choices among such principles, however, were never simply either/or decisions.

As subsequent chapters will show more fully, families that operated farms largely with their own labor – like the Andrews and Johnsons in Beech Creek – created a social world of kinship cooperation and neighborhood reciprocity that contrasted sharply to the entrepreneurial activities and way of life of their more capitalistic neighbors. But the Whites and the Garrards, while pursuing an aggressive course of profit making and marketplace competition, built their world, too, on the basis of cooperative family strategies. Their's, however, called for land speculation, slaveholding, commercial enterprise, and the exercise of political control. Before we can understand more fully how these diverse strategies differed and what each implied for the long-term development of community, wealth, and poverty in Appalachian Kentucky, however, we must first understand more about Clay County's antebellum economy and the depth of its embeddedness in capitalism as gauged by (1) manufacturing, (2) commerce, and (3) slaveholding.

Salt Manufacturing

The scholarly neglect of antebellum industry in Appalachia is unfortunate since, as Mary Beth Pudup has observed, simplistic views of the region's early economy have diverted attention from important questions about how prior indigenous development helped pave the way for the particular forms of dependent capitalist industrial development in the twentieth century for which the region today is famous, as well as how early development also made possible the rise of local elites who influenced the political conditions within which subsequent economic development occurred.[32] Saltmaking was one of Appalachian Kentucky's great antebellum industries, preceding its better-known extractive industries of the modern era such as timbering and coal mining. Like iron making in northeastern Kentucky,[33] saltmaking helped to open the mountain district of southeastern Kentucky to wider commerce by linking it to distant markets, led to the importation of a population of enslaved laborers, and created the socioeconomic foundations for an emergent political elite. Very little, however, has been written about the development or operation of saltmaking in Clay County where the industry achieved its greatest success in Kentucky.[34]

Daniel Boone discovered the salt licks on Goose Creek as early as 1769 by following buffalo and other game there as he explored various Indian routes along the Warrior's Path – the great north-south Native American passageway across the Appalachians, one branch of which passed near the present site of Manchester on route from the Cumberland Gap to the South Fork of the Kentucky River. According to an early nineteenth-century account, the origins of the salt industry in Clay County dated from 1800, when James Collins, an early settler and hunter, first made salt on Goose Creek for his own use by boiling water from a local spring, but probably the manufacture of salt in Clay County began at an even earlier date shortly before the end of the eighteenth century.[35]

The first two commercial establishments in Clay County, Langford's Lick and Outlaw's Saltworks, were located several miles apart on the Collins Fork of Goose Creek (see Figure 3.1). Both made salt by boiling brine in rows of large iron kettles, each weighing hundreds of pounds.[36] Following ownership changes, these two establishments were known afterwards as the Lower Goose Creek Salt Works, located near the present site of Manchester, and the Upper Works, located near the Collins Fork headwaters of Goose Creek. Both salt-

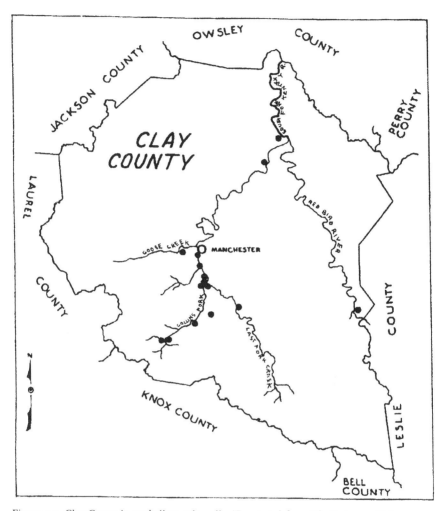

Figure 3.1 Clay County's antebellum salt wells. [Reprinted from *The Register* 50 (July 1952): p. 172, Courtesy of the Kentucky Historical Society].

works were mentioned in state legislation in 1802 that provided for the opening of a road between them and the Bluegrass town of Richmond, suggesting that their commercial significance was already well established by this early date.[37]

By 1810, four firms in Clay County were producing 70,000 bushels of salt annually. Along with a slightly greater amount also produced in Appalachian

Kentucky at the Little Sandy Works, this quantity amounted to nearly half of Kentucky's total salt production that year.[38] Throughout the antebellum era, saltmaking in Clay County was primarily centered on the Collins and East Forks of Goose Creek south of Manchester, the eventual county seat. Additionally, however, Francis Clark, who divided his residence between Clay County and the Bluegrass, operated saltworks near the village of Oneida, where the northern section of Goose Creek joins the Red Bird River to form the South Fork of the Kentucky River, and John Gilbert, one of the area's earliest settlers, operated or leased an additional well and furnaces farther upstream on the Red Bird.

The expansion of the saltmaking industry provoked much conflict and litigation among entrepreneurs and speculators over rental agreements and the ownership of lands containing salt-producing waters during the first decade of the nineteenth century. By the end of that decade, however, the three principal families that dominated the salt industry throughout its subsequent history – the Whites, the Garrards, and the Bates, each with important ties to the Bluegrass region or to Virginia – had arrived in Clay County, defended themselves against challenges to their proprietorship, and established themselves as significant saltmakers.

John Bates first appeared on the docket of civil cases in the Clay County circuit court as early as 1808 when he defended his purchase of an interest in the Lower Goose Creek Saltworks from John Amis, a deceased partner in the firm that ousted the original proprietor of Landford's Lick.[39] In 1820, Bates's saltworks produced 6,000 bushels of salt with nine slaves.[40] Sometime later, he was joined by his brother, Daniel, who expanded operations and outlived him by several years before being murdered in 1844 by Dr. Abner Baker, Jr., an event, as we shall see, that precipitated the infamous Garrard-White "feud." Through the marriage of a sister, the Bates brothers were connected to the prominent Walker family of central Kentucky and Knoxville, Tennessee, and they were joined in business in Clay County by several young male members of the Walker family during the 1830s and 1840s.

Operating first as James Garrard and Sons until 1822, then as Elizabeth Garrard and Sons after the death of the governor, and as Daniel Garrard and Sons after 1835, the Garrard family also played a significant role in the development of antebellum Clay County's salt industry.[41] The Garrards remained active from 1806, when Daniel Garrard first went to the mountains to begin making salt for his father and brothers, until 1908, four years after the death of T. T. Garrard, when the family closed the county's last salt furnace, a tiny operation that by then made salt only periodically for local demand. In 1820, after drought and economic recession had produced three disastrously bad years for the industry, the Garrards manufactured 24,000 bushels of salt with the labor of twenty-two slaves, a quantity amounting to 36% of the local total – probably the highest proportion of the county's production they ever achieved. By 1850, the Garrards' market share had fallen to 8.5% of the county's total when they produced even less salt (20,000 bushels) than thirty years earlier, yet they remained a potent force in local affairs for many years to come.[42]

The Whites, as noted, began the Clay County branch of their saltmaking business in 1804 when James White purchased a share of the Outlaw Saltworks from John Ballenger, an entrepreneur from adjacent Knox County, for $1,100 in merchandise from his store in Abingdon, Virginia, and $50 in cash. He also purchased 400 acres of adjoining land for $2,000.[43] Hugh White came to Clay County later that year to oversee production and manage local trade at the company store. In addition to operating the Upper Goose Creek (Outlaw) Saltworks, Hugh White eventually acquired ownership of the Lower Goose Creek Saltworks (Langford's Lick) as well, and he and his sons built additional furnaces and wells along Goose Creek. Like their competitors the Garrards, the Whites also established wells and furnaces in the North Fork valley of the Kentucky River in today's Perry County.[44]

The White brothers divided their properties in 1824, at which time Hugh's adult sons James and Alexander managed their father's and uncle's works, respectively.[45] Along with his sons Alexander, James, Daugherty, and Benjamin Franklin who went into the salt trade, Hugh White eventually became the largest producer in the county's history. In 1850, the Whites' combined enterprises (including a firm owned by James White's widow, Eliza) had $85,000 of capital invested and made 156,000 bushels of salt, a quantity amounting to two-thirds of the county's total production that year, just after the date when the industry is believed to have reached its all-time peak production of a quarter of a million bushels.[46] The White's control over this much of the local output helped them to influence commodity prices via-à-vis local competitors, a fact that ultimately proved to be a source of tension and conflict among local entrepreneurs, especially the Garrards who also vied with them for control of county government.[47]

Besides members of the Bates, White, and Garrard families, other Clay County merchants and entrepreneurs also attempted to make salt during the industry's early years, including Andrew Bradley, William Bledsoe, Abner Baker, Richard Nicholas, Barton Potter, and John Slaughter. Later, men such as Apperson May, James T. Woodward and Christopher Rand, Mike Horton, John and Hiram Hibbard, and S. M. Dickerson, and at least one woman, Rhoda Taylor, moved in and out of saltmaking in response to market expansions and contractions.[48] Often when their saltmaking attempts failed, as John Murphey's did in 1816 when he could not meet his obligations to several wholesale firms in the Bluegrass, the better-established saltmakers benefited, as Daniel Garrard and John Bates did by acquiring much of Murphey's property from sheriff's auctions at considerable discount.[49]

Early advertisements for renters by the owners of salt licks suggest that persons from beyond Clay County were encouraged as well to take advantage of the economic opportunities that saltmaking promised there. Thus, as early as 1805, John Patrick, the Madison County surveyor and part owner of the saltworks at Landford's Lick, placed an advertisement in the *Kentucky Gazette* offering to rent "two furnaces at the Goose Creek salt works in [then] Madison County with convenient houses for the accommodation of workmen" where, he promised, "the water is good, the wood convenient, and the terms will be reasonable."[50] Civil disputes between renters and local proprietors over breaches of contract for access to furnaces or water, such as the cases by Andrew and Joseph Craig of Knox County against Hugh White and his brother-in-law George Baugh in 1810, or Samuel and James Todd of Virginia against John Bates in 1814, suggest that such lease agreements, generally granting proprietors 1/8 to 1/10 of the salt produced, provided a means for early entrepreneurs both to raise capital and to pass on risks to other investors.[51]

Although rental opportunities represented one entry point into saltmaking, success generally came only to those with sufficient capital, land, and slaves to compete effectively not only against local rivals, but against the obstacles of nature as well. By drilling ever more deeply into the earth's surface, Clay County saltmakers were ensured a continuing supply of brine-rich waters, but the exhaustion of particular wells necessitated the continuous exploration and purchase of additional lands. The ongoing acquisition of land was also prompted by the exhaustion of adjacent supplies of timber, which provided the primary fuel for boiling water during the early years of the industry. Thus, at the end of the nineteenth century, elderly residents of Clay County could recall that when they were children, many years prior to the timber export industry, vast areas surrounding the salt furnaces had already been denuded of trees.[52] Since it was cheaper to transport water than wood, this problem was first solved by pumping brine waters to increasingly distant furnaces near fresh supplies of timber. Beginning in the late 1830s, however, locally mined coal began to be substituted for wood in the evaporation process and the salt furnaces were returned to more convenient locations.[53] In either case, successful saltmaking required capital resources well beyond the means of most Clay Countians.

Table 3.1 reports the growth and decline of the Clay County salt industry from 1820 to 1880 when only one firm was still operating.[54] According to census information, the highest level of employment in the industry was

Table 3.1. *Salt Manufacturing in Clay County, 1820–80*

Year	No. of Firms	Invested Capital ($)	No. of Employees	Quantity (bushels)	Value ($)
1820	7	—	86	73,000	73,000
1840[a]	—	—	148	196,000	—
1850	9	162,000	134	234,500	58,675
1860[b]	5	40,000	59	13,933	21,190
1870	4	16,600	40	64,000	20,920
1880	1	13,000	24	40,000	15,000

[a] Manuscript records for 1840 unavailable.
[b] Firms were "at rest" during most of 1860.

Sources: *U.S. Censuses of Manufacturing* (Clay County Manuscripts), 1820, 1850, 1860, and 1870; 1840 *Aggregate Census of Manufactures* (6th) 26: 262–3.

66

reached in 1840 when 148 hands, mostly slaves, worked in saltmaking. Total production, however, was greater ten years later when nine firms produced just under a quarter of a million bushels of salt, a level reached in the mid-1830s as well.[55] Salt production almost ceased altogether in 1860; even though the amounts produced in 1870 and 1880 were greater than in 1860, they failed to reach the production level of 1820, an off year for the industry because of drought and economic depression.[56]

Table 3.2 shows that all but two of the eleven manufacturing establishments reported in the census for Clay County in 1850 were saltmakers. The only exceptions were two small tanneries. Saltmaking accounted for 95% of all the industrial capital invested in the county that year, as well as 87% of its manufacturing value. Relative to the times, these were not small enterprises. Clay County salt firms averaged about $18,000 in capital and fifteen workers in 1850. The average New England manufacturing firm a decade later had only $12,456 invested capital and nineteen employees. Southern firms averaged only $4,827 in capital and six workers in 1860.[57] With a capital investment of $40,000 in 1850, the largest saltmakers in the county, James and Daugherty White, engaged twenty-five workers to produce 70,000 bushels of salt valued at $17,500. Profit rates for the industry are difficult to estimate since data on important costs such as shipping are not available. It seems likely, however, that despite fairly low ratios of output to number of employees per firm for the county as a whole (only $410 per worker compared with the 1860 rate of $1,196 per worker in New England), many manufacturers prospered since much of their capital was invested in slaves who, as we show later, were also utilized in agriculture so that salt earnings represented only a portion of the value produced by their labor.[58]

Besides its local use in surrounding counties of Appalachian Kentucky, large quantities of salt from Clay County were shipped on flatboats down the Kentucky River to markets in the Bluegrass region. Even as late as the early 1840s, when salt from Appalachian (West) Virginia was flooding western markets including central Kentucky, Clay County salt was still in demand in many Bluegrass communities including Bourbon and Mercer counties and in Frankfort, the state capital.[59] Additional amounts of salt were transported 20 miles overland to adjacent Knox County for shipment down the Cumberland River to markets in southern Kentucky and, in early years, to Nashville and Middle Tennessee. Other quantities of salt were transported by packhorses and wagons on the Wilderness Road through the Cumberland Gap to markets in eastern Tennessee and southwestern Virginia. The booming city of Knoxville, an increasingly important meatpacking town in Appalachian Tennessee in the 1830s, was especially dependent on Clay County salt supplies. Still other quantities of salt were shipped on flatboats from Powell's

Table 3.2. *Clay County: Census of Manufacturing, 1850*

Name of Company	Type of Business	Capital Invested ($)	Kind of Power	Average No. Employed		Annual Product		
				M	F	Quantities	Kinds	Values ($)
D. Garrard & Sons	Saltmakers	20,000	Horse	10	1	20,000	Salt	5,000
Apperson May & Co.	Saltmakers	16,000	Steam	13	1	20,000	Salt	5,000
William & B. F. White	Saltmakers	15,000	Horse	10		16,000	Salt	4,000
Francis Clark	Saltmakers	12,167	Horse	19	1	18,500	Salt	4,675
Alexander White & Sons	Saltmakers	12,000	Horse	11	1	20,000	Salt	5,000
James & D. White	Saltmakers	40,000	Horse	23	2	70,000	Salt	17,500
Eliza White	Saltmakers	12,000	Horse	11	1	30,000	Salt	7,500
Barton Potter	Tanner	5,000	Horse	5	1	1,500	Skins	2,000
Leander Miller	Tanner	3,000	Horse	3		1,000	Skins	4,000
Hugh & D. White	Saltmakers	20,000	Horse	16	1	20,000	Salt	5,000
James T. Woodard	Saltmakers	15,000	Horse	12	1	20,000	Salt	5,000

Source: U.S. Census of Manufacturing (Clay County manuscripts), 1850.

Valley in Virginia via the Holston and Tennessee Rivers to Alabama where prices at one time were reportedly as high as $5.00 a bushel and where, not incidently, James White's descendants achieved wealth and political power from the salt trade and cotton planting.[60]

Despite the significance of Goose Creek salt to the local economy and the backcountry regions of the several southern states, its production was dwarfed in comparison to the vast quantities of salt manufactured in Kanawha County, Virginia (now West Virginia), throughout the antebellum period, where as early as "1817 over 700,000 bushels of salt were being produced annually near Charleston."[61] Kanawha saline virtually dominated antebellum markets throughout the Ohio Valley, including the important meatpacking cities of Cincinnati and Louisville where the otherwise highly competitive manufacturers of (West) Virginia united to monopolize trade by operating exclusive sales agencies. In 1850, thirty-three Kanawha County salt firms combined to produce more than three million bushels of salt with the labor of 3,140 slaves. One firm alone, Dickinson and Schrewsbury, exceeded Clay County's total production that year by almost 20,000 bushels.[62]

The success of Kanawha County saltmaking was due primarily to local innovations in the technology of drilling wells by boring deeply into the rich underground brine waters that were an important Appalachian geological resource tapped during that era. This enabled producers to overcome the initial disadvantages of their remote mountain location by offsetting transportation costs with lowered expenditures for fuel and labor.[63] Many of Kentucky's weaker wells were forced out of business at this time by the cheaper Kanawha salines, which caused prices in many sections of the Ohio Valley to drop from two dollars to one dollar per bushel in 1810, and from one dollar to as little as thirty cents per bushel in 1812.[64] Salt manufacturers in Lewis County, for instance, found that by 1819, sawmills and gristmills in their locality were more profitable than salt furnaces, and by 1850, the salt industry in the northeastern section of Appalachian Kentucky had all but come to an end.[65]

With rich brines comparable to those of the Kanawha region trapped far beneath its surface, however, Clay County was one of the few Kentucky saltmaking communities to adopt and benefit from the early advances in drilling technology pioneered in (West) Virginia.[66] At least in the eyes of local manufacturers, however, geography rather than geology most hindered the growth of the Goose Creek salt industry and prevented it from keeping pace with saltmakers in the Kanawha Valley.

Since the shipment of salt from Clay County posed a huge burden both to producers and consumers because of the area's rugged terrain and initially remote location, the Kentucky legislature passed numerous measures for the improvement of the area's roads expressly for the purpose of facilitating commerce at the Goose Creek saltworks. These included bills authorizing toll-gate (or "turnpike") keepers to collect fees from travelers, excluding salt merchants and their customers, for road construction and repair along designated routes. Among the earliest in Kentucky, these turnpikes were designed to supplement the traditional county militia system whereby local residents (or proxies) were obligated to do annual road work, a system judged insufficient to the task in Appalachian Kentucky where roads leading to the saltworks "pass[ed] through a country but thinly settled and [otherwise] unfavorable for a road," as one legislative bill noted in 1818.[67]

Acts of 1802, 1817, and 1842, in particular, created three major state roads that linked the Clay County saltworks to the all-important Wilderness Road and to important commercial centers in Richmond, Irvine, and London, respectively, and numerous secondary roads linked Manchester to smaller communities in eastern Kentucky such as Hazard in nearby Perry County.[68] Thus, the principal historian of Kentucky mountain transportation notes that "the tributaries of the Wilderness Road were improved chiefly with the object of facilitating the transportation of salt from numerous works located in the vicinity of Manchester," which, she notes, "became, at an early date, a center from which roads radiated in all directions." As a consequence of this early effort, the area's roads, "although steeper and more subject to frequent washouts, were not much inferior to those of Central Kentucky" during the first three decades of the nineteenth century.[69] Although the authors of exaggerated accounts of the county's notorious feuds at the end of the century wrote as if roads had barely penetrated the area, a federal survey in 1904 revealed that, because of early industrial development, Clay County's 1,600 miles of roads gave it the highest ratio of roads per square mile at the time in Kentucky.[70] Thus, earlier, when saltmaking was at its zenith, and despite its rugged terrain, the county was far from being the strange and dissociated place it would be portrayed as a half century later.

Even more important than overland routes, however, were the mountain region's waterways that carried as much as 75% of Clay County's salt to market.[71] The most important of these waterways was the Kentucky River. Crude wooden flatboats 60 feet long and capable of carrying up to 50 tons were used to ship barrels of salt downstream from the headwaters of Goose Creek a distance of twenty-six and one-half miles to its intersection with the Red Bird River. From there, the boats traveled another forty-two miles on the South Fork to the main channel of the Kentucky River and on downstream to markets in central Kentucky.[72] As did the roads of Appalachian Kentucky, small rivers like the Goose Creek and the South Fork presented manufacturers with numerous obstacles and dangers. Although saltmakers in the Kanawha Valley also relied primarily on flatboats to transport their commodities to market, the far greater navigability of the Kanawha and Ohio Rivers made transport on those waterways considerably easier and cheaper than on the rivers of Appalachian Kentucky. So great was the ease of river transportation in West Virginia that a sales agency representing Kanawha manufacturers in 1850 was able to operate a fleet of steamboats between Charleston and St. Louis, offering further important evidence against totalistic images of isolation in antebellum Appalachia.[73]

One of the most severe obstacles faced by Clay County saltmakers, however, was their utter dependence on springtime floods, known locally as "tides," to provide sufficient waters for commercial shipping. Too shallow throughout most of the year for commerce, Goose Creek and the South Fork were both transformed into raging currents by winter thaws and heavy spring rains. During the entire year, only such brief moments, dangerous as they were, permitted salt to be shipped from the saltworks by water routes. Years of severe drought, as in 1818 when only 5,000 bushels of salt were sold in Clay County, brought near ruin to the industry.[74] A report to the House of Representatives in 1836 noted that Goose Creek salt "is shipped in flat boats and sent down during winter and spring, while the water is high, to the country below. The delay and hazard connected with this kind of transportation operates against the interest of the manufacturer, and limits the quantity of salt which he can produce."[75] The industry's vulnerability to the vagaries of weather was further conveyed in a report to the Chief Engineer of Kentucky in 1837 which stated:

> It is necessary to navigate the Goose creek by day, on account of the short bends, and other obstacles to be avoided, so that boats which leave the salt works, above Manchester, arrive at the mouth of Red Bird in the evening, and are obliged to remain over-night; but on the following morning there is seldom water sufficient to pass the Narrows, and they are compelled to await another tide.[76]

Anticipating by more than half a century the daring trips on cumbersome log rafts that would become legendary symbols of Appalachian Kentucky during the timbering era,[77] Clay County boatmen were forced to guide salt-laden vessels on trips made perilous by raging waters. Rapid drops in the river's descent from the Appalachian highlands proved especially troublesome. The most dangerous of these rapids, located in northern Clay County only four miles below the juncture of Goose Creek and the Red Bird River, was known as "the Narrows" (see Photo Essay). Here, the South Fork drops more than twelve feet in little more than a mile.[78] Saltmaker Benjamin F.

White, a son of Hugh White killed piloting a load of salt through the Narrows in 1855, was only the most prominent of many boatmen who lost their lives on the river.

As with highways, the Kentucky legislature passed legislation to improve the headwaters of the Kentucky River for the benefit primarily of the Clay County salt industry. It appointed Daniel Garrard, John Bates, and Beverly Broaddus in 1810 to serve as river commissioners to clear the South Fork and Goose Creek and keep them navigable as far up as the saltworks of James Garrard and Sons. Siding with industrialists against less powerful interests along the river, it gave these commissioners authority to fine persons who obstructed the flow of the river with mill and fish dams. In 1813, the legislature authorized them to raise subscriptions to improve the Red Bird up to John Gilbert's saltworks. Little was accomplished in these early years, however, except by Daniel Garrard who put thirty-two "hands," presumably slaves, to work during the drought of 1818 clearing obstacles and improving the channel of the South Fork at the Narrows.[79]

More than $8,000 were spent in the decade after 1835 improving the headwaters of the Kentucky River, "especially to aid the salt industry," but no additional expenditures on the river were made until after the Civil War.[80] This neglect angered Clay County manufacturers who believed that poor transportation limited the growth of their industry and closed them off from once profitable markets as far away as Nashville, Tennessee. The Kentucky Board of Internal Improvements ratified this complaint in 1835, reporting that in the Cumberland Valley

> salt comes up from Nashville in keel boasts, charged, of course, with a heavy addition to its price, on that account. . . . Were the [Cumberland] river fully opened, the article would come down in abundance from above. . . . One of the proprietors of the Goose Creek salt works, the most extensive establishments of the kind west of the mountains . . . informed me that, in case a certain navigation was provided, they were ready to furnish at once 500,000 bushels per annum, and could so enlarge their establishment as to meet the demand as it might increase from year to year.[81]

Although written to no avail as far as legislative action was concerned, this report was only one of many official state documents imploring antebellum legislators to "look to the mountains of your own proud commonwealth, and see if you can supply your wants; see if you can obtain your salt, iron and lumber from that region." In 1835, state officials estimated that "the market of the city of Louisville, alone," could "be supplied with salt, iron, coal, and lumber, equal in value, to a million dollars annually," if the Kentucky River were canalized to permit the shipment downstream of products from its headwaters in Appalachian Kentucky. A subsequent report of the Board of Internal Improvements in 1840 estimated that as much as six million dollars of "mineral and other resources of our mountains and valleys" were being lost annually to commerce by Kentucky's failure to improve its rivers. Additionally, the report noted "that the valley of the Goose creek [*sic*] furnishes salt water in sufficient abundance, and of the first quality, to supply the States of the west and southwest with the indispensable article of salt, scarcely a bushel of which finds its way to the Ohio River."[82] Although the outside world would eventually come to exploit mountain resources, much of the history of antebellum economic development is the story of the frustration posed to local entrepreneurs by barriers to transportation and the limited will of Kentucky officials to help them overcome these impediments.

Initiated when the fervor for canal building in the United States was at its peak, the most far-reaching antebellum proposal for unlocking the resources of Clay County and Appalachian Kentucky was a bold plan devised by state engineers in 1837 to build a dam and slack water system to improve navigation on Goose Creek and the South Fork and, in the other direction from Clay County, to build a twenty-two-mile canal linking Goose Creek to the Cumberland River at Barbourville. Although twentieth-century writers have pictured the people of Appalachia as slumbering in preindustrial naiveté until some "Mr. Peabody" awakened them to the value of their resources, the plan was launched with the enthusiastic support of mountain entrepreneurs and politicians from Clay and Knox Counties who were eager to ensure the continuing economic viability of the Wilderness Road region at a time when its commercial significance was beginning to wane. This plan, in fact, was part of a larger interstate scheme to build a vast southern canal system to compete with the Erie Canal in the North. Had the whole system of 256 miles of canals and 669 miles of slack water been completed, it would have linked Goose Creek and the South Fork, its most northern points, to ports on the Atlantic Ocean at Savannah and Charleston. Enthusiasm for the plan was diverted, however, to a competing but also uncompleted project with such powerful backers as Henry Clay and John C. Calhoun that called for a railway to traverse roughly the same territory (but not Goose Creek) from Cincinnati, Ohio, to Charleston, South Carolina.[83]

The economic depression that began nationally in 1838 and did not let up in Kentucky until 1844, however, effectively put a stop to all hopes for such grand internal improvements as might have benefited the Goose Creek saltmakers as well as the railroad building others favored. Instead of expansion, saltmakers watched their markets shrink. No longer imagining Goose Creek to be the potential supplier of salt to "the States of the west and southwest," as they had in 1840, state officials in 1848 now described the "great salt wells" of Clay County as being merely "of vast important *to those in its vicinity.*" Later, in 1855, they acknowledged that "because of dangers of navigation," the "salt springs of Virginia are now supplying nearly all the salt that is used in this state."[84]

It is hard to date precisely the demise of the Clay County salt industry. Certainly, it occurred many years prior to the late 1880s, when T. T. Garrard still operated the only remaining saltworks in order to supply local demand, much of it probably due to his own beef and pork slaughtering business. Long before that, Garrard perhaps recognized that the industry's glory days were nearing an end. In 1849 – only ten days after marrying his second wife – he contracted "gold fever" and headed off with friends and two slaves to California. Contrary to the stereotype of Appalachians as being as rooted as the old mountain oaks in their hollows, Garrard had by then already traveled throughout the U.S. Southwest, having earlier raised a company of soldiers from Appalachian Kentucky to fight in the war against Mexico. Accompanied home by one of his slaves (the other of whom would soon make good his promise of sending Garrard $500 "for his liberty"), he returned to Kentucky in 1852 after long trips on a Panama steamer and a Mississippi riverboat.[85]

It was not until 1859, after a stint in the state legislature and the defeat of his bid for the U.S. Congress, that Garrard resumed his partnership with his father in saltmaking. By then, however, the whole Appalachian saltmaking industry had declined greatly because of competition from other regions, especially western rock salt, as well as the relocation of the center of the American meatpacking region from the Ohio Valley to the Midwest.[86] Between 1850 and 1857, "the output of Kanawha furnaces and investment in factories precipitously declined," while several saltworks in Clay County, including ones owned by Alexander White and William White, went broke in the early 1850s as well.[87] By the end of the decade, several of the largest firms that had been active in 1850 were no longer in existence including those of Apperson May and Company and James T. Woodward.

Salt shortages brought on by the Civil War promised briefly to revive the industry in Clay County when prices for Goose Creek salt reached as high as $1.50 per bushel, yet ultimately the industry proved to be but one of that war's many casualties. One of only a small number of salt sources "of such outstanding value as to be of importance for the entire south," "the wells on Goose Creek, in the Kanawha Valley, and in the mountains of southwestern Virginia became the objectives of military attack." According to Ella Lonn, "the confederates boasted that the gaining of the Goose Creek Salt Works in

Kentucky was worth more to them than all the other spoils acquired in that state." Ironically, however, the saltworks of this loyal Union district were destroyed by federal troops to prevent their capture even though the region's most celebrated Union officer, General T. T. Garrard, had earlier defended Goose Creek and the Cumberland Gap region from Confederate invasion.[88] Five hundred soldiers labored thirty-six hours in order to disable or destroy all the furnaces, pumps, wells, and 30,000 bushels of salt they found on Goose Creek to keep them out of rebel hands. Denied their request for federal war-loss compensation, T. T. Garrard and Daugherty White rebuilt their salt-works after the war, but never again was the industry a significant factor in the economic life of the region.[89]

Although Clay County saltmakers and their advocates on the Kentucky Board of Internal Improvements and in the State Engineers office blamed the stagnation of the salt industry throughout the antebellum period on poor transportation, geography – in retrospect – may actually have prolonged the viability of these businesses for several decades by protecting their markets in the southern backcountry, especially Tennessee, that were less easily reached by more distant manufacturers. Thus, in 1810, when the first enormous outpouring of salt from Kanawha County reduced prices throughout much of the Ohio Valley from $2.00 to $1.00 a bushel, Goose Creek salt continued to sell for $2.00. In 1828, shortly after Kanawha salt had dropped to an all time low of 12 cents a bushel in 1826 because of overproduction, Goose Creek salt still sold in some central Kentucky markets for $1.00 a bushel. Finally, according to Benjamin F. White's daybook, salt sold for fifty cents a bushel in 1844 at the saltworks in Manchester when Kanawha salt brought only twenty-two to twenty-five cents per bushel in Cincinnati and sold for only twenty cents three years later.[90] Soon afterwards, however, prices across the two industrial zones became more nearly equal. In the early 1850s, the sales trust representing Kanawha County saltmakers attempted to lock in prices at around twenty-five cents a bushel in Cincinnati, although price violations – through discounts of 25 to 50% – were widespread. Goose Creek saltmakers, however, consistently received twenty-five cents a bushel (before hauling) for salt at their furnaces in Manchester from late 1845 through 1853.[91]

Had the Goose Creek saltmakers not enjoyed access to protected markets, it seems unlikely that the area would have attracted an entrepreneur from the overexpanded Kanawha region such as Gustavius Quarrier, who operated a well and furnace in Clay County but failed there in the depression of the early 1840s.[92] Protected markets may also explain why the saltmakers on Goose Creek were often able to maintain sufficient control over prices to have competed with one another in the bitter price-cutting wars popularly believed to have figured into the rivalries that culminated in Clay County's notorious feuds, even though in the long run, Kanawha manufacturers were helpless to halt the devaluation of their commodity brought about by competition and overproduction.[93]

Benefiting from access to protected markets in the Appalachian hinterland, but limited in how much salt they ultimately could sell there, the Goose Creek saltmakers adapted themselves to a distinctive economic niche that enabled them to survive for several decades. While selectively adopting coal burning and innovative drilling technology to improve productivity, their limited output precluded them from taking advantage of other forms of rationalization that large-scale production afforded. Consequently, they continued to use horses and mules for pumping water and old-style kettles for boiling water many years after Kanawha Valley manufacturers had adopted efficient steam engines for pumping and huge pans weighing close to 2,000 pounds for evaporating massive quantities of salt.[94]

Rather than investing capital primarily in technology, Clay County saltmakers invested more heavily in land and slaves than their Kanawha County peers. Their enterprises more resembling the plantations of the cotton South than modern capitalist industrial firms, they typically operated (or rented out) not only wells and furnaces, but gristmills, sawmills, iron foundries, and farms as well.[95] In contrast to Kanawha County, where their counterparts leased more than half of the slave labor they employed and purchased provisions for them in local markets, and where only one firm is known to have integrated saltmaking with agriculture,[96] manufacturers in Clay County closely coordinated saltmaking with farming and relied on the latter to feed their laborers as well as to provide additional marketable commodities, especially livestock. Thus, in 1838, when Daniel Bates made one of his nephews, Wade Walker, a partner in his saltmaking firm, he expected Walker to oversee each of its vital functions including farming, that is, to "attend to the farm, stock, salt property, and slaves so as to make the same productive." When Bates was taken to court for dissolving the partnership in 1841 and firing Walker as manager, his action, Bates contended, was due as much to Walker's neglect of the farm and livestock as the fact that he had kept the salt furnaces in bad repair.[97]

The self-sufficiency of the saltmakers is a further indication of the importance of farming in the accumulation strategies of local salt manufacturers in Clay County. Daugherty, Alexander, and James White produced 8,697 surplus bushels of food in 1860 beyond the consumption needs of their combined eighty slaves, and Daniel and T. T. Garrard produced 4,093 bushels of food in excess of the amount they needed to feed the twenty-one slaves they owned that year.[98] As a retired saltmaker succinctly recalled in 1898, "James

White had sixty slaves. Dough [White] had a great many, also the Garrards. They raised provisions for the furnace hands, made cloth to clothe them. Had seamstresses to make the goods up."[99]

Although Clay County saltmakers sometimes leased extra slaves to take advantage of increases in the demand for salt,[100] they primarily moved relatively fixed quantities of labor back and forth between their fields and furnaces as changing economic circumstances and opportunities dictated. Saltmakers employed their slaves not only to drill wells, dig coal or cut timber for fuel, tend furnaces, mend kettles, construct barrels, and build, load, and pilot boats, but also to grow crops and raise and slaughter livestock for their own consumption and trade. They put enslaved women to work as well, raising and preparing food and sewing clothes and shoes. Although profitable, this strategy nonetheless helped to limit economic development and diversification in Clay County. By following such a path toward economic accommodation, Goose Creek saltmakers charted a less flexible road of accumulation than the one followed by the Kanawha Valley entrepreneurs that led eventually to greater economic diversification and laid the foundations there for the coal mining, glassmaking, and petrochemical industries that arose later around Charleston, West Virginia.[101]

By protecting themselves, at least in part, from the worst effects of the ups and downs of market demand, as well as the vagaries of droughts and floods that hampered their access to markets, the Goose Creek saltmakers established vertically integrated, slave-based manufacturing and agricultural enterprises that quickly came to resemble islands of self-sufficiency once their industry began to falter. In doing so, they followed a course commonly taken by small manufacturers in other peripheral regions of the world economy. For example, two centuries earlier in the mining regions of Mexico, writes Christopher Chase-Dunn, "market forces generated by the expansion of silver mining linked many farmers and livestock raisers into the commodity chains connected to the European core. When the silver in an area ran out, these cash crop producers reverted to the hacienda economy, a largely self-sufficient rural system containing many of the social attributes of feudalism."[102]

In similar fashion, when saltmaking played out in the Kentucky mountains and before railroads opened the region to further resource extraction and industrialization, the saltmakers of Clay County reduced their slaveholdings and increased their investments in agriculture. Thus, in 1860, after reducing their capital investments in the salt industry by 85% from the previous decade ($85,000 to $13,000) and decreasing their slaveholding by almost one-third, the Whites increased the acres they cultivated on their farms by 15% and doubled their unimproved acreage including grazing land. The Garrards likewise reduced their capital investments in saltmaking from $20,000 in 1850 to only $6,000 a decade later, and they reduced the number of slaves they held from thirty-seven to twelve. On the other hand, they increased the worth of their farms from $12,000 plus $3,563 in animals and machinery in 1850 to $28,000 and $3,555 in animals and machinery in 1860.[103] General commerce, too, was dependent on the salt economy and this sphere of activity went into a decline with the death of the salt trade.

Commerce

To picture Goose Creek manufacturers as tending toward insularity by incorporating as many of the supply elements required for saltmaking as possible, including labor, into their immediate control is not to deny, however, the crucial role their industry played in hooking southeastern Kentucky into the flow of commodities between distant zones of the world economic system. In this regard, saltmaking in Clay County was typical of the small extractive and light manufacturing industries that predominated in antebellum Appalachia. As Wilma Dunaway has shown in an important survey of how the region's early economy functioned on the periphery of global capitalism, such industries were "closely associated with the processing of raw materials – types of economic development that do not generate spinoffs and multipliers required to foster the kind of sustained growth that occurs in the core regions of the capitalist world economy."[104]

Regions that specialize in natural resource extraction and the production of raw materials for further processing elsewhere generally fail to develop locally sustainable and diversified economies. Nevertheless, they often become deeply incorporated into wide networks of economic exchange. Dunaway illustrates this fact by describing the commodity circuits that linked the Kanawha Valley salt industry backwards to east coast merchants and forwards to Ohio Valley meatpackers, southern planters, and New Orleans commission houses where, at last, she says, "Appalachian salt proceeded forward in disguised form: as ancillary investments in other commodities produced for the world market." Describing from the other direction the flow of commodities such as dry goods and coffee into antebellum Kanawha County, Dunaway writes:

> In addition to exporting to international markets, the Philadelphia commission merchant marketed to northeastern manufacturers part of the meats and sugars derived from New Orleans. Relying on company-store advances of imported meats and sugar, northeastern wage laborers generated dry goods. Through turnpike and river networks, the middleman shipped directly to the company store of the West Virginia

salt furnace northeastern dry goods and Brazilian sugar and coffee – which, in addition to the labor needed to move them, aggregated the labor investments of Appalachian salt workers, midwestern meatpackers, southern slaves, European mill workers, and South American slaves.[105]

Although Goose Creek saltmakers operated on a smaller scale and sold products in a more circumscribed zone than their counterparts in antebellum (West) Virginia, they nonetheless contributed to the partial absorption of Clay County into the wider regional economy. In addition to buying local farm products, they created a market for goods and services among local laborers, artisans, tenants, and independent farmers including wood chopping, coal digging, boat building, cooperage, blacksmithing, and farm labor to augment the services of their own enslaved laborers. By paying local suppliers in credits at their company stores, they contributed to the growth of a local consumer economy while, as wholesalers, they linked other local country merchants, to whom they sold imported goods on credit, to extra-local mercantile firms. Additionally, they provided small amounts of cash to local borrowers in the absence of local banks.[106]

In 1898, the Reverend John Jay Dickey, a circuit-riding preacher, interviewed hundreds of Appalachian Kentuckians to test his notions about Appalachian distinctiveness. Still twenty years before the first railroad was to penetrate the county, many Clay Countians told Dickey about the glory days of the early salt trade. Although probably magnifying the volume of past commerce, their memories capture a sense of the extent to which saltmaking had once stimulated the local economy. Thus, in his diary, Dickey noted the recollection of seventy-three-year-old John McDaniel: "There were many six-horse wagons come to Goose Creek when I was a boy, from Louisville, loaded with goods and went back with salt." Melville Johnson, eighty-one, recalled that his father, a hotel keeper, took "in $150 per day. There would be twelve and fifteen salt wagons stay all night. He could stable one hundred horses. . . . That was when I was a boy." J. W. Culton recalled as a child seeing "a train of nine jacks and jennets" carrying salt to Harlan County as well as "wagon trains hauling salt . . . with a hundred wagons in a train, teams of six horses or three yoke of cattle" on the road to the Cumberland Gap through Knox County where he lived as a boy. He also remembered the "[w]agons from Clinch and Powell Rivers [that] would bring barrels of fresh fish, apple brandy, bacon, flour, green apples, [and] cornmeal [to Clay County], everything that was consumed – also jeans, linsey, tow linen, leather, and all sorts of material for clothing." A retired saltmaker and former county official, Judge S. N. Dickerson, told Dickey: "You could see salt wagons going to and from Goose Creek when I was a boy in Tazewell, Tennessee. They went to Jefferson County, Tennessee, and I think to many Tennessee counties. Perhaps as far as Greene. I am satisfied that they hauled salt to Sevier County."[107]

Clay Countians also told Dickey about work they or their ancestors had done for the local saltmakers. Leonidas Nicholson described how his grandfather, an immigrant from northern Ireland, bored salt wells for Hugh White and Francis Clark, and Robert Lynx reported that his grandfather, originally an indentured servant from Germany in the employ of James Garrard, was brought to Clay County by Daniel Garrard to oversee slaves at the saltworks. Henry Lucas, a former overseerer of slaves for James and Daugherty White's salt firm, recalled supervising the slaughter of sixty hogs on one occasion and noted that his father-in-law, Pearce Cottongin "used to steer salt boats" for the Whites. Anderson Philpot, seventy-six, claimed that his father, an English immigrant born in 1749, "made boards to cover the first salt shed put up on Goose Creek," adding that he "gave me the froe he used and I have it yet." Melville Johnson claimed that besides being an innkeeper, his father Thomas Johnson was also "an expert blacksmith" who "made the first auger used in boring salt wells" in Clay County. John Eversole and John McDaniel both recalled working for Hugh White as youths at the peak of the salt trade during the 1840s. J. W. Culton remembered that "cooperage shops were in operation on all the leading roads coming into Goose Creek" and that "wagons bought [their] barrels as they approached the salt works."[108]

Memories of how saltmaking stimulated local demand and employment opportunities are borne out as well in surviving circuit court records such as those documenting the business practices of Daniel Bates in the early 1840s. Bates, whose farming and saltmaking firm was worth approximately $40,000 at the time of his death, employed managers such as Elhanon Murphy and Jacob Phipps to supervise his furnace operation for annual salaries of about $350 and, briefly, he hired a nephew, Wade Walker, to oversee both his farm and furnace enterprises. In addition to owning and leasing slaves, Bates rented portions of his farm to tenants such as Dill Cottingin and he hired farm laborers such as George Frazier and Jarvis Jones (age twelve or fourteen at the time) to tend his livestock, which at the time included as many as 600 hogs and large numbers of cattle, work horses, and mules. During the same period, he hired Samuel Lucas as a farm laborer for $200 a year and asked him as well to make 400 shoes at 50 cents each as well as spend seven days on a flatboat hauling salt down river.[109]

Bates contracted with independent farmers, artisans, and professionals for additional goods and services as well. Between November of 1839 and July of 1841, Bates paid John Woods $566.90 for a variety of services including making 2,000 barrel timbers, 7,500 shingles, and 4,000 boards as well as clearing and improving land, minding stock, providing corn at fifty cents a bushel, and building a flatboat. In exchange, Woods bought $135 worth of goods from Bates including salt, bacon, flour, meal, coffee, sugar, whisky, brandy, and tobacco and he asked Bates to pay off several small debts that he owed to others in Clay County. During roughly the same period, Calvin Handy provided labor services on four occasions and Jesse Colton made a boat for Bates and hauled bark to his tanyard. George Hooker provided him with honeycombs, beef, beef tallow, and labor services worth $200. Bates also paid an attorney, Frank Ballinger, several hundred dollars for giving advice and helping to prepare deeds and mortgages and representing him in various civil actions.[110] When the salt trade diminished after 1850, some of these individuals undoubtedly felt the economic impact of the salt industry's decline and were forced to rely even more than ever on their already considerable self-provisioning and home manufacturing activities.

Merchants' Records of Commercial Development

Experiences documented in court records, like the memories preserved in John Dickey's diary, naturally represent only a small portion of the many forms of commercial activity that the salt trade brought to antebellum Clay County. Additional insights into the depth of market involvement there can be recovered from the surviving daybooks of Hugh White and his son, Benjamin F. White.

Two complete years of business activity are recorded in an account book of the Upper Goose Creek Saltworks (dated 1806–14), the firm Hugh White operated in conjunction with his brother James.[111] Perhaps the oldest surviving business record from Appalachian Kentucky, this daybook affords an indispensable glimpse at Clay County commerce one year before the county's formation when the Goose Creek region was still remote and sparsely settled. As was customary among Upper South merchants at the time, White recorded the value of his transactions in units of British pounds sterling and kept a comprehensive record of who made purchases on behalf of each account, what they bought, and what they paid or traded for such goods and services.

Only two years after moving to Goose Creek, White did business with ninety-five accounts between April 26, 1806, and April 24, 1807. He sold goods and services worth more than $10,000 that year, mostly on credit, to 196 individuals. Roughly 40% of these customers lived in Clay County and another 20% in nearby Knox County, suggesting that a small but significant proportion of households in these two still but lightly populated counties obtained commodities from White or one of his competitors on Goose Creek.[112]

Perhaps not surprisingly since he had only begun to establish himself as a saltmaker in Clay County, yet illustrating the extent to which the salt trade stimulated wider commerce, Hugh White sold only $640 worth of salt (320 bushels) in 1806, some of it to his former partner in a store at the Cumberland Gap, some to a central Kentucky merchant in Jessaimine County, and the rest to local customers in small quantities. His brother James hauled off nearly as much value from Clay County that year ($480) in locally gathered bear, deer, and raccoon skins, bear meat and venison, snakeroot, and ginseng.

Far more impressive than the amount of salt produced or sold in 1806 were the surprising quantity and variety of commodities that the Whites brought into Clay County at such an early date. Based on their purchases, farm families in Appalachian Kentucky – better known for making many of their own household goods and agricultural implements and much of their own clothing – apparently believed that they could benefit from the purchase of labor-saving devices, no matter how determined they may have been to be self-sufficient. Thus, between April 1806 and April 1807, White sold at least one of each the following types of tools and equipment: weeding hoes, saws, "bucher" [*sic*] knives, pen knives and various other knives, scissors, steelyards (for weighing), bridles along with spurs, bits and saddles, handsaw and cross-cut saw files, curry combs, horse collars and bells, scythes, whetstones, padlocks, horseshoes, wool cards, nails, bellows, pails, axes, an iron boring rod, screw augers, and a $20 sword. He also sold quantities of iron, powder, and lead and, once during the year, a wagon, and he provided blacksmithing services such as "steeling axe," "mending jack screw," "making plow irons," and "sharpening and mending auger."

Although household spinning and weaving provided the great bulk of local clothing, White also found a modest market for manufactured cloth and sewing goods. His sales of these items in 1806 included: linnen [*sic*], Irish linnen, calico, silk, muslin (white and coarse), turkey cloth, velvet, colored cloth (blue, scarlet, red, gray), cotton cloth, chintz, velveteen, yellow jean, Forrest cloth, red flannel, lace, moreen, "supefine" broadcloth, furring, and a variety of ribbons, bindings, buttons, needles, thimbles, thread, and vest patterns. White also sold a few items of apparel including gloves, suspenders, wool hats, garters, handkerchiefs, stockings and hose, shoes and shoe leathers, cloaks, overalls, country shirts, mittens, leggings, collars, and one "elegant shawl."

Historians debating the extent of household consumption in frontier Kentucky have discovered evidence of "luxury" goods in the store inventories and probate records of the Kentucky Bluegrass region in the late eighteenth century.[113] That such commodities could soon afterwards be found in Appalachian Kentucky is clear from records of the probated estate of one of White's customers, John Amis. A slave-owning cattle farmer and the part owner of a salt furnace who died in 1806, Amis's household possessed the pewter plates, knives and forks, dishes, pots, ovens, chairs, and bed furniture that even many of the wealthiest third of Louisville's population had lacked twenty years earlier.[114] Hugh White found a market for such household goods on the Kentucky Appalachian frontier as decanters, tumblers, bottles, sets of knives and forks, salt cellars, looking glasses, tin cups, dish glass, blankets, teaspoon sets, small ovens, pots, stew pots, skillets, pot hooks, bed quilts, candle sticks, cups and saucers, room paper, paste board, ladle, and a smoothing iron. He also sold personal goods including combs, spectacles, shaving equipment (razors and razor cases, shaving soap, shaving boxes, and straps), various oils and medicinals, a necklace, a "stran [sic] of beeds," a tobacco pipe, and a watch priced at $30. Additionally, he sold writing materials (a quire of paper, inkstand, inkpowder, and inkpot) and reading matter (a chapbook, a hymn [sic] book, a testament, a "spilling [sic] book" and a "small history").

Finally, and again despite local ideals of self-sufficiency, even foodstuffs could be bought at the Goose Creek saltworks in 1806 since many customers paid for their purchases in country produce and others – landless laborers, for instance – may have lacked the means for producing sufficient quantities on their own. Among the edibles White sold were corn, bacon, meal, flour, turkey, venison, eggs, honey, butter, bear meat, cider, whiskey, tobacco, apples, beef, pork, sweet potatoes, and turnips as well as nonlocal commodities such as sugar, Godfrey's Cordial, and boxed wafers. His livestock sales included cattle and calves, hogs, horses, and oxen.

White's customers varied considerably in independence and wealth. Among them were tenant farmers and laborers as well prosperous farmers like John Amis. An enslaved laborer, "Caperton's Dave," bought shoes, buttons, thread, and a "stran [sic] of beeds." Saltmakers like John Bates, as well as his employees, also made numerous purchases. John Gilbert, a trapper and saltmaker on the Red Bird River, bought fifteen pounds of iron, a bellows pipe, 200 nails, and a pound of steel and was credited with trading White deerskins and corn. Young Daniel Garrard, newly arrived in Clay County that year, traded 291 pounds of powder for forty-six pounds of iron, three-fourths of a pound of steel, and a file and earned a modest credit of six dollars.

Commercial transactions varied widely in the extent to which cash, barter, or credit was used in the exchange between merchants and their customers, during the period from 1790 to 1810 across the Appalachian and trans-

Appalachian regions.[115] In the cash-poor economy of frontier Appalachian Kentucky, however, it is clear that Hugh White exchanged very little money with his customers, although some turned to him for small amounts of cash to pay off their debts to others. In addition to crediting his brother James with more than $11,000 carried over from a previous ledger and $2,500 worth of merchandise received in March of that year, White credited his customers' accounts in 1806 with roughly $4,200 of goods and services – mostly for labor but also furs and farm produce. Thus, besides stimulating consumer demand, White also helped to create a modest demand for labor services in his role as salt manufacturer.

In addition to recording credits of $250 for a slave named "Nate," $73 for "work done by boys," and $300 for the lease of slaves to help him make salt in 1806, as well as paying these workers at the rate of one-sixth the wage level for white labor when they worked nights or at Christmas at his furnace, White employed several local men to supplement his slaves' efforts. These laborers performed something on the order of 766 days of work in 1806 including such tasks as "pumping water," "working on the well," "tending kettles," "working in the shop" or "on the road," "driving wagon," "wood chopping," and "drawing water."[116] Among them, John Stone worked seventy-three days for White between May and December of 1806, mostly tending kettles at the salt furnace. Stone earned just over $70, but he and others on his account purchased food, salt, drygoods, and whiskey costing more than $113. Thomas Nicholson, who worked a total of three months and twenty-eight days for White, earned about $60 and spent about $67 at the company store. Others, like David Mathews, John Irwin, and George Tacket, did not receive regular wages but were periodically credited for supplying wood to White's salt furnace.

Similar patterns of commerce transacted a generation later in Clay County are preserved in the ledgers of Benjamin F. White, which date from 1843 to 1855.[117] The twelfth of thirteen children born to Hugh White and his wife Catherine, Benjamin F. White (1817–55) operated a small country store and saltmaking business until his accidental death while piloting a flatboat down the Kentucky River. Throughout the twelve years of trade logged in his daybook, White did business with 113 customers but sold a restricted range of goods, consisting mostly of food and feed (bacon and pork, beef, corn and meal, flour, oats) and a few drygoods (calico, linen, shirts and pants, shoes and boots). Whiskey made up the bulk of White's sales during his first year in business, but it was soon surpassed by salt. Coffee, along with coffee "potes" and coffee mills, were the only commodities White sold that were not included in his father's more extensive inventory, forty years earlier.

A systematic comparison of the prices White charged for goods with their prices elsewhere is impossible, but impressionistic evidence suggests that Clay County consumers paid dearly for store-bought commodities in the 1840s. Calico cost two to three times more than in Cincinnati, and linen – some varieties of which could be obtained for as little as 25 cents a yard in Cincinnati in the 1840s – sold for as much as $3.20 a yard at White's store. Coffee, typically costing about seven cents a pound in Cincinnati during this period, sold for as much as 25 cents a pound at the beginning of the period and 12 cents at the end. The high cost of transporting such commodities into the Kentucky mountains may explain the relatively high prices they brought locally, but White sold locally made commodities and country produce for high prices as well. He sold small amounts of whiskey for $1.00 a gallon in 1844, nearly ten times its wholesale cost in Cincinnati, and he sold bulk quantities of it to other local merchants for 37$\frac{1}{2}$ cents a gallon. Even corn, costing fifty to seventy-five cents a bushel, was expensive.

Such prices suggest once again that geography partially insulated south-eastern Kentucky merchants and saltmakers from the full impact of national and world price tendencies. Additionally, however, local socioeconomic factors may have augmented the effects of high transportation costs and protected markets on the prices local merchants such as Benjamin F. White could command.

White's customers were distributed across a broad spectrum of wealth and status that ranged from one-time customer Daniel Garrard, who bought a single quantity of salt, to five or six African American men, identified separately by first names in a "black boys account," who purchased hats, coats, shoes, and, occasionally, cash and whiskey. Ranking between these socioeconomic extremes were independent farm owners as well as such local merchants as Stephen Gibson, Leander Miller, and Barton Potter who bought fairly large quantities of salt, whiskey, and other commodities, presumably for resale at their own establishments. An examination of White's busiest accounts, however, reveals that several poor farmers, tenants, and laborers were among White's most persistent and deeply indebted customers, suggesting that employment opportunities at the saltworks may have come at the risk of having to rely heavily on store-bought commodities for subsistence.[118]

Beginning in 1848, James Hooker, the twenty-four-year-old owner of a fifty-acre farm in 1850, appears throughout the log with frequent purchases of bacon, corn, meal, shoes, pork, tobacco, and whiskey, as well as single purchases of other commodities such as sugar and coffee. He was always credited by White for labor services and once, when their accounts were settled, he was ahead by $6.00. Less fortunate was William Bolin, a frequent customer at White's store from 1845 to 1855. Bolin, a thirty-three-year-old tenant farmer with a wife and six children in 1850, often charged pork, bacon, meal, corn, coffee, shoes, and "cash" and, occasionally, flour, whiskey, fabric and thread, and other items. His account noted credits for labor (including plowing), a cow and a corn crop, but such credits never equaled his expenditures.[119]

The ease with which farmers and laborers such as Hooker and Bolin became indebted to their merchant/employers, as John Stone and Thomas Nicholson did before them, suggests that owing one's soul to the company store – a form of dependency indelibly associated in song with the modern Kentucky coal industry – may actually have had deep roots in Appalachia's antebellum era. But White's daybook also hints at how mountain farmers and laborers also may have used store purchases and credits strategically to survive and even prosper. Haywood Gilbert, a forty-year-old farmer with eight children who owned a 400-acre farm and one slave in 1850, bought large quantities of corn and whiskey at White's store and received credits at other times for corn and livestock, a pattern suggesting that Gilbert probably engaged in the merchandising of spirits, as well as farming, in his outlying section of the county.

Jackson Bundy, propertyless at age twenty-nine in 1846, but the owner of 200 acres of land in 1850, never traded at White's store until after the latter date when he began to make purchases almost every month. He frequently charged bacon, corn, and coffee and less frequently meal, flour, pork, beef, salt, and whiskey to his account and received credits for lumber, barrels, and labor. Real Gregory, on the other hand, bought similar quantities and types of commodities from White and was credited with labor from April 1843 until November 1848 when his account was noted "all paid." Soon afterwards, however, he was listed in the 1850 manuscript census of agriculture as operating a 200-acre farm and made no further purchases at White's store. In the case of Bundy, it would appear that acquiring a farm and the timber on it created opportunities to buy goods at White's store by providing wood for salt barrels, whereas in the case of Gregory, farm ownership (or rental[120]) provided the means or motivation to avoid such consumption. Both scenarios suggest that residents of Clay County took "market opportunities" as well as their hazards into account when making household decisions about how best to provide for themselves from an early period.

Networks of Indebtedness and the Depression of 1839–1843

To speak of capitalist "market opportunities" in Clay County or elsewhere as if they were autonomous forces operating independently of the real social relationships constituting them is a theoretical mistake that is referred to in

Marxist theory as "commodity fetishism" or "reification."[121] Although the *ensemble* or *totality* of local and extra-local exchange relations does operate coercively on individuals, "the autonomous market of neoclassical models is virtually nonexistent in economic life" since real-life transactions always are "rife with social connections." Simply put, "all economic activity and institutions are embedded in social relations and structures."[122]

Commerce in early antebellum Clay County, and the dense networks of personal obligation and indebtedness that undergirded it, had a sociological basis in interpersonal relationships of trust and reciprocity, that is, culture, even though the operation of the commercial economy, as we shall we, generated considerable inequality and mistrust along the way. In order to understand the sociological nature of commercial relationships in early Appalachian Kentucky and to search for possible roots of division that may have led to violent community conflict there, we examined all surviving records of civil litigation (772 cases) heard before the Clay County Circuit Court during the periods 1807–50 and 1890–1900 involving a sample of known "disputants" whom we identified from popular and journalistic accounts of the Clay County feuds (see Appendix 1). Since this sample included all members of the saltmaking White, Garrard, and Bates families and several of their associates, it gives us not only a good view of that portion of their commercial activities that ended up being disputed in the courtroom but also a glimpse of their economic endeavors more generally.

It has been said that "in the nineteenth century, as in the twentieth century, the economy sailed on a sea of credit."[123] The dependence on credit was especially significant in the West during the early years of the U.S. republic where specie was rare and banks were only beginning to develop. Even more than in other sections of Kentucky, hard money was particularly scarce in the Kentucky mountains during the early decades of the nineteenth century where, in its stead, promissory notes and less often chattel notes for salt provided the principal circulating media of exchange. In the absence of "real" money, eastern Kentuckians were bound together in dense networks of mutual indebtedness by the exchange of such notes. Debtors and their sureties guaranteed creditors that they were "good" for whatever amounts they promised, often indicating in writing how and when such obligations would be met.

In 168 instances between 1807 and 1850, members of our sample of "disputants" appeared in civil cases before the Clay County Circuit Court, either as plaintiffs or defendants, to argue about the enforcement of such "writings obligatory," that is, promissory notes. This volume of litigation contradicts the facile and erroneous assumptions about Appalachian Kentucky made a half century later by writers as geographer Ellen Churchill Semple who claimed that even at the end of the nineteenth century, "our Kentucky mountaineers have only a semi-developed commercial conscience. They do not appreciate the full moral force of a contract," because, Semple added, they have "little regard for the law."[124] Instructive for what they reveal about the evolution and workings of Appalachian Kentucky's early economy, these cases suggest a surprisingly high volume of commercial activity.[125] Moreover, they document the evolving means of formalized payment by which commercial trade was accomplished and challenge stereotypes of the early Appalachian economy as merely one of direct and simple bartering.

In the first decade after the formation of the county, disputed promissory notes, often written to saltmakers, obligated debtors to repay loans in "good merchantable deerskin, bear skins, or fur skins at the market price," "ginseng at market price," various quantities of slaughtered beef or pork, or livestock as well as – in only one instance – "good and lawful money of the state of Kentucky."[126] Clay County's saltmakers, in turn, were brought to court for failing to supply salt to nonlocal merchants as promised or for failing to pay for goods and services bought locally or on credit from outside wholesale firms.[127]

Beginning in 1820, one can find examples among surviving court records of promissory notes that bore the following inscription: "Notes on the Bank of Kentucky or either of its branches may be received by the officer in discharge of the whole of this judgment." Written in compliance with the state's replevin law of 1820 and calculated to prevent defendants from qualifying for two year's debt replevy, such endorsements suggest the financial and legal sophistication of Appalachian merchants.[128] Later, printed bearer or chattel notes usually written for small quantities of salt began to circulate during the early 1830s alongside traditional promissory notes for the first time.[129] So, too, did the first notes in our sample of cases promising payments in silver and (less often) gold, suggesting both continuing mistrust of paper money issued by banks and the increasing availability of specie in Appalachian Kentucky by this date.[130]

Although our sample cases reveal signs of increasing formalization in the system of promissory notes exchange in Clay County as time went on, they nonetheless demonstrate the fundamentally personal quality of the area's economic transactions. Commercial exchange in Appalachian Kentucky was embedded in local and extra-local social relations in which interpersonal knowledge about debtors and creditors provided the sociological basis for trust. As Lawrence Friedman notes in writing about the wider context of business in the early Republic, "It was a life and death matter to know your debtor and whether he was solvent."[131] Notes written by persons believed to be wealthy and honorable, or notes bearing the endorsements of especially trustworthy persons such as Hugh White or Daniel Garrard, were particularly valuable. Like good coin of the realm, such notes often exchanged hands numerous times, yet unlike hard currency, their validity was often disputed. John Bates sued John Amis's estate in 1808 for payment of a $130 note that Amis had written in 1806 to Robert and James Duff. This note had been assigned to John Riley before the latter endorsed it to Bates. In 1810, John Whitely tested the validity in court of a $40 note signed by the Cumberland Gap firm of Hugh White and George Baugh that Whitely had obtained fourthhand after it had been passed from Wright Smith to Benjamin Tutt and then to Richard Tutt. Samuel Vannoy sued Boling Baker and Issac Johnson (Baker's surety) in 1817 for a $100 note assigned first to Isham Bolin and later endorsed by the latter to William Vannoy who assigned it to the plaintiff. In 1829, Daniel Garrard brought a note to court endorsed four years earlier by Felix Gilbert and John Gilbert, Jr., to Messenger Lewis that had been passed first to Hugh White and by him to Garrard. Finally, John Pullins brought three separate suits against Hugh White for notes acquired third-hand and fourthhand, once rushing to court the very day he was assigned one.[132]

It would be wrong, however, to assume that the paper economy of Clay County was always disputatious. In fact, as estate inventories made at the times of death show, creditors often held promissory notes for many years beyond their due dates, trusting both in the resources and integrity of their debtors and counting such notes as a tangible form of wealth. Thus, when John Gilbert died in 1852, the nineteen notes totaling more than $500 that he held on various individuals were, on average, twelve years past due, fifteen of them dating from the 1830s. The estate of Hugh L. White, a merchant who died at age thirty-nine in 1848, included sixteen notes, half of them past due as well. On his death in 1850, the merchant Stephen Gibson held many notes that had come due in the 1820s but were still uncollected from twenty-five to thirty years later.[133]

Looking at exchange from the other side of the ledger, the administrators of Daniel Bates's estate sold more than $2,000 worth of Bates's livestock in 1844 to apply toward $3,000 worth of outstanding notes that Bates had assigned to creditors before his death.[134] The holding of extensive notes on others, however, was restricted to a small proportion of Clay County's population including wealthy entrepreneurs like Daniel Bates whose estate, including 17,667 acres of land and forty-five slaves worth $16,000, was the product of commercial capitalism.[135] Ordinary Clay Countians, in contrast, were more likely to have resembled Adonirom Andrews III of Beech Creek who, despite being the wealthiest person of his neighborhood, left an estate in 1853 that was settled without mention of outstanding notes.[136]

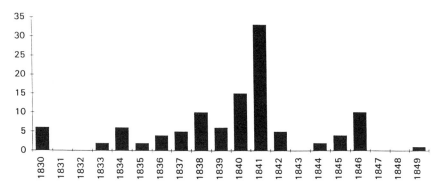

Figure 3.2 Civil suits by bearers of promissory notes, 1830–1849.

If owning an extensive portfolio of promissory notes was an indication of commercial involvement and economic success, the timing of litigations involving such notes was an indirect indicator of the presence of business cycles in Appalachia. Although individuals confidently held notes on their debtors for long periods of time, the frequency of court actions to enforce such notes did not occur randomly. Significantly, such actions reached their greatest peak of the antebellum era during the national economic depression of 1839–43 when, like a house of cards, Clay County's paper economy threatened to collapse. Notes that had been held for a decade past their due dates were suddenly called in.[137] If death provided the routine occasion when promissory notes had to be settled up, economic panics and depressions provided even more dramatic moments of reckoning.

Figure 3.2 plots the frequency of civil suits brought before the Clay County Circuit Court by bearers of promissory notes from 1830 to 1849 in which members of our "Dispute Sample" were either plaintiffs or defendants. Figure 3.3 plots disputes over promissory notes as the percent of *all cases* brought before the Clay County Circuit Court at the beginning of several decades from 1810 through 1900, not just those cases involving our dispute sample. Both figures show that disputes over promissory notes peaked around 1840 when creditors rushed to court to enforce many of the notes they held.

That a national depression would be registered locally in the courtrooms of antebellum Appalachia is surprising only in light of erroneous depictions of the region as having been unconnected to national markets and the global capitalist economy until the end of the nineteenth century. Although geog-

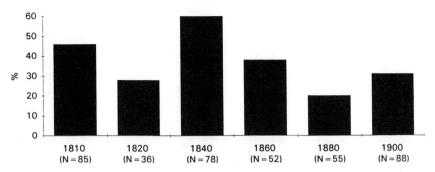

Figure 3.3 Civil suits by bearers of promissory notes, 1810–1900 (percent of all cases in Clay County Circuit Court).

raphy, as we have seen, may have sometimes buffered local manufacturers from moderate price fluctuations in the regional salt market by protecting some markets from the easy reach of competitors, neither these entrepreneurs nor other local merchants were immune to the deeper rhythms of global economic trends. Prices for Clay County's two principal export commodities, salt and livestock, were directly affected by downswings in national prices as Elhanon Murphey, a salt-firm manager, testified to the Clay County Circuit Court in 1843:

> I no [*sic*] that salt and [live]stock of all kind has been on a decline since the year 1839 and salt was not worth as much down the river in 1841 as it was in 1838 by at least twenty five percent and I think there was a like depreciation in [live]stock in the year 1840 and 1841.[138]

The diminishing value of such commodities was felt in even the most remote corners of southeastern Kentucky,[139] reverberating throughout all aspects of commercial life, including even the frequency of apprenticeships and indentures, as Figure 3.4 shows.

Faced with falling prices during these times, several of Clay County's salt-makers found it increasingly difficult to meet their obligations. Thus, in March of 1839, at an early stage of the depression, Hugh L. White mortgaged nine slaves to his father Hugh White, who paid off three of his notes and agreed to serve as security for debts to four other individuals.[140] Two years later in 1841, James H. Garrard, who had already mortgaged three slaves

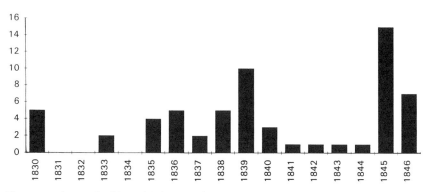

Figure 3.4 Apprenticeship and indenture (frequency).

that year to Hugh White's son-in-law (Lyne Kinningham, an entrepreneur in nearby Knox County) mortgaged his interest in the family's salt well and furnace earnings along with his own lands, livestock, crops, household belongings, and 899 barrels of salt on consignment with various Bluegrass merchants to his father, Daniel Garrard, who agreed to serve as his security for numerous debts to central Kentucky merchants. On the same occasion, T. T. Garrard likewise mortgaged his interest in the saltworks along with his own lands, livestock, crops, household furnishings, and nine slaves to his father to secure $2,700 in outstanding debt. In 1842, James H. Garrard mortgaged a female slave and her two sons to his father for an additional debt of $2,093.[141]

Young entrepreneurs with sufficient backing, like the sons of Hugh White and Daniel Garrard, survived the economic depression of the 1840s, but not all salt manufacturers were as fortunate. The firm of Wilson and Quarrier, active from at least 1832, first began to mortgage properties heavily in 1837 when the Bluegrass firm of Kinkaid and Blackburn agreed to secure $13,363 worth of debt to various eastern merchants. In 1838, they were forced to mortgage or convey additional properties to this firm and to Frank Ballinger, a Knox County attorney representing creditors in Philadelphia, Pittsburgh, Tennessee, Lexington, and elsewhere. In 1840, W. and J. Hollaway Company, one of several Lexington firms to have secured their notes that year, acquired the land from which Wilson and Quarrier drew brine at a public auction for $12,000 but recognized their right to continue to drill there as well. In 1841, they were taken over by the huge Lexington mercantile firm of Robert Wickliffe and Company and managed by J. T. Woodward, the firm's agent and lessee in Clay County. Soon afterward, Woodward married the widow of

Daniel Bates and combined her properties with his to create one of the largest saltmaking businesses in Clay County at the end of the decade. In 1843, all remaining properties belonging to Wilson and Quarrier were purchased by a New York City firm and by Kentucky merchants in Knox and Woodford counties.[142]

Like ripples on a pond, the effects of this five-year period of economic depression spread throughout the commercial sectors of Clay County, sometimes, though, to the benefit of its richest citizens who acquired additional properties at discounted prices. Local merchant Stephen Gibson, for example, mortgaged seven slaves to Daniel Bates in 1843 to protect Bates's security on a $631.76 debt, but Gibson soon afterwards forfeited $150 worth of land to Bates at a sheriff's auction for $16.[143] John House, a tanner, mortgaged three slaves, land, livestock, and personal belongings to Bates to secure a $2,000 debt in 1840. He retained possession of this property until 1850 when Bates's executors forced its sale at public auction.[144] Even the mighty Garrards were forced to sell some of their property at a loss to repay Bates for notes he held, a situation that helped to set Clay County on the violent path to civic and political disorder that the following chapter describes.[145] Others, however, were more fortunate, such as Julius Hacker who mortgaged his land and livestock to his friends Daniel Garrard and John Gilbert, Jr., but managed to weather the troubled period and retain his moderate wealth.[146]

Just as local capitalists were forced to mortgage property to their economic betters, these merchants in turn increased the pressure on their own debtors within the ranks of farmers, tenants, and laborers, thus pushing the effects of economic depression even farther down the social-class ladder in Clay County. For example, Barton Potter secured a $150 note on Thomas Philpot in 1838 by attaching a mortgage to Philpot's livestock and farm equipment. In the following year, he obtained an injunction to prevent Philpot from disposing of this property and forced its sale at public auction where he bought Philpot's colt, three mares, three cows, a steer, and a wagon and gear for the sum of $178 out of which Philpot was required to pay his debt.[147] To secure loans totaling $794 during the nadir of the depression in 1841, Potter became the mortgagee of land belonging to William Morris and farms belonging to William Pigg and Isam Smith as well as Elias Robertson's livestock, James Pigg's livestock, Samuel Burgess's livestock and household goods, and Menom Abner's growing and rental crops, livestock, household goods, and wagon.[148] Through such sharp business practices, the reported value of Potter's own property had increased from $5,000 in 1837 at the beginning of the depression to $12,500 at its end in 1843.[149]

Slaveholding

Despite the fact that slaveholding is a good gauge of market embeddedness, there has been scant scholarly attention to the issue in Appalachia. Mountain slavery has been assumed to be rare and economically inconsequential, little more than isolated incidents of mountaineers buying a few slaves to assist with arduous farm tasks.[150] However, an examination of slavery in Clay County suggests that not all antebellum mountain economic life conformed to this pattern.

Clay County's early economic prominence was built on the abuse of slaves for the most hazardous labor in saltworks and the sale of slave bodies as investments and collateral for loans. In 1850, there were fifty-seven slave owners in Clay County. In 1860, fifty-two people (5.2% of all households) owned slaves in the county. Although few in number, slaveholders – especially those with large numbers of slaves – had considerably larger landholdings and more diverse economic interests than those who did not own slaves. Landowning slaveholders in 1850 averaged $12,286 in real property and 584 total acres (121 improved acres), compared to landowners in the county as a whole, at $1,023 and 465 acres. Ten years later, slaveholders averaged $6,591 in land, with 112 acres of improved acreage, compared to county averages of only $766 and 46 acres. However, among landowners, there was little relationship between the number of acres under cultivation and the number of slaves owned, suggesting that many slaves were purchased for investment and for industrial employment rather than for farm labor only.[151]

More so than for agriculture, the trade in human slaves was a cornerstone of Clay County's profitable salt industry, enriching the owners of saltworks by guaranteeing them a flexible labor force. Thus, the demographic patterns of slaveholding in the county reflect variable labor demand in salt production. In 1850, most (59%) of Clay County's slaves were male, usually adult men and teenage boys used to produce salt. As salt production declined in the following decade, the demand for expensive adult male slaves decreased in favor of cheaper female slaves for domestic and farm work. By 1860, the majority (54%) of Clay County's slaves were women or girls, mirroring the demographic pattern in other parts of Appalachian Kentucky.[152]

In addition to the sizable numbers of African American men, women, and children purchased by Clay Countians, enslaved men and women also were brought into the county through annual or monthly contracts with owners elsewhere to augment the local labor force in the salt industry and to circumvent legal restrictions on slave sales.[153] The hiring of slaves to work in salt manufacturing and the price of hired slave labor peaked at the height of the industry, in 1837, and declined thereafter.[154] Court dockets record frequent disputes between local industrialists and outside slave owners and marketers over the quality of such hired slave labor[155] and its price (from $50 to $150 a year).[156]

Civil court litigation from the turn of the nineteenth century also shows extensive traffic in slaves as investment, as collateral on promissory notes, and as payment on debts. In effect, African American human beings served as another form of currency in the absence of institutional banking.[157] As early as 1810, salt magnate Hugh White rented his slaves to others for prices that ranged from $4.00 to $8.00 a month, garnering funds during slack production times.[158] In addition to bolstering the financial stability of the salt industry and lining the pockets of its owners, slaves were used by Clay County's industrial elite to leverage loans for the new financial opportunities in land and timber that followed the decline in salt.[159] Sales of slaves also could be used to pay off debts, as did the Garrards when they sold seventeen slaves to pay a $7,136 judgment against them.[160] At an average value of $673 in 1850, enslaved persons represented a considerable investment of capital[161] and a lucrative source of further profit making. With financial stakes so high, slave owners accused each other of stealing slaves[162] and of using their influence to force illegal seizure and sale of slaves by the county sheriff.[163]

Wealthy Clay Countians wielded a variety of skillful legal maneuvers to accumulate slaves. John Bates and Daniel Garrard, both affluent salt manufacturers and slaveholders, apparently worked together in what may have been an attempt to defraud the widow of a small slaveholder by convincing the court that a slave in Bates's employ had been purchased rather than mortgaged by her former husband in 1812.[164] Daniel Garrard forced the sale of two slaves in an estate settlement and then, with Alexander White providing security, purchased these same slaves at the resulting commissioner's sale.[165] Claiborne White's firm also acquired several slaves by foreclosing on the mortgages of small slaveholders.[166] Other salt manufacturers bought slaves at court-ordered sheriff's sales and commissioner's auctions.[167] And even more direct financial advantages accrued to wealthy slaveholders who dominated local government: Hugh White was reimbursed $900 by the county when one of his slaves was executed for murder.[168]

Substantial disparities in wealth and landownership divided slave owners from nonslave owners, but there was tremendous variation as well among slaveholders. In 1850, when 9% of slaveholders owned a single slave and 44% owned fewer than five slaves, James White alone owned forty-two slaves. In the next decade, with the decline in the salt industry, the number of slaveholders in the county fell slightly and the distribution of slaveholding in Clay County also changed.[169] Whereas the number of small slaveholders (whose slaves were used in domestic or farm work) remained constant, the number of medium and large slaveholders (owners of slaves used in salt and other industries) decreased substantially. Now 21% of slave owners owned one slave; 42% owned fewer than five.[170]

The decrease in the number of medium and large slaveholders between 1850 and 1860 was due to a decline in the number of slaves per owner, rather than to the abandonment of slaveholding by these owners. In fact, it was those who owned few slaves in 1850 that were the most likely to be without slaves a decade later. Among those who owned four or fewer slaves in 1850, only 29% were slaveholders, in 1860. Among larger slaveholders, 50% of those with between five and ten slaves and fully 89% of those with eleven or more slaves in 1850 still owned slaves in 1860.

Since slaves were used in different types of labor by large and small slaveholders, the gender distribution of slaves varied also by the size of slaveholding. Those who owned a single slave in 1850 typically owned a woman; 73% of these slaveholdings were female. Slaveholders who owned between two and ten slaves owned roughly equal numbers of female and male slaves (47% male). As the size of slaveholding increased, so did the proportion of males. Owners of between eleven and twenty slaves had 67% male slaves. Among the largest slave owners, those owning more than twenty slaves, fully 72% of their slaves were male.

Large Slaveholders

To examine the holdings of large slave owners in Clay County, it is more accurate to analyze family rather than individual holdings. Like the very wealthy in most economic systems, elite Clay Countians held property in networks of extended family and "casual exchange of black labor between family members was common" in the mountains.[171] Moreover, ownership figures capture only a portion of the slave labor force employed by large holders since these also made use of hired slave labor.

The Whites were Clay County's largest slaveholders. In 1850, eight White households collectively owned 162 slaves, or 31% of all slaves owned in Clay County. Most were used as industrial slaves in the White's extensive salt furnaces from which the family realized $39,000 a year in sales. Of the Whites' 162 slaves, 83 were men over twelve years old, 34 were adult women and 45 were children (a ratio of men to women of 2.4/1 and of adults to children of 2.6/1). In addition to this slave labor force, the Whites listed seventy-six other employees (hired slaves and free workers) in their salt works, plus nine servants and farm laborers residing in their households. They controlled directly, either as waged or slave labor, 202 black and white adult workers, and, indirectly, the families and households of these workers. Thus, a significant proportion of Clay County's late antebellum population was economically dependent, owned or hired by the White family, an economic pattern that became particularly significant in the political conflicts discussed in the following chapter.

The task of providing subsistence for this labor pool and wood or coal for salt furnaces required other resources, most notably land and agricultural production. In 1850, the Whites owned land worth $84,700 and operated farms consisting of 815 acres of improved land and 2,312 acres of unimproved land. The value of these farm properties was $36,110, plus $9,732 in live animals, machinery, and slaughtered animals – exclusive of whatever rents they may have received from other, tenants-operated farms.

However, a decade later, with the decline in the salt industry, the Whites' salt works had only $13,000 in capital investment (an 85% drop in one decade) and 23 paid employees (a 70% decline). As the Whites' investments in salt declined, their investments in agriculture increased. In 1860, Alexander, Daugherty, and James White grew more than 4,000 bushels of corn on 721 acres (only a 15% increase in acreage) and almost doubled their unimproved acreage – to 4,000 acre – for a total land value of $40,500, plus another $10,095 in animals and machinery. Between 1850 and 1860, the total slaveholding of the Whites' households dropped 32% – to 110 slaves – although these still comprised 31% of all slaves owned in the county and were worth $129,935. The demographic composition of the Whites' slave labor force also changed with the decline of salt. The ratio of adult men to adult women decreased to 1.6/1 and the ratio of adults to children to 2.4/1, reflecting a labor force more suitable to agricultural and domestic than to industrial work.

Clay County's other major slaveholding family was the Garrards. In 1850, the three Clay County households of the Garrard family owned a total of thirty-seven slaves and housed four nonfamily laborers. Their salt furnaces had eleven employees and produced $5,000 a year. In addition, the Garrards' lands were valued at $32,000, including farms totaling 260 acres in cultivation and 300 acres unimproved for a cash value of $12,000 plus $3,563 in animals and machinery.

By 1860, the Garrards' saltworks still produced $5,000 a year, but other indicators show the imminent collapse of their salt empire as well. The Garrards now owned only twenty-one slaves in Clay County (the bulk of their local personal property of $25,250) and, like the Whites, greatly increased their investment in farm land to 480 acres of improved and 11,800 acres of unimproved land valued at $28,000 on which they grew more than 1,600 bushels of corn and slaughtered animals worth a total of $850, plus another $3,555 in animals and machinery.

Although the Whites and the Garrards had the largest number of slaves in antebellum Clay County, they were not the only large slaveholders. Many owners of the county's saltworks owned sizeable numbers of slaves. In 1850, both James T. Woodward (owner of thirty-one slaves) and Apperson May (owner of twenty-five slaves) owned saltworks nearly as large as those of the Garrard family (although considerably smaller than the White works), producing $5,000 each per year with $15,000 and $16,000 in capital and thirteen and fourteen employees, respectively. Both ran medium-sized farms to produce for their households and slaves. The decline in the salt industry had a particularly devastating effect on these owners; by 1860, both had left the county.

Francis Clark also owned a saltworks, with twenty employees, producing $4,675 in 1850. Together with his twenty-five slaves and one free laborer, Clark owned an astonishing $66,000 in land in Clay County, of which 300 acres were in cultivation and 35,000 acres were unimproved. The cash value of Clark's farms was $12,000, with an additional $1,197 in animals and machinery. Clark's saltworks showed only a slight decline between 1850 and 1860, but he did not reinvest his holdings in land. In 1860, he cultivated only 100 acres (a 67% decline) and held 1,000 acres of unimproved land (an 80% decline) producing only $2,000 with $263 in animals and machinery (a 83% decline). Most remarkably, though, was the increase in Clark's total wealth, which by 1860 included $55,000 in land (presumably much of this rented to tenants) and $120,000 in personal property (including slaves).

Medium and Small Slave Owners

If large slaveholders were universally engaged in the extraction of salt, medium-size slaveholders also tended to be industrialists. Barton Potter, for example, owned seven slaves in 1850 and fourteen slaves in 1860 and ran a tannery in which he had invested $5,000 in 1850 and $6,000 ten years later. Unlike larger slaveholding salt manufacturers, Potter did not operate a farm in 1850, though he did have an $8,000 farm by 1860. Leander Miller, who ran a somewhat smaller Clay County tannery in 1850, owned eleven slaves, but again had no farming enterprise. Several medium-size slaveholders owned small farms, averaging seventy acres of improved land in 1850, approximately midway between the holdings of large and small slaveholders.

Small slave owners had very different patterns of wealth. Unlike in the North Carolina mountains,[172] most small slaveholders in Clay County were dependent on income from farming. Among the twenty-one small slave-holders listed in the 1850 population census, eight (38%) owned no property; of the thirteen landowning slaveholders, the average value of their land was $4,946 – compared to $1,023 for all county landowners and $20,509 for large slaveholders. Ten small slaveholders were listed in the agricultural census as landowners and these averaged 44 improved acres, compared to 151 for large slaveholders. Among those small slaveholders who were landless, one was a merchant, another was a clerk, another a wool carder; one was landless but lived adjacent to a landowning brother and may have worked on that farm. The remaining four were slave-owning tenant farmers.

Contrary to the assumption that small-scale mountain slaveholding was fueled largely by the need for farm laborers beyond that supplied by household and family members, most small-scale slaveholding in Clay County was based on the enslavement of women and children. Among the twenty-five slave owners with four or fewer slaves in 1850, fifteen (60%) owned only adult women and children. An additional three households (12%) owned children under ten years of age, but no adult slaves, suggesting that the children were purchased as long-term capital investments.[173] A mere three owners (12%) had only adult men as slaves; an additional four (16%) owned both adult men and adult women.

Although the slave census does not include information on the occupations of slaves, other studies indicate that on small farms, enslaved men and boys were used almost exclusively as farm laborers; enslaved women and girls typically were used for domestic and household work, but were brought into the fields during times of high labor demand.[174] The gender pattern of small slaveholding thus suggests that domestic work, not farm work, was the more typical task of slaves owned by small slaveholders.

By linking the population and slave censuses, it is possible to examine these small slaveholders more closely. The three small slaveholders who owned only adult men as slaves were all farmers; these slaves were probably used in farming work. But this group had little else in common. Two were young tenant farmers. One couple, the owners of a sixteen-year-old male slave, lived with their three young children and farmed a small fifty-acre plot owned by the wife's mother. Another couple with a baby, also tenant farmers, owned a sixteen-year-old male slave. The third couple were in their seventies and owned $6,000 in land. In their household were four young grandsons, a hired white farm laborer, and a twenty-four-year-old slave man.

Households owning women and child slaves, but not slave men, were similarly diverse. They included several with large numbers of young children, in which slave women may have served as governesses or domestic servants and a household in which a forty-six-year-old mulatto man is recorded as owning a slave woman and three child slaves, perhaps his wife and children.

Women as Slaveholders

Slaveholding is typically viewed as an exclusively male province. Historians have uncovered the history of white women as overseers of domestic slaves,[175] but little attention has focused on women's ownership and control of non-domestic slaves. Typically, slaveholding has been understood through the prism of antebellum gender roles among privileged whites, that is, women working or supervising work within the household; men in the outside world.

A close scrutiny of Clay County's slaveholders suggests that, although this may have been the predominant pattern among slaveholders, it was not universal. Women did own slaves and, with one exception, women slaveholders also headed their own households, often with small children. Several women slaveholders owned farms that they operated with the help of slaves and hired laborers.

Two women in Clay County owned slaves in 1850. Ann Reid, forty-five years old, headed a household with three sons and ran a small farm with $600 worth of land and $50 in livestock. She also owned a thirty-five-year-old woman slave. Martha Murphy, a sixty-three-year-old woman who lived with her twenty-eight-year-old daughter, listed no occupation in the census and owned no land in Clay County, but owned a thirteen-year-old slave girl and a thirty-five-year-old slave man.

In 1860, Clay County had three women slaveholders. Elizabeth Woods lived with her brother, wealthy salt magnate Alexander White, and listed her occupation as "lady." Her two young women slaves presumably served as her personal servants. Lucinda Gilbert, a farmer, headed a household consisting of two young adult sons, both farm laborers, a hired white farm laborer, and nine slaves. Elizabeth Root, also a farmer, supported a household that included her eight-year-old sister, a male farm laborer, a young (non-enslaved) male servant, and a twenty-eight-year-old slave woman.

Thus, Clay County's early industrial success – and some of its financial, agricultural, and commercial strength – was beholden to the exploitation of slave labor and to market exchange of slave bodies. Accounts that acclaim "entrepreneurship" as well as those that laud "cooperation" among frontier businessmen pay insufficient attention to the vicious abuse of human men, women, and children that fueled early market development in places like Clay County. Clay County's antebellum economic practices and markets (both internal and extralocal) depended on access to slaves and to the coersive legal and political power that undergirded slave societies.

Conclusion

The patterns of slave ownership in Clay County, like industrial development and the growth of a commercial economy, contradict simplistic assumptions about the isolation of antebellum Appalachian Kentucky and the primitiveness of its early economy. Nonetheless, as Clay County's once vigorous salt industry declined, this region of Kentucky began a slow process of economic dissociation from the rest of the state that was not overcome until the end of the nineteenth century. Even before such decline, however, many Clay Countians practiced forms of subsistence-first farming that allowed them to live more or less independently of the vicissitudes of capitalist development. The economic and cultural strategies that lay outside the modes of industrial production and market expansion of saltmaking and commerce in antebellum Clay County are important to consider as a lens on the economic dynamics that left rural Appalachian poor in the postbellum period. They also clarify the range of economic alternatives from the past that might serve as building blocks for effective policy strategies in the present. We explore how plain folk's lives were organized in Chapter 5, but, first, the fact of slaveholding points us toward the social organization of coercion and the role of the local state in antebellum Clay County.

III

ANTEBELLUM STATE COERCION

4

STATE MAKING AND THE ORIGINS
OF ELITE CONFLICT

Building capitalist industrial and commercial enterprises in the Appalachian Mountains, as on the Kentucky frontier in general, did not simply depend on the production of commodities and the creation of markets for their exchange, monumental as those tasks were. Coercion and command by the state, even in the relatively laissez-faire economy of antebellum Appalachian Kentucky, also were essential to capitalist development and the making of wealth and poverty.

Generally speaking, local governments in Kentucky were not granted authority to interfere with the operation of markets except in the unique case of taverns where Clay County magistrates set the prices for whiskey, brandy, cider and beer, lodging, meals, horse stabling and feed.[1] Redistribution, too, was minimal except for occasional relief payments to the poor, especially widows and the handicapped.[2] But state force was necessary to en-*force* contracts, adjudicate disputes, and to build the infrastructures that economic development demanded, especially roads and passable waterways. Even more importantly, centralized and legitimate, that is, "public," force was necessary to protect various forms of commodified private property, none more essential to the wealth, prosperity, and class privilege of antebellum Appalachian elites than land and slaves.

In nineteenth-century Kentucky, where "essential governmental functions were in many ways conducted not from Frankfort [the state capital] but from the seats of her multitudinous counties," county courts were the most important units of government.[3] During the first fifty years of the century, each Kentucky county was ruled by non-elected magistrates or justices of the peace whose authority touched the lives of nearly every resident.

So comprehensive and pervasive were the powers and responsibilities of the [county] courts that sooner or later almost everyone in the county, from white adults to slaves, had business with them. People brought their deeds to be recorded, their petitions to be heard, and their crops and livestock to be sold after their official business was completed. Court day was also the occasion for politicking and merrymaking, gossiping, and sometimes brawling.[4]

Functioning as both judicial and administrative bodies, county courts tried civil and criminal cases, arbitrated disputes, and enforced the law. They also assessed property and collected taxes; probated estates; oversaw slave emancipations; administered poor laws and bound out orphaned, illegitimate, and impoverished children as apprentices; determined cases of bastardy and paternity; established schools; authorized the building of mill dams; and built and maintained roads in partnership with the state and with the forced labor of local residents.[5]

The conservative owners of vast amounts of land and slaves who dominated the first two constitutional conventions in 1792 and 1799, which established Kentucky's statehood and the character of its political order, were careful to create, in the words of E. Merton Coulter, "a constitution far removed from the rampant democracy so evidently desired by the masses of the people."[6] They extended suffrage to white males only, excluded free African Americans, Native Americans, and mulattoes from voting altogether, and, after a brief experiment with an electoral college, restricted direct election to the governor, state legislators, and congressional representatives. Finally, the conservatives ensured that the most significant level of government, the county courts, would be ruled nondemocratically by justices of the peace appointed for life by the governor and headed by their most senior member, the sheriff. Possessing great patronage powers, these court officers in turn appointed all other county officials to serve at their discretion. Voice voting, along with the authority to appoint election officials, afforded magistrates and especially sheriffs great powers of intimidation since merely carrying around warrants and summonses on election days was said to have had powerful and chilling effects on voters.[7]

In Kentucky, as throughout the entire antebellum South, county officials tended both to be slave owners and considerably wealthier than their fellow citizens.[8] Clay County, where slave owners and especially salt manufacturers were disproportionately influential, was no exception. Of the seven justices of the peace who convened the inaugural session of the Clay County court in 1807, at least three were slave owners, including the saltmaker John Bates who then owned fifteen slaves. Of five new justices appointed the following year, four were slave owners including saltmakers Daniel Garrard, Beverly Broaddus, and James Todd. The governor commissioned Hugh White, a slave owner and saltmaker, assistant judge of the circuit court in 1807 and he named Daniel Garrard the other assistant judge two years later.[9]

The extent to which justices of the Clay County court were drawn primarily from the ranks of slave owners and wealthy landowners before constitutional reform in 1849 somewhat democratized county governments in Kentucky can be seen by comparing the members of the court with the population of eligible voters in 1841. Although only 7% of Clay County's 758 white male taxpayers owned slaves in 1840, and 56% of them were landless, nine out of the thirteen magistrates in 1841 owned slaves. On average, each of them owned property worth $8,136 in comparison with the county average of $1,090, evidence that Clay County was far from the egalitarian democracy of Appalachian stereotypes.[10]

Even though 1841 was an economically depressed and politically tumultuous year, saltmaking was profoundly important to the capitalist sector of the local economy and several saltmakers served on the court that year, including John Gilbert and David Walker, a nephew and business associate of Daniel Bates. Saltmakers Alexander White, James H. Garrard, and T. T. Garrard were also members of the court, serving where their fathers, Hugh White and Daniel Garrard, had served from the earliest years of the court's existence until their resignations in the late 1820s.

Saltmakers played an even greater political role representing Clay County in the Kentucky General Assembly than in the county, if that were possible. John Bates served in the Kentucky House of Representatives in 1811, 1815, 1817, 1824, and 1832. Daniel Garrard served there in 1822, 1855, and 1857 and in the Kentucky Senate from 1813–17 and 1825–9. His son, James H. Garrard, served in the House in 1836 and another son, T. T. Garrard, served there in 1843 and 1844 and in the Senate from 1857 to 1861. Hugh White's son, Alexander, served in the House in 1825, 1826, and 1861–3 and in the Senate from 1847 to 1850. Other saltmakers with experience in the legislature included John Gilbert, Elhanon Murphy (a salt-firm manager), and John C. Wilson. Robert Brashears, Hugh White's partner in saltmaking on the North Fork of the Kentucky River, once represented Clay and Perry counties in the legislature as well.[11]

The need for legitimate as well as geographically accessible institutions for enforcing law and order in the Kentucky mountains was driven home not only to Clay County's pioneer saltmakers, who soon dominated the local state, but probably to ordinary citizens as well by the occurrence of a violent dispute that took place there in the spring of 1806. Occurring within the vast territory of Madison County, which then included hundreds of sparsely populated square miles and whose courthouse was located nearly seventy-five rugged miles away in Richmond, Kentucky, on the southeastern edge of the Bluegrass region, this conflict was well remembered throughout the nineteenth century by local residents as "the cattle war."[12]

Its political resolution later that year resulted in the formation of Clay County.

Involving several important pioneer families that recently had settled along the headwaters of the three forks of the Kentucky River, the cattle war pitted farmers living within the vicinity of the North Fork of the Kentucky River (now Perry County) – principally the Callahans, Strongs, and David-sons, all interrelated through marriage – against another group of farmers – the Amises, Bowlings, and Gilberts, also intermarried – who lived along the river's Middle and South Forks (now Clay and Leslie counties). The conflict occurred when Middle Fork cattle farmers were in the process of driving their cattle to market in Virginia via the North Fork. According to tradition, when cattle belonging to the North Forkers wandered into a camp that the Middle Forkers had cleared to winter their cattle on the lush canebrake banks of the North Fork, they were slaughtered by a group of the Middle Fork herdsmen led by John Amis, a co-owner of one of the area's first salt furnaces. In retal-iation, fourteen men from the North Fork rode to the Amis camp, seized some of its cattle and killed a prized horse. In response, John Amis raised an armed force of thirty men that included his brother-in-law, John Gilbert (also a pioneer saltmaker and one of the first settlers in the area) and attacked the North Forkers. No one was killed in the resulting battle, but descendants of these combatants figured prominently in subsequent feuds that occurred in Breathitt, Perry, and Clay Counties.[13]

Historical studies of state making in peripheral societies suggest that the local state is born when there is a need for a separate public power to prevail "over armed indigenous societies as well as over the ruling class itself."[14] In Appalachian Kentucky, where there were no indigenous peoples to subdue, the cattle war pointed to the need for the formation of a local county court to resolve disputes among settler groups and "bring some law and order to the three forks area" of the Kentucky River.[15] Although Clay County, autho-rized in 1806, extended over a vast territory that then included the future county seats of Leslie, Perry, Knott, Owsley, and Lee counties, as well as parts of future Jackson, Laurel, Bell, Harlan, and Breathitt counties,[16] its forma-tion nonetheless brought legal proceedings closer to home for the early set-tlers of that section of the Kentucky mountains.

The first meeting of the Clay County court took place at the home of Robert Baker on Bullskin Creek near the source of the South Fork of the Kentucky River in April 1807. A permanent county seat, named "Manchester" in anticipation of Clay County's industrial growth, was soon established on Goose Creek near the center of the region's salt-manufacturing industry. "The records of that first court indicate that men were selected [as justices of the peace] to please both factions" of the cattle war including William Strong and saltmaker John Gilbert along with more neutral parties such as Baker and John Bates, another pioneer salt manufacturer.[17] Two Madison county investors in saltmaking, John White (not related to the Clay County Whites) and John Crooke, served as sureties for the sheriff. Abner Baker, a cousin of both Robert Baker and saltmaker Francis Clark, was chosen as clerk of both the county and circuit courts. Adoniram Andrews, Beech Creek's most prominent citizen, served on the county's first grand jury.[18]

During the proceedings of Clay County's first criminal trial, John Amis, the hotheaded saltmaker who played a key role in the cattle war, was murdered by Joel Elkin, a North Forker employed at the Goose Creek saltworks, who used a loaded gun belonging to Justice of the Peace William Strong, Amis's enemy, to do the killing. Elkin was hanged for this crime, yet despite such a violent and inauspicious beginning, the administration of justice and government in Clay County proved to be stable for the first three and a half decades of the county's existence.

In contrast to prevailing images of early Appalachia as isolated from mainstream social and political affairs, recent studies of antebellum Appalachian political life suggest that the mountain region was more closely integrated with the rest of the nation than previously imagined and that Appalachian local governments, especially in those communities with well-developed commercial ties, did not hesitate to pursue policies aimed at encouraging economic development.[19] Clay County's unswerving loyalty from 1828 to 1851 to Henry Clay's Whig party, a party committed to "enhancing the profitability of property," suggests that it was no different. The strength of its voters' commitment to the principles of Whiggery placed it among Bluegrass and other southeastern Kentucky counties in the "Whig Gibraltar," while the actions of its county court prior to the emergence of political parties suggest that Clay County leaders aggressively pursued policies associated with modernization and economic development.[20]

The earliest surviving records of court actions suggest both the stability of local governance during the county's early years and the fact that county leaders did not hesitate to use the local state to build the infrastructures that capitalist enterprise required.[21] These and later records also document the hegemony of saltmakers and merchants in public affairs throughout the antebellum period. Thus, Hugh White and James Todd were authorized to supervise the building of a public jail in 1807. Land for the first court house, a two-story brick structure, was donated by saltmakers Hugh White, John Bates, John Amis, and John Patrick; Hugh White and Beverly Broaddas supervised its construction in 1812. Daniel Garrard was authorized to establish a town around the courthouse on ten acres of public land in 1817 and he and Claiborne White supervised the building of an office there for the county clerk in 1826. In 1833, Daniel Garrard and his son, T. T. tore down the original courthouse and built a second one. Despite the erection of such public buildings, however, court order books show that the county court and other official bodies sometimes met in the private counting rooms of salt merchants, a spatial indication of the close connections between commerce and governance in antebellum Clay County.[22]

Court orders also show that saltmakers were given authority as highway commissioners to build roads connecting their saltworks to regional highways and to compel the labor of citizens living in those vicinities for road maintenance and improvement. Other entries show them being reimbursed from county tax levies for making river improvements. In the 1820s and 1830s, they were authorized to appoint patrollers to "suppress disorder and disperse all improper collections of slaves." As justices, they also decided when to authorize other citizens to erect enterprises that impacted their neighbors as when, in the second session of 1807, the county court permitted Beech Creek's Adoniram Andrews to build a dam and sawmill on the South Fork. Occasionally, they allotted relief and pensions to widows, the blind, and other paupers, but more frequently they removed children from the homes of poor and especially African American families and bound them as apprentices to wealthy farmers and merchants.[23]

Studies of state building in early modern Europe show both that political development is an uneven process and that the conjunction of state building with an expanding market economy often "breeds widespread corruption as offices become capital assets on which to make profits."[24] Consistent with this pattern, political corruption and the use of public office for private gain were widespread throughout all of early Kentucky, when even the selling of county offices, sometimes at public auction and including the sheriffalty and clerkship, was not uncommon.[25]

A hint that the confusion of public interest with private gain had taken root early in Clay County can be found in a land dispute heard by the Clay County Circuit Court in 1811 when Samuel Todd accused Abner Baker, the county clerk, and John Bates, a justice of the peace, of corruption.[26] Based on enabling legislation from the Kentucky General Assembly, the county court had authorized Baker in 1807 to locate, survey, and sell 6,000 acres of unpatented land in Clay County in order to raise money to build a "seminary," that is, a public school. As compensation for his efforts, Baker was allotted a 569-acre tract of land. Charging that Baker had acted "contrary to equity and good conscience," Todd claimed that the lands Baker had appropriated for the benefit of the seminary were not worth $200 whereas the lands Baker reserved for himself were worth $2,000.

The truth of such claims is difficult to determine from existing materials but it is significant that Baker, who became county clerk as a young man of modest means and whose salary was never more than $40 a year, had managed to acquire $21,000 worth of property including twenty-five slaves after twenty years in office.[27] It is also significant that Todd, who initially lost the case and died before his appeal was heard, managed to enlist Daniel Garrard as the surety for his claims of wrongdoing in what would be the first – but certainly not the most lethal – instance of litigation that would pit a Garrard against a Bates and the only time a Garrard would take sides against a Baker. Finally, that Todd took his complaint of wrongdoing to the local court, rather than acting on it with his rifle as later stereotypes of mountaineers predict that he would have done, suggests that in addition to an orderly and moderately activist local government, Clay County also benefited from effective judicial institutions during its first several decades of existence.

Contemporary research on the role of courts in dispute resolution points out that "litigation is political in the sense that the very act of involving the formal, public authority of the courts in dispute resolution inescapably is part of the political process and has political consequences."[28] Because of the intimate relationship between court use and the "imposition of state legitimated and administered force," court records provide information on the local state as well as local society and thus on how the local state "both exercises its power and makes effective claims to the power it exercises."[29]

In order to evaluate the robustness of Clay County's judicial institutions throughout the nineteenth century, we examined two large samples of court cases. First, we analyzed all civil cases adjudicated in the Clay County Circuit Court from 1807 to 1849 and 1890 to 1901 (772 cases) that included members of families involved in the two periods of sustained violence that became notorious as Clay County's "feuds." Additionally, we aggregated summary data from surviving records for all civil cases filed in the circuit court in 1810, 1820, 1840, 1860, 1880, and 1900 (see Appendix 1). Each of these cases was read by one of three attorneys familiar with nineteenth-century litigation who assisted us in this research. These attorneys concluded that the Clay County Circuit Court was highly effectual in resolving disputes, at least prior to the onset of major violence discussed later. They found these cases unremarkable in the competency, thoroughness, and fairness of the judicial and legal process. Petitions were almost uniformly literate, reasonable, and predictable. Both plaintiffs and defendants were represented by legal counsel and pleadings were correctly formulated. Significantly, outcomes in cases involving feud disputants were more predictable from the evidence presented in the case file than from the familial allegiance of the plaintiff, defendant, or judge, and in only five cases were any procedural irregularities noted.[30]

The attorneys' judgment that competent and professional legal counsel was readily available in nineteenth-century Clay County contradicts the commonplace but erroneous notion that "since his natural environment landlocked him . . . [the Kentucky mountaineer] was denied a sufficient amount of legal knowledge and protection until the past few years."[31] Quite to the contrary, not only were Clay County's eventual feudists and their families consistent and intense litigators, but many of them were practicing attorneys as well, including Daniel Garrard's son William and his grandson Gilbert, as was Hugh White's son John White and his grandson John D. White. Additionally, members of both the Garrard and White families, as we have seen, served frequently as Clay County justices of the peace, and, in their roles as members of the state legislature and even the U.S. Congress, many were lawmakers as well.

Our examination of "feudists'" litigation also shows that both the Garrards and the Whites sought the best attorneys in Kentucky when situations seemed to warrant such. In an early defense of land titles, for instance, the Whites hired future governor William Owsley, John Bates hired future United States Attorney General John J. Crittenden, and the Garrards hired future governor Robert Letcher to represent them.[32] In the 1844 murder trial of Abner Baker, Jr., discussed later, the defense attorney was the most distinguished jurist in antebellum Kentucky, George Robertson, former chief justice of the state supreme court while a key protagonist among the Bakers at the end of the century, George Baker, was himself an attorney. Finally, the early availability of legal expertise in Clay County is suggested by the fact that seven of the jurists who presented credentials in Manchester during the first three years of the court's existence went on to distinguished legal careers that each included terms in the U.S. Congress.[33]

Figure 4.1, which plots the changing composition of Circuit Court cases from 1810 to 1900, shows that Clay Countians did not hesitate to seek legal remedy for a wide range of disputes involving breaches of contract, assault and battery, divorce, conflicts over land and estates, and financial obligations. The figure also illustrates how well court use indexes social change. Throughout all years except 1880, a time of great change in the patterns of family and household life and when divorce represented a remarkably high proportion of civil disputes brought before the court, the greatest volume of litigation was devoted to disputes over promissory notes. Such actions reached an all-time peak during the economic depression surrounding 1840. This heavy reliance on courts to enforce financial obligations and to resolve disputes over debts is hardly surprising, given the heavy reliance of early Clay County commerce on personal notes in an era of scarce cash money. But this volume of litigation does contradict facile and erroneous writings about Appalachian Kentuckians as having "little regard for the law."[34]

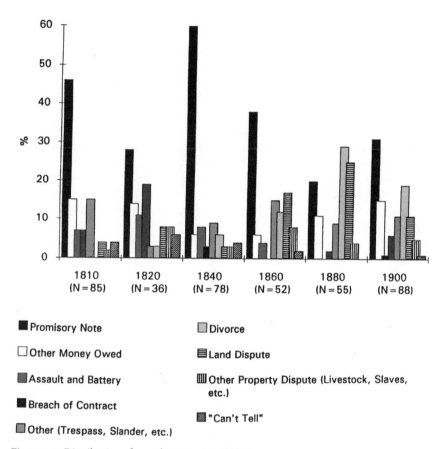

Figure 4.1 Distribution of cases by type, 1810–1900.

As we discuss more fully later, the notion that Kentucky mountain people were "loath to subordinate [themselves] to the body politic" became popular in the late nineteenth century when stories of Kentucky's feuds received extensive national attention. At that time, mountain people began to be depicted either as heirs of a "lawless ancestry" or as having been "a law unto [themselves] too long" to then be able to "look to civil law for protection." Jack Weller echoed this theme in the 1960s in *Yesterday's People* when he claimed that because they had been "determined to establish a life as free from contact with law and restraint as possible," those who settled the Cumberland Plateau had "reverted to a system of private justice based on the personal relationships common to the clan."[35]

The Upper South's sad history of injustice to women, racial minorities, farm tenants, and industrial workers makes it abundantly clear that justice throughout the entire region was not merely "personal, capricious, and uncertain," as one social historian has recently noted, but systematically biased as well.[36] Yet such a history of discrimination does not validate the stereotype of the Appalachian population as a "lawless" people. In her pathbreaking study of the Hatfield and McCoy feud that occurred along the Tug River border between Kentucky and West Virginia, Altina Waller concludes that, contrary to popular beliefs, "Tug Valley residents committed fewer crimes than those in modern communities, but they spent more time in court." "Their willingness to abide by decisions of the local judicial system," she contends, "reflected a confidence that the justice meted out would approximate community consensus and parallel the informal authority structure of family and neighborhood."[37]

Our research on Clay Count courts bears out Waller's claim regarding Appalachians' confidence in the legal process. Although many of the sources of potential conflict in Clay County's developing capitalist economy can be traced to disputes arising specifically in the salt industry over purchase and delivery contracts, rental agreements, and the use of slaves,[38] no issue was more potentially disruptive than disputes over land. Yet time after time, even the feud disputants in our samples of civil litigants turned to local courts to adjudicate property disputes. Despite becoming involved in violent clashes that ultimately crippled the local state and deformed public life in Clay County, these entrepreneurs, as well as other members of the local elite and the common folk, relied on antebellum courts to fend off challenges to their control of land and natural resources.

Contests over the control of land originated from several sources, one of which was simply the poor quality of land surveys in Kentucky that, in the absence of a systematic land policy and in conjunction with multiple and sometimes contradictory patterns of acquisition, resulted in what, as in the rest of Kentucky, was commonly described as a crazy quilt of overlapping and contradictory claims in Clay County. The inexact nature of surveys is evident from the plethora of early deeds recording boundaries marked by streams, rocks, trees, and other natural but changeable aspects of the local environment. One such deed, for example, records the effort of an earnest Clay County surveyor to verify a boundary line by cutting a block out of one of two oak trees marking a corner, counting the tree's annual growth rings, and judging "the different years of growth over the chop of the axe to agree with the date of survey."[39]

Clay County jurors were frequently called on to puzzle out such riddles of inexactitude in the surveying and patenting of land, and often in such cases, the stakes were high. Such was the case in a dispute in 1822 involving Daniel Garrard, Moses Martin, and John Bates over a quarter of an acre of land apparently containing brine. This ejectment case (a form of eviction) was litigated by two future Kentucky governors (Owsley and Letcher) and important enough for the Garrards to obtain a deposition from one William Sweeten, then living in Gallatin County, Illinois, who claimed to have patented and settled the land in question as Governor Garrard's agent in 1798.[40]

As we shall see in the following chapter, however, not all Clay Countians viewed land merely as a disposable commodity. In contrast to the capitalist practice of speculative investments, the subsistence-first farmers of Beech Creek held on tightly to their lands and tended to keep them off the market for transmission within their families since land and family together cemented a noncapitalist way of life for them. But because many others in Clay County and beyond its borders did view land as a speculative commodity, conflicts over inexact and disputable boundaries, exacerbated by the frequent sale and resale of properties that speculation entailed, represented a sizeable problem demanding public adjudication.

The untimely death of business partners also occasioned conflicts over land that ended up in court, perhaps none more dramatic than the murder of John Amis. Shortly before his death, Amis had purchased a one-fourth interest in one of the two earliest saltmaking operations in Clay County, the Goose Creek Saltworks, owned jointly by three Bluegrass (Madison County) entrepreneurs, John Crooke, John White, and John Patrick. Amis purchased Crooke's share for $2,500, half in cash and half in salt, and the latter assigned Amis's debt to John White. Amis died before this debt was paid, but apparently not before assigning his interest in the land to John Bates while retaining some rights to make salt and leasing them to Samuel Todd, a Virginian, in exchange for Todd's clearing the land in question.

Amis's murder in 1807 by an employee of the Goose Creek Saltworks in retaliation for Amis's role in the cattle war of the previous year left this tangle of debts and contracts in considerable confusion, resulting in several years of litigation. Todd sued Bates and Bates sued Todd over wrongful possession, actions that lay behind Todd's charges of public corruption against Bates and his partner, Abner Baker. John White sued his partner Crooke, the administrator of Amis's estate, for interference with his ability to produce salt and for exhausting Amis's estate that White claimed still owed him money for Amis's share in the saltworks. White also sued Lincoln Amis, John Amis's brother, who was himself charged by Samuel Todd with conspiring with Bates to defraud Todd and depleting his water supply. Lincoln Amis likewise accused Crooke of wasting Amis's estate. Finally, to further confuse matters, Hugh and James White purchased 600 acres from the heirs of Stephen

Langford, the saltwork's original proprietor, which they believed included Amis's and Bates's saltworks and they promptly initiated actions that succeeded eventually in ejecting Bates from the property. The point is that all of these actions, with the possible exception of Todd's charges of corruption against Baker and Bates, were apparently litigated without malice and certainly without violence.[41]

Local courts also proved to be an effective instrument of defense against attempts by entrepreneurs from outside the area to gain control over Appalachian resources and enterprises. Prior to the settlement of Clay County, the Commonwealth of Virginia had awarded warrants to unsettled lands throughout all of what would soon be Kentucky as payment for the military service of its citizens in the Revolutionary War. Some of those awarded such warrants, such as Captain Adoniram Andrews of Beech Creek, did in fact survey, patent, and settle in Kentucky, but many others did not, choosing to sell their warrants to urban merchants who accumulated them as investments that eventually allowed speculators to claim vast amounts of land in central and Appalachian Kentucky.

The Clay County deed books record many such large surveys, each representing the aggregation of numerous military warrants, including a 20,000-acre survey originally made in the name of President James Monroe, which was eventually acquired by the Garrards from Pittsburgh investors, a 40,000-acre survey in the name of one Ballard Smith, and a 50,000-acre survey in the name of Philadelphia merchant and steamboat promoter Benjamin Wyncoop. The largest of such claims, combining warrants to cover 116,656 acres between the North and Middle Forks of the Kentucky River, was surveyed in 1783 for Thomas Franklin, a Philadelphia merchant.[42]

Once entrepreneurs demonstrated that salt could be made profitably in Clay County, outsiders attempted to gain control over Goose Creek's brine-rich waters on the basis of such claims, but local courts proved to be an effective means by which Clay Countians could protect their property. One of the most aggressive of these nonlocal speculators was John Savony, a saltmaker from south central Kentucky. Savony brought suits against Hugh White, Daniel Garrard, John Bates, and others in 1810 and 1811, in one case claiming ownership of 5,000 acres, twenty-one houses, four furnaces and two salt wells. In both cases, however, he was unable to eject the local owners.[43] The Whites used local courts to ward off an ejectment effort by William Bledsoe who claimed their furnaces, wells, and houses under a 1792 survey, made well before their arrival in Clay County. The Garrards, besides defending their interests on Goose Creek from John Savony, protected other saltmaking facilities in the North Fork valley (today's Perry County) in 1817 from claimants to a 62,000-acre survey made on behalf of the Reynolds family of Philadelphia.[44]

Origins of the Intraelite Conflict

If Clay County's judicial and governmental institutions proved robust enough to withstand the many conflicts that arose during the county's first three and a half decades of settlement and economic development, the same cannot be said for these institutions' ability to weather the storms brought on locally by the national economic depression that lasted from the end of the 1830s through the mid-1840s. During that long depression, which by 1841 had "burst with full force upon the state," and when, lamented Henry Clay, "[e]very description of property [in Kentucky], without exception, [was] greatly depressed, and still declining in value,"[45] local governmental authority and courts in Clay County were severely tested and in many ways proven inadequate to withstand intraelite disputes.

It is ironic, only in light of a much later discursive tradition that portrayed the Kentucky mountain "feuds" as the consequence of ignorance, isolation, and backwoods primitivism, that the social origins of long-term conflict would take root in the unresolved disputes of that area's leading capitalist entrepreneurs and its best educated, most sophisticated political leaders. Yet such disputes crippled local government and deformed Clay County's nascent public sphere as elite competition and hatred reached deep into civil society to recast the latter along contours shaped by the fractures among elites as they mobilized subaltern allies on behalf of their personal interests and enmities. The most important expression of these disturbances was a bitter, century-long conflict between the county's two greatest families, the Whites and the Garrards.

Initially on the most friendly of terms, the Whites and the Garrards ranked at the top of Clay County's most socially respected and economically powerful families. The memoir of a granddaughter of Hugh White, Bessie White Hager, published after her death in the *Register of the Kentucky Historical Society*, conveys the respect both families initially felt for each other, noting that when Daniel Garrard first arrived in Clay County, he was cordially received by the Whites.

> Being neighborly, Grandfather Hugh sent his son, Alexander, accompanied by a negro servant, bearing a written invitation to the Garrards asking them to dine with him upon their arrival. This started a friendship which terminated with enmity years later as bitter as could be.[46]

Hugh White's genuine affection and respect for Daniel Garrard cannot be doubted since he named his thirteenth and last child, born in 1819, Daniel Garrard White.[47] In 1832, T. T. Garrard celebrated his marriage to his first wife, Nancy Brawner, at the home of his friend Alexander White. A decade later, James White married T. T.'s sister, Mary, three years after the death of his first wife.[48] Since there is no evidence of enmity ever having arisen between Hugh White and Daniel Garrard, it would appear that animosity arose only among members of the second generation of Whites and Garrards in Clay County and their descendants.

All the sources of discord between the Whites and Garrards may never be fully uncovered, but they seem to have resulted from both economic and political competition as well as injuries to the Whites' family honor perceived from actions of the Garrards in the course of events discussed later. Hager, however, wrote only of the keen economic competition between the Whites and Garrards although she was vague about, and may not have known exactly, when it arose.

> James and Daugherty White [her father] continued in the salt business many years, and it was then that enmity or jealousy developed between the White and Garrard families. James and Daugherty soon found that by cutting prices they could sell more salt, so they sold it five cents a bushel cheaper than their competitors. Garrard had to come down too, so he proceeded to undersell them; but only until James and Daugherty heard of it, when they again would lower their prices five cents under that of Garrard. This kept up until at one time James and my father were selling salt at 15 cents a bushel. My father [the larger-scale producer] contended that he could always make it cheaper than Garrard and he did. At times when price cutting became too keen, Garrard would leave his company, only to come back again and give it another trial.[49]

Such economic competition was replicated in the political arena as well, beginning at least as early as 1841 when young T. T. Garrard, a Democrat, ran unsuccessfully against Daugherty White, a Whig, for a seat in the House of Representatives in the Kentucky General Assembly.[50] This was only the first of many electoral contests that would pit a Garrard against a White. Even late in the nineteenth century, when the aging T. T. Garrard still ruled the county Democrats and Hugh White's grandson, John D. White, a U.S. Congressman, was "the Republican boss of his mountain section,"[51] the families continued to vie for local political control.

Perhaps even deeper than economic and political competition, however, were the long-lasting effects of a profound rift between these two preeminent family groups that occurred during a murder trial in 1844 when Dr. Abner Baker, Jr., the mentally deranged husband of Hugh White's young granddaughter Susan, was charged with the slaying of saltmaker Daniel Bates, an antagonist of the Garrards. An understanding of the fallout from this trial and its many causalities, including the quality of public life in Clay County thereafter, takes us to the heart of economic competition and political conflict during that perilous era of economic depression.

At the time violence first broke out among younger members of the county's economic and political elite in 1839, several years before Abner Baker, Jr.'s arrival, economic tensions were already mounting in Clay County. When the saltmaking firm of Wilson and Quarrier began heavily mortgaging its properties in 1837, several years before its eventual collapse, it was only a hint of the bad times that lay ahead for all the areas' saltmakers. In March of 1839, Hugh L. White was forced to mortgage nine slaves to his father to secure the latter's endorsement of his debts to outside creditors. Two years later, James H. Garrard and T. T. Garrard likewise mortgaged all their properties to their father for similar assurances on several thousands of dollars of outstanding debts.[52]

It is against this backdrop that tensions first arose between Daniel Bates and James and T. T. Garrard when Bates petitioned the county court in 1839 for permission to build a dam for a gristmill and sawmill on Little Goose Creek immediately above property on which the Garrards were already operating a sawmill. The Garrards petitioned the county court to deny Bates's request, apparently disputing the boundaries of their respective properties and fearing the effects of Bates's proposed dam on their own water supply. While the court ordered the sheriff to assemble jurors at the site to judge possible damages to the Garrards, the case was continued over a period of many months into the following summer of 1840, but it remained unresolved since the sheriff and jurors – perhaps fearing the repercussions of taking sides on this explosive issue – repeatedly failed to show up to make a judgment.[53] The county court was to have taken up the issue of the conflict between the Bates and the Garrards once again at its July 1840 session, but the court failed to meet that month when events took a violent turn with the first – but not last – shooting of Daniel Bates.

The precise cause of events surrounding the gunshot wound to Bates is unclear, but it seems to trace to an earlier violent episode that had occurred sometime during the previous year of 1839, which had involved several men from the White family and their supporters. A surviving fragment from a civil suit heard before the Clay County Circuit Court in 1839 indicates that Simeon Stivers, a minor son of George Stivers, then county clerk and a frequent business partner of Daniel Bates, had been assaulted by a mob comprised of twenty males including four of Hugh White's adult sons, William, Benjamin F., Daugherty, and Hugh L. Stivers demanded $10,000 in damages but was awarded only $5.00 each against William White and three others and only one cent against each of the other defendants including White's brothers.[54]

No Garrards were named in the action, but they played a central role in a second confrontation between the Whites and the Stivers that occurred a year later. This subsequent event, along with the fact that one of Simeon Stivers's brothers tried to kill T. T. Garrard while serving in Colonel Garrard's regiment more than two decades later during the Civil War, suggests persistent animosity between members of the Stivers and Garrard families as well as the Stivers and Whites.[55]

Exactly who shot Daniel Bates in July 1840 is not clear. The circumstances surrounding the event, however, were described by a witness, Judge Joseph Eve, in a deposition given as evidence in a civil suit brought by Bates against James H., T. T., and William Garrard and others, including five of Hugh White's sons, for assault and battery. The judge's deposition was written hastily the following year as Eve prepared to leave Kentucky to assume his duties as newly appointed chargé d'affaires to the Republic of Texas.[56]

Sitting as the presiding judge of the circuit court in 1840, Eve was informed by Colonel John Gilbert "that there was an armed party of white men and negroes under the hill [below the courthouse] and that unless some person interfered, he was fearful some one would be killed." On consulting with Colonel Daniel Garrard, "who declined to take any interest in the matter," Eve reportedly "went under the hill with the determination to use every exertion to induce the armed party to disarm themselves." Although not indicating why he believed Colonel Garrards's sons to be in command of the mob, which also included several members of the White family, he reports having "intended to go directly to James and T. T. Garrard and try and induce them to desist from any attack upon any individual." Instead of confronting the Garrards directly, however, Eve met with Daugherty White, also a member of the party, and was given the assurance that they would not disturb the court nor make any attack on the Stiverses unless provoked.

Provoked or not, an affray erupted on the courthouse hill the following day during which Daniel Bates, apparently onlooking, was shot in the neck and taken inside Barton Potter's store near the courthouse where he remained for a couple of days until order was restored. On returning from a visit to the Bates family that evening, Judge Eve encountered the armed party below the hill where he confronted James H. Garrard and told him of his surprise to find him and others involved in the conflict since they were "prudent, sober, discrete men," not to mention, in the case of James H. and T. T. Garrard, justices of the county court. Garrard reportedly stated that they had not intended to go on the hill to challenge the Stivers, but some members of the party were induced to go when they heard that the Stiverses claimed that they were afraid to do so. Once there, a fight broke out between David Walker, the wealthiest slave owner then sitting on the county court and a nephew of Daniel Bates, and Julius Hacker, a friend of the Garrards. According to Eve, James H. Garrard stated that "before Mr. Bates was shot that he, Bates, was standing in Mr. Potter's store door and hollowed to him [Garrard] to stop the affray and that he did attempt to keep others from interfering between Mr. Walker and Mr. Hacker."

Judge Eve's deposition carefully avoids speculation about how Daniel Bates came to be shot, but it reports that on the third day of the affair, the judge worked out "terms of peace" between the Garrards and Whites and the Walkers and Bates, both parties of which, significantly, included nonkin allies and armed slaves – a potent harbinger of the warlike mobilization of supporters that lay ahead. Such "peace and friendship between the parties," however, Eve declared at the time, were in their "mutual benefit" as well as "the interest of society" more generally.

In addition to an agreement to disarm, disband, and "forget the past excitement," the "compromise of peace" arranged by the judge included an understanding that "in the future if either party demand anything of the other they were to meet and talk it over as gentlemen and friends." Significantly, Eve's deposition makes little mention of the Stiverses but states that since "a difficulty was likely to arise between Mr. Bates and Colonel [Daniel] Garrard about the boundary of some of their land claims," the truce included a proviso stating that Bates and Garrard "were to leave it to two lawyers to decide between them." It also included a provision that "the difficulty between the Mr. Garrards and Mr. Bates about the mill on Little Goose Creek was to be left to honorable men as the parties were to law it out friendly and as honorable gentlemen."

Eve's deposition acknowledged the judge's sad realization that despite hoping at the time that mediation would ensure that "all would end in peace" and "mutual friendship would be restored," such was far from the case. It concluded with Eve's expression of deep regret for not having thought to request that the parties agree that there should be no future suits for the injury Daniel Bates had sustained from the shooting, for that was exactly the course of action that Bates had chosen.

Three months after the July fray, Daniel Bates presented nine promissory notes worth $5,485 to the Clay County Circuit Court at its October session and demanded their payment with interest. Seven of the notes were signed by Daniel, James H., and T. T. Garrard and two by T. T. Garrard's brother-in-law, Luther Brawner. Brawner's notes were due the past September, but each of the Garrards's notes were due on June 1, 1840, a month before Bates was shot. The court found in Bates's favor but, as if to flaunt his advantage over the Garrards, Bates withdrew the notes from the court in order to prevent their collection. Four days later, he sued James H., T. T., and William Garrard along with Luther Brawner, Julius Hacker, and Sydney Williams as well as William, James, Daugherty, Benjamin F., and Daniel Garrard White for the injuries he had sustained in July from what he termed a "mob attack." Bates demanded $100,000 in damages.[57]

Continued until the case was abated in 1844 on Bates murder, Bates's civil action against his presumed attackers provided a contentious backdrop to the mounting tensions arising from economic depression and business failure throughout the early 1840s. In the meantime, Bates and his friends pursued an aggressive campaign in the Clay County Circuit Court against the Garrards's financial interests. At the height of the depression in 1841, Bates's nephew, William Walker, assigned a note for $4,384 owed him by the Garrards to Bluegrass merchant Ezekiel Fields who brought action against them. Walker also won a default judgment as well against Julius Hacker and his surety, Daniel Garrard, for an $800 debt and George Stivers won a smaller default judgment against James H. and T. T. Garrard. Besides Hacker, who mortgaged all his land and livestock to Daniel Garrard in order to secure the latter's assumption of more than $2,000 worth of debt, other friends whose notes were endorsed by the Garrards were pressed by various court actions as well including Jeremiah Smith, Joseph Cooke, George Wilson, and, in 1842, Bethel Ely.[58]

Also in 1841, Leander Miller, a friend of Bates, won a suit for $1,234 against James H. and T. T. Garrard at the same time that the latter were being sued by the Bluegrass firm of Fields and Holloway for two notes totaling $1,700. Such actions forced the younger Garrards to mortgage all their property to their father for his assumptions of their debts and earlier had forced James H. Garrard to mortgage and convey three slaves to Lyne Kinningham (a son-in-law of Hugh White) for a debt of $1,500. Later that year, Daniel Bates initiated a fresh action on his claims against Daniel, James H., and T. T. Garrard and Luther Brawner to win a default judgment for $7,136 against them. In May 1843, the Garrards and Brawner mortgaged seventeen slaves and 300 acres of land to Bates to honor this claim. Finally, in 1846, Stivers and Walker, administrators for the deceased Bates, forced the sale of these properties at public auction to pay off the balance of the Garrards's debt to Bates estate.[59]

As Clay County's paper economy of obligations and mutual indebtedness began to collapse like a house of cards, partly through strategic actions bred by antagonism and partly through the inexorable effects of depression, the local state – ruled by many of the same protagonists who waged war in the

Clay County Circuit Court – soon became crippled as well. In 1842, Elijah McWhorter was nominated by the county court as sheriff, but, perhaps unable to raise the $10,000 bond from supporters as the law required, failed to qualify for office. From this point on, local governance was largely ineffective. A memorandum from the state auditor to Governor Robert Letcher in April 1843 reported that Clay County had failed to appoint a revenue collector for the years 1842 and 1843. In response to an inquiry from the governor, George Stivers, the county clerk, assured the governor a few days later that Felix Gilbert, county surveyor, would engage in the discharge of the duties of sheriff as the law required and enter a bond for the collection of taxes. Later that same year, Circuit Court Judge Tungston Quarles voided all decisions made by the circuit court from April 1842 to May 1843, there being no sheriff in the county to serve orders throughout that period. This decision had an especially devastating effect on creditors who had tried to use the authority of civil court to recover loans.[60]

Political conflicts in Clay County again came to Governor Letcher's attention in July 1843 when he received letters from Samuel Ensworth, a citizen, and T. T. Garrard, a member of the court, in regard to a dispute over appointments to fill two vacancies on the county court occasioned by the formation of Owsley County from part of the territory of Clay County earlier that year. By a close and contested vote, a controlling faction of Clay County magistrates had recommended Stephen Bates and Barton Potter over Job Baker and Abijah Gilbert to the governor in June. Samuel Ensworth petitioned Letcher to commission Bates and Potter whom he described as "independent" men who would "change the character of our court" so that it would "be able to do business hereafter." He also complained to the governor that "our county court has been ruled by party spirit and it has been impossible sometimes to do any business at all in court, only such they saw cause to have done to forward their party interests."[61]

T. T. Garrard, on the other hand, complained to the governor that the recommendations made to him by the court were "contrary to the constitution" since there were only twelve justices in commission at the time because of the forced departure of two others to Owsley County. Garrard claimed that since only six of the remaining justices concurred in the appointment of Bates and Potter, these candidates did not enjoy a majority of the court's favor as the court's recommendation to the governor had implied. "If the court has erred," Garrard wrote, "it ought to be taught a lesson by higher authority."[62]

Clearly troubled by these developments, Governor Letcher sought an opinion from the Attorney General regarding his duty to issue the commissions as recommended by the court and asking whether he might as governor "go behind the court to ascertain the individual opinions of the justices

who are on the bench." Advised that he could not query the justices individually and that he was obligated to accept the recommendation from the
court at face value, Letcher granted commissions to Bates and Potter to serve
as magistrates on the Clay County Court. In December of the same year, he
commissioned George Stivers as sheriff.[63] It was to this seething caldron of
Clay County's economic and political antagonisms that the criminal lunacy
of Dr. Abner Baker, Jr., would soon add an indelible ingredient.

The Murder Trial of Dr. Abner Baker, Jr.

Abner Baker, Jr., born in 1813, grew up in Clay County, the youngest child
of Abner Baker who had served as clerk of the Clay County court for many
years before his removal to Garrard County in the 1830s. Like his male age-
mates among the Garrards and Whites, Baker had been sent outside the
Kentucky mountains for an education, first to East Tennessee College in
Knoxville. After following in his father's footsteps briefly as clerk of the
county and circuit courts in Clay County from 1834 to 1836, he completed
a medical education at the Louisville Medical Institute in 1839, being the
fourth of Abner Baker's sons to become a physician. It was in Louisville, some
claimed, that he first showed signs of the madness that he soon would inject
into Clay County. After practicing medicine for a time in Knoxville, he
returned to Manchester around 1842. In 1844, he married Susan White, the
fifteen-year-old daughter of James White by his first marriage. Baker's marriage to Susan lasted only three months before ending in tragedy and death.[64]

Some found it odd that Baker would take his young bride to live in the
home of his sister Polly and brother-in-law Daniel Bates despite Baker's
public proclamations that Bates was a "black hearted man" who opposed his
marriage. Many persons claimed that Bates treated Baker kindly, but Baker
later told acquaintances that Bates "only kept him there at his house to
protect him from the Garrards and others." The acknowledgment by Bates's
associates that "Daniel Bates went armed from the time of the difficulty
between the Garrards and Bates," along with Baker's claim that Bates "kept
a band of lawless men and negroes about him" at all times, suggests the
climate of fear in Clay County produced by the conflict between these powerful enemies. But it was possibly Bates's refusal to loan Baker several thousand dollars to go into business that enraged Baker and ultimately led him
to murder his patron and brother-in-law.[65]

It was not greed, however, but madness that friends and kinfolk most
noticed in Abner Baker. Soon after his marriage, along with expressing his
hatred of Daniel Bates, Baker began to call his young wife "the damnest
whore living." He also told many acquaintances that his young wife was a

"nymphomaniac" who had had intercourse with numerous individuals, including, from age nine, her former schoolmaster in the Bluegrass and her uncles Daugherty and Benjamin F. White, and that often she had been pregnant and aborted. He claimed as well that Daniel Bates had had intercourse with her on several occasions, sometimes in Baker's presence, once on the floor of Baker's bedroom while a slave held him at bay with a Bowie knife. Further, Baker claimed that Bates was plotting to ruin his own wife's reputation in order to divorce her and have Susan to himself. It was only his determination to protect his sister from harm, Baker told others, that kept him living in Bates's household.[66]

In the summer of 1844, only three months after his wedding, Baker got into a violent argument with Bates. Mad perhaps, but understanding how to take advantage of the bitterness that divided his community, Baker went to T. T. Garrard to borrow a pistol. Garrard reportedly first refused, saying that he was no friend of Baker and that he did not want to see one of his friends shot, but relented when Baker told him that Daniel Bates was the "rascal" whom he feared and that he only wanted a gun for self-defense. Soon thereafter, Baker drew a gun on Bates before being subdued by Bates's armed slaves. According to later testimony, Bates asked J. T. Woodward, another saltmaker present at the time, "to see Baker out of the country – that he did not want to hurt him or be hurt."[67]

Baker stayed away from Clay County only a short while, and on his return, asked everyone he encountered if Bates or any of the Whites had made threatening statements about him, expressing fears that Bates's slaves had been told to kill him. Later the same day, Baker found Bates at his furnace, shot him fatally, and fled. To friends George Stivers and Barton Potter as he lay dying, Bates – described by his enemies as "a man of a deep, dark, revengeful mind" – pledged $10,000 from his estate for Baker's prosecution and freedom to his trusted slave Pompey for Baker's slaying. He further extracted a promise that should all else fail, his young son would take Baker's "scalp" when he grew up.[68]

At least in this instance able to discern his friends from his enemies, Baker fled the scene of his crime and surrendered himself to the Garrards. In their capacity as justices of the peace, James H. and T. T. Garrard refused to hand over Baker to other officials who came to arrest him. They agreed on mutually acceptable guards with James White and David Walker whose demands for custody of Baker they also denied, instead detaining the prisoner at the home of their father, Colonel Daniel Garrard. Some days later, two justices of the peace, T. T. Garrard and John Gilbert, held an official court of inquiry to determine whether Baker should be handed over to a grand jury for consideration of the charge of murder, but the Whites and Walkers refused to participate. Not doubting Baker's guilt but finding the defendant legally insane, Garrard and Gilbert released him to the custody of two of his brothers, Tennessee physicians who sent Baker to Cuba in hopes that he might there regain his health.[69]

The Walkers, outraged at the "unjust" killing of their uncle, and the Whites, their honor damaged by Baker's slanderous charges against Susan White of adultery and her uncles of incest, began a legal campaign to undo the judicial actions of their erstwhile friends the Garrards in order to bring Dr. Abner Baker, Jr., to trial for murder. In January 1845, they succeeded in petitioning Governor William Owsley to issue a $150 reward for Baker, whom the governor described as having "fled from justice" and "running at large." As executors of Daniel Bates's estate, David Walker and George Stivers added an additional $850 reward for Baker, which they advertised in the New York *Courier and Enquirer*, the Charleston, South Carolina *Mercury*, and the New Orleans *Picayune*. Abner Baker, Sr., remonstrated in the same newspapers that his "absent and persecuted son" was not guilty and pled for his mercy. Not knowing that their father intended to request a change of venue from the Kentucky legislature should his son show up, Baker's brothers advised Abner, Jr., to return from Cuba to stand trial and they turned him over to Clay County authorities.[70]

Abner Baker's trial is well-documented, transcripts of its proceedings and related petitions having been preserved in the papers of Governor William Owsley and by Baker's brother-in-law, C. W. Crozier, who published them in 1846 in a book entitled *Life and Trial of Dr. Abner Baker, Jr. (a Monomaniac)*, which he dedicated to "the independent, manly, and praiseworthy conduct of the Garrard family, in Clay County, in desiring that justice and humanity be exercised towards an unfortunate lunatic." These records show that Abner Baker was brought to trial on the first Monday of July 1845. His prosecution was led by a commonwealth's attorney and three privately paid prosecutors from Laurel, Knox, and Madison counties who were rumored to have been promised a contingent fee for Baker's conviction. Baker was defended by the state's most distinguished jurist, George Robertson, former chief justice of the Kentucky Court of Appeals, along with William Garrard, J. Hays, the independent-minded attorney Samuel Ensworth, who earlier had opposed T. T. Garrard's challenge to county court appointments, and two other attorneys.[71]

Baker's attorneys succeeded immediately in getting a jury selected by George Stivers dismissed on grounds that the sheriff, one of Bates's executors, was known to have pledged Baker's conviction to the dying Daniel Bates. Judge Tungston Quarles subsequently appointed Anderson Clark and Job Andrews, the latter of Beech Creek, as court elisors. They in turn selected twelve farmers largely from the Beech Creek area, including several

Andrewses and Johnsons and their neighbors, to serve on the jury, providing the citizens of that obscure rural neighborhood a rare opportunity to play a public role in making Clay County history.[72]

Once the jury was empaneled, testimony and arguments in the Baker trial took less than three days. Little time was spent proving that Baker shot Bates; most was devoted to the question of Baker's sanity. Baker's defense attorneys presented evidence, including testimony from a psychiatrist from the state mental hospital in Lexington, that Baker's mental competency in other areas of his life, apart from his obsessive delusions about his wife's sexuality and infidelity, was indicative of "monomania" and that he should be found not guilty of the murder of Daniel Bates by reason of insanity.[73]

A few persons admitted initial doubts about Susan White's chastity. A letter from Baker's brother William to his sister, Bates's wife, and referring to Bates's reputation for cohabitation with female slaves, suggests that he suspected Susan White of infidelity and his sister of covering it up. James H. Garrard was suspicious because Susan had earlier signed affidavits of confession that Baker had presented to her father and because, said Garrard, James White had not killed Baker on the spot. One can only wonder if the suicide of one of Susan's uncles, John White, the distinguished Court of Appeals jurist and former speaker of the U.S. House of Representatives, only days before Baker was to be hanged, renewed such doubts. But ultimately nineteenth-century assumptions about gender, unchallenged by today's revelations of sexual behavior and abuse within families and expressed again by James H. Garrard in the belief that no "woman in the world would act in the manner he charge[d] her with acting," prevented even Baker's supporters from imagining that his ravings were anything but lunacy.[74]

The friends of Daniel Bates and sympathizers with the Whites's hurt pride, however, claimed otherwise. Abner Baker was evil, not insane. His mind was "sound and strong," they claimed; he was "a smarter man than those who [had] tried [and released] him" in the prior court of inquiry.[75]

In contrast to George Robertson's eloquent but highly technical exposition of medical theories of insanity and monomania and their legal ramifications in his closing arguments to Baker's trial, the private prosecutors stooped to demagoguery by warning the uneducated jurors from Beech Creek not to be fooled by "Lexington Doctors" brought in "to enlighten and astonish ignorant mountaineers." They urged them not to allow "one of the ruffle-shirt gentry" to escape his just punishment. After deliberating for a day, the jury found Baker guilty and he was sentenced to be hanged. Shocked at having lost their case at a time in Kentucky courtrooms when felony convictions could not be appealed, Baker's attorneys and supporters initiated a vigorous and widespread effort to persuade the governor to grant a pardon while the Walkers and Whites mounted an equally vigorous campaign opposing pardon.[76]

Persons on both sides of the conflict with personal connections to Governor Owsley undoubtedly hoped to influence his decision. John White, a leader of Owsley's party, had studied law with the governor years before in his private practice. Abner Baker, Sr., brother-in-law to Oswley's immediate gubernatorial predecessor Robert Letcher, had counted him as a personal friend for more than forty years. George Robertson, who presented Owsley with transcripts of the trial along with eloquent and passionate letters from the convicted man's father, assured the elder Baker that the governor, also a former Court of Appeals justice, was certain to "decide in a few days favorably."[77]

In addition to Abner Baker's many letters to Owsley on behalf of his "deranged and unfortunate son," many other individuals wrote the governor, including the commonwealth attorney who prosecuted the case but advocated pardon, or signed petitions originated by the trial's partisans. Some of the most revealing letters came from the attorneys on both sides. Baker's attorney Samuel Ensworth reported the

> great excitement in the county against the prisoner, brought about by the wealthy connexions of Daniel Bates, and the wife of the prisoner, who, it was, and is thought, was badly injured – the effect of which was to be seen upon the trial, by some of the wealthy and influential, standing or sitting in front of the jury – and when anything was said against the prisoner, or anything read which they thought was against him, they would nod their assent, but on the contrary, when anything was said which operated in his favor, you could see the marks of dissent – which in exciting cases have a tendency to influence the minds of jury men particularly where the jury have been in the habit of looking up to them for advice.

Ensworth told the governor that "immediately after the jury had returned their verdict they were taken to the tavern where the Walkers and others of Bates connection put up and got their dinners and were roomed for some time." In correspondence to a sympathizer, attorney William Garrard called the trial "one of the most relentless, savage, overawing, corrupt prosecutions that ever disgraced a free state." To Ensworth's account, he added that Daniel Bates's executors first "marched an armed force, of forty or fifty persons to town" to intimidate the court and that "during the trial, they had arms and armed men so placed, as to be confident everything and every person was in their power."[78]

Bates's supporters and at least one of Baker's private prosecutors were no less adamant than his defenders about the rightness of their cause. Pointing factually to the breakdown of government in the county but painting less credibly the Bates faction as the "party of law and order," A. J. Caldwell, a prosecutor, advised Governor Owsley that

> In the County of Clay, a lawless spirit prevailed for several years, and the county has no administration of law. Murder after murder was committed during the period of about three years, until the well disposed part of the community saw that a lawless state could be borne no longer; they determined to organize and enforce the laws. They did organize and they have succeeded in the case of Baker so far in properly enforcing them. There seems to be a proper spirit in the county a larger majority in favor of law. Those who are anxious and zealous for the pardon of Baker are the bitter personal enemies of Daniel Bates, and the leaders of the disorganizing party.

Even more slanderous was a letter from a future U.S. Congressman from nearby Barbourville, Green Adams, asserting that the officers who conducted Baker's original court of inquiry that had freed Baker to his brothers' custody "had instigated [Baker] to kill Bates and were determined to protect him regardless of any principles which would activate an honorable man and an orderly citizen."[79]

Both sides claimed that the collapse of government in Clay County had either jeopardized or invalidated the jury's verdict. Abner Baker, Sr., complained to the governor that it was "difficult to estimate the pernicious influence of highly excited, large and wealthy family connections in a place and among a people composing the major part without laws for the last three or four years past." "How," he asked, "could a fair and impartial trial be expected under such circumstances and previous discipline [*sic*]." The sincerity of many letters may be doubted, however, if William Garrard's complaint about the mischievous effects of the Bates and White partisans in bearing arms in the courtroom is to be believed. Thus, one must question the candor of ten prominent members of the Bates/White faction who signed a remonstrance against pardon, stating that since "for a long time the practice of wearing concealed weapons has been carried to an alarming extent and to the terror of many peaceable citizens and that the laws in consequence thereof have been trodden underfoot," they believed Baker to be "a proper subject for punishment."[80]

In addition to writing lengthy and often inflammatory letters to Governor Owsley, both sides sent the governor petitions as they reached deeply into ranks of Clay County society and beyond for signatures, forcing even the common folk of the county, many who signed with marks, to choose sides between elite factions. Ultimately, some 730 persons wrote letters to the governor or signed petitions favoring Baker's pardon; another 360 opposed it.

While petitions were being prepared during the weeks when both sides awaited the governor's decision, rumors began to circulate that Abner Baker, Sr., and the Garrards were raising an armed force, some claimed with cannon, to free Dr. Baker from the Clay County jail. Although local authorities had already assigned 150 men to guard Baker and, it was rumored, planted the jail with dynamite if all else failed to prevent their prisoner's rescue, they demanded more protection from the governor. In early September, Governor Owsley ordered the state adjutant general, Peter Dudley, a brother-in-law of Daniel Garrard, to mobilize state militia from surrounding counties to quell "an insurrection against the law of the Commonwealth [that] is imminently threatened in Clay County." Whether thwarted by the presence of militia or never more than a rumor planted to alienate the governor from Baker's plea, an insurrectionary force did not materialize. Owsley finally decided against pardon at the end of the month and on October 3, 1845, Dr. Abner Baker, Jr., was hanged in Manchester.[81]

Allowed to utter his final words, Baker expressed no remorse at his execution. Instead, he proclaimed himself "the victim of a whore and a whore's friends . . . a man offered up to the gallows by the foulest means to save the wreck of a whore's family." After reiterating his claims that Daugherty White "had made a mistress of his brother's daughter up to the very night before" Baker had married her, and that he had killed Daniel Bates "not because he liked Daniel Bates less, but honor more," Baker turned to the hangman and said, "'Tis all the work of a whore! I am ready, let a whore's work be done."[82]

Baker's well-publicized trial and execution were rebuked by many observers, some even beyond Kentucky. An authority on legal insanity wrote in the *American Journal of Insanity* in 1846 that Baker's conviction and hanging were the result of "judicial ignorance and barbarity." The *Knoxville Register*, a newspaper in the town where two of Baker's brothers practiced medicine, condemned "the unhallowed deed of hurrying a *lunatic* from time to eternity" as "judicial murder." In a recent analysis of the case, the contemporary legal historian Robert Ireland has concurred: "vengeance propelled by wealth and political influence, a flawed criminal justice system made all the more deficient by negligent defense lawyers and an ignorant jury, and an insensitive governor combined to send Abner Baker to the gallows. In many ways," Ireland concludes, "the case [indeed] amounted to judicial murder."[83]

Remarkably, however, despite all the excitement caused by Abner Baker's trial and execution, things began to calm down in Clay County soon afterwards. The horrible economic depression that had wrought so much havoc on the local economy and especially its salt industry was over. The

White/Bates faction was comfortably in control of Manchester, but local antagonisms were soon overshadowed by national events in 1846 when many Clay Countians, T. T. Garrard foremost among them, answered the governor's call to help wage an imperialist war against Mexico. In 1849, the authors of a new state constitution, including Clay County's convention representative James H. Garrard, introduced modest democratic reforms to Kentucky government, including, most importantly, the direct election of county officers. In 1851, Clay Countians elected county officers who, though still richer than average, were closer to the common folk than ever before, including for the first time only one slave owner on the county court. At about the same time, the hanging of another Baker for murder, this time a distant kinsman of Abner Baker, produced interest but no civic unrest. Yet the schisms produced by elite conflicts in the 1840s continued to simmer never far beneath the surface of political life in Clay County until they would explode with greater violence than ever at the end of the nineteenth century.[84]

Discussion and Conclusion

Political factionalism and the violence it fostered in antebellum Clay County did not result from lawlessness, nor the prolongation of frontier individualism as many would later claim, but from elite competition and its ruinous effects on the local state and civil society. The expression of hostilities in Clay County that culminated in the trial and execution of Abner Baker, Jr., was made visible in public documents that allow not only a glimpse into the social origins of elite conflict not generally afforded during the passage of more mundane times, but also early evidence of three contradictions to effective state making in Appalachian Kentucky: *clientelism, corruption,* and a *stunted public sphere.*

Clientelism

Patron-client relationships are defined as "instrumental friendships" in which higher-status persons use resources and influence on behalf of lower-status persons in exchange for the latter's expressions of esteem, personal assistance, or political support.[85] Clientelist politics, common to many less developed nations, did not originate in Clay County in the schism that arose between the supporters and enemies of Abner Baker or Daniel Bates. But clientelism, as Eric Wolf has shown, thrives where personal security and material well-being cannot be guaranteed by law and other impersonal social institutions.[86] The collapse of political authority in Clay County in the 1840s, as later, made it important for ordinary folks to choose, in the words of an Appalachian labor song, "which side they were on" in elite schisms as did the pressure to do so that came from the elites themselves.

Roots of clientelism can be found in many of the earliest social practices of frontier Clay County, from the militaristic reliance on kinfolk and friends in the cattle war of 1806 that prompted the formation of local government, to the priority placed on endorsements by wealthy sureties in the county's paper economy of "writings obligatory." Reliance on the influence and connections of prominent men was routinely reinforced, as, for example, in 1815, when seventeen "private soldiers" appointed former commanders William Phelps and Thomas McGitton, a future Clay County sheriff, to broker payments for their military service in the War of 1812.[87]

When their support was needed, as in the mobilization of sympathies for and against the pardon of Abner Baker, Clay County's most powerful patrons did not hesitate to call on their friends and followers to declare publicly their loyalties. Thus, we find among the signatures garnered on behalf of Baker's pardon by the Garrards, the individual and family names of persons whom Daniel Garrard had vouched for as surety during the depression – Wilsons, Hackers, and Bethel Ely. Against pardon were Benjamin F. White's frequent customers Stephen Gibson, Howard Redman, and Haywood Gilbert; his hired laborer Jackson Bundy, and a future employee Real Gregory (see Chapter 3). The long-lasting nature of some of these loyalties is suggested by the fact that the Garrards's agent in a violent clash between the Garrard and White factions in 1886 was Andrew Hacker, son of Julius Hacker, the Garrard friend whose fray with David Walker had provided the context for the first shooting of Daniel Bates in 1840.[88]

Analysis of petitions shows that to a remarkably similar extent partisans on both sides reached equally far across social strata to include both genders and all socioeconomic levels of civil society except African Americans. Of Clay County residents that we could identify on the 1845 or 1846 tax lists, only 38% of petitioners for pardon and 37% of those who opposed it were landowners, suggesting that an equally broad spectrum of citizens was encouraged by both sides to sign petitions. Thus, whereas a group of self-identified "ladies of Clay County" sent a petition for pardon to the governor, other petitions, pro and con, were signed by individuals whose marks indicate illiteracy.[89]

Both sides had solicited support from beyond Clay County, but the Garrards and Bakers went farthest. Only 22% of their petitions were signed by residents of Clay County compared to 51% of those opposed. Physicians from various parts of the state, including Lexington, Louisville, and Frankfort along with the medical faculty at Transylvania University and the superintendent of the state lunatic asylum, numbered prominently among those from beyond Clay County who recommended pardon.

Here, too, in the relative ability of elite factions to mobilize supporters beyond Clay County, is another instance of what would be a persistent pattern. Being the most socially prominent family with extensive statewide connections, but Democrats in a predominantly Whig/Republican county, the Garrards would fare best in their political competition with the Whites throughout the rest of the century when they ran for offices whose jurisdictions went beyond solidly Republican Clay County and drew on a wider following. Thus, James H. Garrard was elected to represent Clay County in the constitutional convention of 1849 when his district included surrounding Democratic counties and in 1857 when he was elected to the first of five terms as state treasurer.[90]

The petitions yield further insight into the social organization of patronage and elite competition as well. In a letter to the governor, the adjutant general reported that "Parties are represented to me as being about equally divided here, and as I suggested to you in a previous communication that I might find 'neighbor arrayed against neighbor' I find not only that *true* but I find *brother* arrayed against *brother*."[91] Although one can indeed find many family names on opposing petitions – the courageous dissent of Barton Potter's wife from the opinion of her husband, a strong supporter of Daniel Bates, being a prominent example – an equally striking pattern in the petitions is the inclusion of the names from large family groups favoring one side or the other almost exclusively. Significant numbers of Gabbards, Wilsons, Houses, Hollandsworths, Nances, Norths, Morgans, Roarks, and Robertsons, for instance, signed petitions for pardon submitted by the Garrards, but few or none for execution. Most notable were the many Philpots, a majority of whom signed petitions for pardon with marks, who would again side with the Bakers and Garrards a half-century later to play an especially violent role in the latter's renewed war with the Whites. Such patterns of loyalty suggest the social organization of whole families into the grids of clientelism that later observers have so frequently identified as a defining characteristic of Kentucky mountain politics.[92]

Corruption

Political clientelism such as the leadership-centered cliques and factions apparent in antebellum Clay County often "undermine[s] the formal structure of authority" in the weak governments of economically backward societies.[93] In a recent comparative study of differential state capacity among developing nations, Peter Evans has shown that effective governance results from what he calls "embedded autonomy." That is, at the same time that effective states have strong ties to important groups in civil society, they also enjoy autonomy from manipulation by "rent-seeking" groups outside the state.[94] The competition between Garrard and White factions for control of the local state that followed for decades after these families' initial conflict in the 1840s, and their subsequent use of the local state in the postbellum era to advance their own interests and those whom they favored, ensured that Clay County's government was deeply embedded in civil society but far from autonomous from factional manipulation.

Knowledge that control over the local state could be financially beneficial was not news to members of the antebellum political elite, including former sheriffs and career politicians like Abner Baker, Sr., who amassed an economic fortune during his many years as county clerk, nor to the county's saltmakers who depended on the state's coercive powers for disciplining their slaves and compelling ordinary citizens to maintain the roads and waterways on which their commerce depended. But the Baker crisis taught their followers as well new lessons about the revenue-generating potential of county government and the advantage of being on the right side of its controlling faction.

Analysis of court orders assigning guards to Baker while he awaited execution shows that partisans who signed remonstrances against Baker's pardon, including several persons from Beech Creek, were rewarded with lucrative opportunities to prevent Baker's rescue or escape. These records show that 229 persons were paid 75 cents per day for a total of 4,736 days for guarding Baker, amounting to $3,352. More than 100 of these guards were employed twenty-one days or more for a minimum of $15.75; 40 of them worked thirty days or more. Eight men earned more than $50 each, some more than $80, no small sum in the 1840s when cash was scarce in Clay County and land often sold for less than one dollar per acre. Although a few of Baker's supporters, most notably his brothers and four Philpots, were allowed to guard him, most were not. Of those who signed petitions favoring his pardon, only fourteen were given guard duties while seventy-five men who signed petitions against Baker's pardon were given such duties (33% versus 6% of the guard force).[95] Moreover, since payment for guard duties was made by the Commonwealth of Kentucky, the imprisonment of Abner Baker proved to be a significant new source of extralocal income. Thus, the idea of the state as a revenue-generating machine in a poor economy was another lesson from the Baker trial both Clay County patrons and clients would remember long afterwards.

A *Stunted Public Sphere*

If state capacity to solve problems, like economic development, depends on a necessary degree of autonomy from corruption by factions in civil society, democracy, on the other hand, depends on a robust public sphere for its defense. On this dimension of political development, too, Clay County proved lacking.

Jürgen Habermas has argued that democracy is advanced and protected by a public life that institutionalizes rational-critical discourse among autonomous citizens on political matters whereby their decisions are made on the basis of good arguments rather than the effects of status, power, or influence.[96] In publicly debating the sanity of Abner Baker, the quality of his trial, and the justness of his possible execution, Clay County citizens were potentially engaged in the sort of discourse that Habermas advocates as being essential for a healthy democracy.

Many citizens, Mrs. Barton Potter being a good example, undoubtedly thought through the issues for themselves to form a reasoned position on the merits of a pardon. To the extent that such independence and rationality characterized their public discourse, Clay Countians approximated Habermas's ideal of a "public making use of its reason."[97] However, in the context of clientelism such as existed in Clay County, not only good reasons but loyalty, esteem, and expectations of future favors, to say nothing of fear and intimidation, influenced the positions people advocated.

That fear and intimidation were indeed factors influencing support or opposition to Baker's pardon is suggested by several letters to Governor Owsley. William Morris wrote: "I must confess I was afraid to sign the remonstrance for fear of an assault being made on me for so doing as I know I have got some bitter enemies for taking Bateses' part." The fact that considerable pressure was being exerted on some Clay Countians to choose one side or the other is evident from the fact that a number of individuals, including several members of the jury, signed petitions for both sides and others later renounced their endorsements. Thomas Cook, foreman of the jury, wrote that although he was convinced that Baker was of sound mind, he had been induced to sign a petition for pardon, but in writing the governor, he was withdrawing his name from it. Two other jurors, both from Beech Creek, likewise wrote that Baker was "most righteously convicted." However, they explained that since "immediately after said conviction they were induced to sign a petition for the pardon of said Baker under certain representations or conditions which [had] since been violated," they no longer wished to be regarded as favoring his pardon. In light of such letters, Abner Baker, Sr.'s, contention that "fear, favor, and monied influence" had "caused the names of men, women, and children ignorant of the merits of the case to be subscribed to the Remonstrance" should not be interpreted as indicating that only one faction in the dispute resorted to such unprincipled tactics.[98]

As heirs to the U.S. Republican tradition, Kentuckians were the beneficiaries of democratic institutions, compromised as these were by the forms of coercion on which Kentucky's antebellum slaveocracy was premised. But like its capitalist economy, public life in Kentucky developed unevenly across the state. At one extreme were certain Bluegrass communities like Danville, whose "Political Club" in the eighteenth century debated such issues as the merits of each of the clauses of the federal Constitution and of Kentucky's separation from Virginia.[99] Even Lexington, although hierarchical and including many landless citizens, had numerous reading rooms and coffeehouses that nurtured political debate and participation, at least among the white men of its leading classes. Although court days brought many of the common folk of Clay County together monthly, the conditions there, however, were much less favorable for the development of a vigorous public life where even public business was sometimes conducted in the private counting rooms of its hegemonic merchants.

Some Clay County citizens such as Daniel Garrard, whose father had been a participant in the Danville Political Club's debates, took seriously their public leadership roles. As a presidential elector, Garrard had troubled himself in 1840 to publish a twenty-nine-page pamphlet stating some of his reasons for opposing the Whig candidacy of William Henry Harrison.[100] But, traditionally, such political activism in Clay County was the prerogative of wealth and status as well as gender and race. Partisans of the Abner Baker, Jr., trial, however, helped to encourage the expansion of a local sphere in Clay County in 1845 by mobilizing supporters and opponents of Baker's execution.

The extent of this mobilization is remarkable in the absence of local newspapers and public meeting spaces and in the context of a subsistence-farming economy that kept many rural families outside the orbit of commercial affairs.[101] But mobilization was also cooptation. The creation of a public life from the top down ultimately reinforced clientelism instead of a robust democracy in Clay County and political corruption rather than political development.

In the context of clientelism, corruption, and a manipulated public sphere, the state building in antebellum Clay County failed to produce public institutions with the capacity to address local problems effectively. The next two chapters, examining the patriarchal moral economy of Beech Creek and racial dynamics in Clay County, explore the social origins of poverty and economic stagnation in the rural agricultural economy, problems an ineffective state could not confront.

PHOTO ESSAY

There is little visual record of Clay County in the early years of the nineteenth century. We have located no surviving images of the saltworks, early stores, or slavery. For the late nineteenth and early twentieth centuries, the visual record is more extensive, although biased. National magazines and newspapers printed drawings and cartoons that sensationalized violence in Clay County. Although misleading as historical depictions of the county itself, these images usefully indicate how stereotypes of mountain people were constructed in a national discourse.

There is also a collection of photographs of Clay County taken in the early years of the twentieth century by Claude M. Matlock, a lighting manufacturer from Louisville, who became interested in the work of the Oneida Baptist College. Matlock spent several years traveling to Clay County to photograph the area and its people. His photos (the CCM Collection) provide a unique visual image of mountain life in a period of rapid social and economic change. Like the images of feud life, however, Matlock's images of Clay County were circumscribed by his sense of the county and its future. Many photographs depict placid farms, industrious but impoverished families, and flattering images of Oneida Baptist College. African Americans are not found in his photos. Neither are scenes that suggest the conflict and exploitation that lay beneath the surface of Clay County's economic life.

Photo Essay

Farm on South Fork of the Kentucky River in Clay County, ca. 1913. CCM
#311. Courtesy of Photographic Archives, University of Louisville.

A group of men "snake" logs from the forest, ca. 1906. CCM #136. Courtesy of Photographic Archives, University of Louisville.

Logging practices in the late nineteenth century were brutal on loggers and animals alike and left Clay County's land and creek beds scarred. Typically, loggers hitched oxen to drag (or "snake") timber along narrow paths. Logs were then rolled down hillsides into streams and held behind handmade splash dams until ready to float downstream to market.

A watermill and splash dam on Bullskin Creek, ca. 1913. CCM #481. Courtesy of Photographic Archives, University of Louisville.

The "Narrows," a notorious stretch of the South Fork of the Kentucky River that claimed many log rafts and loggers, ca. 1910. CCM #207. Courtesy of Photographic Archives, University of Louisville.

A woman spinner, ca. 1906. CCM #75. Courtesy of Photographic Archives, University of Louisville.

Home manufacturing and the labor of women and children were key to the survival of subsistence agriculture, suggesting that the conventional image of self-sufficient mountain men distorts the vital role of family labor in the rural Appalachian economy. Despite the availability of a wide variety of commodities in local stores, rural mountain families produced many goods at home. Children provided essential, unpaid labor to family farms.

Adult and children boiling molasses while visitor watches, ca. 1913. CCM #361. Courtesy of Photographic Archives, University of Louisville.

Father and children gathering corn from a hillside patch, ca. 1906. CCM #74. Courtesy of Photographic Archives, University of Louisville.

Travel by horseback near mouth of Buffalo Creek, 1906.
CCM #405. Courtesy of Photographic Archives, University
of Louisville.

Covered wagon with merchandise traveling to Oneida,
ca. 1906. CCM #51. Courtesy of Photographic Archives,
University of Louisville.

A federal survey in 1904 revealed that, because of early industrial
development, Clay County's 1,600 miles of roads gave it the
highest ratio of roads per square mile at the time in Kentucky.
However, rugged terrain and the uncertain condition of creekbeds
made travel hazardous and the transportation of merchandise
uncertain well into the twentieth century in parts of the county.

Clay County's elite lived in material luxury, but political conflict within the county prevented the creation of a significant local civic and economic infrastructure. Compare the home of Manchester merchants R. G. and N. C. Potter (ca. 1906) with a view of the Manchester town square, ca. 1910. CCM #37, 229. Courtesy of Photographic Archives, University of Louisville.

Martha Bowling (Coldiron) Hogg was an influential
Clay County entrepreneur. When her first husband,
Calvin Coldiron, died, Martha inherited substantial
property. A prenuptial agreement and a court decree
declaring her a "femme sole" allowed Martha to retain
control of her property after she married Stephen
Hogg in 1895. She was a major financial power in the
county, acquiring extensive real estate holdings and a
considerable fortune, and donating land for the
establishment of Oneida Baptist College. Photo ca.
1906. CCM #10. Courtesy of Photographic Archives,
University of Louisville.

Ameridth Combs speculated in land in Clay County in the nineteenth century at a time when local land trade was still largely mediated by kinship and neighborhood ties. Combs also invested in commerce, becoming a major creditor of the Manchester merchant Robert Potter. Shortly before his death in 1908, he was involved with Martha Hogg and others in an unsuccessful effort to secure a railway line to run through his property in northern Clay County. He is pictured with his wife Ester Allen Combs. Also pictured is Lee Combs, son of Ameridth and Ester, who also was involved in local land ventures. Photos ca. 1906. CCM #71; 8. Courtesy of Photographic Archives, University of Louisville.

Clay County was formed in 1806 when a conflict between cattle farmers pointed to the need for a local court to resolve disputes. Saltmakers and merchants dominated county politics and did not hesitate to use public institutions and public funds for private gain and to solidify their positions in disputes with other elites. A magistrate court meeting in Clay County, ca. 1913. CCM #406. Courtesy of Photographic Archives, University of Louisville.

Clay County's institutions of local governance were tightly controlled by competing elite families. As these families fought each other for economic and political advantage throughout the nineteenth century, their conflicts spilled over into violence, known locally as "wars" and outside the region as "feuds." Such violence undermined local courts and legal systems. Clay County courthouse surrounded by the tents of the state militia, ordered to Manchester to quell civil unrest, and Tom Baker on the courthouse grounds, moments before he was murdered by a hidden sniper, 1899. Both reprinted from John Ed Pearce, *Days of Darkness*. (Lexington: University Press of Kentucky, 1994.)

Although Clay County's feuds were the result of struggles between elite families to control county power during periods of rapid economic and political change, the popular press portrayed such violence as irrational responses to petty conflict. Line drawing from Hartley Davis and Clifford Symth, "The Land of Feuds" in *Muncey's Magazine*, 1903. Courtesy of Special Collections and Archives, University of Kentucky.

Agents of social reform and educational improvement in Appalachian Kentucky worked to keep an image of mountain feuds before the public eye. President Frost of Berea College recounted stories of the Clay County feud to potential northern benefactors and described education as key to destroying the "feud spirit" in the mountains. Cover from *Berea Quarterly* (January 1913). Courtesy of Special Collections and Archives, University of Kentucky.

The Berea Quarterly

Vol. XVI.   BEREA, KENTUCKY, JANUARY, 1913   No. 4

Men Proud of Being "Dangerous"

ONE DOLLAR PER YEAR   THIRTY CENTS PER COPY

As speculators began to eye Clay County as a rich source for resource extraction, many mountaineers took legal measures to protect their coal and mineral rights against exploitation by local and outside entrepreneurs. Coal was never as prominent in Clay County as in other parts of Appalachian Kentucky, but small-scale coal mines were developed in the late nineteenth and early twentieth centuries. Clay Countians displaced from subsistence agriculture provided an exploitable labor force for the new coal industry. Coal mine near Crane Creek, ca. 1910. CCM #162. Courtesy of Photographic Archives, University of Louisville.

Despite the image of rural Appalachia as uniformly isolated and impoverished, Clay County retained a middle class even after the local salt industry collapsed and its agricultural and commercial bases began to erode. Frequent lecture tours of northern cities by J. A. Burns on behalf of Oneida Baptist College drew attention and funding to the area. Dr. C. Adeline McConville of New York established a medical clinic in Oneida in 1909 after hearing Burns speak. Photo ca. 1912. CCM #369. Courtesy of Photographic Archives, University of Louisville.

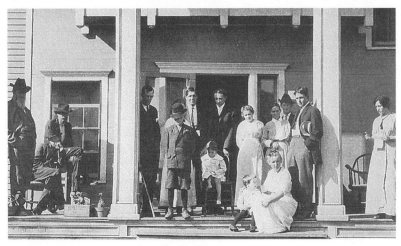

The War on Poverty was launched in Appalachia. Public support for federal antipoverty programs was garnered in part by widely disseminated photographs of impoverished mountain children. Here, children gather in Clay County, near Manchester. Courtesy of *Louisville Courier-Journal* and *Louisville Times*.

James S. Brown (*photo on right*) began an ethnographic and genealogical study of a series of creekbed neighborhoods in Clay County in 1942. His research on the residents of this area and their descendants resulted in the landmark "Beech Creek" studies of family and migration and made this historical study possible. Brown's involvement with the Beech Creek families has lasted more than fifty years and stands as a model of perceptive, sensitive, and ethical ethnographic research. Brown is pictured in front of a general store near Oneida, Kentucky. Photo by Paul Weingartner.

IV
CULTURAL STRATEGIES

5

THE PATRIARCHAL MORAL
ECONOMY OF AGRICULTURE

For over a century, writers and policymakers have attributed the chronic poverty of Appalachia to the supposed backward characteristics of the region and the arrested culture of its population. Their explanations, the antecedents of culture-of-poverty theories, strip away the historical dynamics of regional poverty by attributing modern-day economic problems to supposed timeless qualities of Appalachian culture. Like those writers, we, too, find a connection between modern-day Appalachian poverty and the conditions of an earlier era. However, we trace the roots of poverty to the structural limitations of subsistence agriculture within particular sets of social relations rather than to pathological individual traits or irrational forms of economic production. Cultural factors did play a part in the historical process whereby Clay County lost its economic vitality, but these cultural strategies cannot be understood apart from the larger context of capitalist markets and state coercion. In earlier chapters, we scrutinized how markets and politics shaped the accumulation of wealth by a few Clay Countians who were well-positioned in local commerce and manufacturing. We look now at how cultural strategies also shaped economic accumulation as well as a life of increasing impoverishment for many in the county as a robust system of subsistence agriculture in the antebellum period began a long decline in the postbellum era.

Nonmarket-Based Cultural Strategies

American writers paid little attention to social or economic conditions in the southern mountains until after the Civil War, when, in comparison with national patterns of industrialization and urbanization, "Appalachia," as the region was soon named, began to be perceived as out of step with the more rapid pace of U.S. development.[1] Thus, by the time social scientists systematically began to study rural Appalachian communities, they had inherited a discursive tradition about the region as a place apart, a traditional society in the midst of modern America that was isolated in space and frozen in time, that is, the place "where time stood still."[2] That this depiction was false detracted little from its force or longevity.

Despite being heirs to a discursive tradition that marked Appalachia as stagnant and underdeveloped, twentieth-century ethnographers preserved eyewitness accounts of daily life in the mountains. Although it can be misleading to project ethnographic depictions of Appalachian community life back in time, these observations provide some of the best clues about the cultural strategies that shaped earlier patterns of economic and social life. We thus begin an investigation of Clay County's subsistence agriculture, what we call its "patriarchal moral economy," by examining ethnographic accounts. These ethnographic studies can be misleading if read as some of their authors intended – as anthropological notes on a society oddly fixed at the brink of modernity. Thus, their empirical observations of mountain culture must be rescued from the theoretical webs in which they were caught before they can be put to use. Two conceptual shrouds in particular mask the specificity of social relations that Appalachian ethnographers observed when they assembled invaluable observational data on the everyday practices of near-subsistence agricultural production in the Appalachian mountains. These are *familism* and *traditionalism*.

Familism

The strength of kinship bonds and the lack of extra-kin cooperation in Appalachia were universally noted in early ethnographic studies of the Appalachian mountains. In describing Beech Creek, Brown wrote:

> [T]he family rather than the individual was the unit of Beech Creek.
> . . . Through their daily, intimate contacts the members of a family
> group built up a strong feeling of group solidarity. They thought of
> themselves as a group, and the neighborhood thought of them as
> solidary groups. . . .[3]

In her study of Little Smoky Ridge, an impoverished Tennessee mountain community a decade later, the anthropologist Marion Pearsall noted:

> The family is the center of the individual's universe. To a remarkable
> degree, it is his universe. . . . [The individual] develops a strong sense
> of unity with his family but finds little or no opportunity to learn to
> co-operate with persons outside his family and much of what he learns
> tells him *not* to co-operate with others.[4]

Finally, in Shiloh, a roadside settlement in western North Carolina observed in the 1960s, the sociologist John Stephenson observed that:

> It is often said that families are closer in the mountains than elsewhere, and informants in Shiloh certainly gave verbal testimony to this. . . . There is little inclination to [extra-kin] cooperative group action and very little background training for such cooperation.[5]

Read through the veil of modernization theory, the observed pattern of social cooperation based in kinship and family bonds was denoted as a culture of "familism" – a social network of expectations and actions out of synch with a society in which economic and social life had long since ceased to be kin-defined. In their attempts to document the "familistic" character of mountain life, however, all three ethnographers recorded important details of family behaviors and patterns of interaction including household divisions of labor by age and gender, methods of childrearing, patterns of decision making, networks of solidarity, and lines of antagonism within and between family groups.

Whereas ethnographers observed and preserved the raw behaviors of family life, they failed to conceptualize explicitly the social relations around which these behaviors were organized. Particularly slighted were the social practices of patriarchal authority that privileged adult men at the expense of women and children. As anthropologist Mary Anglin notes, "We are left to conclude that, in antebellum Appalachia, rules about gender were underwritten by traditions of (nuclear) familism and that history was the province of men."[6] Mountain ethnographers aggregated behaviors of family life into the gender-neutral concept of "familism," a cultural ethos that included both kin-based relations of economic and social life and a psychological sense of affectional ties to kin.[7] For Pearsall, family ties were an element of traditional culture that was caused by and reproduced premodern local society.

> [T]he individual interacts almost exclusively with relatives. . . . The situation is ideal for absorbing traditional behavior. The ways and values acquired in this manner happen not to be suited to an industrial civilization but they make for security and self-assurance as long as the individual remains in the traditional setting.[8]

Writing some years later, Stephenson found Shiloh to be less marked by familistic orientations, but still observed:

... certain indications of familism, such as the tendency to stand together, the maintenance of family relationships over time and space, the existence of family work groups (particularly in the traditional occupations), and the prevalent social identification through kinship.[9]

The specificity of family interaction consolidated under the rubric of "familism" in these studies can be unlocked by deconstructing that concept into three sets of social relationships.[10] First, ethnographic accounts of "familism" reveal the process by which decisions were made – how, for example, the patterning of transitions of the life course was the product of patriarchal family strategy rather than individual choice alone.[11] In Beech Creek, according to Brown, family groups were "exceedingly important in controlling the actions of an individual, for hardly any decision was made without all the other members of the group knowing about it, discussing it, and reaching a common decision on it."[12] In a society in which access to land and occupations was almost completely reserved for men,[13] fathers and husbands had the major role in shaping family decisions, although court records of divorce actions initiated by women and judgments awarding women child custody, property, and even restoration of maiden names suggests that patriarchal authority in Clay County was not absolute.[14] Second, "familism" encompasses family behaviors in economic production through patrilineal property transmission and cooperative labor among adult males. In Beech Creek, sons were more likely to remain on the parental land than were daughters. This meant that family groups in the 1940s were formed around the procreative families of brothers and that cooperative farming activities were built through fraternal relationships.[15] Finally, one can discern in ethnographic descriptions the role of family networks in economic exchange and distribution – particularly the role of adult male kin in allocations of surplus and aid during crisis times. Brown's concept of "family groups" in Beech Creek was based in part on this dimension. In Beech Creek, "there were frequent exchanges of food among the families . . . through their daily, intimate contacts the members of a family group built up a strong feeling of group solidarity . . . in crises the family stood together."[16] Modern ethnographic studies of rural Appalachia also point to the continuing importance of kinship units in structuring obligations of economic assistance.[17]

Traditionalism

To the ethnographers who scrutinized Appalachia in the mid-twentieth century, the very goals and values of mountain society seemed to contradict the principles of individualism, achievement motivation, and universalism that were said to underlay an advanced capitalist society. Pearsall, studying Little Smoky Ridge as it was beginning to face capitalist market pressures, stressed the lax work ethic of a populace that she judged to be indifferent to commercial farming ("no one in the neighborhood considers farming a worthy year-round profession for a 'real man'") and where formalized bookkeeping and profitable agricultural marketing were absent ("no long range planning for land use. A man 'takes a notion' to put a particular hillside into corn or beans or something else."). In Little Smoky Ridge, "[w]hatever the actual net income, many potential profits [were] lost under the current system of handling and marketing produce." Economic traditionalism implied satisfaction with what had been "good enough for Grampa." Life was "geared to self-sufficient survival with no special emphasis on the acquisition of material possessions as status symbols and even as laborsaving devices." In the rural locality that Pearsall observed, the increasing availability of consumer goods was beginning to influence the definition of "minimum essentials," but life there was not yet organized around acquisition for the sake of acquisition. Desire for a mail-order guitar, for instance, did not yet "commit a man to working steadily after he [had] acquired the guitar." Even in "Shiloh," a more strongly consumer-oriented community, Stephenson quotes an informant as saying, "I just like a full belly and take one day at a time."[18]

Modernization perspectives aggregated these behaviors into a cultural orientation, the expression of "traditional mountain subculture."[19]

> Contemporary Little Smoky Ridge is the product of such clinging to outmoded ways, and the values supporting the old system work against easy and rapid incorporation into a different way of life. . . . [A]djustment to the more secular outside world is thwarted by the local family system and the cultural world it imparts to its members.[20]

Pearsall's description of Little Smoky Ridge residents as having a traditional "frontier" orientation and experiencing problems of adjustment to the modern world, although negative and reductionistic, nonetheless is built on recoverable observations of limited consumption desires and of an agricultural production system that was at odds with the social logic of the capitalist marketplace, yet one that was rational within the social relations of subsistence production and cooperative exchange.

Pearsall's concept of frontier traditionalism in Appalachia, like its successor in the 1960s, "culture-of-poverty" theory, portrays a society trapped in its own cultural apparatus – barred from the class mobility of industrial capitalism by a cyclical reproduction of antiquated cultural traits. It explains social stasis at the expense of change. Read from another perspective, however, the cultural strategies and social relations embedded within the concept of traditionalism begin to emerge. What Pearsall and Stephenson capture *implicitly* are traces of a social logic distinct from those of advanced capitalist societies but nonetheless shaped by economic rationality. The indifference to practices and desires of an industrial market society that is implicit in Pearsall's report of a "casual" attitude toward work is consistent with a society geared toward self-sufficient production and consumption networks. Similarly, muted hierarchies of worth and achievement seen in the largely ascribed statuses of Beech Creek described by Brown reflect a social stratification system still somewhat shaped by mutual exchange as well as by competitive gain.[21]

If we enlarge discourse to look for relations of power, resistance/accommodation, and class formation/class antagonism, the ethnographic notes become even more revealing. Pearsall hints at opposition to forms of capitalist workplace control, although she depicts this as a cultural deficiency. She decries "the sense of personal independence" and "resentment of being bossed" as "perhaps more important than near-illiteracy and lack of technical skills" in barring Little Smoky Ridge men from outside labor markets. Yet, the clash of noncapitalist and capitalist work life is captured in Pearsall's description of men "easily angered at real and fanciful attacks on their freedom to come and go, work or not, as they please."[22]

Stephenson likewise reports the persistence of egalitarian norms in Shiloh in the cautious and polite manner with which people made suggestions to one another as well as in resistance to workplace authority. One informant "quit his factory position" because his foreman was "pushing and pushing, always after you." Another commented, "I don't tell anybody else what to do, and I don't want anybody else telling me what to do." Although, curiously, Stephenson argued strongly against the analytic applicability of the concept of class to Shiloh, he nevertheless provided a graphic picture of class conflict at the workplace:

> One local story that has been handed down with embellishment over the years tells of a man who helped built the "scenic," a parkway through the mountains nearby. Although his was not a factory job, the story illustrates well one local attitude toward close work supervision. The man's job involved hauling loose dirt and rock away from a construction site and dumping it over a nearby cliff. After dumping each load, he would lean on his wheelbarrow and watch the dirt cascade to the bottom of the cliff. The supervisor, after watching the worker enjoy several episodes of this time wasting spectator sport, walked over to him and said gruffly, "Why don't you get another and watch it chase

the first one down?" To which the worker is said to have replied: "Why don't let's watch the *wheelbarrow* chase it?" At this he pushed the wheelbarrow over the cliff and "went to the house" (walked off the job).[23]

Stephenson uses this story to illustrate the presence of a traditionalist subculture that inhibits adjustment to the "new type of work." However, from another perspective, this daily life incident also documents resistance to the capitalist separation of work and control. As an anecdote, a narrative existing in local folk culture, this story can be read as one that preserves a remembrance of the noncapitalist meanings of work and personhood of an earlier era while it encodes a local tradition of opposition to capitalist workplace hegemony both for those who repeat it and for those who hear it (unless modernization theory has deafened them). Stephenson's story complements social history accounts of the collective expression of resistance that emerged in Appalachian coalfield towns and it preserves a glimpse of a declining way of life not easily captured in traditional sources of sociohistorical data.[24]

Besides diverting attention from actual social relations to values and attitudes, ethnographies also can be misleading if they treat the social relations signifying traditionalism as unique to Appalachia. By many accounts, the entrepreneurial spirit of competitive individualism was not an intrinsic component of early American rural life, or at least not exclusively so. Comparative research done since the completion of these ethnographies draws attention to other American regions, notably early New England and sections of the nonmountain South where Cotton was not King, where trade was secondary to subsistence, where personal gain and achievement were typically subordinated to family security, and where culture, especially kinship norms, operated alongside market signals to integrate economic life.[25]

There are several theoretical shortcomings in much of this work, however. First has been the tendency to oppose so-called "moral economies" and "market economies" as either/ors rather than to investigate differences in the relative importance of normative factors and market-based decisions, as well as the much overlooked role of the state, in shaping variations in economic life across U.S. communities and historical periods.[26] The question is not whether early Appalachia was predominantly a moral economy or a market economy, but rather how economic life there was structured simultaneously by culture, markets, and power.

A second shortcoming follows from the tendency among scholars in the moral economy/market economy debate to focus exclusively on the psychological motivations of producers, that is, their "mentalité," rather than on actual social relations of production, whatever the mix of reciprocity and commerce found among them. That the totality of social relations, rather than the intentions of individual actors, ultimately shapes the forms and trajectories of regional economic development is illustrated by the case of formerly subsistence farmers in the Georgia Upcountry who attempted to maintain their way of life by shifting from general, subsistence farming to cotton cultivation once railroads penetrated their communities in the postbellum era but whose increasing dependence on the market resulted for many in tenancy rather than continued autonomy.[27]

Third, the counterposition of market versus moral economies obscures the extent to which subsistence farm economies were constructed within patriarchal family relations. The image of independent, autonomous entrepreneurs forging a market in which to exchange goods neglects the extent to which adult men were the beneficiaries of nonmarket patriarchal restrictions on the labor force participation of women and children, even in highly market-oriented economies. Moreover, as feminist scholars have shown, the idea of yeoman farmers as the agents of a precapitalist mentalité of cooperation and egalitarianism effectively diverts attention from the patriarchal control that male farmers exercised over their wives, children, and other household members as well as the strategies of resistance exercised by household subordinates.[28]

Finally, just as the focus on individual motivation diverts attention from social relations to psychology, a focus on the mere fact of market involvement or its quantitative expansion also obscures the effects of social relations on economic development. Scholars are beginning to appreciate the far greater extent of commerce in early Appalachia than previously recognized,[29] yet the sheer volume of trade in the region does not determine the social dynamics of Appalachia. The question is not really how much early economic actors *produced* for exchange (which may have been extensive), nor whether they *consumed* certain quantities of manufactured commodities (which the early account books of the Goose Creek salt merchants show they did), but rather to what extent early households were able structurally to *reproduce* themselves independently of these exchanges, that is, independently of capitalism. The degree to which households had access to means of production and subsistence and were able to renew these means of production, including their own labor power, without having to rely solely on buying and selling commodities, determined whether they could live autonomously from capitalism or at least resist being fully dependent on it.[30]

In Chapter 3, we used *slaveholding*, *manufacturing*, and *commerce* to gauge the development of capitalist markets in antebellum Clay County. Now, we look from the opposite direction to examine the extent to which economic actions there also were organized independently of markets. That is, we scrutinize the influence of nonmarket-based cultural strategies, especially kinship reciprocity, on economic life in Clay County and Beech Creek. We begin by examining decision making in the rural neighborhoods of Beech Creek in three areas of economic action where market signals, in a more fully developed capitalist system, would typically govern transactions. These decisions involve how households and families secured *goods*, *labor*, and *credit*. We then explore agricultural production in Clay County and Beech Creek to examine how subsistence production was intertwined with social relations of coercion, patriarchy, and market, as well as those of reciprocity and kinship.

Economic Decision Making

Our use of the term "patriarchal moral economy" to describe Clay County's subsistence agriculture draws on historian E. P. Thompson's brilliant conceptualization of moral economy as "a consistent traditional view of social norms and obligations, of the proper economic functions of several parties within the community" and on economist Nancy Folbre's path-breaking work on patriarchy as a "particular site of social and economic activity . . . a social institution with a division of authority and labor based largely on age and gender [and] . . . a system that reflects gender interests."[31] Patriarchal moral economy thus is defined by the social practices and relations (rather than by the attitudes or psychological orientations) that form the intersection of family and economy in Clay County's subsistence agriculture.

Before turning to a discussion of subsistence agriculture, however, it is important to remember that although the majority of Clay County's nineteenth-century farms were modest, there were a small number of comparatively well-to-do farmers, especially slave owners. Tables 5.1 and 5.2 show that slave owners operated relatively large farm enterprises worth nearly five times the cash value of other owner-operated farms in the county and owned livestock inventories worth twice as much. They grew twice as much corn and slaughtered animals worth three times as much as other farm owners.[32] The scale of these farms is a good reminder that although self-subsistence, as we show in what follows, was a key to the reproductive strategies of many Clay County farm families, agricultural marketing also played an important role in the local economy. Geographical isolation and poor transportation facilities, however, limited the full development of agricultural marketing, especially export. Thus, the Kentucky Commissioner of Agriculture reported in 1879 that "export crops" in Clay County "are small owing to want of transportation, but enough is produced for home consumption, and quite a large surplus could

Table 5.1. *Farm Size and Values in Clay County, 1860*

	Owner/Operators			Tenants			Slave Owners			Beech Creek Farms		
	Mean	No.	%	Mean	No.	%	Mean	No.	%	Mean	No.	%
Improved acres	52	92	100	35	28	97	109	37	100	60	59	100
Unimproved acres	424	92	100	463	11	40	1,041	34	92	679	46	78
Cash value of farm	$935	91	99	—	—	—	$4,419	32	86	$1,437	47	80
Cash value of livestock	$410	91	99	$210	29	100	$880	37	100	$373	59	100
Cash value of machinery	$38	92	100	$19	29	100	$83	36	97	$38	59	100
Cash value of home manufacturing	$28	82	89	$18	16	55	$54	26	70	$26	45	76

Source: Eighth Census of the United States, 1860: Agriculture (manuscripts).

Table 5.2. *Farm Production in Clay County, 1860*

	Owner/Operators			Tenants			Slave Owners			Beech Creek Farms		
	Mean	No.	%	Mean	No.	%	Mean	No.	%	Mean	No.	%
Bushels of corn	406	92	100	420	29	100	831	35	95	450	59	100
Cash value of slaughtered animals	$91	90	98	$62	29	100	$270	36	97	$98	58	98
Number of cows	3.6	92	100	2.9	29	100	7	37	100	3.8	56	95
Number of cattle	6	80	87	3.3	21	72	16	30	81	5.1	48	81
Number of oxen	2.7	55	60	2.3	12	41	5	29	78	3.9	38	64
Number of sheep	15.3	77	84	8.8	11	38	26	25	68	14.1	31	53
Number of hogs	23	83	90	16	27	93	27	35	95	21.2	56	95
Cash value of garden products	$145	7	8	—	—	—	$67	4	11	—	—	—

Source: Eighth Census of the United States, 1860: Agriculture (manuscripts).

be spared each year, if there was a convenient market." The Commissioner's report in 1891 likewise noted that "nearly all of [Clay County's] agricultural products are consumed in the county."[33]

Goods: Home Manufacturing and Land

One important indication of the ability of mountain farmers to reproduce themselves without heavy reliance on store-bought commodities or having to sell their labor, is the remarkably high per-farm values of household manufacturing in Beech Creek and Clay County, compared to the rest of the nation. According to one authority, "as a factor in the economic life and prosperity of the country as a whole," home manufacturing "was practically nil at the end of the sixth decade of the nineteenth century."[34] Northeastern farms manufactured on average only $4 worth of goods at home in 1860, and midwestern farms produced only a little more, valued at $9. In sharp contrast, however, Clay County farm owners produced significantly more homemade goods in 1860, valued at $28. Beech Creek farmers manufactured an average $26 of products that year. Farms benefiting from slave labor in Clay County manufactured still more goods ($54 worth), almost eight times the northern average. Tenant farmers had less labor time to devote to home manufacturing – only 55% made goods at home, perhaps indicating not only greater dependence on merchants or landlords, but also their younger ages and thus lesser family labor resources – but those who could afford the time to do so also produced considerably more goods ($18) than did northern farmers.

From the earliest years of settlement, many rural inhabitants of Clay County, from enslaved laborers to independent farmers, traded with the Goose Creek saltmakers and other country merchants. The livelihood of some – waged employees at the saltworks, especially – was heavily predicated on access to store-bought commodities. But such dependency was not the rule for most subsistence farm owners and tenants in Beech Creek throughout much of the nineteenth century. The federal census stopped gathering information on home manufacturing after 1870 when it was no longer significant nationally but Kentucky's first annual report on agriculture, published in 1878, noted the continued significance of home manufacturing in Clay County.

> The sensible, industrious women of Clay are the true source of its manu-
> facturing energies. They still ply the shuttle, hold the distaff, and chant
> to the chorus of the spinning wheel. Flax, wool, and cotton are grown
> for home consumption, and large quantities of home-made jeans,
> linseys, linens, and cottonade, &c., are manufactured by the old process
> of hand labor. Besides this, there are produced, for home consumption

and traffic, large quantities of butter, eggs, chickens, ducks, geese, turkeys, guineas, feathers, beeswax, honey, ginseng, maple sugar, molasses,
shuck and bark collars, leather, home-made shoes, &c.,&c.[35]

This description highlights the often overlooked role of women producers of
home manufactured goods and importantly suggests the overlap between economic strategies of production for the home and petty commodity production in subsistence economies where homewares occasionally would be
brought into the "traffic" of the market.[36]

By the time that Brown interviewed Beech Creekers in 1942, home manufacturing had largely disappeared. Noting the increasing commodification
that had taken place there around the turn of the century, Brown wrote that
"when lumbering came to the area and made more money available, [Beech
Creekers] gave up such domestic crafts as weaving and shoemaking and
bought clothing and shoes. Eventually they spent large portions of cash
income for flour, sugar, lard, and meat, which they had formerly produced."

Significantly, some of the oldest people in Beech Creek in 1942 could still
recall how important home manufacturing had once been to their way of life.
Brown writes:

Farm life at the time of the Civil War [was] still well remembered by
one old man still living on Beech Creek, Preston [Johnson]. His father
. . . owned most of the creek, and the [Elisha Johnsons] were considered "good livers." They lived in a log house with three or four rooms
and a "lean-to" kitchen. Most of their furniture and kitchen utensils
were homemade. . . . Wheat and corn, grown exclusively for use at
home, were ground in the early days at a mill down-river. . . . Beef
cattle and sheep were slaughtered for home use. . . . They bought salt
from wells not too far away and produced their own sugar from groves
of maple trees ("sugar orchards," they were called). Wild honey was not
uncommon, and most families had beegums on the hill behind the
house. Sorghum molasses were made in the fall. Sheep were numerous;
their wool was spun into thread and woven into cloth for winter clothes.
Some people raised cotton, but flax seems to have been commoner, and
women took pride in the linen they wove. (The oldest woman on the
creek remembered the whole process of linen-making and recalled with
nostalgia how stiff and hard new linen was and how soft and white it
became with long, hard use.) [Elisha Johnson] tanned hides and made
shoes for his family (and his youngest son, Preston, remembered the last
shoes he had made, probably in the 1880s). About the only things the
[Johnsons] had to buy were needles and coffee.[37]

That the replacement of this pattern of self-sufficiency by commodification was a slow process, and one that proceeded in stages, is indicated by one informant from Beech Creek, born around 1910, who told us in an interview that even when her comparatively well-do-to family (the Andrews) no longer practiced the art of spinning during her childhood, she could remember their shearing the wool from their sheep and shipping it annually to mills in Knoxville, Tennessee, in exchange for a portion given back as woven cloth from which they made clothes at home.

Since there was a thriving market in the real estate of Appalachian Kentucky well before settlement, mountain people's self-sufficiency was predicated on the most highly commodified of goods, land. On the surface, this dependency might appear to undermine the conditions for a "moral economy" yet even this most thoroughly capitalist institution, private property, was not free of the normative hand of culture nor ruled imperiously by an invisible hand of the market. For many in Clay County, at least in part, kinship mediated access to land and thus exerted a profound influence on social reproduction. Coersion, too, played an important role, especially for African Americans whose ACCESS TO LAND, as we discuss in the following chapter, was severely limited.

Writing about the early Shenandoah Valley in colonial Virginia, Robert Mitchell claims that "[i]n their acquisition of land for settlement," the early immigrants "viewed land less in terms of a carefully nurtured garden to be transmitted intact to the next generation than as a commodity to be bought, sold and leased in the open market."[38] Certainly, the Whites, Garrards and other Clay County entrepreneurs shared this view of land as a speculative commodity and its possession (along with slaves) as their road to wealth and political power as suggested by the thousands of transactions to buy and sell land, mostly with nonkinfolk, that they recorded in Clay County deed books. But theirs was not the only strategy toward the land in Clay County where meanings and practices of land acquisition and transmission varied among population groups.[39]

In order to probe the relationships among land, family, community, and economic development in Beech Creek, we examined all the land actions recorded in county deed books for members of the Andrews family from initial settlement of Beech Creek until 1900 and for those of the Johnson family through 1910, a total of just over 250 deeds for both families.[40] This research confirms Brown's observation that the members of the Andrews family had always been more prosperous and more market-involved than the Johnsons. Despite being comparably sized, the Andrews were involved in 50% more transactions than the Johnsons (roughly 150 out of 250). Though poor like everyone else in Beech Creek by the 1940s, the Andrews still ranked at the top of the local stratification hierarchy of wealth and prestige when Brown lived among them. From the earliest days of settlement, their lands on the South Fork of the Kentucky River in the Laurel neighborhood of Beech Creek had been more valuable than the steep slopes occupied by the Johnsons in the Beech Creek basin. Their first occupant of the area, Adoniram Andrews, initially patented 400 acres along the river where he built a saw mill at the beginning of the nineteenth century. He and his earliest descendants actively sought to increase their landholdings. Twenty out of the 32 transactions they engaged in before 1850 involved purchases of land from nonkin, mostly neighbors. By 1850, Adoniram Andrews III was the wealthiest person in the Beech Creek community, owning fifteen tracts of land worth between $5,000 and $6,000.

In the 1850s and especially during the 1860s, members of the Andrews family began to sell more tracts of land than they purchased, several of these going to members of the Johnson family with whom they were increasingly interrelated through marriage, but they also continued to purchase lands. The Johnsons initially owned much less land than the Andrews but they, too, added to their holdings by buying land from neighbors, and especially in-laws, whenever they could. Of their twenty-four transactions before 1870, ten were purchases from nonkin neighbors but only three were sales to nonkin. Land transactions intensified for both families during the 1880s and 1890s when the third and fourth generations of Beech Creekers inherited lands and subdivided parents's estates. The majority of the Andrews's transactions during these years, however, were restricted to their circle of kin, as members of the Andrews family gave, sold, and traded tracts or agreed to conditional boundary lines among themselves. Significantly, however, the Johnsons sold more land during the same years to nonkin than to other family members. As Brown's ethnographic work shows, this departure from normative expectations among kin had a profound impact on community solidarity within the Beech Creek basin where the Johnsons were concentrated.

Prior to 1900, land purchases and sales in the Beech Creek neighborhoods had been confined to a very large degree to kinfolk and nearby neighbors. Land prices in the 1880s were very similar to the 1850s, reflecting the relative lack of commercialization in the area. But for a number of reasons in the 1890s, including economic expansion but also bad feelings among some of Elisha Johnson's adult children, two of the Johnsons decided to leave Beech Creek and sell portions of their holdings to outsiders. Before that, from 1810 to 1880, population increase in the Beech Creek basin had been due, in Brown's words, "to the natural increase of children and grandchildren of Samuel and Daniel Johnson."[41] But John Johnson's decision to sell the tracts of land he inherited from his father Elisha opened up the neighborhood to outsiders from other Clay County communities for the first time in its history. By 1920, about half of the population in the basin area were not closely related to the Johnsons.

Among the newcomers to move onto the creek were the Barnetts and the Carters. The latter, especially, were considered "low down" by the older families and never well accepted in the community. In only a short amount of time, according to Brown's oral history of the neighborhood, the Carters and the Barnetts became bitter enemies, at times embroiling the Johnsons and even the Andrews in their conflicts and occasionally taking legal action against one another as well as engaging in barn burnings and ambushes. The local school and the church, the only nonkinship-based organizations in the basin, soon collapsed as did cooperative efforts such as the local roadworking system. According to Brown, the result by 1942 was that the "the Beech Creek [basin] neighborhood" – in sharp contrast to the Andrews's Laurel neighborhood where 47% of people were first cousins or closer and where mutual cooperation and visiting were prominent features of everyday social life – was no longer

> a strongly integrated group in which people felt great loyalty to the neighborhood itself, were individually immersed in it, and had a strong cooperative tie with everybody in the group. There was little neighborhood pride, little cooperation in common tasks for the good of the group, and considerable conflict and bitterness among the people.

Thus, we see that the people of Beech Creek were intensely concerned about the "sufficiency" of their landholdings. The self-sufficiency they achieved in agriculture did not result in the disregard for land as a commodity. In fact, as we show in what follows, the voracious spatial requirements of their farming practices and the demands posed by their large families challenged them to seek actively to expand landholdings. Even so, kinship expectations and neighborhood considerations mediated the purchase and sale of land in Beech Creek throughout much of the nineteenth century. Significantly, when some parcels of land there were marketed openly to outsiders in the 1890s beyond the immediate network of neighbors and kin, this action in part grew out of hard feelings among family members and resulted in a noticeable decline in the quality of community life. That conflicts resulted from opening up land in the Beech Creek basin to outside buyers affirms both the presence of a market in land there and the cultural forces that constrained and gave moral meaning to it.[42]

The social practices associated with land ownership and transfer were based in cultural strategies that were patriarchal as well as "moral," although patriarchal control of land was not monolithic. Certainly, few women (outside of an elite group, discussed in a later chapter) owned land in their own right. Although we have no direct evidence from nineteenth-century Clay County, studies from other rural areas suggest that the women who controlled land in their own name were more likely to have power and influence in the community.[43]

At least some women, however, were able to secure land as widows through dower rights. Nancy McCollum was left nearly destitute when her husband died in 1888. Although his estate included land on Crane Creek worth $800, he also left $143 in debts to G. W. and A. W. Baker and John Coldiron. The Bakers and Coldirons forced sale of the land to satisfy debts of the estate and the Bakers then purchased the land for $246, less than one-third its value; a mere one acre was reserved for Nancy and her children. Remarkably, within four years Nancy was able to parlay her meager parcel into sufficient capital to buy back some of the original land from the Bakers and to establish herself as an independent landowner.[44]

As legal strictures against married women owning property began to lift in the late nineteenth century, some Clay County women used their newly won access to the courtroom to defend their land and property, even against the encroachment of family members. One woman fought bitterly – and successfully – against her husband and son to preserve her rights to land she had inherited from her father. Another sued her attorney for illegally bonding a sheriff's sale of her mule.[45] Even in divorce, women sometimes made successful claims on the property of their husbands. One woman who sued for divorce on the grounds of cruelty and abandonment, swearing that her husband had "driven her away" and left her with no means of support, was allotted one-half of her husband's property, including land. Another, declaring that her husband has left her in "desolate condition" was awarded $1,000 as a divorce settlement.[46]

Labor

In a previous chapter, we noted the importance of slaveholding, a common form of commodifying labor by force in capitalist economic peripheries and thus a gauge of both market involvement and coercion among merchants, saltmakers, and some large farmers in Clay County. Wealthy individuals such as these also made use of waged labor and considerable but unknown amounts of farm tenancy, suggesting that social class differentiation was already well advanced in Appalachian Kentucky prior to the modern era. Scholars have begun to recognize the extent of coercive and exploitative labor patterns in early Appalachia. Especially in the zone of the Goose Creek saltmakers, kinship obligations combined with class and racially based coercion to supply labor needs by a combination of obligation, exchange, and force.[47]

Although attention to force and coercion is an important corrective to romanticized images of the region's past as a Jeffersonian Eden, it is important not to err in the opposite direction by picturing Appalachia in totalistic terms as one recent scholar has done who claims that nearly two-thirds of Appalachia's agricultural households in 1860 were "semi-proletarianized."[48] Such a misleading conclusion results from aggregating the considerable number of Appalachian tenant farmers, farm laborers, and slaves at a single moment in time while ignoring the fact that, except for slaves, the statuses of tenant and farm worker were often functions of life course and position within the family as well as social class. The labor procurement process in Beech Creek shows how this was so.

Slaveholding was almost non-existent in Beech Creek where family labor predominated. Tenants and farm laborers provided important labor resources in Beech Creek, but family relationships, more than social class inequality, guided economic action. We shall have much more to say about the interaction of social class and kinship, and also race, later, but one way to show how family relationships mediated labor procurement in Beech Creek and Clay County is to examine the relationship between farming households and the farm laborers they employed. Together, farmers and farm laborers made up 85% of the employed population in Clay County in 1860, but the distinction between the two had more to do with household status than social class. Whereas 94% of persons classified in the federal census as farmers were household heads, only 15% of farm laborers headed their own households. Farmers' average age in 1860 was 39 years, but farm laborers on average were only 23 years old; 60% of them in 1860 were still attending school. Both of these demographic facts suggest that farm laborers' status was more the expression of a transitory stage in the life cycle than a permanent station in the class structure.[49] Data from Beech Creek, which permit us to evaluate the kinship relationships of both laborers and employers, confirm that impression.

In Beech Creek, the proportion of farm laborers among the adult employed population reached a peak of 60% in 1900 before declining to 47% the next decade yet only 4 out of 141 farm laborers in 1900 headed their own households. Sons and daughters in agricultural households made up fully 76% of the total number of laborers. Table 5.3 reports the relationship of the remaining farm laborers to heads of households in 1900, the census year when, as we discuss later, households in Beech Creek were most widely extended horizontally and vertically to bring in siblings, grandchildren, nephews, and parents-in-laws as farm laborers. Indeed, a total of only five farm laborers

Table 5.3. *Farm Laborers' Relationships to Beech Creek Heads of Households (Excluding Sons and Daughters), 1990*

Relationship	Number
Same	4
Wife	—
Mother	1
Father	—
Sister	1
Brother	1
Mother-in-law	1
Father-in-law	2
Brother-in-law	4
Uncle	1
Nephew	3
Son-in-law	2
Granddaughter	3
Grandson	5
Stepson	1
Different last name	0
Servants	5

living in other's households were unrelated to the head of the household in 1900, a pattern that reveals the extent to which social relations of agricultural production in Beech Creek remained grounded in kinship rather than purely market-mediated processes.

The powerful influence of kinship ties, however, does not mean that labor procurement in Beech Creek was egalitarian. Indeed, Beech Creek's labor system was shaped by authoritative patriarchal family norms as well as by social class, expressed as land ownership. During most of the nineteenth century, the majority of women were effectively excluded from remunerative labor in agriculture, whereas young men's place in the economy was dictated by the life span and inheritance decisions of their fathers. In such a system, the growth of a wage labor market in mining and timbering at the turn of the century – drawing members away from the family farm – would ultimately prove to be more disruptive to social relations in Beech Creek than would the participation of households in commodity markets.[50]

Credit

Along with commodities and labor, the third market relationship that is central to the operation of a capitalist economy involves credit.[51] In the absence of complete records from creditors, the best indirect indicator of the volume of credit relationships (and commercial involvement more generally) is court usage. In the previous chapter, we showed that slaveholders, salt-makers, and other entrepreneurs and merchants relied heavily on local courts to enforce their transactions, especially since promissory notes were commonly used in the absence of specie and reliable paper money. This reliance on courts allows us to use the record of involvement in local court actions as a proxy measure for commercial and especially credit transactions. In order to compare economically marginal subsistence farmers with elite, market-embedded, commercial farmers and entrepreneurs, we compared all court actions from 1807 to 1900 that involved members of the Johnson family in Beech Creek with those of commercially engaged litigants from the wider county, the Whites and the Garrards.

Members of the large Johnson family were involved in far less litigation than were members of either the White or Garrard families; collectively, they were involved in only thirty-seven court actions over nearly a hundred years. By comparison, the Whites were involved in 176 cases and the Garrards in 234 cases in just the decade of the 1890s. Although a Johnson was involved in Clay County court proceedings as early as the second year of the court's founding (1808), the majority of cases involving Johnsons occurred after 1860 (84%), most of these during the 1890s (62%).

Significantly, most of the Johnson's social and economic transactions – and disputes – took place within the context of close relationships among kin and neighbors. In nearly one-third of the actions they were involved in – these primarily having to do with estate settlements, divorces, and land disputes – both the plaintiff(s) and the defendant(s) were Johnsons. In contrast, in less than 20% of cases involving Whites (or any of their allies in our dispute sample[52]) in the 1890s, Whites were both plaintiff and defendant; the comparable figure for the Garrards and their allies was 17%. Additionally, because of their commercially marginal economic status, the Johnsons tended to be defendants (65%) much more often than they were plaintiffs (35%). For the more commercially active Whites and Garrards, however, the plaintiff/defendant ratios were more nearly equal; Whites were plaintiffs in 94 cases, defendant in 84; Garrards were plaintiffs in 112 cases, defendants in 122.

As Table 5.4 indicates, there were differences also in the types of cases in which the Johnsons were involved, compared with those of litigants who were more deeply involved in the marketplace. Overall, 71% of the Johnsons's

Table 5.4. *Case Docket Comparison: Johnson Family, Feudists, and Total Clay County*

| | Johnsons[a] | | Feudists[b] | | Total for Clay County | | | | | | | | | | | |
| | | | | | 1810 | | 1820 | | 1840 | | 1860 | | 1880 | | 1900 | |
	No.	%	No.	%	No.	%	No.	%	No.	%	No.	%	No.	%	No.	%
Promissory notes	9	24	165	49	39	46	10	28	46	59	20	38	11	20	27	31
Money dispute	8	22	78	23	21	24	15	41	9	12	7	13	9	17	22	26
Estate settlements[c]	5	14	16	5	0	0	0	0	0	0	0	0	0	0	0	0
Land dispute	4	11	30	9	3	4	3	8	2	3	9	17	14	25	10	11
Assaults	3	8	2	1	6	7	4	11	6	8	2	4	0	0	1	1
Other tort cases	5	14	34	10	16	19	3	9	10	13	9	17	5	9	11	12
Divorce	3	8	11	3	0	0	1	3	5	6	6	11	16	29	17	19
Total	37	100	336	100	85	100	36	100	78	100	53	100	55	100	88	100

[a] Cumulative, 1807–1900.
[b] Cumulative, 1890–9.
[c] In the survey of decennial dockets, we do not distinguish estate conflicts from other financial and property disputes as we did in examining cases involving Johnson family members and feudists.

court cases involved contract disputes, such as failure to pay promissory notes or other financial disputes, a proportion virtually identical to that of the county as a whole. Most of these occurred in the 1890s as the pace of commercial activity quickened in Clay County and the Johnsons were increasingly involved in economic disputes, especially around logging, and when several generations of large families disputed inheritance and farm subdivision. Among the commercial litigants in the 1890s, in contrast, a full 86% of cases involved contract disputes.

Tort actions, involving assaults, constituted 22% of the Johnsons's total docket; divorces constituted another 8%. Thus, in contrast to the finding from contemporary communities in which tort actions are relatively rare,[53] it was not uncommon for the Johnsons to go to or be brought to court for various injuries. The fact that they were not adverse to seeking legal remedies to redress personal wrongs as some stereotypes of Appalachian people might suggest, implies that their low level of court involvement indeed can be taken to indicate a low level of commercial activity, not simply a reluctance to use courts altogether. The Whites and Garrards, by comparison, were involved in a lower rate of tort actions (only 11% of cases), but used the courts much more frequently than the Johnsons to resolve contract and other credit disputes.

Thus, Clay County's economic life was organized in part by social relations that operated outside of the market forces that governed economic transactions in other, more commercially embedded regions. But as an examination of Clay County's agriculture at mid-century demonstrates, such nonmarket-based social relations, what we call a "patriarchal moral economy," initially did not hamper the economic productivity of mountain agriculture.

Clay County Agriculture in 1860

Understanding the long-term trajectory of rural Appalachian development and the institutional sources of economic decline requires a close look at how the vast majority of people in the region made a living before the modern era. Yet, like so many other aspects of the region's preindustrial social life, farming in Appalachia has received but scant attention until very recently. Early, casual observers from Frederick Law Olmstead to Horace Kephart undoubtedly exaggerated the "rude and destructive" character of mountain farming.[54] Such stereotypes have been carried over into cultural interpretations that link Appalachian poverty to the presumed backwardness of mountain culture (and agriculture), often without systematic evidence.[55] Subsequent scholars, advancing the model of Appalachia as an internal colony, attributed the decline of the Appalachian farming economy to the intrusion of absentee land and mineral ownership and to the corporate domination of the region by multinational energy businesses. Thus, Eller claimed that "the small, marginal farm usually associated with the stereotyped picture of Appalachia was in fact a product of modernization" and the Appalachian Land Ownership Task Force asserted that "with th[e] intrusion [of coal and timber interests] began the decline of mountain agriculture."[56] Yet these scholars, too, failed to devote sufficient attention to the history, internal dynamics, and developmental consequences of Appalachian farming.

New studies, however, are beginning to focus more directly on Appalachian agriculture and its impact on the economic and social development of the region. Following up on the earlier work of L. C. Gray, Forrest McDonald and Grady McWhiney have shown the importance and economic viability of animal husbandry throughout the nineteenth-century South including open-range herding in the upland, backcountry, and mountain regions.[57] Horticultural practices in the southern mountains, too, have begun to be reappraised, appearing in a far more favorable light than as stereotyped in traditional accounts. Thus, John Otto and his coauthors have shown that the "slash-and-burn" technique of "forest farming," commonly practiced throughout the Appalachian and Ozark highlands in the nineteenth and early twentieth centuries, was a viable and effective form of agriculture within certain ecological and demographic limits.[58]

On the other hand, studies of preindustrial life in the more isolated sections of eastern Kentucky and West Virginia, such as Altina Waller's analysis of the Tug River Valley, describe farming there as having been largely subsistence-oriented prior to 1900, a finding supported by an early USDA study that reported that 58.4% of all farms in the Allegheny-Cumberland plateaus were still non-commercial in 1935.[59]

Tables 5.1 and 5.2 (above) report farm sizes and values, corn production, and livestock inventories for Clay County in 1860 (along with comparable values for Beech Creek farms) for three categories of farm operators: owners, tenants, and slaveholders.[60] (The Beech Creek community included almost no slaveowners.) The designation of slaveowners is straightforward in the census manuscripts but the determination of owners and tenants, and their relationship to a third category (farm laborers) is problematic as are the social dynamics of tenancy in the mountains. At best, tenancy levels are estimates.[61]

Using techniques suggested by agricultural historians Frederick Bode and Donald Ginter,[62] we estimate that no less than 22% and perhaps as many as 41% of the 230 farmers who headed their own households in our Clay County sample were tenants in 1860. Higher estimates, according to Bode and Ginter, are less certain yet more likely to be correct. Our higher estimate includes 44 "farmers without farms" as well as the 22 "farm laborers" in our

Table 5.5. *Average Sample Farm Characteristics for Northern U.S. Farms with Three or More Improved Acres, 1860*

State/Region	Farm Value ($)	Value of Implements ($)	Improved Acreage	Unimproved Acreage	Horses	Oxen	Milk Cows	Cattle	Sheep
		Farm Statistics					Livestock Inventories		
Eastern region	3,581	125	79	39	2.4	0.8	4.9	4.2	15.8
Western region	2,367	90	65	72	3.1	0.8	3.0	4.9	9.2
North	2,819	103	70	59	2.9	0.8	3.7	4.6	11.6

Note: Eastern region = Connecticut, New Hampshire, New Jersey, New York, Pennsylvania, Vermont; Western region = Illinois, Indiana, Iowa, Kansas, Michigan, Minnesota, Ohio, Wisconsin.
Source: Atack and Bateman, *To Their Own Soil*, 111-12.

sample who headed their own households in 1860. (Most farm laborers, however, were not tenants but rather members of farm households related by kinship to the household head; 80% of these were sons of the household head.) Since the analysis that follows, however, is necessarily restricted to farm families and individuals listed in the census of agriculture, we compare the farms operated by owners (75%) with tenant farms defined as those operated by individuals with no property and/or missing values for improved acres and cash value of farms (25%).

Contrary to stereotypes about Appalachian farms, Table 5.1 shows that most farms in Clay County, even those operated by tenants, were extremely large in comparison with other regions. Owner-operated farms in 1860 averaged 476 total acres in the county at a time when farms in the northern United States, including the Midwest, averaged only 129 acres (Table 5.5). Farms operated by slave owners were even larger, averaging 1,150 acres – almost ten times the size of average northern farms (though small in comparison with large southern slaveholding operations). But because land in the mountains of Kentucky was comparatively cheap, the cash value of Clay County farms in 1860 was low. Owner-operated farms averaged only about one-fourth of the value of northeastern farms and even the large farms owned by slaveholders – these, presumably, occupying some of the best bottomlands in the county – were less than 25% more valuable than average farms in the Northeast one-tenth their size. In fact, the largest farms in Kentucky were those of the Kentucky mountains. Farm sizes *increased* and the value of farms *decreased* as one traveled east from the Blue Grass region across the rugged Cumberland Mountains, reflecting both the patterns of large landholdings and low level of commercialization in Appalachia.[63]

	Livestock Inventories		Output of Principal Crops and Products (rounded to whole numbers)							
		Value of								
	Value of	Livestock					Irish			Home
	Livestock	Slaughtered	Wheat	Corn	Oats	Wool	Potatoes	Butter	Cheese	Manufactures
Hogs	($)	($)	(bu.)	(bu.)	(bu.)	(lbs.)	(bu.)	(lbs.)	(lbs.)	($)
4.7	493	88	38	139	169	57	82	421	221	4
15.7	420	77	105	520	58	26	37	166	22	9
11.6	447	80	80	378	99	37	54	261	96	7

Consistent with the model of slash-and-burn forest farming described by Otto, Clay County farmers, including slave owners, improved only small portions – roughly 10% – of their farmlands, allowing "old ground" to return to forest or to be used for pasture and leaving much of their total acreage unimproved. On the 121 owner-operated and tenant farms in our sample, improved lands averaged only forty-eight acres, ranging from only three acres (the minimum for inclusion in the census) to one large farm operation with 300 improved acres. Almost half of all farmers in Clay County (48%) cultivated thirty acres or less in 1860, despite owning large amounts of unimproved hillside forest land, whereas the largest farms – the top 10% – cultivated 100 or more acres. Owner-operated farms cultivated, on average, only fifty-two acres – an area roughly three-fourths that of farms in the North.

Because enumerators did not report the cash values and unimproved acreages of tenant farms, it is impossible to know exactly what resources tenants had at their disposal, but their farms, too, were large. The ones with known values averaged 498 acres. Nonetheless, tenants cultivated even smaller acreages than farm owners, averaging plots of only thirty-five acres. This size difference, in part, probably reflected life-cycle differences between tenants and owners. Some tenants rented farm lands in addition to pursuing other occupations – our sample included a cooper, a blacksmith, a coal digger, a constable, a gunsmith, and a saltmaker – but most were young farmers. Tenants, averaging thirty-three years old, were an average of six years younger than farm owners and they were more likely to head simple (nuclear) families. Forty-one percent of the farm owners in our sample headed extended and multiple family units or had others living in their households but only 27.5% of the tenant farmers headed such households. Consequently, tenant farmers commanded less labor resources from family members and others in their households than did owners to clear lands and cultivate crops while their younger ages permitted them less time to have accumulated other farm resources such as livestock and machinery.

Other than the fact that Beech Creek farms were small in 1942 – necessitating at least periodic off-farm employment to supplement income – it is unlikely that farm activities in 1860 differed greatly from the daily and seasonal work rhythms and the age and sex division of labor that Brown described so well for the Beech Creek farms he observed in 1942. Farmers in Clay County, as well as in Beech Creek, pursued forms of general (or diversified) subsistence-oriented farming in 1860 that stressed meeting the needs of their households first before bartering or selling whatever surplus in crops and animal products were left over.

Comparison of Clay County farm production (Table 5.2) with data from northern farms the same year (Table 5.5) reveals the surprising finding that these Appalachian farms – including farms in the Beech Creek neighborhoods – were on average at least as productive as their northern counterparts and even surpassed them in important farm products such as corn.[64] Clay County farm owners, on average, produced 340% more corn on their farms than did farmers in the Northeast and only 22% less than Midwest farmers, the nation's leading grain producers. Their livestock inventories included roughly the same number of cows, cattle, and sheep, but considerably more hogs and more oxen (important for the heavy work of clearing and hauling in a rugged environment) as northern farms. Owner-operated farms in Clay County and all farms in Beech Creek averaged higher returns (in cash or kind) for slaughtered animals than did farms in either the Northeast or the Midwest. Although corn was by far the most important field crop in Appalachia, the comparison of Beech Creek farm values for 1860 (Table 5.6) with northern farms suggests that farmers' production of other crops in Clay County was also reasonably competitive with other regions. Beech Creek farmers produced more wheat than northeastern farmers and more wool than midwestern farmers. They produced considerably less oats than both subregions of the North, but the Appalachian practice of allowing livestock, especially hogs and cattle, unrestricted range to feed on forest masts is likely to have compensated for this deficiency.

Although these data do not take into account, as we do in later in this chapter, the size of farm families that had to be supported in the region, they nonetheless suggest the viability of agriculture in this section of the Kentucky mountains at the midpoint of the nineteenth century. Even to other Kentuckians at the time, however, the productivity of mountain farms was largely overlooked, probably because these were subsistence rather than

Table 5.6. *Beech Creek Farm Values, 1850–80*

	1850			1860			1870			1880		
	Mean	No.	%	Mean	No.	%	Mean	No.	%	Mean	No.	%
Improved acres	41	41	79	60	59	100	39	106	80	24.9[a]	60	71
										14.6[b]	48	56
Unimproved acres	287	30	58	679	46	78	221	110	83	168[c]	57	67
Cash value of farm	$527	41	79	$1,437	47	80	$782	111	84	$582[d]	61	72
	($596)						($524)			($442)		
										$474[e]	85	100
										($360)		
Cash value of home manufacturing	$26	45	87	$26	45	76	$31	115	87	—	—	
	($29)						($21)					
Cash value of machinery	$17	49	94	$39	59	100	$23	130	98	$23	81	95
	($19)						($15)			($17)		

Note: Dollar values in parentheses are standardized to 1860 dollar values.
[a] Acres in tillage.
[b] Acres in pasture.
[c] Acres in woodland.
[d] Owners only.
[e] All farmers.
Sources: U.S. Censuses of Agriculture, 1850, 1860, 1870, 1880.

commodity producing units. Thus, in 1854, when the Kentucky Agricultural Society was organized for the improvement of farming in the commonwealth, the mountains of Eastern Kentucky were excluded from its three farm districts and, later in the century, the University of Kentucky Agricultural Experiment Station largely ignored the problems of mountain farmers by devoting exclusive aid and research to commercial farm interests in the central and western sections of the state.[65] Geographical isolation, statewide ignorance about mountain farming, and the prevalence of subsistence practices, rather than economic insufficiency, stimulated erroneous impressions about eastern Kentucky farming during the middle of the nineteenth century that would contribute to twentieth-century stereotypes about Appalachia.

Postbellum Trends in Agriculture

If the picture of Clay County and Beech Creek farming in 1860 was one of relatively high agricultural production in comparison with farm operations in the northern United States, the story of farming there over the next two decades is one of dramatic and rapid agricultural decline. Whereas farms in the North – especially but not only in the Midwest – increased the value, productivity, and efficiency of their operations through improvements in transportation, mechanization, specialization, and the use of chemical fertilizers, our longitudinal data on agriculture in Beech Creek indicate that farms there decreased dramatically in size and productivity throughout the remainder of the nineteenth century.

Beech Creek witnessed dramatic declines in the size and value of farms, livestock inventories, and crop production from 1860 to 1880. By almost all measures, 1860 was a peak year of agricultural abundance. Between 1850 and 1860, the average farm in Beech Creek had more than doubled in size from a total of 328 improved and unimproved acres to 739 total acres in 1860. The value of farms increased by 240% from $596 in 1850 (as expressed in 1860 dollars) to $1,437 in 1860 (Table 5.6). Although the average number of animals on each farm actually fell somewhat between 1850 and 1860, the values of livestock holdings and slaughtered animals rose considerably (Table 5.7). Crop production, too, reached peak levels (Table 5.8). Corn, the most important crop in the mountains, increased by 25%. The production of oats fell, but more farms grew wheat in 1860 than in 1850 and the number of farms making butter, and the quantity produced, had skyrocketed by 1860.

During the next two decades, however, these improvements vanished as livestock holdings, production levels, and farm values fell precipitously. Most farm variables fell to levels even lower than those of 1850. By 1880, Beech Creek farms averaged only 208 acres and were only 28% as large and 31%

Table 5.7. *Beech Creek Livestock Inventories, 1850-80*

	1850			1860			1870			1880		
	Mean	No.	%	Mean	No.	%	Mean	No.	%	Mean	No.	%
Hogs	26.2	51	98	21.1	56	95	9.8	114	86	12.8	44	51
Milk cows	2.9	52	100	3.8	56	95	2.3	125	95	1.9	73	85
Cattle	9.7	41	79	5.1	48	81	3.8	80	61	3.1	58	67
Oxen	2.8	16	31	3.8	38	64	2.9	48	37	2.3	18	21
Sheep	17.6	40	77	14.1	31	53	12.0	99	75	14.3	46	53
Horses	2	48	92	2.1	49	83	1.5	87	66	1.4	47	55
Value of livestock	$192	51	100	$374	59	100	$257	131	99	$142	84	98
	($217)			—			($172)			($108)		
Value of slaughtered animals	$60	48	92	$98	58	98	$88	123	93	$107[a]	84	98
	($68)						($59)			($81)		

Note: Dollar values in parentheses are standardized to 1860 dollar values.

[a] Estimated by the formula ((((livestock value × 0.3) 10.04) × 0.76)/7.6), where 0.3 is the average ratio of the value of slaughtered animals to value of livestock for 1850 to 1870 and 0.04 is average price per pound.

Sources: *U.S. Censuses of Agriculture*, 1850, 1860, 1870, 1880 (manuscripts).

Table 5.8. *Output of Principal Crops and Products in Beech Creek, 1850–80*

	1850			1860			1870			1880		
	Mean	No.	%	Mean	No.	%	Mean	No.	%	Mean	No.	%
Corn (bushels)	362	51	98	450	59	100	234	129	98	247	76	88
Wheat (bushels)	35	8	15	60	31	53	36	51	39	39	37	43
Oats (bushels)	111	23	44	34	12	20	48	40	30	37	26	30
Irish potatoes (bushels)	20	27	52	27	25	42	18	103	78	13	8	9
Beans (bushels)	9	37	71	7	57	97	8	106	80	—	—	—
Butter (pounds)	28	6	12	373	53	90	72	100	76	78	71	83
Wool (pounds)	21	37	71	26	28	47	22	95	72	20	45	52

Sources: U.S. *Censuses of Agriculture,* 1850, 1860, 1870, 1880 (manuscripts).

as valuable as farms had been in 1860. Livestock inventories, valued at only 29% of 1860 holdings, declined for all animals except sheep with hog production falling sharply from twenty-one hogs per farm in 1860 to only thirteen in 1880. Even more dramatic than the decline in the numbers of animals was the increase in the proportion of farms that no longer owned certain species of livestock. Hogs, for instance, were nearly universal on farms in 1860, but only about half of the farmers in Beech Creek owned hogs two decades later. Oxen were present on 64% of the farms in 1860, but only 21% of the farmers owned them in 1880. Farm products derived from livestock fell proportionately. Milk cows, for instance, declined by 50% and butter production fell far below the 1860 level. Because sheep holdings remained constant, the average production of wool did not drop as dramatically as butter, yet fewer farms produced wool than in 1860. Crop production, too, fell more or less in proportion to the decrease in farm sizes while the smaller size of farms forced a reallocation of acreage allotments among crop mixes. The number of farmers growing wheat and potatoes declined, but oat production increased by a modest amount (perhaps necessitated by the impact of timbering on livestock grazing). Most importantly, corn production averaged only 247 bushels per farm in 1880, an amount only 55% of the 1860 corn crop that had averaged 450 bushels.

Because the manuscripts of the 1890 census were destroyed by fire, the manuscript record for U.S. farms ends in 1880. This is especially unfortunate for the study of Appalachian agriculture since mountain farms were obviously undergoing considerable changes during the last decades of the nineteenth century. Data on agricultural holdings reported in county tax rolls for 1892, however, extend a partial view of Beech Creek farms another dozen years beyond 1880[66] and suggest further modest declines in farm production, especially livestock, from 1880 to 1892 (Table 5.9).

Between 1880 and 1892, average corn production in Beech Creek held steady, but the number of cattle (milk cows, oxen, and beef cattle) and hogs per farm fell, along with the proportion of farmers owing each. Only 41% of the farmers listed in the tax rolls, for instance, owned hogs in 1892 (down from the 1880 census level of 51%). The average number of horses per farm remained steady (at 1.3), but the proportion of farmers owning horses declined from 55% in 1880 to 39% in 1892. A portion of such decreases may reflect the fact that marginal farmers excluded from the agricultural censuses were included on the county tax lists, but the comparison of data from 1860 and 1892 tax lists confirms the unmistakable conclusion that Beech Creek farmers in 1892 were significantly poorer than those of a generation earlier. On all variables, except ownership of mules, the monetary values (in constant dollars), the amounts produced, and – except for corn growing – the

Table 5.9. *Corn Production and Livestock in Beech Creek, 1860 and 1892*

Year	No. of Taxpayers	Corn (bu.)	%	Horses Value	No.	%	Mules Value	No.	%	Cattle[a] Value	No.	%	Hogs Value	No.	%	Total Personal and Real Estate
1860	70	504	71	$116	1.8	70	$91	1.5	11	$97	8.8	77	—	9.5	59	$1,183 ($n$ = 60) ($\%$ = 86)
1892	56	246	71	$69	1.3	39	$93	1.3	21	$70	5.8	46	$12	5	41	$427 ($n$ = 41) ($\%$ = 73)

Note: The dollar values for 1892 are expressed in 1860 dollars.
[a] Cattle in 1892 is cattle plus bulls.
Source: Clay County tax rolls.

Table 5.10. *Change in Beech Creek Household Size, 1850-1942*

Number of persons	Year						
	1850	1860	1870	1880	1900	1910	1942[a]
One	5%	0%	0.6%	1%	0%	1%	3%
Two	8	9	14	11	7	15	13
Three	6	9	13	9	20	13	16
Four	6	19	16	14	11	13	16
Five	6	12	15	11	15	15	9
Six	11	11	11	13	15	11	14
Seven or more	57	41	30	42	32	32	30
	100%	100%	100%	100%	100%	100%	100%
Number of households	63	87	180	149	83	80	77
Household population	433	527	945	902	481	414	391
Mean	6.87	6.06	5.25	6.05	5.80	5.18	5.08

[a] Reported in Brown, *Beech Creek*, 468.

proportion of farmers reporting production fell dramatically between these years. Most significantly of all, as a reflection of the declining prosperity of agriculture, Beech Creek farmers in 1892 were far less wealthy than their ancestors of the previous generation, their estates valued at only 36% (in standardized dollars) of those in the earlier era.

Surplus Production

Thus far, we have examined aggregate trends in animal and crop production, but the data indicating these trends have not been standardized to take into account the changing nutritional needs of Beech Creek farm households nor the variable feed requirements of their livestock. During the years under investigation, the average size of Beech Creek households declined (Table 5.10).[67] This factor, along with the decreasing size of farms and their diminished livestock inventories, imply that over time Beech Creek farmers may have needed to grow less food and feed to reproduce their households. The changing mix of crop allocations, too, suggests the importance of standardization, but since Beech Creek farms did not primarily produce agricultural commodities for market, the value of products sold does not capture variations in output. Consequently, we have utilized well-documented techniques developed by economic historians to measure the output of nineteenth-century farms in order to assess changes in the productivity of Beech Creek farms.[68]

Table 5.11 reports surplus agricultural production in Clay County for 1860. It shows surprisingly high levels of production on even the smallest farm units. Even those below the median of thirty-five improved acres averaged 150 bushels of produce above and beyond the subsistence and reproduction requirements of their households and farms. Only 21% of these small units failed to meet their own needs. Larger farms did even better, those above the median producing 508 bushels of surplus and those cultivating more than 100 acres producing 684 bushels. Perhaps not surprisingly, since tenant farm families were smaller and had fewer members to feed than households headed by farm owners, farms operated by owners and tenants were almost identically productive although it should be noted that a few of the largest farms in our sample – including one with 300 acres of improved lands – were operated by nonowners, implying that some "tenants" were actually professional farm managers. Furthermore, the fact that one elderly salt manufacturer, Francis Clark, owned lands worth $120,000 in 1860, but, according to the farm census, operated only a 1,000-acre farm with very limited production suggests that a significant portion of the value of farm products raised by tenant farmers may have gone to such large landowners as well.

In addition to the sample farms, Table 5.11 also reports data on all farms in the county that were operated with slave labor. These, too, were able to produce large food surpluses that went well beyond the consumption requirements of their own households as well as that of their slaves. The largest of these, with improved acreages greater than 100 acres, averaged 1,512 surplus bushels. The existence of large surpluses on such farms confirms the existence of potentially marketable quantities of foodstuffs in Clay County during the late antebellum period just as the production of modest surpluses on smaller units confirms the latter's self-sufficiency. Additionally, the production of surpluses on the farms of the largest slaveholders suggests that these operations produced ample food for slaves employed in off-farm enterprises such as saltmaking. Thus, for example, salt manufacturers Daugherty, Alexander, and James White produced 8,697 surplus bushels of food beyond the consumption needs of their combined eighty slaves, and Daniel and T. T. Garrard produced a surplus of 4,093 bushels of food in excess of the amount they needed to feed the twenty-one slaves they owned.

In comparison with other farm regions, Clay County farms were surprisingly productive. Atack and Bateman report average farm surpluses of 359 and 175 bushels, respectively, for owner-occupied farms in the Midwest and the Northeast in 1860.[69] Assuming that hogs were fed entirely on forest masts, both tenants and farm owners in Clay County produced, on average,

Table 5.11. *Surplus Agricultural Production in Clay County, 1860*

Size of Farm Unit				Land				Tenure				Slaveowners		
Number of Improved Acres	Mean Surplus (bu.)	% Producing Surplus	No.	Tenure	Mean Surplus (bu.)	% Producing Surplus	No.	Slaveowners	Mean Surplus (bu.)	% Producing Surplus	No.	Mean Surplus (bu.)	% Producing Surplus	No.
Below or equal median of 35 acres	150	79	63	Owners	314	87	92	Large[a]				1,512	94	18
Above median of 35 acres	508	95	56	Tenants	334	85	27	Small[b]				501	85	13
Above 100 acres	684	100	8					All				1,087	90	31
All farms	318	87	119											

[a] Large slave owners operated farms with more than 100 improved acres.
[b] Small slave owners operated farms with less than 100 improved acres.
Source: *Eighth Census of the United States, 1860: Agriculture* (manuscripts).

Table 5.12. *Surplus Production in Beech Creek, 1850-80*

	1850	1860	1870	1880
Tenant farmers	51 bu.	331 bu.	108 bu.	17 bu.
	(*n* = 29)	(*n* = 16)	(*n* = 32)	(*n* = 23)
Farm owners	327 bu.	414 bu.	247 bu.	139 bu.
	(*n* = 23)	(*n* = 37)	(*n* = 100)	(*n* = 61)
Small owners	158 bu.	223 bu.	102 bu.	85 bu.
	(*n* = 12)	(*n* = 20)	(*n* = 52)	(*n* = 24)
Large owners	512 bu.	639 bu.	404 bu.	174 bu.
	(*n* = 11)	(*n* = 17)	(*n* = 48)	(*n* = 37)
All farmers	173 bu.	389 bu.	213 bu.	106 bu.
	(*n* = 52)	(*n* = 53)	(*n* = 132)	(*n* = 84)

Sources: Calculated from *U.S. Censuses of Agriculture*, 1850, 1860, 1870, 1880 (manuscripts).

roughly comparable levels of surplus to those of farm owners in either subregion of the northern United States at the time of the Civil War. Clay County slave owners produced three times as much surplus as Midwest farm owners and six times as much as northeastern farm owners.

Table 5.12 and Figure 5.1 report trends in surplus production among Beech Creek farmers from 1850 to 1880. All categories of farmers, tenants as well as large and small owners, improved production significantly between 1850 and 1860, but saw these improvements reversed by 1880 when surpluses fell to levels well below those of 1850. Surpluses on owner-operated farms fell 66% from 1860 to 1880 and all farmers experienced declines that averaged almost 300 bushels (73%). Tenant farmers were more severely affected. Not even taking into account the sizeable portion of their production that went toward rent (generally, one-third), their surplus production fell by almost 95% to an average of only seventeen bushels, suggesting that oral history recollections of particularly hard times among this group in the twentieth century are probably quite accurate.[70] Table 5.13 shows that the number of farms experiencing food deficits rose from only 9% in 1860 to 36% in 1880. As argued before, the most realistic way to model Appalachian farm practices is to assume that farmers did not give their hogs significant quantities of feed throughout the year. Nevertheless, the fact that simply adding hog consumption to farm requirements in 1880 would have lowered

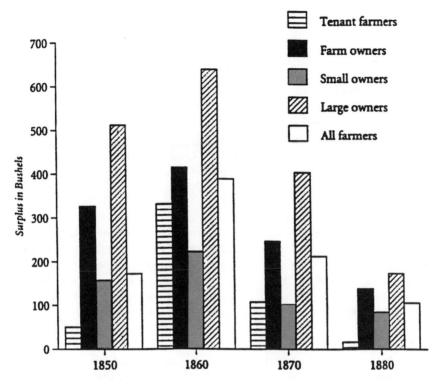

Figure 5.1 Trends in farm productivity.

the average surplus for all farms to only thirty-five bushels and created food deficits for 48% of Beech Creek's farmers suggests how economically vulnerable Beech Creek farms were becoming by 1880.[71]

A number of possible factors may explain the decline in Beech Creek farming between 1860 and 1880. Even though Clay County was not a major battleground, some reductions in livestock holdings may have been caused by conflicts that occurred there during the Civil War. The South as a whole experienced vast declines in its livestock supply because of the destruction of animals during the war. Eight former slave states, for example, produced nearly three million fewer hogs in 1880 than 1860 because of wartime losses.[72] Minor battles and raids in Clay County undoubtedly caused some hardship including the murder of one resident of Beech Creek by Confederate cavalry. In addition to the destruction of saltmaking facilities by federal troops, Confederate troops are known to have captured 150 head of cattle

Table 5.13. *Beech Creek Farms Not Producing Agricultural Surpluses*

	1850	1860	1870	1880
Percentage	36.5	9	20	36
Number	19	5	26	30
Total number of farms	52	53	132	84

Sources: Calculated from *U.S. Censuses of Agriculture*, 1850, 1860, 1870, 1880 (manuscripts).

during a raid on Goose Creek and the guerrilla forces of John Hunt Morgan are said to have "stole[n], robbed, and burned nearly everything [owned by] the people of Red Bird Creek, Goose Creek and South Fork."[73] The Union officer who oversaw the destruction of the county's salt wells and furnaces reported that the armies had taken "nearly all of [the local farmers'] available personal property – cattle, horses, and crops – and are generally in a destitute condition."[74]

Declining soil fertility, too, may have reduced farm output, but this is difficult to determine since the agricultural censuses did not report acreage allotments by crop before 1880. Beech Creek's soil was almost certainly less fertile in 1942 when Brown observed the community than it had been in 1860. But an analysis of county-level aggregate census data shows that per acre yields of corn, though low,[75] did not fall between 1880 and 1910, suggesting that the worst impacts of soil erosion in Clay County probably occurred during the twentieth century rather than during the period immediately after the Civil War.

A more likely explanation for the decline of Beech Creek farming in the nineteenth century is the changing balance of land and population. The Appalachian population experienced one of the highest reproduction rates in the United States during the period covered by our investigation.[76] With children under age ten constituting from 30% and 41% of the population in Beech Creek between 1850 and 1910 (37% of the 1860 population in Clay County), natural increase was remarkably high even by Third World standards today. Economic historians speculate that commercial farm families elsewhere limited fertility out of fear of failing to provide adequate land and capital for their offspring in response to the pressure of mounting economic competition.[77] The fact that subsistence-oriented farmers in Appalachia do not seem to have subscribed to this rationale reinforces our assertion of the need to examine the social and familial relations within subsistence agriculture.

An important clue to the relationship between production modes and household and family patterns is the observation that patriarchy provides strong incentives to high fertility in noncapitalist economies by positioning fathers to use and benefit from the labor of all family members, including children.[78] Although operating within a capitalist national economy, the subsistence agriculture of Clay County similarly prompted high fertility because of constant demand for labor and the ability of children to contribute significantly to sparsely mechanized farms. A Clay County farmer born in 1824 noted the utility of a large family: "We had 15 children – 10 sons and 5 daughters are living. When I was cleaning up my farm of 1,200 acres we would have a log rolling within ourselves."[79]

The value of a big family was heightened further by severe obstacles to the acquisition of nonfamily labor. Labor by slaves was integral to the making of salt in some parts of the county, but by the mid-nineteenth century, adult slaves sold for $500 to $1,000 and more in Kentucky markets, making such labor prohibitively expensive for Clay County's subsistence farmers. Wage labor, too, was both scare and unusually expensive in Clay County. In 1890, the prevailing wage for farm laborers in Clay County was $12.75 a month, only slightly less than the $13.50 a month paid to farm laborers in the highly commercialized Bluegrass county of Clark, although Clay County land was worth a mere $5.18 an acre, whereas Clark County land commanded more than six times as much: $33.22 an acre.[80] The persistent shortage of wage labor, combined with the financial inability to invest in slaves, kept fertility high in Clay County's subsistence farming areas long after it had declined in other, more market-oriented, regions of the country.

The effect of rapid population growth on limited land resources – in this case, due largely to the reproduction of only a handful of families – can be illustrated by its impact on farming along the rugged creek-bed portion of Beech Creek, one of the three neighborhoods that made up the whole Beech Creek community.

Beech Creek itself, that is, the creek from which the Beech Creek community derives its name, runs a distance of only five miles from its headwaters to its mouth at the South Fork of the Kentucky River. The creek flows through hilly terrain on which valley bottoms are rare, amounting to less than 10% of the basin's total land area. "From the air the Beech Creek basin looks like a great gully with many subsidiary ditches branching off in vine-like fashion."[81] Unlike the broad valleys that run alongside a few sections of Goose Creek and the Kentucky River in Clay County, the Beech Creek basin is not an area in which a large population can sustain itself through the practice of subsistence farming.

In 1810, only one household lived on the creek itself, Daniel Johnson's family with six members. According to Brown, twenty-six people lived along the creek in 1850, all of them located near the mouth of the stream. By 1880, forty-nine people in seven households lived along the creek from its mouth almost to its headwaters in the rugged hills high above the river. Population on the creek increased further from 86 in 1900 to 164 in 1920, after which it remained almost stationary until 1942 because of the outmigration of 95 people.[82]

Such population growth directly influenced the quality of Beech Creek agriculture through its impact on farm size. The custom of equitable partible inheritance meant that mountain farms had to be divided and redivided to accommodate new generations of farm families. Thus, it seems likely that by 1880, Beech Creekers were already beginning to approach a point of diminishing returns as they subdivided their farms to provide a means of livelihood for their children and grandchildren.[83]

An intergenerational analysis of two original Beech Creek farm families, the Andrews and the Johnsons,[84] confirms the diminishing prospects that Beech Creek farmers faced from 1850 to 1892 as a consequence of the declining scale of their farm operations. Adoniram Andrews (1734–1838) came to the Kentucky mountains from New England after serving in the Continental Army during the American Revolution and fighting in the Battle of King's Mountain in North Carolina. He traveled through the Cumberland Gap to the Beech Creek section of Clay County where he established a farm on the south fork of the Kentucky River and built a sawmill on the river. He was elected to serve on the first grand jury that was formed in Clay County in 1805. "Squirrelman" Job Andrews, believed to be his brother, settled nearby. Soon afterwards, Daniel Johnson patented one hundred acres on the river at the mouth of Beech Creek in 1816, not far from the more extensive landholdings of Adoniram Andrews. In 1826, his brother, Richard Johnson, purchased fifty of his acres and also began to raise a family. Andrews descendants, along with those of a few other settlers, soon populated the Laurel neighborhood of Beech Creek along the Kentucky River and descendants of the Johnsons populated adjacent tributaries of the river in the Beech Creek basin. Much of the history of the Beech Creek community revolved around the activities of these two families and members of both still live in or near the Beech Creek neighborhoods today.

The changing patterns of land ownership and farm production among the Andrews and Johnson families in Beech Creek between 1850 and 1880 are evident in a comparison of five fathers with their same-age sons thirty years later that reveals that the sons were unable to accumulate as much land, or grow as much food, as their fathers had done before them at a comparable age. The reason for this is simply the fact that they had to share the estates that had been built up by their fathers with other siblings. Thus, in 1850, at age fifty-one, Adoniram Andrews III – the wealthiest farmer in Beech Creek – owned 5,603 acres. Thirty years later, his son Daniel, age forty-eight, owned 600 acres. Elisha Johnson owned 1,400 acres in 1860 when he was forty-seven, but his son Alex owned only 400 acres at age fifty-one in 1892. Abel Johnson owned 700 acres at age forty-eight in 1860, but his son Samuel owned only 100 acres when he was the same age in 1892. Job Andrews owned 350 acres in 1860 when he was thirty-five, but his son, Morris, at age thirty-three, owned only 50 acres in 1892. William Johnson owned 500 acres in 1870 at age fifty-five, but his son, Squire, at fifty-one – fairing better than many of his generation, given the extent of his father's possessions – owned 350 acres in 1892.

Additional analysis of farm outputs for eighteen fathers and their adult children in Beech Creek from 1850 to 1892 reveals that in no case did members of the younger generation of farmers – the third generation in Beech Creek after its initial settlement – produce surpluses in the 1880s as great as those produced by their fathers at the peak of their productivity in the earlier period from 1850 to 1860.[85] Although this generation was not poor, the diminished levels of its landholding, wealth, and farm production point to the social origins of the poverty of subsequent generations.

Family size, the quantity of initial land holdings, and the acquisition of additional acres influenced how well the fathers of each generation could position their sons and daughters for the next generation of farm life in Beech Creek. Both the effects of life cycle and family formation on farming outcomes, as well as the long-term impacts of farm subdivision, can be shown by a detailed examination of the Elisha Johnson family, a family that for several years dominated the Beech Creek basin area. Indeed, the experience of this single family summarizes the whole journey from prosperity to poverty that marks the history of Beech Creek from 1860 to 1942.

Elisha Johnson, whose home manufacturing was described earlier, was the son of one of the original settlers of Beech Creek. According to Brown, he married in 1836 and had eight children, including Preston Johnson, with whom Brown lived in 1942 while he carried out his first fieldwork. In 1850, at age thirty-seven, Elisha operated a farm of 250 acres (30 improved) that included $200 worth of livestock. He slaughtered $35 worth of meat that year, grew 500 bushels of corn, and managed to produce a good surplus of food (equivalent to 254 bushels) beyond the immediate needs of his family. During the next decade, he managed to buy many additional tracts of land from neighbors and relatives, enabling him both to increase his farm production and to prepare for his children's future. By 1860, his household had increased in size but so, too, had his farming operation which would soon comprise virtually the entire basin area of Beech Creek from its mouth to its headwaters. He still only cultivated about thirty-five acres, but owned more than 1,400 acres in 1860. His livestock inventory had increased considerably to include three horses, five cows, six oxen, six cattle, four sheep, and twenty hogs worth nearly $600. He slaughtered $120 worth of animals that year and produced a surplus that was the equivalent of 430 bushels of food.

By 1870, Elisha still produced a sizeable food surplus (334 bushels), but he farmed only 300 acres, having begun to distribute his property among his sons and daughters who were establishing their own farms and families on portions of his lands, though he still retained legal title to their farms. Some sons and daughters left Beech Creek, but a married daughter and two sons, Alex and John, were listed in the agricultural census in 1880. Elisha, age sixty-seven, produced a good surplus (186 bushels) in 1880 as did his daughter, Mary Polly, and his son Alex. Another son, John, also operated a farm that was reported in the census, but he was unable to produce a surplus on his smaller holding, producing only enough food for his family and livestock.[86]

According to Brown, when Elisha Johnson died, some time after 1880, his widow, a second wife, retained 280 acres as a "widow's dower" that was subsequently divided into seven tracts, each containing about forty acres, at the time of her death. Several of Elisha's children passed on land to their children, but the eldest, John (as we noted before), had conflicts with his siblings and sold his property to nonkin, thus opening up lands within the creek basin to nonkin for the first time since the days of original settlement.[87]

By 1942, Elisha Johnson's lands – which according to Brown's estimate may have totaled as much as 2,200 acres at their peak – had been subdivided into twenty-four tracts owned by twenty-one different owners. *"At that time, 21 families lived on parts of the original farm, on which only one family was living in 1860.* Three of these families lived on what was the widow's dower; one lived on the part Preston was given; seven lived on what was John's; two on Eliza's; three on Alex's; and four on James' farm."[88]

Only one of Elisha's children, Preston, was still alive when Brown first observed Beech Creek. Brown wrote:

The youngest son of Elisha Johnson (Preston) was still living in 1942. Unlike his brother Alex, Preston never had a civil war pension, and unlike his brother James, who had only two children, Preston had a family of 16 children. To support this big family, Preston sold parts of his original farm. By far the biggest block, some 350 acres, was sold to

Calvin Andrews, a Laurel neighborhood man who bought it for the timber. Two small tracts – one of 35 acres and the other of 15 acres – he sold to his daughter Sarah Johnson Williams and to his son-in-law Ernest West. The farmhouse itself, which Preston built [around 1880] and the 75 acres surrounding it, were deeded to his daughter Ellen J. West [in 1932] in return for her assuming care for her old parents as long as they lived. In 1942, Preston himself owned only one steep, forested tract of some 66 acres.[89]

Thus, by 1942, 156 people in thirty-two impoverished households lived in an area (the Beech Creek basin) where only twenty-six people in three households had lived ninety years earlier in relative plenty.

The same high rate of population growth that eventually destroyed the balance of people, land, and resources in Beech Creek had its impact throughout the rest of Clay County. As Harry Caudill once said of Appalachian Kentucky in general, "the stork outran the grubbing hoe and plow."[90] For each decade from 1850 to 1900, the county's population grew by 22 to 25%, primarily through natural increase. Only the decade between 1900 and 1910 registered a slower rate of growth (with an increase of 16%) when many young people had begun to leave the county to search for opportunities elsewhere.[91] Such population growth resulted in reduced farm sizes and more intensive land-use practices.

In 1880, 1,414 Clay County families farmed a total of 239,896 improved and unimproved acres for an average of 170 acres per farm, but by 1910, more than twice as many families (2,916) farmed only slightly more space (244,214 acres) on farms that averaged only 86 acres. Per capita farm acreage declined in the county from 38 acres in 1860 to less than 14 acres in 1910. By the time that Brown entered the Beech Creek neighborhoods on the eve of World War II, farms averaged less than ten acres in crops and nine of the twenty-nine farms that Brown studied exhaustively averaged fewer than thirty total acres of improved and unimproved land. This was comparable to Clay County as a whole where 34% of all farms were less than thirty acres and 50% were less than fifty acres.

The consequences of enormous population growth and farm subdivision were undoubtedly worsened by the inherent limitations of forest farming. Forest farming was an effective adaptation that substituted land for labor and capital, but its continued success "required an abundance of woodlands for new fields and range."[92] *Time* and *space* both worked against the long-term success of successive generations of mountain farmers.

In regard to space, it has been estimated that "omnivorous hogs required less range land than cattle . . . [but] even a small herd of cattle required hundreds of acres of unfenced range in order to find sufficient native forage."[93] Farm subdivision reduced the space available for livestock foraging by forcing farmers to use their increasingly scarce lands ever more intensely.[94] Thus, the proportion of each farm that was improved in Clay County rose steadily from 12% in 1860 to 42.4% in 1910, bringing more and more woodland into cultivation. Additionally, the commercial timber industry further accelerated forest clearances during the logging boom that occurred between 1890 and 1925.[95] These changes were registered in declining livestock inventories. The average Clay County farm had 13.4 hogs and 5.1 cattle (of all types) in 1880 and but only 5.8 hogs and 3.9 cattle in 1910. (As Table 5.7 reported earlier, the average Beech Creek farmer had 21 hogs and 12.7 cattle fifty years earlier in 1860.)

Time requirements, too, worked against later generations of Appalachian farmers. The practice of "forest fallowing" required long amounts of time, usually a generation or more, for reforestation to restore old soil to its original productivity. "After an old field was reforested, it could be cleared and farmed anew. But if the field was again cultivated before reforestation and restoration of nutrients in the forest growth was completed, then declining yields, soil exhaustion, and soil erosion resulted."[96] When farms began to shrink in Clay County as a consequence of intergenerational subdivision and, as less "new grounds" became available, farmers became pressured both to cultivate steeper and poorer quality acreages as well as to shorten the length of time their lands remained out of production. Thus, an informant Hubert Collins, recalling Beech Creek farming during his youth in the 1930s, told our interviewer that his parents and their neighbors would typically "let their old grounds lay out . . . a couple or three years." When asked if the landscape he recalled as a boy looked different from today's, he replied, "Wouldn't be no trees. Everything'd be in corn." In Beech Creek, Brown found that although some good bottomlands remained, many portions "[had] been cultivated since the early days and [were] so exhausted by continual cropping and erosion [that by 1942 they were] rocky, unproductive, and thin."[97] "Evidence of erosion [was] everywhere – slips, slides, gullies, rock-choked stream beds, washed banks and bare, scarred fields."[98]

The long-term limitations of forest farming in Appalachia were apparent even to contemporary observers during the nineteenth century. In 1873, J. B. Killebrew noted that "the people in no portion of the state [of Tennessee] live so well or have their tables so bountifully furnished" as the farmers of the Cumberland Mountains of East Tennessee, yet he foresaw what would soon become the Achilles heel of mountain farming when he pointed out that already by the 1870s "in the matter of the subdivision of farms, East Tennessee ha[d] gone quite as far as seems desirable."[99] Sixty years later,

Table 5.14. *Household Types in Beech Creek, 1850-1942*

Household Types	Year						
	1850	1860	1870	1880	1900	1910	1942
Solitary or nonfamily	5%	2%	1%	1%	1%	3%	3%
Simple family	70	77	82	63	55	76	74
Simple family with others	8	7	9	9	4	5	—
Extended family	10	12	7	20	33	15	14
Multiple family	5	2	0	7	7	1	9
	100%	100%	100%	100%	100%	100%	100%
N =	63	87	180	149	83	80	77

Source: For 1942: Brown, *Beech Creek*, 470; author did not distinguish "simple family" from "simple family with others."

Tennessee farmers, like their counterparts in the hills of Kentucky, were impoverished.[100]

In the face of economic crisis, Clay County's subsistence farming households drew on the same resource that had supplied labor and land in times of plenty: the patriarchal family. Economic crisis provoked the extension and expansion of the households of Beech Creek as newly impoverished brothers, uncles, and cousins – and their wives and children – were brought into more economically stable households. Earlier, simple (nuclear) families had been the overwhelming majority of Beech Creek households, constituting between 70% (in 1850) and 82% (in 1870) of all households (Table 5.14); in the twentieth century, this pattern would be restored again. As the agricultural crisis of the late nineteenth century deepened, however, the proportion of nuclear households declined, to a low of 55% in 1900, while extended family households increased sharply, from 7% in 1870 to 33% three decades later.[101]

Not surprisingly, the ability of a household to take in additional members was a privilege of the age and economic status of its members, especially adult men. Households formed around a landowning man were more likely to take in grandparents or grandchildren (extended family), brothers or cousins and their families (multiple family), or, less commonly, nonkin (simple with others) than were tenant farming households (Table 5.15). Similarly, households formed around older men were more likely to absorb others than were

Table 5.15. *Household Type by Land Ownership of Household Heads in Beech Creek, 1850-1910*

Household Types	Year									
	1850		1860		1870		1990[a]		1910[b]	
	Owners	Nonowners	Owners	Nonowners	Owners	Nonowners	Owners	Nonowners	Owners	Nonowners
Simple family	71%	70%	78%	75%	80%	86%	51%	68%	73%	84%
Simple with others	6	10	7	6	11	6	4	4	5	5
Extended family	9	10	11	13	8	6	40	18	18	11
Multiple family	12	3	2	3	—	—	6	11	2	2
Solitary or nonfamily	3	7	2	3	1	2	—	—	2	—
	100%	100%	100%	100%	100%	100%	100%	100%	100%	100%
N =	34	29	55	32	117	63	53	28	57	19

[a] Missing data = 2.
[b] Missing data = 4.

Table 5.16. *Mean Age of Household Heads by Household Composition in Beech Creek, 1850-1910*

Household Composition	Year					
	1850	1860	1870	1880	1900[a]	1910
Simple	37.9	38.9	36.6	36.4	40.0	38.1
	(N = 44)	(N = 67)	(N = 148)	(N = 94)	(N = 46)	(N = 61)
Simple with others	38.6	42.8	36.4	38.8	41.3	39.3
	(N = 5)	(N = 6)	(N = 17)	(N = 13)	(N = 3)	(N = 4)
Extended	30.6	48.8	35.4	40.0	45.3	59.0
	(N = 6)	(N = 10)	(N = 13)	(N = 30)	(N = 26)	(N = 12)
Multiple	58.0	44.5	—	45.0	50.2	52.0
	(N = 5)	(N = 2)		(N = 10)	(N = 6)	(N = 1)
Nonfamily	44.67	55.5	36.0	28.5	—	32.0
	(N = 3)	(N = 2)	(N = 2)	(N = 2)	(N = 2)	(N = 2)

[a] Missing data = 2.

households formed around younger men (Table 5.16). That such household extension was a response to crisis, rather than an entrepreneurial effort to maximize production by adding additional laborers, is evidenced by the fact that the ratio of persons of "nonproductive" ages to all household members (the "burden of dependency") was roughly equivalent across household types in 1880.[102] Moreover, fully 34% of all these 1880 farms were producing below a subsistence level.[103] Nuclear farm families averaged slightly lower food residuals (sixty-one bushels) than extended households (seventy-four bushels), as expected. Yet, on average, both were producing very near the threshold of reproduction. Multiple families, too, were living in economically marginal situations, averaging 5.5 bushels less than necessary for reproduction. Only the nuclear-with-others households – that is, the few households that went outside the kinship network for labor – produced significantly above the subsistence level, averaging 184 bushels above reproduction.

How did so many farm families in Beech Creek survive below the level of subsistence in the late nineteenth century? A study of eighteenth-century Massachusetts, which found that 38% of all farms fell below the standard for self-sufficiency, suggested that New England farms were integrated into local networks of production, cooperation, and exchange that made "subsistence possible on farms that were not sufficient."[104] A similar interhousehold economic subsistence network operated in Beech Creek. Some farm households supplemented below-reproduction-level farming with the proceeds of hunting, fishing, and trapping, sources of food supply not measured in the subsistence equation. We speculate that although these were important factors in their survival, the kin network was an even more important component. Among families producing below subsistence, 68% were related to a nearby family producing at or above subsistence. Thus, for example, Samuel Dill, age twenty-two, lived with his seventeen-year-old wife Sarah on only five acres of land and barely produced at a subsistence level. Living nearby, however, was his father Elisha Dill, who operated a 300-acre farm, and an older brother, Issac, who rented a farm, both of whom produced well over what they needed to reproduce their own families and farms. Similarly, Ulysses Creech's rental farm yielded far less than was required for subsistence, but his father William owned 100 acres nearby and produced a large surplus. We can only infer what the census records imply, that is, that these kinsfolk survived through interdependence. Our oral history interviews confirm the importance of such family ties in the 1920s. As Hazel Collins told us: "When we ran out of potatoes, well . . . Daddy had a brother to give us plenty. And meat, they'd give us milk and butter, if we was out, and we shared, you know, our extras."[105] Landownership thus provided at least some Beech Creek farmers with the opportunity to support dependent kinfolk during times of economic hardship. Household expansion in Beech Creek was not a strategy to allow farming families to pursue opportunities in an emerging market economy; instead, it was a response to scarcity based in longstanding bonds of kinship and family solidarity. The strength of family groups that made possible the reproduction of marginal and below-subsistence farms through interhousehold strategies of survival was rooted in patterns of interdependent subsistence within a patriarchal moral economy.

In this regard, the family strategies of subsistence farmers differed in scale, not in objective, from those of the county's commercial elites. For the Whites, Garrards, Bakers, and other wealthy Clay Countians, it was family connections that linked the wealth of the eastern seaboard to the financial opportunities of frontier Kentucky. No differently than marginal subsistence farmers, the sons of the elite were beholden to the financial largess of family members for their economic futures. Hugh White prospered in a salt business established by his wealthy saltmaking brother from Virginia. Daniel Garrard grew rich on land surveyed and patented by his father, a Virginia-born Bluegrass planter and, later, Goveror of Kentucky. Abner Baker, too, was set up in Clay County by a wealthy Virginia father. The tradition of relying on kin to provide the conditions for making a living did not cease with the settlement of Clay County. Long before his death, Hugh White dispersed slaves, land, furniture, livestock, and cash to his sons, daughters and sons-in-law, setting them up to be the new generation of county elite. Such bequests provided a tremendous economic advantage to their recipients although they did not always secure family harmony. After receiving more than $2,300 in cash, slaves, and property from his father-in-law Hugh White, Lyne Kinningham chided White for showing a "great deal of disrespect" by failing to provide another $530 that Kinningham regarded as his due.[106]

Conclusion

The consequences of slow economic growth, population increase, land short-age, and soil depletion in Appalachia were obvious to twentieth-century ethnographers. In Beech Creek, scarce bottomland remained in the control of a few families, but "by the time the grandchildren of the original land-owners were grown, the area was so thickly populated relative to the agri-cultural potential of the land that families had moved up hollows and coves until the entire length of Beech Creek and its tributary valleys was inhab-ited."[107] In the Tennessee community of Little Smoky Ridge, likewise, "suc-cessive divisions of property and loss of soil fertility" had made cultivable land "scarce even by local standards." Family tracts of 100 to 600 acres had been reduced by inheritance to small plots of only 15 to 40 acres in the 1950s.[108]

Ethnographers were wrong, however, to attribute this structural limitation to a flaw in Appalachia culture. Pearsall, for instance, contributed to the erro-neous assumption of Appalachian exceptionalism when she wrote that moun-tain farmers "were committed to the destructive extensive methods of their forebearers, and they could be successful only so long as the supply of new land was unlimited. The result is the *cultural blind alley* in which they find themselves."[109] But mountain farmers were led down no more blind an alley than were their predecessors in other U.S. farm regions before them. What occurred in Appalachia in the late nineteenth century was simply the repe-tition of events that had already happened in older regions such as New England during the late eighteenth century when "mounting [population] pressure on the land supply" had led to "sharply diminished landholdings and a greater cultivation of marginal lands."[110] The only things exceptional in Appalachia were the timing of the demographic upheaval – since the lack of modern means of transportation and extensive market linkages permitted the relatively late survival of subsistence agriculture in the mountains – and the fact that trained social scientists were on hand to observe firsthand and to record the outcome of processes that had occurred earlier and been forgotten elsewhere.

In early New England, as later in Appalachia, "family lands were divided again and again to accommodate the increasing numbers of young men."[111] Charles Grant, for instance, reports that the "economic opportunity" that had once been "exceptionally bright" for the first generation that peopled the town of Kent, Connecticut, from 1740 to 1770 became "darkened . . . by the pressure of population . . . against a limited supply of land" by the time of its third generation.[112] The regionwide result was a massive exodus of population from New England between 1790 and 1830. New Englanders adapted to the crisis of their agricultural society by sending many of their sons and daughters into the new factories than had begun to dot their rural landscape, but many more moved to new lands on the western frontier, including Kentucky, where they were able to continue farming as their ancestors had done before them with little cultural discontinuity. It was during this period that Adoniram Andrews left New Hampshire to settle in the Kentucky mountains and it was his greatgrandchildren's generation in Beech Creek – the third generation after settlement – whose way of life was becoming "darkened" by the increasing scarcity of land.

The pattern of economic crisis and outmigration was repeated in Appalachia, but not for a century later. For Appalachians, moving into an extended family household represented an initial strategy for economic survival for those whose farms were unable to sustain them, but, like New Englanders, seeking work elsewhere was an additional option that many were forced to choose. Brown found that a small part of the income of Beech Creek families in 1942 was derived from family members working "outside" in southern Ohio factories, indicating that extraregional migration and employment were already important factors in the life of Beech Creek. After World War II, hundreds of thousands of impoverished rural Appalachians followed their kinfolk to the new urban and industrial frontiers in the cities of the Midwest, creating massive outmigration from the Appalachian mountains.

Other indicators, too, suggest that what ethnographers described as Appalachian cultural traits of familism and traditionalism were simply social patterns that had happened at an earlier, but economically comparable, time in other regions. The dense networks of kin living in close proximity that characterized Appalachia at the turn of the twentieth century, giving rise to characterizations of Appalachia as familistic, in fact is virtually identical to the residential pattern in New England in the late eighteenth century; both are characteristic of settled communities. Similarly, the massive outmigration after those time periods resulted in a lower residential density of kinship for New England in the late nineteenth century and for Appalachia in the twentieth. The juxtaposition of these regions at the same period of time implies a cultural lag in Appalachia that is better understood as differences in the timing of social and economic transformation.[113]

After the turn of the twentyth century, outmigration and the search for waged employment replaced family extension as the predominant family strategy for coping with rural economic crises.[114] But the bonds of solidarity that originated in subsistence networks persisted. The extensive kin-based chains of migrants from Appalachia to the industrial cities of the Midwest represented simply another type of family strategic response – a response now shaped by new market-based constraints of paid labor and class stratification. Extrahousehold strategies of cooperation, which researchers found to be so important for understanding the migration experience and urban adjustment of rural Appalachians as they relocated in midwestern cities after World War II, were an essential feature of the social relations that underlay the patriarchal moral economy in the nineteenth century.

Family survival strategies, rooted in a nonmarket system of social production and reproduction, thus helped rural Appalachians to cope both with the hardships they encountered during the capitalist-industrial transformation of the mountain region and with the hardships millions faced in the urban Midwest as economic refugees from rural poverty. Further, rural traditions of reciprocity contributed to the emergence of labor militancy in the twentieth century.[115] At the same time, however, the failure of Appalachia's subsistence economy to sustain an expanding population contributed to the destructive contours of modern Appalachia, including the predominance of exploitation and poverty. Limits on agricultural capacity contributed to the development of an underemployed labor pool that could be utilized cheaply in railroad, timber, and mining industries, whereas noncommoditized agricultural production, by setting limits on indigenous capital accumulation, contributed to dependence on outside capital for the development of the region's natural resources.[116] This dependency has made Appalachia one of the most visible symbols of economic exploitation and political subordination in capitalist America.

6

RACIAL DYNAMICS AND THE
CREATION OF POVERTY

Poverty in the United States has both racial and spatial dimensions. The poor are clustered by skin color and by place: African Americans in urban centers and the Mississippi Delta, Native Americans on reservations, Hispanics in the Southwest. With its overwhelmingly white population, race appears not to be a factor in the poverty of Central Appalachia. But as the history of Clay County shows, the racial dimension of poverty is not absent in Appalachia; it is simply more complex. Just as Clay County was not always poor, so, too, it was not always white. During the nineteenth and twentieth centuries, as Clay County became economically poorer and more isolated, its population became more predominantly white.[1] The racial composition of Clay County, like its poverty, was historically created.

Despite its present-day racial homogeneity (only 1.7% African American in 1990), Clay County had significant numbers of both enslaved and free African Americans in the nineteenth century. Racial stratification in the county thus was embedded within two distinct sets of economic relations: the coercive relations of slavery and the market relations of free labor. Moreover, in both sets of economic relations, inequalities of race and class overlapped. Both African Americans and whites experienced high rates of impoverishment, but they traveled different routes to chronic poverty in Clay County.[2]

Much research views race and poverty as individual attributes, with race acting as a filter on access to economic opportunity. Such an approach, however, is of limited value for understanding the racial dynamics that underlie the collapse of opportunity structures and the creation of regionwide poverty in Appalachia. We approach race differently, as an historically constructed social relation that shapes, and is shaped by, the conditions of historical development in specific regional contexts. Such an approach exposes the racial subtext in the story of Clay County's historically deepening poverty. The historical pathways that eroded the county's economic viability also depleted its racial diversity. In turn, the county's changing racial composition modified its economic dynamic.[3]

Table 6.1. *Number of Free African Americans in*
Clay County and Number of Whites in Beech Creek,
by Gender and Census Year, 1850-1910

Year	African American		White	
	Male	Female	Male	Female
1850	82	96	222	206
1860	116	142	258	247
1870	212	269	477	458
1880	324	352	458	441
1900	253	296	244	234
1910	257	238	213	197

Note: We include those designated in the census as
"mulatto" in the sample of African Americans, since the
census distinction between these groups is unreliable.

In this chapter, we explore the racial dimensions of poverty in nineteenth-century Clay County, seeking to understand the different historical trajectories that led African Americans and whites into poverty. We examine the experiences of enslaved Clay Countians and compare the county's free African American population with whites in the rural Beech Creek neighborhoods (Table 6.1). Racial comparison within Clay County's free population allows us to explore historical changes in the ways in which race shaped economic conditions and opportunities in the late antebellum and early postbellum periods.

The Dynamics of Race

Clay County was most racially diverse during slavery. As was true for the southern Appalachian region as a whole, most antebellum African American residents of the county were enslaved. Slaves comprised more than three-quarters of the county's African American population between white settlement and the Civil War. In 1850, there were 515 enslaved persons in Clay County, constituting nearly 10% of the population. Although low in comparison with the state of Kentucky as a whole (in which 21% of the population was enslaved), this was the highest rate of slaveholding in the Kentucky mountains. Ten years later, enslaved Clay Countians declined 31% to only 5% of the population, but still constituted the third highest proportion of slaves in the Kentucky mountains.[4] Although numerically small, free African Americans were a larger proportion of Clay County's African American population than that of the southern Appalachian region as a whole. In 1860, when less than 10% of southern Appalachian African Americans were free, almost one-half (43%) of African Americans in Clay County were free. At the onset of the Civil War, Clay County's free African Americans represented 25% of the entire free African American population of Appalachian Kentucky.[5]

The population of free African Americans in Clay County increased steadily, if slowly, throughout the antebellum and early postbellum period, growing most dramatically in the decades immediately after emancipation. Rapid white population increase during the same period, however, caused the ratio of African Americans to whites in the county to decline virtually every decade after 1840. After 1880, African Americans in the county decreased both as a percentage of the population and in absolute numbers. In this, Clay County was not unique. The late nineteenth and early twentieth centuries witnessed the near disappearance of African Americans from most nonmining areas of the southern Appalachians.[6] This trend was not confined to the Appalachian regions of Kentucky. African Americans constituted 24% of the population of the state of Kentucky as a whole in 1840 (96% of whom were enslaved), but less than 15% by 1890.

Social Relations of Slavery

As we have seen, from its beginning, the salt industry depended on slave labor. Slaves were forced to work at the most dangerous jobs in the salt industry: tending salt furnaces and boiling salt kettles, cutting timber, navigating salt boats, and digging coal to supply fuel for salt furnaces. In his study of the antebellum salt industry in the Kanawha Valley of West Virginia, John Stealey documents numerous gruesome accidents suffered by slaves. Slave owners who leased their slaves to salt manufacturers were cognizant of the hazards of working in the salt industry and sometimes wrote leases that restricted their slaves from the most perilous occupations. Despite such efforts, many slaves were injured or even killed in the salt industry. In 1812, for example, Archer Dickerson, a Clay County slave owner, mortgaged his slave Jack to John Bates for a $250 loan. A decade later, Dickerson's widow, Mary, sued Bates on the grounds that an accident in Bates's salt furnace left Jack "ugly and disfigured" from injuries that caused his face to pull to one side, decreasing his sale value from $600 to $250 and his rental value from $100 to $40 a year.[7]

Although the working conditions of slaves in the salt industry were extremely brutal, some historians argue that mountain slaves overall faced less harsh treatment than did those on southern plantations, largely because the low proportion of slaves in the mountain population made them seem less of a threat to the security of whites. Economics, too, may have dissuaded masters from some punishments since physical injuries, even cosmetic ones, could dramatically reduce a slave's value and those who hired slaves were liable for such damages.[8] However, there is little evidence that Clay County's slaves actually fared better than southern plantation slaves. In 1847, Harriet, a slave, filed a civil lawsuit with the help of the law firm of Hays and Garrard, charging that she had been hired out to William White, who beat and detained her. White responded only that Harriet had been "moderately chastised."[9]

The oral testimony of former slaves also suggests that many slaves faced harsh treatment in Clay County. Amelia Jones, born enslaved to Daugherty White, described her owner as "good to the slaves," noting that "he fed us well and had good places for us to sleep and didn't whip us only when it was necessary." But, Jones added, in Clay County "most masters treated [slaves] cruel and beat them most of the time. They were underfed at most places." Another former slave described Hugh White as "so mean to his slaves that I know of two gals that killt themselfs. [One was] found across the bed with a pen knife in her hand. He whipped another . . . most to death fer fergiting to put onions in the stew. The next day she went down to the river and fer nine days they searched fer her and her body finally washed upon the shore."[10]

In stark contrast to the image of mountain society as distant from the antebellum slave trade, Clay County's county seat, Manchester, was a bustling slave marketing center. Here, slave traders, salt manufacturers, and farmers crowded around an auction block from which slave men, women, and children were bought, sold, and leased. One former slave remembered seeing lines of slaves standing on an outdoor elevated wooden platform erected in the city center while an auctioneer gave "a general description of [their] ability and physical standing" and traders beat them with long whips "to see if they could jump around and wuz strong." Another recounted the day her twelve-year-old sister was sold for $1,220 to be sent to a southern plantation and her father was "sold at that place." "[A]fter they were sold and a good price paid for each they were handcuffed and marched away to the South." Yet another remembered that her master, "a better man than most of them," did not "auction off his slaves as the other masters would. . . . When he started to sale one of us he would go out and talk to the old slave trader like he wuz g'wine to sale a cow or sometin and then he would come back to git the slave he wanted. This wuz the way my mothers' brother and sister wuz sold."[11]

Despite such evidence of cruelty and brutality, the wills left by some Clay County slave owners show evidence of concern for the welfare of at least a few of their slaves. A few slaveholders bequeathed slaves in family groups – parents and children, or more commonly, mothers and children – to the same heir, although others specified separate heirs for even very young children and their parents. Some ordered their slaves freed on their death, or specified that slaves should be emancipated after an additional five to eight years of servitude. As discussed in Chapter 4, Daniel Bates's deathbed statement naming Abner Baker, Jr., as his murderer set free his slaves, "Joe, Nash and his wife Lucy, and his negro man Pompey."[12] It is unclear, however, if these somewhat benevolent provisions by slave owners were always carried out on their deaths. Legal cases involving contested estates show that slaves were far more likely to be bequeathed or sold than to be freed on their owner's death.[13] Instances of manumission and the sale of family units do appear in county court records and on bills of sale for Manchester slaves, but these are rare. In civil actions in which slaves were mortgaged to settle estates or promissory notes, there is only one case in our sample in which parents and children were mortgaged together and only three cases in which a parent was mortgaged along with a child.[14]

Even during the lifetime of their owners, Clay County's slaves were not spared the horrors of family dissolution through sale. One former slave noted that her owner "didn't hesitate to sell any of his slaves, he said 'You all belong to me and if you don't like it, I'll put you in my pocket' meaning of course that he would sell that slave and put the money in his pocket." The breakup of slave families in sale was commonplace; what differentiated humane from cruel owners in the oral testimony of the county's former slaves could be simply the measures an owner took to distract slaves from witnessing the sale of their children or spouse:

> The day [my owner] was to sell the children from their mother he would tell that mother to go to some other place to do some work and in her absence he would sell the children. It was the same when he would sell a man's wife, he also sent him to another job and when he returned his wife would be gone. The master only said, "don't worry you can get another one."[15]

Amidst the terrors and disruption of slavery, Clay County's slaves displayed remarkable acts of resistance. As early as 1809, a slave named Joe ran away to avoid being sold at a sheriff's auction to settle a judgment against his owner.[16] Other slaves recall more direct acts of resistance and retaliation. In an interview conducted in the 1930s, Sophia Word recounts an episode from her adolescence in Clay County:

The Mistress had an old parrot and one day I wuz in the kitchen making cookies, and I decided I wanted some of them so I tooks me out some and put them on a chair and when I did this the mistress entered the door, I picks up a cushion and throws over the pile of cookies on the chair and mistress came near the chair and the old parrot cries out, Mistress burn, Mistress burn, then the mistress looks under the cushion and she had me whupped but the next day I killed the parrot, and she often wondered who or what killed the bird.[17]

Not all resistance was as covert. Word also recalled an episode of direct violence against her owner:

One day my Mistress Lyndia called fer me to come in the house, but no, I wouldn't go. She walks out and says she is gowine make me go. So she takes and drags me in the house. Then I grabs that white woman, when she turned her back, and shook her until she begged for mercy. When the master comes in, I wuz given a terrible beating with a whip but I didn't care fer I give the mistress a good'un too.[18]

Although the Clay County criminal record is fragmentary, it contains several cases of slaves accused of burglary, assault, and murder – crimes that may have reflected rage against owners or other whites. In the October 1840 term of court alone, there were two proceedings against enslaved African Americas. Allen, a slave, was charged with shooting Daniel Bates with intent to kill; his $1,000 bail was provided by James H. Garrard. Dick, a slave owned by Hugh White, was found guilty in a jury trial of murder. The court ordered the executioner to "hang the said Dick by the neck until he is dead, dead, dead." After pronouncing sentence on Dick, the court heard evidence from White about Dick's worth and ordered that White be reimbursed $900 after producing a "certificate of execution" of Dick.[19] Justice in Kentucky operated largely in favor of whites and the propertied, but slaves were not automatically found guilty in Clay County criminal trials. Several were able to have their charges dismissed or were acquitted in court, as in the case of "Jasper, a slave," who was found not guilty of a charge of intent to kill in 1841.[20]

The most extraordinary litigation involving Clay County slaves was a series of cases in the mid-1840s in which slaves, with prominent white attorneys, sued their owners for freedom and monetary compensation for unlawful enslavement. Initially filed at the height of the first prolonged period of feuding between the Garrards and White/Bates faction, these cases pitted feuding slaveholders against each other. For these politically powerful slave-holders, the attempt to secure freedom for an enemy's slaves was another avenue for venting hostility. But such fissures among the elite did afford the possibility of legal redress to at least some slaves.

The earliest such legal action was filed in 1844 by "Allison of Color," represented by attorney James H. Garrard, against Stephen Bates.[21] Allison claimed that under the will of John Bates, his original owner, he was to be freed after eight years of service to Bates's son, Stephen. Eight other slaves brought suit against Stephen Bates for freedom under the same will. The cases were ultimately decided in favor of the plaintiffs by the Kentucky Court of Appeals after seven years of intense litigation (during which time the slaves were hired out through sheriffs' auctions), but each slave received only a penny in damages.[22]

By 1847, Bates's slaves developed a new legal tactic, suing him for the value of their labor while unlawfully detained. Claiborn "(of Color)" Theophilis, also represented by Garrard attorneys, asked for $500 in damages from Bates for unlawfully detaining him and forcing him to labor for five years.[23] Harriet "of Color" brought an action claiming her freedom from William White who had hired her from Stephen and Daniel Bates.[24] Like Theophilis, Harriet sued for damages based on the value of her labor – also set at $100 a year – and charged White with unlawful detention and cruelty.

In 1852, another remarkable case pitted slave against owner. Wesley Walker, a slave, sued his owner, William Walker, for the value of all labor performed after 1848 when, Wesley argued, William had granted him a deed of emancipation. In his petition, Wesley detailed his work for William – digging nettle out of the ground, working in the garden, cutting work, pasturing horses, and bringing coal – which he valued at $111. The Clay County court sided with Wesley and ordered the sheriff of Madison County, where William now resided, to collect the full $111 judgment, plus $48.96 in court costs.

Social Relations of Race

If there is a paucity of records documenting slavery in Clay County, the historical record is nearly mute on the nature of social relations between white and free African Americans. Certainly, interracial marriages and families were not unknown, even in antebellum Clay County. The diary kept by the Reverend Dickey records the case of Salim Sturgeon of Clay County, a white woman, who lived as the "concubine or wife" of George, an African American slave owned by William Turner, and who was described by her neighbors as a "witch." The 1850 census also lists three African American women with white husbands (17% of non-enslaved African American married women). Six of these marriages (representing 38% of African American married women) appear in the 1860 census.[25] In addition, nine African American children resided with a white father in 1850 and 19 in 1860.

Records of mercantile firms show that whites and African Americans also were bound together through complex market ties. White business owners relied on continual transactions with African Americans and African Americans depended on white businessmen and white-owned firms for credit and loans. Even slaves could be accorded credit on their master's accounts at local stores; the merchant Elhanon Murphy recalls "having let Lewis [a slave] have shoes on Daniel Bates account."[26] But if race determined the relative positions of African Americans and whites in such market relations, it did less to structure the terms of these exchanges. White business owners sold products to African American customers at prices identical to those they charged other whites. African Americans and whites borrowed money from, and deferred payment to, white retailers with similar rates of monetary repayment although different prevailing wage rates for African Americans and whites extended the time that African Americans were required to work to repay loans with their labor.[27]

Another site at which free African Americans came into contact with whites was the local judiciary. Court actions preserved records of numerous routine financial transactions between African Americans and whites. Monetary disputes involving African Americans usually pitted them as defendants against white plaintiffs, reflecting the economic dependence of African Americans on whites. Numerous cases involved African Americans mortgaging or selling property to satisfy debts to whites. But such disputes also suggest how relations of financial credit and obligation bound impoverished African Americans and wealthy white businessmen together. White entrepreneurs sought to make money through loans to African Americans. Also, whites relied on African American suppliers and producers. William Collins, a free African American, for example, was sued repeatedly in the 1840s and 1850s by white salt manufacturers for substantial unpaid loans and for failing to build and deliver a salt boat.

A particularly detailed account of the economic ties between white merchants and African Americans is found in a ledger book that recorded all transactions during 1845 and 1846 between James Jones, a landless eighteen-year-old African American farm laborer, and Frank Ballinger and Company, a local retail firm. This rare account book was filed in evidence for a 1849 civil case by Ballinger against Jones. The ledger indicates that during this two-year period, Jones purchased substantial amounts of cloth and leather ($31.39), farm equipment and supplies ($18.04), food and salt

($80.04), tobacco ($3.08), and other household items ($0.76) from the Ballinger company. Most purchases were made on credit. For these goods and as cash advances against other loans and tax debts, the Ballinger company extended Jones $46.58 in small increments over two years. Jones repaid the Ballinger firm by building delivery boats, slaughtering hogs, and repairing equipment.

Not only were the economic fortunes of free African Americans tied to those of whites, but in antebellum Kentucky, their very status as free citizens was at the discretion of white officials and employers. Emancipated slaves, a Kentucky historian notes, "were never secure in their freedom and could always be enslaved. They were required to carry certificates of freedom, be gainfully employed under penalty of imprisonment, observe curfews, and exercise restraint and discretion in their associations."[28]

Thus, the coercive relations of slavery and the market-embedded race relations of free society overlapped. Coercion often lay beneath the surface of ostensibly free market exchanges between whites and free African Americans, as when a lack of credit forced African American farmers to mortgage their crops and equipment or sell their land to whites. On the other hand, slaves sometimes were allowed surprising access to the structures of free society, for example, in cases in which slaves attempted to redress wrongs by their owners through the courts. In what follows, we examine how the intertwined social relations of coercion and market affected the long-term economic prospects of African Americans and whites in Clay County. We explore racial differences in three factors that are commonly associated with economic well-being or impoverishment in emerging market economies: migration and persistence, resource accumulation, and household and family structure. Together, these shaped the historical pathways of economic opportunity or constraint for Clay County's African American and white populations.

Migration and Persistence

In 1840, 15% of Clay Countians were African American. Fifty years later, this proportion had dropped to 3%. What caused such a rapid decline in the county's racial diversity? At least some of the decline, and in some cases virtual disappearance, of African Americans was due to factors that also motivated many whites to leave: a heightened concentration of landownership that made small farming increasingly problematic and the expansion of employment opportunities elsewhere in mining, lumbering, and industry. Additionally, racial violence and organized racial terrorism certainly played a role in the exodus of African Americans.[29] What were the characteristics of those who remained and those who left? And how did patterns of persistence or

Table 6.2. *Persistence Rates of African Americans and Whites: All Household Heads and Landowning Household Heads, Clay County, 1850-1910*

Race	1850-60	1860-70	1870-80	1880-90	1900-1910
African American					
Total	0.41	0.24	0.27	0.29	0.27
Owners	0.38	0.60	0.48	n/a	0.24
White					
Total	0.29	0.27	0.34	0.15	0.40
Owners	0.41	0.40	0.38	n/a	0.41

Notes: Persistence is the number of household heads from the base year found in the subsequent census divided by the number of household heads in the base year (see Burton, *Father's House*, 349 n. 69). Analysis is based on free household heads only. Owners are defined as those reporting ownership of real property in the 1850, 1860, and 1870 censuses and residing in an owned (not rented) home in 1900 and 1910. The 1880 census did not collect information on property ownership. Because the 1900 and 1910 censuses instructed enumerators to regard the family as the statistical unit in recording data on homeownership (thus crediting ownership to all members of the family unit), the extent of ownership is inflated overall. Thus, this table is restricted to household heads.
Sources: *U.S. Bureau of the Census*, 1850-80, 1900-10.

mobility affect the long-term economic situations of those who remained in Clay County?[30]

Since the U.S. census failed to record slaves by name, it is impossible to measure precisely the geographic mobility of all slaves who were emancipated in Clay County. However, an analysis of county wills allows us to trace those slaves who were mentioned by name in the wills of their owners. These data suggest that emancipated slaves rarely remained in Clay County for very long. John Bates, a wealthy salt manufacturer, left a will that specified the terms of emancipation of fifty-one of his slaves. Some were freed and given "a spot of ground to make a support on"; some were freed but given no land; and some were bequeathed to Bates's heirs for eight years, after which they were to be set free. None of these slaves ever bought land in the county and only seven appear in any subsequent county records. Most quickly left the county. None appears in subsequent tax rolls or censuses.[31]

Free African Americans and whites can be traced over time by linking individual and household census and tax records. Table 6.2 compares rates of persistence of Clay County's African American household heads with those of whites in the Beech Creek neighborhood and compares rates of persistence of landowners with total persistence rates at each period and across race.[32] Several patterns are evident. Both African Americans and whites had fairly low rates of persistence, mirroring the pattern found in other southeastern areas.[33] Only in the case of African Americans from 1860 to 1870 were more than one-half of household heads found a decade later. Nearly half the time, fewer than one-third of them could be found. Thus, the stereotype of early rural Appalachia as stable and isolated is wrong on both counts. Here, as in much of the nation in the nineteenth and early twentieth centuries, communities and neighborhoods underwent frequent and substantial population turnover.[34]

Surprisingly, the persistence rates of African Americans and whites were similar, averaging about 30% over this period, although a decade-by-decade examination of the data hints at racially specific factors for persistence and migration. With the exception of 1850–60, the rate of persistence of African American household heads was stable. White household heads had more variable persistence rates, including a dramatically low rate of 15% from 1880 to 1900. Such a racial difference may indicate that whites were more likely than African Americans to respond to the pull of economic opportunities elsewhere, such as the lumbering and mining booms between 1880 and 1900. The decisions of African American families may have reflected instead the more constant push of economic instability and racial tension.

Usually, but not always, landownership increased the chance that a family would remain in Clay County over time. Among white household heads, property owners were always more likely to persist than the landless. Among African American household heads, however, property ownership was associated with higher rates of persistence in only two of the four periods.[35] Further, the occupations of persisters varied across race. White household heads who remained over time were nearly all landowning farmers, reflecting outmigration among white landless households.[36] African American household heads who remained, especially in the late nineteenth century, were nearly as likely to be landless farm laborers as landowning farmers. For African Americans at the end of the nineteenth century, more than for whites, property may have provided the economic means for a family to emigrate from Clay County.

In contrast to Orville Burton's finding that African American persisters in a Deep South community tended to acquire significant amounts of property,[37] African Americans who persisted over time in Clay County began with, but did not continue to accumulate, substantially more property than average. The few African American household heads who were present in both 1850 and 1860 held real property worth an average of $1,700 in 1850, more than twice the average holdings of $775 for all African American landowners in Clay County that year. Ten years later, the economic advantages of persisters had greatly declined. They now held property worth only $900, on average, just slightly more than the average of $880 for all African American property owners in Clay County.[38]

Finally, the similar persistence rates across race suggest that it was racial differences in rates of natural increase and of migration *into* (but not out of) Clay County that led to the increasing racial disparity in population.[39] Beginning in 1808, Kentucky enacted a series of laws that sought to restrict the migration of free African Americans into the state.[40] The effect of these laws is evident in census data on place of birth, which reveal that large numbers of whites continued to arrive until the 1880s, but that only negligible numbers of nonenslaved African Americans did after 1850. Virtually all free African Americans who resided in Clay County, especially after the Civil War, were born in Kentucky. Although there were increasing numbers of free African Americans in Clay County over time, this resulted from emancipation and natural population increase, not from immigration into the county.

The patterns of persistence and migration suggest that Clay County had little to offer and much to repel African Americans in search of economic opportunity. Those who had the financial means to do so left. Those who did not were forced to remain in the county, where they faced increasing economic hardship in a declining economy. If geographical stability could brighten the fortunes of landholding whites, it often portended a financial downfall for African Americans.

Resource Accumulation

Race determined both wealth and opportunity in nineteenth-century Clay County. In the early decades, wealth and the ability to accumulate it were based fundamentally on land ownership.[41] Later, educational and occupational resources began to supplant landownership as the foundation of economic stratification. As assets of individual achievement, occupational position and literacy appear to be more congruent than landownership with the principles of equity that buttress market exchanges. But in Clay County, possession of these, no less than of land, was circumscribed by race. Indeed, inequities of property holding in the early and mid-nineteenth century differentially positioned white and African American Clay Countians to acquire jobs and education in the late nineteenth and twentieth centuries. As racial dynamics structured land ownership, they etched the racial contours of enduring patterns of wealth and poverty.

Table 6.3. *Characteristics of Landowners, by Race, Clay County, 1850-70*

Characteristic	1850		1860		1870	
	African American	White	African American	White	African American	White
Number of landowners	8	37	10	57	21	120
% of household heads owning land	22	54	24	64	24	64
Mean value of land	$775	$945	$880	$1,281	$486	$700
Aggregate value of land	$6,200	$34,962	$9,300	$73,306	$10,200	$86,087
Mean per capita value of land	$35	$82	$36	$145	$21	$92

Sources: U.S. Bureau of the Census, 1850-70.

Landownership was exceedingly uncommon among African Americans in antebellum Clay County, as it was throughout the South.[42] Only ten African Americans in Clay County owned land in 1860 (only eight in 1850) and seven of these came from just three families. This represented 24% of free African American–headed households in 1860 (22% in 1850), compared to 64% of white households in 1860 (54% in 1850) (Table 6.3). Together, all free African Americans in Clay County in 1850 owned only $6,200 in farmland (less than 2% of the county total), or $35 per capita. By 1860, this amount had barely increased, to $9,300 or $36 per capita. By comparison, whites living in Beech Creek owned more than twice as much per capita in 1850 ($82) and four times as much ($145) ten years later. If slaves (none of whom owned land) are included, the racial disparity in per capita antebellum land ownership is even more pronounced. There are also striking differences in the value of land owned by whites and African Americans. In 1850, the average African American landowner in Clay County owned $775 worth of land, compared to $945, or 22% more, for Beech Creek whites. Ten years later, the disparity had increased significantly. African American landowners owned $880, whereas Beech Creek whites owned $1,281, or 45% more.

A few slaveholders left wills giving property to their slaves, but it is unclear if these bequests were satisfied. In 1842, for example, David Clark ordered all his land and property (valued at $3,298) divided among his seven slaves with specific instructions on the exact disposition of each tract of land and each bed, piece of furniture and farm animal. Each was given a bed. One man and woman were also given furniture and two women received cows and a mare. But none of these former slaves appears in subsequent records, indicating either that they did not receive the land or that they quickly sold it and left the county.

Too, the slaves emancipated by John Bates's will after a specified number of years of service to his heirs were unable to retain their "spot of ground to make a support on." Several of Bates's former slaves appeared in subsequent tax rolls and censuses, but all were landless and very poor, with total property values of $25 to $75 in the 1840s. One former slave, Sharper Bates, was ordered freed five years after Bates's death with "a spot of land," but the censuses of 1850, 1860, and 1870 show him as a landless tenant farmer with only a small number of livestock. Hannah Bates, another slave awarded land in Bates's will, also was landless in both 1850 and 1860, heading a household in 1850 but living as a servant in a white-headed household ten years later.

Slaves who were emancipated but not given land under Bates's will also fared poorly. Milam Bates, freed at Bates's death, became a landless tenant farmer. Claiborne Bates, assigned to John Bates's nephew for eight years, appears in the 1860 census as a propertyless farm laborer living in a white-headed household. Both Milam and Claiborne Bates left Clay County after 1860. Harriet Bates, a teenager at Bates's death, remained propertyless and unmarried, living in her father's household. Joe Nash, also landless, headed his own household, but had accumulated only $150 in property by 1860. A number of other African Americans with the Bates surname appear in county records (presumably earlier freed slaves and their descendants), but only one – Ephram Bates with a small $50 tract in 1850 – ever owned land in a census year.[43]

The pattern of African American landlessness continued almost unchanged into the postbellum period. In 1870, whites in Beech Creek still owned more than 400% as much real property per capita as Clay County's African Americans. Although the percentage of African American households that owned land that year was slightly higher in Clay County than in the upper South states on average (24% versus 19%), it was considerably lower than the percentage of local white landowning households (64%). The value of property held by Clay County's postbellum African Americans was low even by the standards of southern states. In 1870, African Americans in the upper South averaged real estate holdings of $746; in the state of Kentucky, $684; in Clay County, only $486 (Table 6.3).[44]

As in the Deep South,[45] racial differences in the availability of credit partly accounted for the difference in landownership between African Americans and whites. An analysis of county deed books indicates that African Americans, far more so than whites, purchased land with cash, especially in the antebellum period. For example, Nicholas Cotton, one of Clay County's largest African American landowners, used cash for all his land purchases before 1860; only during the Civil War years could he secure mortgages, primarily from Daniel Garrard. His brother, Nelson, was the only African American able to obtain mortgages to purchase land in antebellum Clay County, and this required significant other property. He acquired a $210 mortgage from T. T. Garrard in 1857 by pledging a horse, a yoke of oxen, four cows, two calves, a yearling, two sows, and five shoats, in addition to the land. Whites, with better access to mortgages and other credit, were far better positioned to acquire land in Clay County.[46]

Despite the difficult time that African Americans had securing loans and mortgages, however, they were not without any resources to acquire land. African Americans, like whites, obtained land through court-ordered sales and as the result of civil lawsuits.[47] Also, African Americans and whites sold land back and forth between them and in several cases African Americans served as creditors for both African Americans and whites.[48]

The life history of Elijah Griffin, a free African American man, indicates that there were possibilities for economic success for a few African Americans in antebellum Clay County. Griffin, one of twelve children, was born in 1804 in Virginia, but his family soon migrated to Kentucky. In 1827, the Clay County clerk attested that the Griffin family had lived in the county for many years, ". . . ever reputed as free people here . . . they are commonly orderly, honest and industrious people, possessing a competency for support." At his death, Elijah's father divided the family's land among five sons. Elijah received no land – only $10 in cash – but his fortunes rose quickly. By 1835, still landless, he had a taxable worth of $150. Soon thereafter, one of his brothers left the county and Elijah was able to purchase a 1,200-acre tract of land on Goose Creek worth $4,000. Elijah used this land to make loans to both African Americans and whites and to leverage the purchase of additional tracts. William Collins, an African American, gave Elijah his livestock to satisfy a $43.50 loan. Similarly, Perry Hollinsworth, a white tenant farmer with a total worth of $415, was forced to mortgage not only his livestock, but also a loom, furniture, and his yearly crop to satisfy a $200 loan from Elijah in 1840. And Elijah did not hesitate to use the court to enforce his property rights. In 1853, he sued the heirs of a landowner who died owing him $40 and collected the full amount, plus $12 in court costs. During this time, Elijah continued to purchase land, buying 300 acres in 1854 and an additional 500 acres from Daniel Garrard in 1862. By 1860, he owned $7,000 in taxable property and land. His farm included $400 of livestock and produced substantial amounts of wheat, corn, wool, peas, potatoes, butter, beeswax, honey, and meat.[49] However, the story of Elijah Griffin is telling, but exceptional. Landownership in Clay County was a visible indicator of a system of racial dynamics that privileged some whites by disadvantaging virtually all African Americans. Even African Americans who gained access to land seldom had the financial means or the backing of local creditors to retain it over a long period.

Occupational data provide additional insight into how racial dynamics structured resource accumulation in Clay County. Virtually all adult males in the antebellum Clay County census reported themselves as farmers. But the apparent racial similarity in occupations masked significant differences. Perhaps three-fourths of African American farmers in 1850 were landless tenant farmers, compared to less than one-half of white farmers in Beech Creek.[50] Since the 1850 census failed to record any occupation for 68% of the primarily rural African American–headed households in Clay County, it is difficult to estimate farm ownership with any precision. If we assume that most rural African Americans were engaged in agricultural pursuits, the actual number of free African American household heads working on land owned by someone else may have been as high as 78%. In addition, substantial numbers of enslaved African Americans labored as farm laborers, as servants, or in Clay County's salt industry.[51]

The 1860 census gives a more complete picture of occupations and wealth holdings of the free population of Clay County. Among African Americans, sixteen listed themselves as farmers, seven of whom were owners and nine tenants, and an additional thirty African Americans were farm laborers. Among Beech Creek whites, there were seventy-four farmers, of whom only twenty were tenants, plus fifty-three farm laborers. Thus, 85% of African Americans working on farms, compared to 57% of whites, worked as sharecroppers, tenants, or hired laborers in 1860.[52]

Agricultural life in postbellum Clay County remained rigidly defined by race. Increasing proportions of both white and African American farmers owned the land they farmed, but, like Orville Burton found for Edgefield, South Carolina, tenant farmers and farm laborers in postbellum Clay County were disproportionately African American. Of the sixty-four African American household heads engaged in agriculture in 1870, only eighteen (28%) were owner-operators; the rest were tenants or farm laborers. Nine years later, only 22% were owner-operators. Moreover, the farms of most postbellum African American owner–operators were tiny, typically yielding fewer than 100 bushels of corn. African American–owned farms in 1870 produced

Table 6.4. *Farm Equipment and Livestock Holdings of Tenant Farmers, by Race, Clay County, 1850-70 (Number of Cases in Parentheses)*

Holdings	1850		1860		1870	
	African American	White	African American	White	African American	White
Value of machinery	$12	$13	$10	$34	$14	$11
	(8)[a]	(27)	(5)	(15)	(14)	(29)
Value of livestock	$100	$162	$285	$355	$170	$153
	(14)	(34)	(5)	(15)	(17)	(30)

[a] Number reporting value > 0.
Sources: *U.S. Bureau of the Census*, 1850-70.

only slightly more than $200, compared to nearly $400 for the farms of Beech Creek whites. By 1879, this racial disparity had widened even further. African American–owned farms generated only $172, compared to $375 for Beech Creek white-owned farms. The most successful African American farmer in these years, Cotton Nimrod, grew $400 worth of corn and owned $700 in livestock and farm equipment on land inherited from his father.[53]

If the experience of landownership differed substantially between African Americans and whites, so, too, did the experience of tenancy, especially in the antebellum years. White tenant farmers, although younger on average, owned more farm equipment and machinery and had substantially more valuable livestock holdings than did African American tenants. In 1850, there was little racial difference in the average value of farm equipment ($12 for African Americans and $13 for whites), but only 57% of Clay County's African American tenants, compared to 79% of Beech Creek's white tenants, owned any farm implements at all (Table 6.4). By 1860, all tenants reported some farm equipment, but its value averaged $10 for African Americans and $34 for whites. Livestock holdings showed a similar pattern. In 1850, African Americans averaged $100 in livestock, compared to $162 for whites. Ten years later, African Americans averaged $285 and whites $355. In 1850, 21% of both African American and white tenants owned no horses, asses, or oxen, animals that were important in farming and as mortgageable resources for tenants seeking to acquire land.[54] Another 50% of African American, but only another 38% of white, tenants owned only one of these animals. By 1860, all tenants owned at least one horse, ass, or ox, but 20% of African

American and 27% of white tenants owned no more than one. Virtually all tenants of both races owned either milk cows or cattle in both these years.[55]

Postbellum racial differences in tenancy were less pervasive. Although 22% of African American tenants owned no farm equipment in 1870, compared to only 6% of white tenants, they averaged more of it ($14 versus $11) and also more valuable livestock ($170 versus $153) than the younger white tenant farmers (Table 6.4). White tenants were more likely than African American tenants to own no (26% versus 22%) or only a single (52% versus 44%) horse, ass, or ox.[56]

In a rural society, tenancy can represent either a lifelong agricultural class position or a stage in the family life cycle as sons wait to inherit their fathers' land. Our data allow us to distinguish these two forms of tenancy by following tenants over time and linking records across generations. These data show that in nineteenth-century Clay County, permanent tenancy was more common among African Americans, whereas tenancy awaiting inheritance was more common for whites. White tenants were significantly younger than white owners and more likely than African American tenants to live near property-owning family members. Such inheritance, combined with outmigration of the landless, meant that there were few white permanent tenants in Beech Creek. Between 1850 and 1870, only two whites remained as tenants in two consecutive census years: Nathaniel Baker and William Parker, both of whom owned livestock worth less than the average holdings of white tenants and much less than the average holdings of white owners.[57] In contrast, lifelong tenancy was common among African Americans; in fact, it was not even confined to the poorest of them. Because of the difficulty that even African Americans with substantial farm equipment faced obtaining credit for land purchases, livestock and machinery holdings do not predict which farmers were able to make the transition from tenant to owner. African American permanent tenants in some years had livestock holdings that exceeded those of other African American tenants, and even some owners.[58]

Personal property ownership was more widespread among both African Americans and whites than land ownership. African Americans were less likely than whites in comparable occupations to own personal property, but, surprisingly, given the obstacles that African Americans faced in obtaining employment, education, and training, property ownership was by no means unknown among Clay County's African American population.[59] Farmers were the most likely to possess property – livestock and farm equipment – but small amounts of personal property also were reported by both men and women of both races in virtually every occupation, including servants, washerwomen, seamstresses, and field hands. Unlike in the Deep South, where Jacqueline Jones has found that African American landowners owned less

Table 6.5. *Literacy, by Gender and Race, Clay County, 1850-1910 (Percentages)*

Year	African American		White	
	Men	Women	Men	Women
1850	6	0	39	27
1860	33	11	57	23
1870	29	19	69	47
1880	30	16	57	34
1900	66	56	84	70
1910	75	64	86	77

Note: The sample includes only those at least fourteen years of age.
Sources: U.S. Bureau of the Census, 1850-80, 1900-10.

property than white tenants,[60] in Clay County, there was little difference in the amounts that they owned.

As the economy of Clay County became more extensively commercialized, education and occupation rather than land conferred wealth and status. But the opportunities opened by expanding commerce were rigidly segregated by race. In antebellum Clay County, African Americans were almost entirely restricted to service occupations: servants, washerwomen, seamstresses, and cake bakers. In contrast, some whites in rural Beech Creek established themselves in retail trade, craft production, and semiprofessions. Very few whites worked as servants. This pattern continued in the postbellum decades. Occupational openings for African Americans came as cooks, washerwomen, and laborers, whereas Beech Creek whites secured positions as coopers, physicians, lumber dealers, salesmen, and teamsters, though farming remained their principal occupation.

Educational opportunities for non-enslaved African Americans in Clay County initially were highly restricted. Only two attended school in 1850. Later, as education was opened to both races in postbellum Clay County, African American household heads gained somewhat proportionately to whites, but fewer than one-third of them, compared to almost one-half of white heads, could read by 1880. Further, as indicated in Table 6.5, literacy was possessed disproportionately by men during every time period and for both races, although the gender gap was wider among whites than among African Americans. The unique advantages, and perhaps the particular marketable value, of education for white men is evident in the fact that fewer than one-half of white women, African American women, and African American men could read and write before 1900, a threshold reached by white men by 1860. Indeed, more than three-quarters of white women were illiterate before 1870 and more than four-fifths of African American women were before 1900.

Despite the obstacles, however, some African Americans did acquire literacy skills in the nineteenth century. As expected, literacy and economic advantage were found together in Clay County, although it is not clear whether literacy bestowed wealth or the reverse. For both African Americans and whites, those who could read and write were much more likely to own land than those who could not. The few African Americans in professional occupations (e.g., clerks and teachers) were literate, but surprisingly, literacy among African Americans was not confined to particular occupations. Literate African Americans worked as farmers, servants, laborers, cooks, and wagonmakers. The sole African American recorded as literate in the 1850 census, for example, Franklin Hide, was a thirty-one-year-old tenant farmer. Ten years later, eighteen African Americans were listed as literate; of these, six were farm owner-operators, two were women married to white husbands, one was a woman tenant farmer, and two were male field hands. Four of the eighteen were members of the same family.

Finally, as Loren Schweninger found in her study of southern African American female property owners, barriers of race and gender reinforced each other in Clay County, restricting the property and opportunities of white and African American women in different ways.[61] This is most clear in the range of occupations that census takers listed as being held by women and girls, outside of their unrecorded labor in home manufacturing, family farming, and housekeeping. White and African American women differed not only in the likelihood they were employed for wages, but also in the occupations that they held and in the family and household situations that led them to seek paid work.

Women constituted only 20% of Beech Creek whites with recorded occupations in 1860, and virtually all of them were widowed women operating farms. But contrary to stereotypes of Appalachian frontier widows, not all these women were owners in title only. In 1850, for example, twenty-seven-year-old Nancy Andrews was married to a farmer and raising a young child. Ten years later she appeared in the census as unmarried (presumably widowed, though possibly deserted) and operating a $1,000 farm with the help of her fourteen-year-old daughter. By 1870, now nearly fifty, she transferred all her land (which had increased in value by $800) to her daughter, who was operating the farm. Similarly, Sarah Johnson headed a farm household of co-resident daughters and granddaughters; the value of her farm more than doubled (from $130 to $300) between 1850 to 1860. Tenant farming, less common among Beech Creek's white women, mostly consisted of unmarried women supporting minor children.

African American women were much more likely than white women to report paid occupations. In 1860, 42% of employed African Americans were women, who held a variety of service and farming occupations. There were two African American women farmers, Nancy Hughes and Sally Potter. Like the white women farmers, both were both unmarried (probably widowed) and had co-resident minor children. Unlike the white women, however, they were tenant farmers and neither remained in Clay County for more than a decade. Clay County's three African American seamstresses included a nineteen-year-old woman married to a white man, a forty-year-old woman living with her adult children, and a thirty-two-year-old woman heading a household of four minor children. Female farm laborers included three household heads supporting minor children and two young adults living with white farm-owning families.

In postbellum Clay County, African American women held a smaller range of occupations than they had in earlier decades. In 1870, thirty-one of thirty-three African American women with identified occupations were servants, as were ten of sixteen white women, a pattern that continued in 1880.[62] One interesting exception was Julia Clark, an African American mother and household head. In 1870, thirty-four-year-old Clark worked as a seamstress to support her four minor children living at home; her twelve-year-old daughter had been boarded out as a servant. By 1880, Clark had all her children living with her and was operating a farm as a tenant farmer.

Tenant farming was less common, but not unknown among Beech Creek's white women. Jane Christain, for example, also supported her two minor children by working as a tenant farmer. Three African American women (but no white women) owned land and other property in 1870, although none of them was listed in the census as a farmer. Two of them were widows (one the widow of a white man) and both were supporting minor children at home. The other was a forty-year-old single woman who did not appear in earlier censuses, either because she was recently arrived or recently freed.

The twentieth century saw some opening of occupations to African American women, but again in very race-segregated occupations: laborers, washerwomen, cooks, and servants. White women were largely without occupations, except through inheritance of farms from deceased husbands although the 1900 census recorded one white woman physician. An African American woman schoolteacher also was included.[63]

It is clear that gender and race interacted to shape the opportunity structure for white and African American women in Clay County. Like African
American men, African American women faced tremendous legal and financial obstacles to retaining their property. African American women, who were
much more likely than white women to head their own households (discussed
in what follows) or to live in households headed by impoverished male laborers or tenant farmers, relied on wage employment for their economic survival.
Although African American women were somewhat more likely than white
women to work in agriculture, such pursuits rarely translated into economic
security or opportunity, as they often did for white men. Rather, agricultural
work, like wage employment, represented a survival mechanism for those
severely dispossessed by both race and gender.

By linking a variety of historical records, we can reconstruct the lives of
two African American women for a glimpse into the interaction of race and
gender in nineteenth-century Clay County. The life of Ellen White – who
first appeared in the census of free persons in 1870 at the age of fifty –
illustrates that at least some African American women were able to sustain
households and amass property in postbellum Clay County. In 1870, White
headed a household consisting of three daughters; the tax rolls that year show
her as owning no property. Ten years later, still landless, she headed a household with one now-grown daughter and two adult grandsons. But within the
next few years, White accumulated both land and money. In 1885, facing ill
health, she hired a white attorney, B. P. White, to write her will. She left $35
to each of three daughters, but to a fourth daughter and a grandson (the son
of a small farmer but himself landless) she left the bulk of her estate, both
land and property, "they having been kind in nursing and caring for me in
my old days." As was true of African American property owners in general,
neither the daughter nor the grandson were able to retain ownership of the
land they inherited for very long. By 1892, the grandson owned only a $60
mare; the daughter owned no property.[64]

The story of Alice Freeman illustrates a different outcome for African
American women property owners. Alice acquired land through inheritance
from her father, George Freeman. In 1832, George, a forty-two-year-old free
African American farmer, bought fifty acres of land from a white man for
$200 cash. With this land, George accumulated sufficient resources to begin
loaning money; he subsequently held debts from both white and African
American farmers. At some point, however, George found himself in legal
trouble and in 1852 was forced to mortgage all his land, property, and debts
owed to him to secure the services of a local attorney. Again, George recovered enough real and personal property to leave a tract of land and some livestock to his daughter Alice. But, like her father, Alice quickly lost the land

when she was forced to retain an attorney to defend her against charges of stealing a hog in 1861.[65]

In postbellum Clay County, propertied white men were able to translate their financial advantages in the earlier, land-based economy into skills and occupational positions that conferred privilege in a more intensively wage labor-based system. Landless whites and African Americans, with few resources in land, had little access to the educational and occupational opportunities of the commercial marketplace. They either left the county or remained as its poor.

Household and Family Structure

Studies of poor populations indicate that kinship networks and household arrangements can either ameliorate or magnify financial hardships over time and across generations. At times, household and family structures serve as strategic resources for their members, providing a margin of security against financial disaster. But family obligations can also deepen financial distress and make economic viability impossible.[66] In Clay County, household and family structures varied by race, and African Americans and whites differed in how they drew on kinship ties and household living arrangements to cope with poverty.

Few firsthand accounts of Clay County slavery have survived, thus making it difficult to reconstruct the nature of family and household arrangements among the county's enslaved population. But in census and court records, one factor is striking: because of their use as industrial slaves, the majority of Clay County's slaves, unlike those in other mountain counties, lived in large groups. Although most slaveholders in Clay County owned relatively few slaves, the extremely large numbers of slaves owned by a few wealthy salt manufacturing families meant that slaves typically lived with sizeable numbers of other slaves. In 1850, a mere 2% of slaves (11) lived in situations in which they were the only slave. Another 9% (36) lived in households in which two, three, or four other slaves resided. Eighteen percent (92) lived in slave groups of between 5 and 10, and 29% (147) lived in slave groups of 11 to 20. Almost half, 44%, or 229, of Clay County's enslaved population lived in groups larger than 20.[67]

Between 1850 and 1860, the declining fortunes of salt – and the resultant reduction in demand for slave labor – reduced the number of slaves in Clay County and changed the living situations of those enslaved persons who remained.[68] Still only 3% (11) of slaves lived in households in which they were the only slave and another 8% (29) lived with 1 to 3 other slaves. But a substantially larger number – 140, or 40%, of the slave population – lived in midsized groups of 5 to 10 slaves. And, in sharp contrast to a decade before, relatively few slaves lived in large groups. Only 23% (83) lived with 11 to 20 slaves and 26% (91) in groups larger than 20.

The demographic distribution of slaves suggests that few of Clay County's slaves lived with family members. In 1850, among the twenty-one slave-holders who owned four or fewer slaves, only one owned a man and woman of similar ages. Another three owned adult women and men of greatly dissimilar ages. The remaining 17 (81%) owned only adult women, only adult men, or only child slaves. Moreover, most enslaved children lived with only one parent, almost always a mother. Records of a three- and nine-year-old who were the sole slaves of a white family – and other households who owned preteen girls as their only slaves – indicate that at least some enslaved children were separated from both parents and other adult kin at very young ages.

In 1860 (the only year with census data on slave dwellings), few of Clay County's slaves lived in single-family residences and few lived in the same house as their owners. Most slaves lived in large groups on the property, an arrangement that one former slave described as "the old 'master's' home [with] the negro shacks all in a row behind the home."[69] Slave dwellings, especially for those owned by large slaveholders, were crowded. The seventy-one slaves owned by James and Daugherty White lived in only eight houses. Seventeen slaves owned by Sylvann Gibson lived in only two dwellings, and twenty-one slaves owned by Francis Clark were provided a total of three houses.

Moreover, slaves were unlikely even to stay with the same owner over time. We estimate the proportion of slaves in the 1850 census who were owned by the same person or household in 1860 by comparing the age and sex distributions of slaves owned by each slave holder in those years. To make this a conservative test, we count as present in 1860 every slave of the same sex who was between five and fifteen years older than a slave recorded in the 1850 census. By using this criteria, at most 111 out of the 241 slaves living in Clay County in 1850 were living in the same household a decade later. More than half, possibly many more, had been disrupted from the social ties that they had formed. The level of residential disruption was much higher for slaves who lived in large slaveholding groups in 1850 than for those in smaller groups, reflecting the shifting labor market of salt manufacturing. For slaves who lived with ten or more other slaves in 1850, only 41% (74 out of 179) were found in 1860. In contrast, among slaves owned by slave-holders in 1850 who had 4 or fewer slaves, 64% (7 out of 11) were found a decade later.

The living situations of Clay County's free African Americans, especially between 1850 and 1880, were also markedly different from those of whites.

Table 6.6. *Persons Unrelated to Household Head, by*
Race, Clay County, 1850-1910 (Percentages)

Year	African American	White
1850	22	2
1860	25	3
1870	24	3
1880	7	2
1900	3	2
1910	8	1

Sources: *U.S. Bureau of the Census*, 1850-80, 1900-10.

Antebellum African American–headed households were far more likely to be female-headed than were households headed by whites. Of the Clay County households in 1850 that had a free African American household head, fully 32% were headed by women, compared to only 8% of the white-headed households. In 1860, the gap widened: 45% of free African American households were female-headed, compared to only 6% of white households. But ten years later, with emancipation, the race difference in female headship almost vanished: 19% of African American and 13% of white households were headed by women.

The situation of persons living in households headed by nonkin shows a similar pattern, but also reveals the extent to which family life was disrupted for many free African Americans in antebellum Clay County. As shown in Table 6.6, over 20% of all free African Americans in Clay County, but no more than 3% of Beech Creek whites, lived in households headed by nonkin in every decade from 1850 to 1870. Thus, African Americans were about eight times as likely as whites to live with nonrelatives. After 1870, the percentage of African Americans who lived with nonkin fell sharply, to fewer than 10% every year through 1910, but it remained higher than the very low rate for whites. A small part of this racial disparity in antebellum patterns may have resulted in part from the manumission of some members of Clay County' slave families, causing a prior overcount of one-parent and female-headed households in the census of free persons, rather than from more deeply rooted cultural differences in household and family formation. But it is impossible to tell from these census data.[70]

Table 6.7. *Mean Age of Persons Unrelated to Household Head, Clay County,*
1850-1910

	African American				White			
	Male		Female		Male		Female	
Year	Mean Age	N	Mean Age	N	Mean Age	N	Mean Age	N
1850	18	17	27	23	19	7	9	2
1860	23	27	22	37	21	10	20	5
1870	19	36	25	79	21	15	24	11
1880	22	22	33	24	23	11	12	9
1900	23	10	31	8	21	4	27	2
1910	17	2	45	6	22	3	—	0

Sources: *U.S. Bureau of the Census,* 1850-80, 1900-10.

African American women living with nonkin were, on average, older than
white women in similar living situations. Living in the household of nonkin
may have been a life-course stage for white females who served as servants
or governesses during their late teen and early adult years. For African
American women, in contrast, living with nonkin was often an arrangement
of servitude or labor that continued well into adulthood. Among whites, men
were more likely to reside in a white nonkin household, primarily as farm
laborers. Among African Americans, women were most likely to do so, principally as servants.[71] Table 6.7 indicates that lifelong servitude in another's
household may have been more characteristic of African American females
than of males. In almost every year, African American women living with
white nonkin were significantly older, on average, than men. For whites, the
sex differences in age were more variable over time, largely due to the smaller
number of whites in this situation.

The ranges of occupations and ages of those living with nonkin – largely
female servants or male farm laborers – further underscore how different this
experience was for whites and African Americans. Among whites in Beech
Creek, those who lived in a nonrelative's household as a farm laborer were
typically in their early twenties. African American farm laborers in that
situation were much older, from their late twenties to late thirties. Moreover,
white farm laborers living with nonkin were mostly of similar, young ages.
African American farm laborers living with white nonkin ranged in age from

their early teens to over sixty years. The situation of female servants was similar. African American servants living in a nonrelative's home were much older than comparable white servants, from their late twenties to early forties. The few white female servants residing with nonkin tended to be much younger, generally in their early twenties.

A close examination of the living situations of Clay County's most depedent populations, the elderly and children, underlines the extent to which race shaped one's chances of living with family or living with nonkin, and, as the historian Steven Ruggles points out, provides a different picture of race differences in family structure than does analysis at the level of the household.[72] For elderly persons, racial differences in living arrangements were associated with differential access to land since property ownership greatly increased one's chances of continuing to head a household in old age.[73] Thus, elderly whites, who were much more likely than elderly African Americans to own property and to own more valuable property, also were more likely to head households in most years. Overall, the majority of both white and African Americans elderly persons (except African Americans in 1870) lived in their own households as heads or spouses of heads (Table 6.8).

The living situations of those who did not head households are also revealing. Daniel Scott Smith and his colleagues found that in the late nineteenth-century South "co-residence of older southern blacks with their children was less influenced by the motives of production and inheritance" than by economic marginality.[74] This pattern was even more pronounced in Clay County in the mid-nineteenth century. Before 1880, elderly African Americans who did not head their own households were much more likely to be employed as servants or laborers in the households of nonrelatives than to live with children or other relatives. Indeed, substantial numbers of elderly African Americans, as many as 53% in 1870, lived apart from kin, usually by living in households headed by white nonkin. In contrast, few white elderly persons in any year lived in nonkin-headed households. This racial difference reflected the extreme economic marginality of most households headed by free African Americans and their consequent inability to absorb additional dependents, as well as perhaps their drive not to accept or to avoid economic dependence on others.[75] Before 1880, not a single elderly African American lived in a household headed by a relative, whereas significant numbers of elderly whites did.

As Table 6.9 shows, elderly women, none of whom owned property in their own names, found living situations that differed greatly by race. White elderly women lived in their own homes, as household heads or wives of heads; lived with their adult children; or, in one case, with a sister. Elderly African American women who did not live in their own homes as heads or

Table 6.8. *Racial Differences in Landholding and Family Relationships among the Elderly, Clay County, 1850-1910*

Characteristic	1850		1860		1870		1880		1900		1910	
	A	W	A	W	A	W	A	W	A	W	A	W
N	19	10	17	13	17	17	25	33	40	22	35	20
% who owned land[a]	21	30	12	38	6	41	—	—	32	77	43	92
Average value of land owned ($)	338	583	1,600	2,040	1,999	571	—	—	—	—	—	—
Household position:												
% head or wife of head	68	70	53	85	47	77	68	70	70	82	80	85
% related to head but not head or wife	0	30	0	15	0	17	20	27	25	18	14	15
% not related to head or wife	32	0	47	0	53	6	12	3	5	0	6	0

Notes: We define *elderly* as sixty years of age and over, instead of the more conventional sixty-five years of age, because of a marked pattern of "age heaping" at decade intervals in census data on reported age, especially for African Americans. A = African American; W = white.
[a] Property ownership figures may be inflated for 1900 and 1910, because the census reported whether someone lived in a home that was owned or rented rather than who owned the property. These figures are reported for assessing racial differences rather than absolute levels of property ownership.
Sources: *U.S. Bureau of the Census*, 1850-80, 1900-10.

wives of heads lived as servants, boarders, lodgers, or with grown children or other relatives. Across the entire South, one-third of African American and one-quarter of white elderly unmarried (single, divorced, widowed) women headed their own households in 1880, but, perhaps due to the scarcity of employment opportunities for elderly women, this was not true in Clay County. In 1880, all white unmarried women lived with their adult children. Among unmarried African American women, 73% lived with their adult children; the other 27% lived as boarders, as household heads, or in the homes of white nonkin.[76] Except in 1870, there were substantial race differences in the chances that an elderly woman lived with a spouse. In every census year

Table 6.9. *Relationship to Head of Household for Elderly Women, by Race, Clay County, 1850-1910 (Percentages)*

	1850	1860	1870	1880	1900	1910
African American women						
Heads	22	0	11	8	17	47
Wives	33	43	0	33	33	21
Mothers, grandmothers (in law)	0	0	0	43	38	21
Sisters	0	0	0	0	4	0
Servants	0	14	0	0	4	11
Boarders	0	0	0	8	4	0
Unrelated to head	44	43	89	8	0	0
White women						
Heads	17	17	44	0	18	25
Wives	50	50	0	53	54	50
Mothers, grandmothers (in law)	33	33	44	47	18	25
Sisters	0	0	0	0	9	0
Servants	0	0	0	0	0	0
Boarders	0	0	0	0	0	0
Unrelated to head	0	0	11	0	0	0

Note: Some columns do not add up to 100 because of rounding.
Sources: *U.S. Bureau of the Census*, 1850-80, 1900-10.

except 1870, more than half of all white elderly women lived with husbands. For elderly African American women, however, no more than half, and in most years a third or fewer, lived with a spouse.[77]

If the lives of Clay County's adult population differed radically by race, the lives of its children did not. Children worked as farm laborers, field hands, and servants. For whites, the labor experiences of childhood constituted a rite of passage that preceded the acquisition of a home and land. For many African Americans, however, labor in the employ and household of another extended throughout a lifetime. In nineteenth-century America, as in early modern Europe, childhood was, for many whites as well as African Americans, a period of servitude and labor.[78] As Table 6.10 indicates, there was little consistent racial difference in the percentages of Clay County's children who reported paid employment; they ranged from 26% of African American and

Table 6.10. *Living Arrangements of African American and White Children, Clay County, 1850-1910 (Percentages)*

	1850		1860		1870		1880		1900		1910	
Arrangement	A	W	A	W	A	W	A	W	A	W	A	W
Live with parent(s)	76	93	76	94	73	94	90	90	84	84	87	93
Live with other family	0	4	3	4	1	3	6	7	13	13	11	6
Head or spouse of head	1	0	0	1	2	1	1	1	1	2	1	1
Live with nonkin	23	3	21	2	24	2	3	2	2	1	1	0
N	92	256	142	299	240	502	356	514	271	228	253	205

Notes: Children are those 16 years of age and younger. A = African American; W = white. Some columns do not add up to 100 because of rounding.
Sources: *U.S. Bureau of the Census*, 1850-80, 1900-10.

20% of white children in 1870 to 5% of African American and 11% of white children ten years later.

One major racial difference stemmed from an 1825 Kentucky state law that allowed for the arbitrary seizure and forced apprenticeship of free African American children, especially those from poor families. Work conditions for these children sometimes differed little from slavery and economically marginal African American families were deprived of their children's contributions to household production.[79] In 1839, for example, the Clay County Court separated for apprenticeships nine children ranging in age from two to seven, all but one of them living in a mother-only household. Three of these were the young sons of Lucinda Freeman, an extremely poor African American tenant farmer. By 1850, Lucinda had regained her three sons, but with a total taxable property of $30 (three cows and fifty bushels of corn), she could provide only a meager living for a household that then included four sons, her sister Minerva, and three young nieces. Things improved only a little within the next decade. By 1860, Lucinda's sons had left the county, but she still reported only $60 in property and now supported three minor grandchildren. Her sister Minerva headed a separate nearby household with six minor children, but reported no property or occupation.[80]

The living arrangements of Clay County's children also differed by race, especially in the early years. Virtually all white children lived with at least one parent between 1850 and 1870, but nearly one-fourth of the African American children lived with someone else, usually as a servant or laborer in a white nonkin household (Table 6.10). From 1880 to 1910, though, there was a racial convergence in living arrangements. The percentage of white children living with at least one parent declined, to a low of 84% in 1900, whereas the percentage of African American children living with a parent increased, to a high of 93% in 1910. The percentage of African American children living with nonkin dropped sharply, approaching the negligible level for whites, whereas the number of both African American and white children who lived with family members other than parents increased.

These patterns suggest that the common scholarly practice of viewing households and families as universal strategic resources for the poor is problematic. Among the very poor – Clay County's landless African Americans – the combined assets of households or families were simply too meager to sustain additional dependent members. Many, especially the dependent elderly and children, were forced to find living arrangements as servants or laborers at the places of employment. Such strategic use of kinship networks required financial stability that was simply inaccessible to most African Americans in early Clay County.

Conclusion

The comparison of African American and white Clay Countians in the nineteenth century suggests several conclusions about the relationship between race and poverty, or its reverse, economic opportunity. First, there are racial differences in the relationship between persistent poverty and outmigration. In most research, outmigration has been understood as an individual or family response to chronic regional poverty.[81] Further, large-scale outmigration typically is viewed as heightening overall poverty in the region of origin, since it is usually the very old, the very young, and the unemployable who persist in a poverty region during periods of economic opportunity elsewhere. A comparison of whites and African Americans in Clay County, however, suggests a more complex relationship between regional poverty and migration. In the nineteenth century, possessing the means of economic security (i.e., landownership) increased the likelihood of persisting in the county among whites but increased the likelihood of leaving during some periods for African Americans. White persisters, often property owners, increased their property accumulation over time, whereas African American persisters, without an initial base of property, tended to sink more deeply into poverty. Thus, the incidence of poverty among whites initially decreased in the nineteenth century due to the outmigration of landless whites. Among African Americans, in contrast, the poorest remained in Clay County, creating significant impoverishment in this group. Economic opportunity outside Clay County, in the coal and timber industries of Appalachia or in the emerging industrial centers of midwestern cities, did not operate in the same way across race and thus shaped racially distinct trajectories for those who remained in the county.

Second, resource accumulation in nineteenth-century Clay County was in part a function of age and life-cycle stage for whites but not for African Americans. For many white young men, a lack of resources, and particularly land, was a characteristic of young adulthood as they awaited land inheritance from their fathers. Among African Americans, however, age did not often lead to ownership; landlessness was likely to be a lifelong condition. Moreover, whereas whites typically accumulated greater amounts of property over time (often by using small amounts of land to purchase additional land), African Americans did not. The ability of an economically marginal household to maintain or increase its financial base was a function not only of its initial holdings, but also of racial factors.

Third, as rural Clay County began to change from a subsistence-farming economy to an economy based increasingly on waged work, white men were better positioned than African American men or than women to take advantage of new economic, educational, and occupational opportunities. Rather than reduce the economic disparities between whites and African Americans (and between men and women) that had been built up in a system of household-based agricultural production, commercialization, and industrialization exacerbated inequalities and heightened the advantages of whites and men.

Finally, the ability to expand or contract households provided a means of survival for economically marginal rural whites, but not for African Americans in nineteenth-century Clay County. Among white Beech Creekers, marginal and below-subsistence farming households were sustained during economic crises by family and kinship networks as Beech Creek farming households producing above subsistence levels absorbed additional household members from economically troubled kin households. But such household-based strategies were possible only among kinship groups in which at least some households were economically secure. Among African Americans, kinship ties linked households of similar economic precariousness. In times of economic crisis, therefore, some members of African American households (typically, the elderly and the young) were forced to live in nonkin, and often white-headed, households as domestic or agricultural laborers. Household situations adopted only during economic hard times by whites more often became permanent, impoverishing situations for African Americans.

When James Brown entered Beech Creek on horseback on the eve of World War II, Clay County was, as it has remained, seriously poor. Economic decline throughout Appalachia impoverished nearly all who remained in the region. But the common economic destination of whites and African Americans there should not obscure the racially specific historical paths that each group followed into chronic poverty.

V

POSTBELLUM CAPITALIST
MARKETS AND THE LOCAL STATE

7

FROM MARGINALITY TO
INTEGRATION

Virtually all African Americans and most whites who remained in Clay County in the postbellum decades faced increasing impoverishment as eastern Kentucky in general and Clay County in particular began what the geographer Mary Verhoeff referred to as a "gradual dissociation" from the central section of the state.[1] In antebellum times, Clay County was integrated into regional networks of transportation and commerce as a center of salt production and a base for prominent political and economic elites. As salt manufacturing dwindled and the use of the Wilderness Road declined, however, the county slipped into an era of deepening economic and geographical isolation that lasted more than a generation, ending only with a massive plunder of timber and mineral resources at the end of the nineteenth century.

Moreover, the reintegration of Clay County into wider commercial and financial markets that occurred as a result of large-scale resource extraction was on terms much different than those a half-century earlier. No longer were local and regional entrepreneurs the primary actors who dictated the county's economic direction and profited from its resources. Now national and international corporations, sometimes employing local capitalists, charted Clay County's economic path. As a result, the county assumed a new place in the global economic landscape. Like much of the southern Appalachian region, Clay County became a peripheral, dependent region of resource extraction. For some (outside corporate owners as well as local elites), this future portended great wealth. For most of Clay County's population, it meant generations of poverty.

How did Clay County lose its economic vitality in the space of a few generations? What caused its slide from relative prosperity in the nineteenth century to abject poverty in the twentieth century? Why did its storehouse of wealth – its timber, coal, gas – generate wealth for so few in the county? Answering these questions requires not only that we take a careful look at how local and outside actors responded to economic constraints and opportunities during the decades of decline and economic reintegration, but also that we examine legacies from earlier, more prosperous periods in the county. Clay County's journey from integration to isolation, from wealth to impoverishment, and from local to outsider control was not inevitable, nor the result solely of economic conditions at the turn of the century. Rather, the lingering effects of earlier economic and political relations also shaped the county's trajectory through the twentieth century and beyond.

In the next chapter, we examine the nature of postbellum political conflict and violence in the county. Here, we focus more narrowly on economic concerns, particularly on three contradictory forces operating in the late nineteenth century: the generation of wealth without significant accumulation of capital; the vulnerability of local merchants and financiers to national economic trends; and the exploitative and highly contentious relationships among outside capitalists and Clay County's local elites and non-elites. Each of these had a role in fashioning the economic vulnerability that would characterize Clay County into the twenty-first century.

Land and Wealth

By seeing Clay County in the late antebellum years, it would be difficult to imagine how economically insignificant it would become a century later. On the eve of the Civil War, a combination of salt manufacturing and land acquisition, together with the economic marginality of much of the population, resulted in great fortunes for a small number of local families. In 1860, the top 5% of households owned one-third of all wealth in the county, with the top 10% owning 48%, or almost half. Although Clay County was not quite as economically stratified as most U.S. cities or as the Cotton South, it was slightly less egalitarian than the rural northern farm region.[2]

Even among farmers, wealth holding was highly skewed. Those whose wealth (personal and real property) totaled less than $100 comprised 17% of all farmers. These averaged only $24 of personal property and $4 in real estate in 1860. Those with wealth totaling between $100 and $1,999 made up 72% of farmers. Their estates averaged $665 ($308 personal property and $357 in land). Only 11% of farmers had wealth valued at $2,000 or more and these averaged $1,807 in personal property and $2,274 in real property, for total estates of $4,081.

Despite the contention of some historians that rural neighborhoods – as opposed to wider county contexts – were relatively egalitarian, that, for example, "in remote mountain neighborhoods . . . economic differences were minimal" and "measures of social prestige and privilege" were based on status distinctions, not control of resources such as land,[3] rural Beech Creek mirrored the county's pattern. The top 10% of Beech Creek households owned

37.5% of real estate value in 1860, almost identical to the 37% figure for the county as a whole. Land ownership was even more concentrated among the top one-fifth of household heads in Beech Creek – where the top 20% owned 61% of the land value – than countywide, where the top 20% owned 53.7%.[4]

Although a small elite in Clay County held a vastly disproportionate amount of personal wealth and land, they did not invest these resources in the diversified industries or local infrastructure that might generate sustained economic development. Rather, some invested their fortunes outside the county, in areas such as the Bluegrass. Others used their fortunes to leverage lucrative financial arrangements with outside resource extractive industries intent on plundering the riches of Clay County. When salt manufacturing declined, therefore, Clay County was left with few local industries or employ-ment possibilities. Manufacturing establishments in the county, with the exception of those producing salt, were small, poorly capitalized, and gener-ated employment for a total of only twenty employees in 1860. That year, a mere 15% of Clay County's employed population held nonfarm occupations, making the county considerably less economically diversified than compara-ble rural communities elsewhere.[5]

Ten years later, despite a salt supply described as "inexhaustible" by one state agency, the failure to develop local transportation, combined with vigorous competition from other salt-producing regions, meant that the county retained only four establishments engaged in saltmaking, collectively employing but thirty-nine men and generating a relatively paltry $20,000 annually. Clay County also was home to two small sawmills, two tanneries, two blacksmith shops, and a steam carding mill for producing wool, but none generated significant amounts of employment or revenue and most failed within a decade.[6]

Those who embarked on entrepreneurial careers in the early postbellum years had little success. James Mayham tried manufacturing salt and operat-ing a steam-powered sawmill and gristmill for five years but was reported "broke" in 1871. James Murphy operated a sawmill and gristmill in the late 1860s, but had "returned to farming" by 1870. Herman Hayes' gristmill and sawmill failed in 1871. Suggesting its increasing economic isolation from other areas of the United States, Clay County also lagged far behind most other nonsouthern rural counties in literacy, a highly marketable skill in an industrial economy. Whereas 67% of the *poorest* 1% of all household heads in the rural Northeast were literate in 1860, only 52% of *all* Clay County farmers (and only 15% of workers) were literate the same year.[7]

The county's increasing economic marginalization produced complicated outcomes for the wealth holding of its inhabitants. In the county as a whole, the proportion of total wealth owned by its richest residents remained fairly stable during the latter part of the nineteenth century, as a small elite continued to dominate Clay County's limited commercial and industrial development and to own a vastly disproportionate share of the county's land. In 1892, the top 5% of household heads owned 37% of the county's wealth, whereas the top 10% owned 49%, virtually identical to the ownership patterns of 1860.

In Beech Creek, outside the area in which the very wealthiest Clay County families resided, however, the postbellum years brought greater equality in wealth holding. Here, the share of wealth owned by the top 10% of households dropped from 59% in 1860, to 41% in 1870, and then to 36% in 1892. Moreover, in contrast to the increasing landlessness that often is associated with industrializing areas, Beech Creek experienced a decline in farm tenancy over time. Tenancy decreased from 46% in 1850, to 37% in 1860, and to 25% in 1910 and the proportion of household heads who owned property increased.

Beech Creek's increasing equality of wealth and landownership was one outcome of the declining viability of subsistence agriculture in rural Appalachian Kentucky. The growing agricultural crisis after the Civil War pushed many of the white landless who were dependent on payments or reciprocity from landowners, together with a large proportion of both landowning and landless African Americans, out of the county. Among Beech Creek landless household heads listed in the 1850 census, only 19% were still present in the county when the census enumerator arrived a decade later, compared with 42% of those with land. A mere 38% of Beech Creek's 1860 landless were present ten years later, but 70% of landowners remained. Between 1900 and 1910, when landlessness declined to its lowest level, 36% of 1900 landowning heads still lived in Clay County in 1910, but no one who was landless in 1900 could be found in the county the next decade.[8] In Beech Creek, the outmigration of landless whites resulted in a sharp decline in landlessness and an overall increase in economic equality.[9]

Despite household networks of reciprocity, the ability to produce an adequate supply of food to meet the needs of farm households and livestock also was an important determinant of whether families remained in Beech Creek over long periods of time. Of the sixty-six farmers who produced a surplus in 1880, fourteen were living in Beech Creek in 1900 and all but one owned land. In contrast, only one of the seventeen farmers who did not produce a food surplus was still living in the county twenty years later.[10]

The outmigration of propertyless and economically marginal farm families meant that as generations succeeded each other in the rural neighborhoods of Beech Creek, greater parity of land ownership was achieved, leading later ethnographers to misperceive rural Appalachia as a region of long-standing egalitarianism. But even with increasing equality, landowning remained the crucial resource in the interplay of power, privilege, and prestige. It is commonly said that Appalachia's subsistence farmers needed only small amounts of cash in order to pay taxes and buy a few necessities that could not be manufactured at home. But this assertion does not accord with the large and potentially marketable surpluses of agricultural goods that Clay County and Beech Creek farmers produced around the midpoint of the nineteenth century. It also ignores mountain people's desire for the principal commodity on which their way of life depended: land.

What has been said of early New England is no less true of nineteenth-century Appalachia: "Land was the essence of life throughout the region; a sufficiency of land was a vital concern of the great majority of men."[11] Earlier, we demonstrated that the acquisition or loss of land determined, at least in part, how well farmers were able to help secure the future well-being of their descendants. Elisha Johnson, as we have seen, was concerned enough to achieve a "sufficiency" of land for his children that he managed to buy up almost all the land in the Beech Creek basin before he died. Similarly, the career of Ameredith Combs, ancestor of Bert Combs, one of the few governors of Kentucky to come from the mountains, is only one of many showing how far from "lackadaisical" nineteenth-century farmers were in their pursuit of land.

Ameredith Combs was a farmer and surveyor who owned land on the south fork of the Kentucky River near the Andrews and the Johnsons. As a surveyor, his frequent dealings with the farmers who lived in his vicinity – along with his knowledge of their property – led to numerous opportunities for him to buy and sell land. Between 1850 and 1908, Combs purchased twenty-seven tracts of land for at least $10,000 (not all deeds recorded the purchase price) and sold a number of others. As one traces the history of his transactions through the Clay County deed books, the impression emerges that he had become a small entrepreneur and land speculator at a time when local land trade was still largely mediated by kinship and neighborhood ties. The Andrews (related by marriage) and the Johnsons numbered among his earliest trading partners. Job Andrews sold Combs 150 acres of land for $200 in 1850 and later the same year, on the death of his mother, William Johnson sold Combs an eleven-acre share of his father's estate for an undisclosed amount. Perhaps regretting his decision – and apparently paying a good price for the lesson – Johnson bought the tract back from Combs more than a decade later for $250.

One particular incident, somewhat cloudy in detail, suggests that Combs could be both shrewd and tough in his transactions. Sometime during the

1870s, Combs entered into a business arrangement with A. E. Robinson and Robert Potter, the merchant whose meteoric rise and fall we describe in what follows. For reasons that are unclear in the records, one Thomas Beatty obtained a judgment against the three men for $6,754.37 in 1877. In order to secure the judgment, the sheriff of Clay County publicly advertised and auctioned a tract of property appraised at $9,000 that was owned by Robert Porter. The buyer, for the sum of $6,005, was Ameridith Combs. In addition to gaining control of his fellow defendant's property for two-thirds of its value, Combs paid Robinson's portion of the debt and, nine years later, gained title to his home on Goose Creek as repayment.

One may perhaps infer from a deed dated May 11, 1895, that Combs passed on his acquisitive values to his offspring. The deed reports that "A. M. Combs, being sick and not expected to live on 25 January 1894, and wishing to have his estate settled in such a way as not to sacrifice same, was induced to make, sign, and acknowledge a deed of conveyance, conveying all his property . . . and also his personal estate" to his sons, Lee, William, and John. But Combs surprised his sons by recovering. Five months later, John and William swore that "A. M. Combs – on account of his bad health and not in a condition to fully investigate, understand, and transact business, and not fully understanding said deed at the time of making, signing, and acknowledging same" had by then "recovered his health" and asked them to "relinquish and waive all right, title, and future claims" to his property, which they did. Combs continued to deal in real estate for at least another decade.[12]

As late as 1942, James Brown found that in Beech Creek, status continued to be intertwined with landownership. The families that Brown termed "high class" all owned land, were descended from large landowners, and "conformed more closely to the mores of [Beech Creek]," which were centered about "a good income, ownership of property, and economic well-being." The ancestors of Beech Creek residents ranked as "low class," on the other hand, had descended from those who owned little or no land.[13]

As economists have demonstrated, the ability of families to accumulate property has a direct connection to the economic growth potential of the regions they inhabit. Households tend to accumulate property over the life cycle of the household head, with wealth increasing during adult years, then decreasing with retirement or transfer of property to adult children in older years. On average, then, wealth is correlated with age of the household head during all but the oldest period of adulthood. Although there was a relationship between age of head and landholding in Clay County, the relationship weakened over time, indicating reduced accumulation in households. In Beech Creek in 1850, every year of age translated into an average increase of

$94 in real property; by 1870, this had dropped to $23. In the county as a whole, the economic gain from a year of age of the household head declined from $104 to $12 between 1860 and 1892, suggesting a drastic secular decline in the income earning potential of the area, a sure signpost on the road to poverty. The declining association between age and accumulation also was a visible marker of the decline of patriarchal relations, as an increasingly waged economy began to erode, although not destroy, the economic privileges of age that accrue to landowning adult men in subsistence agricultural economies.[14]

Earlier, we saw that Clay County and Beech Creek farmers produced relatively large agricultural surpluses in the antebellum period. In 1860, before the related processes of population increase and farm subdivision lowered the productivity of their farms, they managed to outproduce many of their counterparts in the northern United States. Despite this accomplishment, the low level of commercialization in the Kentucky mountains meant that farmers were unable to accumulate large quantities of wealth. Also because of the lack of commercialization, their lands – ever decreasing in the average size of individual holdings – did not significantly appreciate in value.

Moreover, the county's continuing basis in subsistence agriculture meant that little agricultural product left the county. Apart from modest livestock sales, of the large quantities of corn, wheat, barley, oats, hay, tobacco, butter, eggs, chickens, ducks, geese, turkeys, guineas, feathers, beeswax, honey, ginseng, maple sugar, and molasses produced on Clay County's postbellum farms, only corn was grown for market.[15] Thus, agriculture generated neither a sufficient quantity of buying power in local markets nor a sufficient infusion of cash from export and extralocal markets to stimulate indigenous industrial and urban development as in other U.S. farm regions.

Despite postbellum trends toward land equity in Beech Creek, and the stability of wealth distribution in the county as a whole, fairly little wealth was generated in Clay County in the decades after the local salt industry began to decline. The lack of economic diversification and the decrease in the productivity of subsistence agriculture caused Clay County's economy to stagnate in the postbellum decades and its wealthholding to deteriorate. In 1850, the average Beech Creek household owned land worth $1,022; by 1870, this had dropped to $467 (in constant dollars). Total property declined even more dramatically, from an average of $1,342 in 1860 to a mere $361 by 1892. These property levels were substantially lower than those in other regions. Beech Creek farmers at their peaks of earning power, between the ages 48 of 62, averaged estates of $1,998 in 1860, almost $600 below the U.S. average and $1,980 below that of free males in the South. At roughly comparable peak ages of accumulation, mature farmers' estates in the Northeast were worth $4,200, whereas in the Midwest, estates averaged $3,550. Only one member of the Beech Creek community, Adoniram Andrews III, had an estate valued above $5,000 in 1860, but one-fourth of all the farm households in the state of Texas were worth that much or more the same year.[16]

Lacking the capital to finance extensive transportation systems or commercial farming endeavors, nineteenth-century farmers in Beech Creek and Clay County made the best living they could through subsistence agriculture. But theirs was increasingly a journey from prosperity to poverty and to deepening economic and geographical isolation.

Commerce and Markets

Neither agriculture nor salt launched Clay County as an industrial region. But what of the county's other, if limited, economic sectors? Why was the county unable to capitalize on the commercial and mercantile networks that supported local development in other regions of the United States? To fully understand the nature of local economic stagnation – a road to Clay County's contemporary poverty – we need to look also at the nature of its early commercial ventures and local markets. In so doing, we can uncover not only the indigenous obstacles to development, but also the complicated relationships between local and national economies that shaped Clay County's economic progress, and its lack.

Unfortunately, rural Appalachia has left little record of its commercial past. Only one set of postbellum nineteenth-century merchant accounts – the records of Robert Potter, discussed in what follows – still exist for Clay County. But the nature and economic robustness of mercantile activity over this time period can be discerned through manuscript records of the Robert G. Dun (later Dun and Bradstreet) credit rating company. Between 1840 and 1880, about seventy-five individuals engaged in business enterprises to a great enough extent that businesses outside the mountains wanted information on their credit worthiness, earning them a visit from a Dun credit rater. In the words of an historian of the South, Dun representatives "came to town, visited stores, talked with people who knew of important information – marital difficulties, drinking problems, a propensity to gamble, a rich father-in-law, a spendthrift son – and sent a report to headquarters." At Dun headquarters, "[a]ll the tangible and intangible evidence, sifted and reduced, emerged in the books as a letter and a number."[17]

Dun records chart mercantile careers in Clay County that rose and fell with trends in the salt industry and national economy. Seven merchants were operating in 1850, but of this group, only Hugh White, Robert Potter, and

Edward Gibson remained in 1870 when the salt industry was only a shadow of its antebellum strength. For the most part, Clay County's postbellum merchants were engaged in very small and economically marginal enterprises, indicated both by their poor credit ratings and the fact that few were listed by census takers as full-time merchants. Tyra Gibson, who owned a 300-acre farm and three slaves in 1858, was listed in Dun records as doing a "small business" that year on Otter Creek with about $700 of capital. John Gilbert was operating a "safe but small business" in Manchester the same year with $2,000 capital. Reuben and James Baker, who owned a general store on Goose Creek, were described in 1870 as "good and prompt [in paying their debts] but small capital." They did not merit a listing as merchants in the 1870 census. By 1876, they had "quit business." Similarly, Elizabeth Benge operated a general store at Houses Store, Kentucky, with "small capital." Creed Rowland and Thomas Brown, who owned a dry goods store on Horse Creek from 1870 until at least 1880, were "perfectly safe" but did "not trade largely." The firm of Coldiron and Hornsley on Laurel Creek was described as "good but pressed."[18]

Most who received Dun reports had entries for only a few years. A good number of them went broke. Robert Allen and Nathan McDowell were described as "doing a thriving business and making money" on Buffalo Creek in 1857, but by 1863, Robert Allen's credit was "not good" and he was out of business the following year. Merchants Gilbert and Runs operated a grocery and dry goods business in Manchester for only one year before returning to Tennessee in 1865. William McDaniel, a man with "small capital," began selling dry goods and groceries in Manchester in 1864 but was "broke" by the summer of 1868. John S. M. Dickinson and James Smith, also of Manchester, suspended business the same summer and were "thought to be embarrassed." The druggist firm of Mills and Morgan on Laurel Creek was described as "punctual" in 1870 but "broke" in 1871. William Cook and M. G. Horton, merchants on Goose Creek, went out of business in 1867 after only two or three years.

New merchants were attracted to Clay County later in the 1870s, but they, too, experienced uneven results. At age twenty-two, Henry Lezinski, married to a granddaughter of Daniel Garrard, came from Louisville in 1857 to operate a grocery store in Manchester. In 1878, he was described as having $3,500 in capital invested in his business, but in 1880, he sold out and returned to Louisville. John Garnett came to Clay County from Madison County (near Lexington) in 1878 to open a store at Houses Store, but in 1879, there was "no such man here." J. J. Brooks, age twenty-three, and his twenty-one-year-old brother came to Manchester from West Vernon, Kentucky, in

1874 to open a pharmacy, but by 1877, they had relocated in Richmond, Kentucky. J. L. Yeager and his brother went broke on Otter Creek in 1877.

Even merchants with considerably greater experience or assets found those to be difficult times. John Lucas had done business in Clay County since at least 1855 but went broke in 1877. In 1873, John Link, in business since 1853, had $15,000 capital invested in a general store and flour mill at Houses Store and owned $10,000 "clear" in real estate. Although these assets placed him considerably above many of the county's merchants and businessmen, by 1878, he had been "pressed for some time" with several judgments made against him. In 1879, he was "hard pressed," and by the spring of 1880, he was described as "embarrassed and becoming intemperate." Ed Gibson operated a successful general store in Manchester and weathered the decade of the 1870s only by drawing on his thriving farm operation run largely by tenant labor.

Despite this bleak picture, however, a few merchants did well in Clay County and a handful grew to be very wealthy by local standards. John Hyden, an antebellum merchant, slave owner, and one of the few southern sympathizers in the county,[19] took his slaves with him to Virginia during the Civil War and returned to do business in Clay County in 1869 after spending a few years in Missouri. In 1875, he was described in the Dun manuscripts as "wealthy for the county" with an estimated worth of $10,000. In 1880, he remained a "wealthy man . . . experienced . . . and safe." Paul House, who operated a general store at Houses Store, Kentucky, from 1866 until at least 1880, was described as a "good, desirable customer" owning $4,000 in real estate. W. J. Candell – listed in the 1880 population census as a merchant and in the farm census as owning a $1,250 farm – operated a store at the mouth of Big Creek near Manchester for a good number of years and was described by the Dun correspondent in 1880 as "a merchant of considerable experience" who "owns valuable real estate."

In an important study of economic development in the southeastern Kentucky coal mining counties of Floyd, Perry, and Harlan, Mary Beth Pudup has shown that "middle class formation was supported by the twin pillars of longevity and kinship." She writes: "The intersection of professional occupation, political office, county-seat residence, and property ownership – all within the compass of a certain few families – was the rule, not the exception, governing middle-class formation in southeast Kentucky."[20] So, too, in Clay County were kinship connections fundamental to the success of local merchants.

John Gilbert's business prospects were good in 1856 because he began business in partnership with, and later succeeded, his father Felix Gilbert whose estimated worth in land and slaves was $20,000 when he died in 1859. His marriage to the daughter of a "wealthy" man in the Virginia mountains in 1860 only helped to buttress his economic assets and prospects before poor health forced an early retirement. When W. J. Candell (earlier) commenced business in 1873, he was described as "a young man of good habits and business capacity and fine promise although not wealthy." That "promise" was secured two years later when he married the daughter of his partner, Hiram Marcum, a "sober, industrious money-making man" who had been active as a merchant in the 1850s and 1860s and owned $12,000 worth of property at the time of his daughter's marriage.

Even more important for the commercial success of postbellum merchants were family connections with men who had prospered during the peak of the antebellum salt trade. The case of Hugh L. White illustrates the fact that a prior generation's accumulation of wealth could be translated into new levels of economic achievement, even during bad times. Landless except for a $600 town lot in Manchester, Hugh L. White owned $2,000 capital in his merchandising business in 1860 as well as another $2,500 in notes, cash, and credit. Even more important than these considerable assets, however, was the fact that he was a grandson of the salt manufacturer Hugh White. Although the Dun correspondent had reported in 1861 that the "times are desperately hard here now," in 1864, he called Hugh L. White "the best merchant in the mountains of Kentucky" and reported that he had "made from $15,000 to $20,000 in dry goods within the last three years" and was then worth about $40,000. During the 1870s, White was described as being "very wealthy" with real estate and "a great deal of stock in good banks." (His descendant J. H. White was the president of the First National Bank of Manchester in 1907.)

Beverly P. White's success stands out for having been accomplished largely on the basis of the potential for accumulation that trade could bring for at least a small number of persons. Yet he, too, had kinship connections that were called on to influence his success. The son of antebellum merchant Benjamin F. White, Beverly P. White first appeared as a merchant in the 1880 census when he was age 38. Dun manuscript records for White, however, date back to 1867 when he was operating a store in Manchester with funds provided by his sister-in-law, Martha Ramsey. Ramsey, a granddaughter of Daniel Garrard, was the widow of C. C. Ramsey, a "good trader," who died in 1863 leaving his wife "good town property and a good farm" besides the capital in his grocery and merchandising business. In 1867, she married William Letcher White. By January of 1873, Beverly P. White was "selling more goods than any man in the county" and – owning $5,000 in real estate – was considered "wealthy for this county." In June of the same year, he entered partnership with his much wealthier relative, Hugh L. White. Their joint venture lasted little more than a year before being dissolved and Beverly P. White commenced business briefly with Robert Potter. Their firm, too, lasted for only a year or so before B. P. returned to business on his own. That same year, the *Dun and Company Reference Book* gave him a "good" credit rating for $10,000 to $25,000. In 1890, his credit was still good for that amount.

White's career shows that a moderate amount of wealth could be accumulated through commercial activities in Clay County during the 1870s. With starting capital provided by his sister-in-law and business associations bequeathed him by his father, White established a successful merchandising enterprise and won respect among the small middle class in the county. In the late 1870s, his economic position translated into political power as well when he won office as the presiding judge of the Clay County court.

Although White was able to parlay family advantage into financial success, the very different career of Clay County merchant Robert Potter shows that even a favored-class position and good connections were not guarantees of economic invulnerability in Clay County. His dramatic rise and fall demonstrates that the financial fortunes of Clay County's merchants were not simply the product of local economic circumstances, but also reflected the cyclical nature of distant financial and consumer markets.

Robert Potter's prospects were great in 1858 when he began his business career at age nineteen, principally because he was the son of Barton Potter, described by Dun and Company as a "rich, smart, and clever Yankee from Massachusetts" who had "made his wealth himself." In 1854, Barton Potter had been engaged in a "large and profitable [tanning] business" that was "increasing capital rapidly." Having already been in business for twenty years, including salt manufacturing in the 1840s, his estimated worth was $40,000. Described in 1863 as "one of the oldest merchants in the mountains," he bequeathed a great estate to his son Robert on his death in 1867. Three years later, Robert liquidated much of his late father's farming operations to concentrate on running his Manchester store. And Robert's personal fortune increased again in 1872 when his mother Elizabeth transferred to him all her property in exchange for a support payment of $1,000 a year. The following year, the Dun credit rater predicted that Robert Potter would "be the wealthiest man in the mountains of Kentucky in a few years." In 1874, the Dun representative described Robert Potter as "the wealthiest man of his age in this part of the state" with an estimated worth of $40,000 to $50,000. By 1876, when his estimated worth was "near $60,000," his "good" rating for credit between $50,000 and $100,000 surpassed even that of T. T. Garrard.[21]

Rare surviving logs of daily transactions and accounts at Robert Potter's store from the 1870s into the 1890s[22] – which register 1,427 account transactions – preserve a detailed record of Robert's financial dealings. Like other Southern merchants,[23] Potter transacted few of his exchanges with money. Most exchanges were on credit, sometimes secured with mortgages on land, animals, or other possessions; other times they were reimbursed through periodic work around the store or his farm or paid with bull calves, turkeys, hogs, corn, mares, mules, hay, or whiskey barrels. As did Hugh White a generation earlier, Potter's store functioned also as a quasi-bank, buying and issuing credit for various currencies and notes, including promissory notes, jury claims, and checks and providing cash to his customers. During normal times, Potter also acted as a loan agent, permitting his customers' accounts to carry sizeable amounts of debt over extended periods of time.

Potter's store sold large quantities of food to its mostly local customers. At his store, it was possible to buy a great variety of foods not grown locally (such as coffee, sugar, mustard, pepper, spices, ginger, and lemons) and foods processed or manufactured elsewhere (candy, soda, vinegar, crackers, and flour). That not all Clay Countians had access to land, however, is underscored by the large amounts of locally produced foods also sold at Potter's store, such things as peaches, apples, potatoes, onions, molasses, salt, and eggs, as well as bacon and beef.

Potter also carried a wide range of medicines, including pain killers, castor oil, cinnamon bark, gargling oil, liniment, strengthening cordial, God's cordial, Bates drops, various pills, sulphur iodine, bitters, and balsam of nitre, suggesting that traditional healing methods and products were giving way to new, highly advertised, medical goods. Consumer demand for household items also seemed robust, as Potter sold items ranging from kitchenware (silverware, dishes, bottles, sifters, tinware, coffee mills, stoveware, and tea kettles) to general products for the household, like matches, washboards, lamp chimneys, string, buckets, and irons. Goods that in an earlier era were manufactured at home (soap, candles, and brooms) or retrieved from the ground (coal) could now be purchased from Potter. Luxury goods had made their way to Clay County as well. Potter's shelves featured snuff, pipes, spectacle cases, hairbrushes, combs, and satchels. By the end of the nineteenth century, Potter's store even dealt in expensive consumer durables: sewing machines, organs, and cooking stoves.[24]

In postbellum Clay County, most people continued to make their own clothes at home even as clothing was readily available for sale. From Potter, it was possible to buy ready-to-wear leggings, hats, shirts, and belts, but also to buy the materials for home manufacture of clothing: ribbon, thimbles, shirt fronts, collars, binding, feathers, batting, tacks, blocking, needles, calico thread, buttons, and pins, fabrics like alpaca, wool, and flannel, and popular dies like indigo.[25] Finished boots and shoes could be purchased, but also the materials for shoemaking: hide and shoe leather, heel plates, and shoe knives. Despite the high illiteracy among Clay Countians, Potter's store carried pens, lead, blank writing books, history books, grammar books, readers, and general books and served as the local post office.

For local farmers, Potter offered a range of farm implements and services, including animals (bay horses, mares, cows, and heifers), hunting and fishing supplies (fish lines and buckshot), horse and team supplies (stirrups, side saddles, and axle grease), building supplies (hand axes and handsaws, hammers, paintbrushes, padlocks, chains, augers, drills, bolts, nails, and hinges), and logs and boards from nearby sawmills. Potter's store also served as a labor exchange, taking contract for services such as wagon repair, rental of horses and wagons, drilling, and hauling hay or corn.

With cash still scarce in Clay County in the latter half of the nineteenth century, transactions at Potter's store involved a variety of different strategies of exchange. The strategies of James Hibbard, a young, single, illiterate, and landless farm laborer who purchased items from Potter's store three or four times a week, were typical of those used by Clay Countians of limited means. Although he lived with Isaac Swafford, for whom he worked as a farm laborer, Hibbard apparently did not have full access to Swafford's meals since he regularly bought foods produced on Swafford's farm, including small amounts of beef, pork, and bacon. Between August 1876 and May 1879, Hibbard also bought coffee, medicines, spices, farm implements, and shoes and used Potter's store as a bank, withdrawing cash and securing payment of debts to other people.

Like others of modest means, Hibbard repaid Potter with his own labor, generally earning a credit of $1 a day. His transactions of October 1876 were typical. On October 3, Hibbard borrowed $4 from Potter to pay the Clay County merchant Henry Lezinski. The next day he bought salt, mutton, and shoe pegs for a total of $1.45, and two days later, a bucket and beef for $1.76. He then was credited $8.50 for 8.5 days of work. Between October 10 and 19, Hibbing bought more beef and coffee, borrowed funds from Potter to pay two other debts, and received credit for another four days of work. As his debts grew, Hibbard's work for Potter increased dramatically. By 1879, he essentially had become Potter's employee, working a full 26.5 days in March 1879. Apparently, this strategy was successful. Hibbard's debt to Potter never exceeded $5 and, unlike many of Potter's customers, he was never sued by Potter for outstanding debts.[26]

The account of Levi Andrews, a moderately prosperous farmer in Beech Creek with a family of seven, shows that different strategies of exchange were possible for those with some means. Andrews paid his debts by selling Potter molasses and ox calves, and by assigning to Potter $32 of his own claims on debtors. Over a nine-month period in 1876–7, this strategy garnered Andrews $126. Unlike Hibbard's purchases of basic foodstuffs, Andrews was able to buy luxury items like shoe polish and candy, as well as farm equipment. His farm must have produced well since Andrews bought no foods except apples and spices. In contrast to the continuing work that he demanded of poor customers, Potter was willing to extend greater credit to men of means. Typically, Andrews carried a balance of more than $350 at Potter's store. When his account ended in June of 1877, he still owed Potter $220.[27]

Like other Clay County merchants, Potter differentiated financially between whites and African Americans as employees, but not as customers. For example, John Herd, a landless African American farm laborer living in a white-headed household, patronized Potter's store in 1886. His account shows small purchases of bacon and meats, tobacco, salt, molasses, and coffee and withdrawals of cash. For these, he paid the same prices as did white customers. As he worked to repay his debts to Potter, however, Herd was at a decided disadvantage. For his forty-seven days of labor in 1886, he was credited only $23.50, half the customary wage paid for work by white debtors.[28]

The networks of indebtedness that bound Potter and his customers (and also Potter and his creditors and suppliers) served as local currency in Clay County. Debts were incurred and paid through complicated exchanges of goods and labor. Although this system was highly practical in a cash-poor economy, it also was fragile. At Barton Potter's death in 1867, the bulk of his massive estate consisted of debts that others owed him, some many years in default. As his estate was settled, his widow Elizabeth correctly predicted a "great loss" if each debtor were pressed for immediate settlement and authorized her son Robert, as administrator of the estate, to "indulge debtors and extend the time of payment."[29]

The barter- and labor-based system of exchange at Potter's store, and throughout much of rural Appalachian in the nineteenth century, is often taken as an indication of the region's economic insularity from national and international financial systems. Despite the low level of currency in circulation at Potter's store, however, an examination of Potter's accounts and lawsuits during the mid-1870s makes it clear that Clay County was firmly integrated into larger networks of commerce and finance.

When the national financial panic of 1873 hit Clay County, it sent reverberations through the webs of liabilities that bound Potter to his customers and suppliers. In a single year, land prices in the county tumbled more than

50%, from an average of $2.16 an acre in 1872 to $1.07 an acre in 1873; prices did not recover for more than a decade. Collapsing real estate values were a disaster for merchants like Potter who held large numbers of mortgages. In 1877, the Dun representative noted that Potter was said to be carrying a heavy load of "unproductive real estate" and it was reported that "those who have known him for years do not now care for his trade." Later the same year, he was described as being "rather embarrassed," perhaps due to the court-ordered auction of his land to satisfy debts of more than $13,000, but the rater nonetheless predicted that he would "come out all right." However, in 1878, the Dun correspondent reporter estimated that it would take all his property to pay his debts and the Dun ratings published shortly thereafter no longer listed him as a Clay County businessman. Adding to Potter's troubles was the 1878 arrest of his nephew Barton P. Simpson for the murder of James White, requiring substantial family funds and the assumption of additional debt for bail and attorneys.[30]

The cause of Potter's collapse can be found in the linkages between Clay County's economy and the national structure of finance and commerce in which it was embedded. Despite its integration into national markets, Clay County's economic practices relied on the local circulation of debts and credit as well as on forms of barter exchange that had long ago been eroded by the circulation of money in most regions of the nation. But when the national panic of 1873 sent land values tumbling, thus undermining the value of mortgage debts, Potter could no longer sustain the extensive network of barter, debt, and delayed repayment on which many of his patrons had come to rely and on which much of the local economy depended. Abruptly, the terms of Potter's loans changed, with dire consequences for many in the county. In 1878, Potter sued William Begley to force repayment of a mere $31.80 remaining on a promissory note issued that same year, although Begley had carried a $60 debt for a much longer period two years earlier.[31]

Although Potter would extend loans for long periods when he was financially stable, he was quick to sue those who owed him money during times of national financial panics and recessions. Between 1835 and 1919, the Potter family (including Robert, his parents, and his wife) filed 199 lawsuits in Clay County Circuit Court. Few of these cases were filed in the early years. The Potters's litigation peaked in the early 1870s, and then again in the aftermath of the 1893 depression, largely in the form of cases to force payment of delinquent promissory notes or real estate mortgages. As wealthy plaintiffs, the Potters almost always won civil suits against their debtors. Most of Potters's defendants were compelled to auction their land to satisfy the court judgments.

As he tried to stave off financial collapse, Potter also took advantage of his status and legal savvy to extract payment from his debtors through more coercive means. In a particularly well-documented incident, Potter rode to the home of an elderly couple who owed a $1,500 mortgage to his father, Barton, and demanded immediate payment. The couple agreed to forfeit most of their land, excepting their home, which was protected from seizure for debt by state homestead acts. Since they could not read or write, the couple asked Potter to write a deed conveying their homestead to their daughter. Apparently without their knowledge, Potter instead wrote the deed to transfer the couple's homestead to his own wife, Nancy.[32]

Potter's efforts to regain his financial footing victimized members of his family as well as his customers and debtors. When Robert's mother Elizabeth died in 1881, she bequeathed her estate to Robert, another son (James) and a son-in-law (William Simpson). Perhaps to repay debt, James and William transferred their shares of Elizabeth's real estate holdings to Robert, but they retained superior liens on the land to prevent it from being seized by Robert's creditors. The effect on James was severe. When he forfeited his mother's land, James became propertyless and was forced to survive as a tenant farmer. Shortly thereafter, his wife died and an accident resulted in the loss of one of his hands, leaving him unable to farm and without means of support. Desperate, James turned to Robert, insisting that his brother return some of their mother's land. Robert refused and instead transferred the most valuable parcels of land to his wife Nancy. Frustrated and nearly destitute, James's children then sued Nancy Potter, testifying that Robert's actions had left them homeless and unable to obtain a "good English education." The lawsuit continued in court for almost twenty years. Eventually, James's family was awarded a paltry $2,900 judgment against Robert, but collected only $1,500 from the then late Robert Potter's estate.[33]

By the late 1870s, Potter's failing finances attracted the attention of his creditors. Local elites had provided much of the capital that sustained Potter's business and, as it declined, Potter faced Clay County's most prominent families in court. The Whites began legal proceedings against Potter to collect on outstanding notes, forcing Potter to sell tracts of land to cover his debts. A. M. Combs also turned to the legal system to protect himself against a financial catastrophe with Potter's collapse, battling Potter and his estate in court for over twenty years and forcing to judicial sale numerous tracts in three counties owned by Potter and his debtors.[34]

By 1879, in the face of enormous sums still owed to A. M. Combs and many others, Potter had little choice but to file for bankruptcy. Although he still had vast real estate holdings, depressed prices for land continued to undermine Potter's ability to repay his debts.[35] Faced with imminent receivership, Potter seized on his wife's financial independence as a way to protect some of his business assets. With Robert insolvent and his estate in receivership, Nancy now became a major economic actor in Clay County.

From the beginning, Nancy proved herself to be a shrewd businesswoman, a judgment shared by her descendants. When Robert's receivers forced the sale of mortgaged land to recover debts owed to the Potter business, she attended the commissioner's auctions and purchased land at deep discounts.[36] In the first years after Robert's collapse, Nancy could not raise enough funds even to pay the sales bonds on these tracts, and she often forfeited her purchases. But, drawing on her contacts with Clay County's financial elite, Nancy convinced Vincent Boreing, president of the Bank of London, a buyer for the New Jersey–based New York and Kentucky Land Company and later a congressman from 1899 to 1903, and other local elites to act as backers on her sale bonds. This allowed her to retain her purchases and thereby acquire a large amount of land, even as Robert's financial empire was in decline. When land prices escalated in the early 1890s, Nancy sold this real estate at a tremendous profit.[37]

Nancy aggressively pursued a variety of financial options available to a person of means in nineteenth-century Clay County. By leveraging her real estate holdings, she was able to buy unpaid judgments against propertyless debtors at public auctions and to hold these, often for years, awaiting subsequent property purchases against which she could levy at a substantial profit. Even while her husband's estate was in receivership, Nancy was an active litigator against Robert's debtors. She sued to force the sale of land, raft logs, and other property, actions that continued well after Robert's death in 1896. Not even the county's most powerful families were immune from Nancy's efforts to regain her financial standing. In 1899, a local judge and three others had given bond for W. H. Treadway, a debtor of Potter. When one of the group could not pay on the bond, Nancy levied on his Manchester house and store, forced them to be sold at a commissioner auction, and then bought the properties herself.[38]

Nancy was also an astute entrepreneur, moving her assets to take advantage of Clay County's changing economy. As real estate began to recover its value, she began to buy and sell land. When timbering became profitable, she contracted with local loggers and raftsmen to cut trees and deliver them to market. As late as 1922, at the age of eighty-three, she continued to deal in real estate, careful to reserve for herself the now valuable coal and mineral rights. According to one family member, Nancy's entrepreneurship was so successful that her descendants were able to live off the proceeds of her estate well into the mid-twentieth century.[39]

Nancy was not alone among women from Clay County's elite families in her involvement in business and commerce. Until late in the nineteenth century, Kentucky law did not permit married women to control their own property.[40] Women from financially powerful families, however, were able to evade these restrictions by petitioning the court to have themselves declared "femme sole," thus be able to control their financial affairs independently. Ellen C. Jett Lyttle, the wife of David Yancey Lyttle, a lawyer, farmer, and Democratic state senator, is an example. In 1879, Ellen and David jointly filed a suit in equity stating that Ellen had property from her father's estate and that she "be empowered to use, enjoy, sell and convey, for her own benefit any property that she may now own or hereafter acquire free from the choice of her husband." The court granted the petition, allowing Ellen to "make contracts as a single woman, sue and be sued, to trade in her own name, to dispose of her property by will or deed free from the control of her husband and in regard to the disposition of her property [have] all the rights and privileges and powers of a femme sole."[41] Ellen exercised her newly acquired independent legal status to deal in real estate. When she died in 1890, her estate included land holdings in four counties.[42]

An equally striking example of Clay County's women entrepreneurs is that of Martha Coldiron Hogg, who gave the land on which Oneida Baptist College was built. Martha's first husband, Calvin L. Coldiron, died in 1892, leaving Martha with a sizeable estate that she determined to retain and manage herself. When she decided to marry Stephen P. Hogg, the county judge of neighboring Owsley County and the 1891 Kentucky constitutional convention delegate from Clay and Owsley Counties, she convinced him to sign a prenuptial agreement, stating that she would retain ownership of all her real and personal property and have the ability to transact financial matters on her own.[43] Martha and Stephen then filed a petition in court to have Martha declared a "femme sole" so that she might "continue to have, own and control for her own separate use and benefit all the real and personal property she now owns and all the profits and increase of so . . . also to all the property and . . . she may hereafter buy or become possessed of, in any way and she reserves the full right to own, control, buy and sell said property as she chooses."[44]

As a married woman, and later as a widow, Martha wielded major financial power in Clay County. Like her male counterparts, Martha kept close ties to local politicians by posting bonds for deputy sheriffs. She also profited by the time-honored practices of other financial elites, increasing her fortune considerably by foreclosing on property and by buying undervalued real estate at court-ordered auctions to resell it for a profit.[45] In 1895, for example, Martha acted as surety for a $100 land purchase by Lucy Collins. When Lucy defaulted, Martha quickly repossessed the land and sold it at a 50% profit to

Beverly P. White.[46] The following year, Martha purchased land from Samuel Combs at a Manchester sheriff's auction for $500, less than two-thirds of its appraised value.[47]

Martha showed little hesitancy to use the courts to defend her financial interests. One series of transactions is especially revealing. In 1896, Martha rented a farm on Red Bird to A. B. Howard, the former sheriff and a central actor in the 1890s feud discussed in the next chapter. In their precise rental agreement, Martha agreed to rent to Howard for one year; in turn, Howard was to pay her 900 bushels of "good average corn" harvested "at the usual gathering time . . . and put up in good condition in a new barn" as well as to sow oats and grass seed, paying Martha one-third of the oat crop. Despite the stipulation that he would raise crops himself on the farm, Howard sublet the farm to Jules Webb, James B. Howard, Steven Barrett, and Andy Howard, who then refused to provide Martha with a share of their crops. Martha immediately brought a civil suit against the renters, charging that the subletters "are threatening to and will unless prevented destroy and dispose of the corn raised upon said farm." Further, Martha charged that all of them were insolvent and demanded an attachment against their crops to ensure her payment.[48]

Even Martha's grant of land to a local private academy, which made her a legendary figure in the 1890s feud, reflected painstaking efforts to control the disposition of her property. In two separate deeds in 1899, she conveyed one-quarter acre valued at $25 to the college for the construction of a school building. She specified that the school building must be worth not less than $600, that it must be built within two years, and that the college must use the building only for school or church purposes. Martha also donated an additional ten acres worth $1,000, stipulating that the college must erect a school building worth not less than $5,000 within ten years, that the building must open onto a street fifty feet wide, and that no other buildings could be built on the land. Moreover, Martha retained a lien on the land and specified that the property would revert to her if the school closed.[49]

The economic successes of Nancy Potter, Ellen Lyttle, and Martha Coldiron Hogg, however counter to stereotypes of mountain women in the late nineteenth century, paralleled those of their male counterparts in one respect: They were wrought largely through speculative financial investments, ventures that left little lasting mark on the local economy. Describing the southern Appalachian region, Pudup noted that, "[s]ubsistence production and barter terms of trade did not permit local accumulation of money capital. Both direct producers [farmers] and nonproducers [merchants], therefore, lacked the financial means to become a vanguard class and to finance regional capitalist development."[50] In Clay County, as elsewhere in

Appalachia, commerce (like agriculture) provided a prosperous life for some, a marginal livelihood for many. But commerce based on the local exchange of goods and services – like production based on home consumption – provided little means to accumulate substantial local capital.

Practices of barter and credit – prevalent during the cash-poor decades after the Civil War – began to decline in the late nineteenth century as exploration of Clay County's natural resources brought outside capitalists and additional cash into the area and created demand for new businesses. Signs of change in the local economy, however, were slow to emerge. Capitalizing on the presence of early timber and land scouts, Clay County's first hotel (the Lucas Hotel in Manchester) opened in 1877, but as late as 1880, only ten full-time merchants, including a father-and-son partnership, appear in the census. It was not until 1887, well into the lumber boom, that a tiny liquor store and a small millinery opened in Manchester, becoming the first businesses other than sawmills, general stores, and pharmacies to operate in the county. It was nearly a decade later that other establishments opened, first the Bank of Manchester in 1895 backed by the money of T. T. and Gilbert Garrard and two men from London, Kentucky, then a jeweler in 1899, followed by a publisher, printer, and telephone company. Even by comparison to other parts of the South, turn-of-the-century Clay County had very few mercantile establishments. Although southern counties in 1900 averaged about 144 stores, Clay County in that year had only 26, most of which were in the vicinity of Manchester except for a tiny general store in the outlying village of Oneida; a mere 36 persons were engaged as merchants.[51]

Throughout the nineteenth century, almost all Clay County merchants operated with very small amounts of capital. Of the Dun credit ratings published in 1900, only one besides T. T. Garrard's evaluation was rated above $2,000 and that was a small timber and merchandising firm rated "fair" for credit up to $5,000. In the context of such a commercial environment, a "good" rating for credit between $50,000 and $100,000 made T. T. Garrard stand out as an economic giant. Thirty-six merchants were also listed in the census of 1910, but only three of them were among the group listed a decade earlier, suggesting that most merchants either failed in business or left the county that decade. In that same year, Clay County had twenty-three manufacturing establishments, but these averaged only $1,023 in capital and twenty employees and generated an average annual value of $2,004.[52]

For much of the nineteenth century, Clay County's immense stands of hard and soft wood, including walnut, cherry, oak, locust, and hickory, were renowned as one of the most intensely timbered areas of Kentucky. Similarly, its coal, iron, and natural gas reserves were well known long before the massive exploitation of these resources began at the turn of the twentieth

century. But low levels of capital in local commerce and agriculture generated little local capital for the huge expense of building an industrial and
transportation infrastructure for large-scale development, including especially the costly enterprise of railroad building. This task would fall to capitalists from outside the region.[53]

Resource Extraction

The exploitation of Clay County's natural resources began long before Mr.
Peabody's coal train reached its borders. Although outside corporations
played a major role in the massive turn-of-the-century plundering of Clay
County, initial forays into resource extraction began much earlier, orches-
trated by its local business and financial elite. As the local salt industry
declined, merchants, salt manufacturers, and landowners looked for opportunities to benefit from whatever economic improvements might increase the
value of their lands. The county's rich timberlands were a prime target. Large
owners like the Whites and the Garrards pursued logging and, later, coal
development. Smaller owners like the Johnsons and Andrews of Beech Creek
sold mineral rights and cut timber on their land or on their neighbors' lands
to float downriver for sale in regional sawmills. Some, including residents of
Beech Creek, even went so far as to subscribe to a railroad company around
the turn of the century that they hoped might build a trunk line through
their property. Timber extraction and sale, like later efforts at coal mining
and natural gas and oil production, involved complicated relationships among
local elites, outside industrial and financial corporations, and the majority of
Clay County's population. Over time, these relationships shaped the nature
of investment, the processes of resource extraction, and the building of transportation in Clay County. In turn, the possibilities and constraints on development transformed economic relationships within the county and between
county and outside actors.

Timber

A certain amount of Clay County's timber was razed long before it became a
viable commodity for large-scale export. Early white settlers burned large
amounts of timber to clear land for planting crops. Salt manufacturers
stripped nearby forests to fuel salt kettles, in the process deforesting vast areas
near the Goose Creek saltworks. As early as the 1840s, timber also began to
have an external market. Local entrepreneurs paid farmers for selective
walnut, yellow poplar, and ash trees located near rivers and streams that they
piloted downstream to sawmills in Frankfort.[54]

The practice of marketing local lumber to sawmills outside the county continued even as timbering became more widespread in the postbellum years. In 1870, only two sawmills, both steam-powered, operated in Clay County. One was owned by T. T. Garrard to provide, in part, timber for his saltworks. Both were fairly small operations with only two employees and an investment of $600 each. Together, the two mills processed $3,200 in lumber annually, less than 20% of the $17,983 worth of timber harvested in the county that year. No large timber producers yet existed in the county. Most of the nineteen farmers listed in the census of agriculture that year as producing timber produced less than $300 annually.[55]

Ten years later, timber production was much more widespread in Clay County, with 80% of all farmers reporting some timber harvesting, compared to less than 35% of farmers in 1870, and a total county production of more than $30,000 in timber. But the inaccessibility of eastern Kentucky's timberlands to rail transportation and the consequent reliance on unpredictable rivers and barely navigable streams to transport logs to mills continued to put severe limits on local timbering. An 1880 census report on the nation's forests described those of eastern Kentucky as "practically uninjured [although] probably unsurpassed in the amount, quality and value." Even as late as 1891, the state agricultural commissioner reported that Clay County's forests were "almost as unbroken as . . . a hundred years ago."[56]

In the early decades of timbering, a few trees were processed at portable sawmills, but most were hauled to a stream or creek and then floated downriver to sawmills, first to Frankfort and later to the Kentucky towns of Jackson, Beattyville, Valley View, and Clay City. To bring timber to waterways, loggers typically built narrow paths, along which as many as eight yoke of oxen would drag (or "snake") logs until they reached a place steep enough to roll them down a hillside. Less frequently, crews built logging roads through the woods and hauled timber out on ox-drawn wagons. At the water, loggers used hand spikes to push timber into the water where it was held behind handmade "splash dams." When the logs were ready to float, gates in the splash dams would be opened, pushing the timber downstream to market. Such logging practices were brutal for loggers and animals alike and left Clay County's land marred by log tramways, snake roads, and hillside log dumps and its creek beds scarred by the remains of splash dams.[57]

In the river, loggers constructed log rafts (or "raaves") from seventy or eighty logs lashed side by side with hickory tie poles and pins, creating rafts 100 to 200 feet long. These huge log rafts, typically driven by a steersman and five crewmen, known as "pikers," were carried downstream on river tides.[58] Adventurous loggers might attempt a raft trip as early as February or as late as November, hoping to garner extra cash. But these trips were dangerous and risky. Ice-coated logs were difficult to stand on and timber could not be notched for safety without lowering the value of the logs. Moreover, ice-filled rivers could crush a timber crop. Thus, most logs were cut in autumn and winter and brought to market with the spring floods, known locally as "tides."

The first spring tide, usually in March or April, was described by one observer as "the most exciting time of the whole year." Streams swelled and crowds "gathered on the creek bank to watch the raftsmen depart." As one crew left, "other loggers were assembling more, many of them standing up to their belts in icy water. Some men were up on the hillsides 'snaking' more logs down to the river with oxen."[59] Since log rafts at best traveled about four miles an hour, and only during daylight, the trip to Frankfort took a week to complete. Steersmen guided the rafts by memorizing all landmarks on the river and stream. Among raftsmen, "[p]ractically every twist and turn of the river, as well as certain rapids, bars, and eddies had been given their own special names." Along the way, raftsmen camped on their rafts or stopped at riverside farm houses for meals and shelter. Once in Frankfort, river men collected their wages and profits and, flush with cash, turned to Frankfort's many saloons and its notorious gambling parlors and houses of prostitution before walking home, or later, making their way by train to London and by foot back to Clay County.[60]

Rafting logs was an arduous and risky proposition. One logman remembered leaving one April after "[r]ain had fallen during the night and the river had swollen into a tide." A high river gave the promise of a quick trip, but also meant that "logs were water-soaked which made it difficult to steer." Nonetheless, the crew left, with "one of the best river men as our steersman. He chose his own men, six of them, and the raft was unloosed on rising water." At the last leg of their journey, however, tragedy struck. The raft "began to 'bow' and turn," throwing the crew into the deep, churning water where they grasped for submerged branches, and watched helplessly as the raft "went on into the South Fork and broke up."[61]

Particularly dangerous stretches of river required those with special skills and provided opportunities for additional money. Daring, or cash-hungry, men would offer to take log rafts down these stretches, then walk back to solicit another trip. One notable area was the "narrows," a long gorge in Clay County between two cliffs on the South Fork. Generally acknowledged to be the most treacherous mile of navigable water around, the narrows caused breakers six to ten feet high. A logman recalled that

> the sound of the breakers was so great that the crew could not even hear
> the screams of the steersman in his effort to tell them how to pull at

the oars. One man usually stood in the middle of the raft with all the coats and valuables held as high as he could hold them. Water splashed through the cracks of the logs as high as 6 feet. At times men have floated off clinging to an oar and have been picked up in the "basin" just below this great gorge, drowned or badly bruised by the rocks.

When a raft entered the narrows, "it took hard fighting on the part of the logmen to bring it through right side up and with its spine in good condition," and when a raft capsized, "it sometimes took a luckless piker to a watery grave. The slightest mistake on the part of the steersman resulted in a calamity."[62]

Even in the early decades, labor arrangements for harvesting and marketing lumber varied. Some farmers controlled the entire timbering process, cutting their own trees and floating them to market. Since most harvesting took place during slack periods in agriculture, however, most landowners hired local farmers or farm laborers to do part of the labor. Men were hired to cut trees and to haul logs to the head of a creek where representatives of timbering companies and independent entrepreneurs bought logs at a price that would ensure the owner a small profit. More money could be made by those willing to float their own logs to Frankfort, but this strategy left the landowner vulnerable to the vagrancies of weather and rains.[63]

To reduce their financial risk further, many landowners subcontracted even more of their timbering. Landowners sold timber to a local contractor or to a scout for a timber company who paid cutters to harvest the trees and saw them into logs. Timber was generally purchased standing, by the tree or by the cut board measure, and prices varied tremendously for different types of trees. Many hardwoods were highly valued and could fetch a good price, but trees like low-grade poplar sold for little more than the cost of labor to haul it to a stream. Contractors then arranged with a team of haulers to drag the logs to a river in exchange for one-half of the timber. At riverside, the logs were sold to another agent who bargained with a timber company to float the logs to a mill.[64]

The days of river transport by independent raftsmen and selective cutting by local timber contractors, however, were short-lived. Corporations that sought to benefit from Appalachia's rich timberlands saw local control over timbering as intolerably wasteful and inefficient. When timber was purchased "on the stump" from local landowners, both its price and supply were unpredictable, creating problems for sawmills and for the eventual timber buyers. Too many logs became waterlogged on the river during the journey to the sawmill, were lost as splash dams collapsed, or fell prey to timber thieves. As Eller points out, such uncertainties convinced many timber companies of the advantages of controlling all aspects of lumber production themselves and this they did by "acquiring tracts of timberlands in unexploited areas of the mountains, [then] hiring a logging crew, opening a sawmill, and constructing a timber camp."[65]

As the railroads reached into the southern Appalachian mountains, though not as yet into Clay County, in the late nineteenth century, larger corporations arrived as well, beginning a period of massive systematic timbering. Between the late 1880s and 1920, vast tracts of mountain timberland were felled in a frenzy of profit taking. Burt and Brabb Lumber Company, a Michigan firm that bought out the lumber interests of local timber titan Thomas Jefferson Asher, contracted for 602,817 board feet of Appalachian pine and poplar in a single float contract in 1890. Although a railroad line would not penetrate its borders until well into the twentieth century, Clay County was not immune from the reach of corporate timber giants. Companies bought or leased vast tracts of Clay County land and timber, frequently reserving future rights to subsurface minerals, oil, gas, and coal deposits. Mowbray and Robinson, a Cincinnati firm, purchased 60,000 acres of timberland in Clay and Leslie Counties.[66]

By 1900, the southern Appalachian region was providing 30% of the total hardwood cut in the United States More than 3.5 million board feet of timber were taken from the states of Kentucky, West Virginia, and Tennessee alone. At the peak of timber production in 1909, the region produced four million board feet, or 40% of the U.S. total.[67] This corporate timber harvest resulted in what historians describe as the "wanton destruction of the Southern forests." Eager to maximize investor profits, corporate timber giants made no attempt to preserve young growth or to ensure future forests, and their methods of harvesting left dry forest debris scattered about, fueling massive forest fires and significant erosion of desirable farming bottom lands. The Reverend Dr. A. E. Brown recalled that in 1880, "the forests were untouched . . . the mountains were full of sparkling brooks and creeks." Thirty years later, "many of the mountain streams are dry throughout the summer and fall, while in winter, the waters descend in torrents and do vast damage, rendering worthless the bottom lands which used to be the most desirable for farming purposes."[68]

Corporate plunder of Appalachia's timber also transformed the nature of work in logging. Timbering ceased to be a supplement to agriculture as companies assembled large full-time crews housed in timber camps and logging towns. By 1906, over 10,000 workers were employed in the eastern Kentucky logging industry. Most would never return to now idle farms. Thus, when logging declined in the early decades of the twentieth century, many of these wage-dependent workers formed a ready labor pool for the newly opened coal mines and textile mills of the southeast; others continued the historical migration of the poor out of Appalachia.[69]

Minerals

In 1887, W. H. Horsley, a land agent from the coal fields of western Virginia, visited the homes of farmers in Beech Creek and other Clay County neighborhoods in order to purchase the rights to mineral, oil, gas, and coal resources that lay beneath their land.[70] Elisha Johnson and his sons John, Preston, James, and Alex sold him mineral rights to approximately 1,750 acres in the Beech Creek basin for $700. Horsley also visited the Johnsons's nearby neighbors and kinfolk along the Southfork of the Kentucky River where he acquired mineral rights to 4,825 acres. He bought rights to at least 3,275 acres from various members of the Andrews family. Repeating the same transactions along other tributaries to the Kentucky River such as Sexon Creek, Goose Creek, and Bullskin, Horsley eventually purchased the mineral rights to a total of 72,424 acres on 250 tracts of land in the County. In 1903, he transferred the ownership of these titles to the Kenton Coal and Oil Company for an undisclosed price.[71]

As Alan Banks has shown, the lack of control of land and mineral resources was one of the major obstacles to industrialization that capitalist investors had to overcome before they could profitably develop the vast resources of the Appalachian mountains.[72] Along with corporate timbering, acquisitions like Horsley's – only a small, local example of the massive accumulation of property that absentee capitalists were achieving throughout the mountain region at the time[73] – initiated a new era in Clay County history. No longer would the history of the county be shaped almost exclusively by the dealings of local people. For better or worse, the land and people of Clay County were becoming incorporated more firmly into wider networks of industrial and commercial power.

It is wrong, however, to portray these mountain people as hapless victims blindly handing their fortunes to slick-talking corporate agents.[74] Horsley's offers of forty and fifty cents an acre – for unknown quantities of minerals that local people had no way to mine or sell on their own – must have seemed like a pretty good deal to the Johnsons, the Andrews, and other Clay County farmers at the time. Experienced merchants as well, such as Hiram Marcum and John C. Coldiron, took up Horsley's offer to earn some extra money from their land. Since, according to our analysis of deeds, land in the Beech Creek neighborhoods sold for around $2 an acre in the 1880s, the opportunity to earn 20% of the value of an acre, while retaining rights to the surface, was not an opportunity to be taken lightly.

Despite the fact it is only with considerable hindsight that mountain people's decision to sell their mineral rights can be faulted, it is common for writers to present Appalachian people as the innocent but ignorant victims of outside exploiters. Thus, Harry Caudill claimed that "the mountaineer lack[ed] fundamental knowledge about his land . . ." and was "exceedingly lackadaisical about such things as land titles, taxes, and laws."[75] Similarly, Warren Wright, a prominent opponent of strip mining in East Kentucky, claimed that "[The mountain man] didn't even know what he was selling. . . . Of course, it was a truism that he also didn't care what he was selling. You must understand this if you want to understand eastern Kentucky."[76] The gross stereotyping and, indeed, the latent class hostility that often lurks behind such interpretations, is blatantly asserted by Chid Wright, son of "Devil" John Wright (alternatively an outlaw and a land agent) who said, "Some people would sell the land *and* the mineral rights. I think they were willing to sell it and glad to be rid of it. They didn't have any idea about what they were selling. Not a bit. All the people knew how to do was take a pick and a little black powder and shoot out enough coal to last them through the winter."[77]

But stereotypes about East Kentuckian's ignorance and carelessness about such things as property, land titles, and the law do not hold up to close scrutiny and can be discounted as yet another misleading implication of the internal colonialism and culture-of-poverty models of Appalachian development and their depiction of Appalachians as victims. Even the most cursory examination of the thousands of deeds, wills, mortgages, indentures, and contracts that are registered in every Appalachian courthouse attests to the care with which mountain people sought to secure their economic transactions among neighbors, kin, and business associates.

Often, even understandings within families were publicly recorded, as the following examples from transactions among kinfolk in Beech Creek show. When William Johnson deeded two tracts of land on the Southfork to his minor son Robert in 1865, he noted that he was thereby granting his son, who was then wishing to marry, "the liberty of working for himself and transacting his own affairs." Abel and Nancy Johnson sold 100 acres of land to their sons James and Columbus for $400 in 1877, but reserved for themselves four acres for gardening around the home place and rights to all the timber they would need for the rest of their lives. Similarly, in 1898, when William Johnson's son William B. and his wife Mary deeded property to their adult children Hugh, Laura, John, James, Nancy, and Jane, they formalized the expectation that their children would take care of them throughout the remainder of their lives, "furnishing each of them with suitable diet, clothing, and when sick nursing and medical attendance and at their death to have them decently buried." A provision added that the children's deeds would be "null and void if they fail to perform any part of their contract." Finally, Elisha Johnson's daughter Tina, described by family members as "quare" and "childish," deeded land she had inherited from her father to Govan Jones "to take care of [her] has long as she lives as one of his family." The contract also specified that Tina would "mind and obey" her keeper "in as far as what is right."[78]

Also revealing are Clay County cases involving efforts of women to use legal means to safeguard their land, even against family members. One such case involved a sixty-five-year-old widow who had given one-half interest in her farm to her twenty-year-old son in exchange for managing the farm and providing for her during her lifetime. In 1894, with the help of a prominent local attorney, C. B. Lyttle, she filed a lawsuit against her son, charging that he had failed to provide for her as promised and had sold his interest in the farm to Anderson Baker for $300. Her son, represented by A. W. Baker, countered that he had made no such agreement with his mother and produced a deed showing that he had paid her $100 for the land and use of the upper rooms of her house. Despite this evidence, the court ruled in favor of the mother and voided the land transfer.[79]

Widows especially took care to protect their land legally because without a land base, it was more difficult to extract full care from their adult children. In an 1890 lawsuit over a debtor's note, for example, one of the parties claimed to spend $1.50 a week boarding and caring for his mother-in-law, but noted that she had agreed to work in the household and to furnish articles for her own keep to offset this cost.[80] Also, Ellen C. Lyttle's 1888 will carefully spells out that her daughter was at liberty to take possession of Ellen's land before her death but that she would be required to pay a "reasonable rent" to support her parents until their death.[81]

A series of land transactions by the Howard family illustrates that ordinary people could use property law in complicated and sophisticated ways to their advantage. In 1890, G. T. Howard sold 250 acres to Lee Combs for $5,500, or $22 an acre. Combs paid Howard by giving him title to another parcel of land, owned jointly with A. M. Combs. The following year, G. T.'s parents, Lewis and Elizabeth Howard, sold 204 acres to New York and Kentucky Land Company (NYK), a New Jersey corporation, for $20,320, or nearly $100 an acre. After that, land sales between Combs and the Howards continued for several years, at prices far below what the Howards had been able to command from the land company.

It is tempting to think that the transfers between Combs and Howard were priced below value out of neighborly goodwill. But the reasons were more complex, and far less noble. In 1894, the state of Kentucky sued G. T. and

Lee Howard for fraudulent transfer of land, claiming that both the sale of land to Combs and transfers from Lewis Howard to G. T. were intended to avoid paying $5,000 the Howards owed on a bail bond in Knox County. The state tried to collect the money by forcing a sale of Howard land until A. B. Howard, a relative and sheriff, testified that no land could be sold because the Howards were propertyless. If the Howards were indeed landless, they did not stay that way for long. Within a few years, Lewis and Elizabeth Howard were once more selling land to NYK for $100 an acre.[82]

The Howards were not alone in their savvy dealing with outside investors. Many mountaineers, even those in modest circumstances or in remote areas of the county, realized the potential value of the minerals, oil, and gas that lay beneath their land and negotiated significant prices for these. Even some property owners with virtually no experience in cash land transactions were able to command substantial prices and favorable terms from Horsley and other corporate scouts. The experiences of the Bakers on Crane Creek were not uncommon. As late as 1899, parts of Crane Creek had never been owned by anyone outside the Baker family; all sales were to relatives, a pattern resembling that of Beech Creek described in Chapter 5. Yet this lack of experience with nonfamilial property transactions did not mean that the Bakers were strangers to legal formalities. In fact, all transfers of land, even among kin, had been duly recorded with the county clerk for decades. When Horsley arrived at the home of Thomas Baker, he may have anticipated an easy sale. But Baker was able to secure $15 in cash and an additional $102 when "good deeds are presented" for mineral and mining rights to his 250-acre tract and had the remarkable foresight to conserve some of the coal reserves for himself.[83]

Such actions contrast sharply with one historian's depiction of a mineral buyer "greeted hospitably" by mountain residents who were hungry "for the opportunity for conversation and a change from the rhythms of daily life" who therefore found it difficult to resist when "the traveler would casually produce a bag of coins" for land or mineral rights. This historian may be correct that it "was difficult for the mountaineer to envision the scale and impact of industrial change," but, as the case of Thomas Baker illustrates, mountaineers did make efforts to secure themselves a place in the changing economic order.[84]

If many Clay Countians were able to command nonnegligible amounts for their subsurface rights, within a few years, it was clear that the value of these mineral rights far exceeded these prices. Thomas Baker's sale of subsurface rights in 1887 for forty-seven cents an acre gained him around 20% of the value of the land. A mere four years later, however, a buyer agreed to pay only half of the previously negotiated $5,000 sale price for a tract of land on

Sexton's Creek when he discovered that the mineral rights had earlier been sold to Horsley.[85] In some cases, mineral values were equal to, or even exceeded, the value of the land's surface.

Pressure on Clay Countians to sell their resources mounted as the synergy between railroads and financial and industrial corporations led to a flurry of interest in the resource potential of the county in the 1890s. Corporate fervor for Clay County's minerals and land grew as rumors developed of possible railway development in the county; attention to its minerals spurred further efforts to build rail lines. As early as 1854, the Kentucky state legislature had tried to develop a railway line connecting the Bluegrass to Virginia by transversing the eastern Kentucky coalfields, but these efforts never came to fruition. By the late 1880s, the Louisville and Nashville (L & N) Railroad had been convinced of the potential for coal and timber development in the southern Appalachians and was building rail lines throughout the region, including a line from Corbin to Pineville, although not into Clay County.[86] In 1892, the Kentucky Coal, Iron and Development Corporation obtained 20,435 acres in the county, valued at $94,194. That same year, Kentucky Mineral and Timber (KTM), a New Jersey corporation with offices in New York City, floated a $750 million bond issue, largely through the Western National Bank of New York, to finance 184 separate land purchases, including 40,000 acres in Clay and Leslie Counties.[87] Perhaps following the suggestion of Kentucky Governor Stevenson in 1869 that the state "look to Europe for capital [to] develop our industrial and mineral wealth,"[88] corporations from Europe soon joined the Appalachian landgrab. By 1894, La Societé Anonyme du Centre des Appalaches (Kentucky, U.S.A.), a Belgian corporation, had acquired 72,000 acres in Clay and other southeastern Kentucky counties, secured with a mortgage of $160,000.[89]

With the corporate land rush, property in the county changed hands at a dizzying rate. When A. W. Chastain, a local "lunatic," died in 1889, for example, his real estate was sold and resold seven times in less than three years. At first, Chastain's land was bought and sold by local investors; eventually it ended up in the hands of the Kentucky Coal, Iron and Development Corporation, which sold it to Central Appalachian Corporation from which it was ultimately bought by the International Development Corporation.[90]

As speculators (both local and from the outside) vied for Clay County's resources, they pushed the value of land up dramatically. In 1889, land in the county was worth an average of $2.86 an acre. The following year it sold for $3.23 an acre; the year after, $5.18 – an 81% increase in two years. Some parcels underwent even more spectacular price inflation. The land that KTM bought in 1892 for around $5 an acre was worth $10–$30 an acre two years later. Yet, even with this dramatic increase, the value of most land in Clay County still lagged far behind the rest of the state where land averaged $9.13 to $10.96 an acre. At its peak in 1891, Clay County's land was worth only slightly more than half (54%) that of the rest of the state. Within two years, it was worth only one-third the state average. Further, it was not all Clay Countians who benefited from the local land inflation. Even by 1890, much of the county's land was no longer owned by its residents. Sales to outside investors and companies, together with migration of some landowners to the West and North, had created substantial absentee ownership in the county.[91]

In addition to their success in buying land for what later would be clear had been bargain prices, outside corporations did not always even stand by the agreements they made with local residents. Corporate agents typically offered a combination of cash and bonds or promissory notes as payment for land, timber, or mineral rights. Thomas and Franklin Baker and Hiram Smith sold fifty-six acres to NYK for $43 in cash, with another $181 in six-month and one-year promissory bonds. The Bakers and Smith, like many mountaineers, were careful not to relinquish their land until the sale price was paid in full. But others were less cautious. Clay County's courtroom was the site of several lawsuits by local residents seeking redress against outside corporations who sold their land to another corporate entity before paying bonds to the original landowner. Jesse Allen, for example, sued NYK in 1895 when the company transferred the deed to his land to KMT after paying only $325 of the $2,500 owed to Allen.[92]

It was not only Clay County's small farmers who were vulnerable to the financial maneuvers of large outside corporations. Even local economic elites fell prey to dishonest or unscrupulous corporations and their monetary agents. When John D. White sold substantial stands of his timber and land to NYK, the company refused to pay him the contracted price before reselling the land to KMT, which in turn mortgaged the land to Brayton Ives of New York's Western National Bank as part of KTM's $750,000 bond issue.[93]

If Clay Countians of different economic means faced similar treatment by outside corporations, however, they had vastly different abilities to challenge it. B. P. and John C. White sold land in 1895 to NYK for $21,040, or $11 an acre, but received only $420 before the land was resold to KMT and then to Western National Bank. The Whites brought suit against all three corporations and succeeded in forcing the land to be sold at judicial auction, where they repurchased it at a substantial discount. Clay Countians of more modest means had much less success against dishonest corporate practices. Martin Davidson sold land in 1890 to NYK for $4.50 an acre, which the company quickly resold to KMT after paying Davidson only $135 of the contracted $706. Although Davidson's heirs brought suit against the two corporations – and won – they ultimately were forced to sell part of their remaining land to pay a $50 bill to the attorney who argued the case.[94]

The Davidson's situation was not unique. Ironically, those without significant resources often were forced to sell their land to pay the attorney fees necessitated by legal challenges to their land title. Nevertheless, Clay Countians – even those of modest means – continued to turn to the local courts to protect them against outside corporations. At times, the courts obliged, forcing monetary settlements or sale of corporate land to satisfy claims by local residents. But outside corporations also used Clay County courts to safeguard their property rights. Central Appalachian Company, for example, filed suit in Clay County against Henry Hensley for illegally cutting and removing timber from their land. When the stakes were high, corporate interests could draw on tremendous political resources to prevail in the courtroom. In 1891, NYK sued former Clay County sheriff A. B. Howard, claiming that he had overvalued 12,740 acres of Clay County land for the purposes of tax assessment and also taxed them on an additional 23,282 acres that they did not own. During the trial, Kentucky Governor John Y. Brown intervened on behalf of the corporation. NYK won a reduction in taxes and Howard was enjoined from further efforts to collect the original amount.[95]

Governor Brown's intercession to safeguard the interests of a New Jersey corporation was one example of the often overlooked role of Kentucky's elites in corporate exploitation of the mountain region's natural resources. Although, as we will see, Clay County's wealthy families were able to finance some timbering and a limited amount of mining themselves, they lacked the resources and access to credit that would allow them to finance large-scale resource and industrial development in the mountains. Instead, local elites acted as the agents of outside corporations. Gilbert Garrard and Thomas J. White contracted to provide timber for Kentucky Mineral and Timber. Edward G. and William T. Garrard signed an agreement with a New York City timber magnate to protect his Clay County lands from trespassers, to aid in securing tenants to occupy the land, and to procure the rights of way for the removal of timber in exchange for half of the net timber proceeds.[96]

However, relationships between corporations and their local agents were often contentious. NYK signed a contract with Beverly P. and John C. White, authorizing them to purchase 20,000 acres in Clay, Leslie, and Owsley Counties for $5.50 an acre. After the Whites had bought large tracts of land, the corporation refused to reimburse them for $50,000 of the purchases, claiming that the Whites had not provided clear title to the land because of competing patent claims. The Whites then sued the corporation, setting off a protracted and sophisticated legal battle between these two economic giants that eventually ended in federal court.[97]

Despite friction, local elites were strategically located to benefit handsomely by their connections to outside corporations. As the county's largest landowners, they profited immensely from the speculation in real estate and the boom in land values that resulted from outside interest in the area's potential resource wealth. Between 1889 and 1891, the average value of Clay County land increased 81% and the value of timbered land increased even more sharply. In 1891, John G. White sold 2,422 acres of timber to NYK for the impressive sum of $9,293, or nearly $4 an acre of timber, and Beverly P. and John C. White netted $21,000 (at $11 an acre) for land sold to NYK, and substantial amounts in subsequent years. Gilbert Garrard and Thomas J. White acted as partners in 1894 to buy timber from the land that KMT had earlier purchased from Clay Countians. Beverly P. and John C. White sold 3,786 acres of land to NYK for $11 an acre, over $40,000. John E. White sold timber to Asher and Hensley, who acted as buyers for Ford Lumber Company. William T. and Edward Garrard, sons of T. T. Garrard, sold land to NYK in 1891, to Clay County Mining Company in 1910, to investors (for $18,000) in 1907, to a railroad in 1909, and to coal companies between 1915 and 1918. Later, the Garrards sold land to Fordson Coal Company (a Henry Ford company) for $19,000 and formed a partnership with Laura R. White to buy and sell Clay County timber. With White, they contracted to make wheel spokes for automobiles and whiskey staves for distilleries. However, the boom in land did not reach all parties in Clay County. In the same year that Whites and Garrards were commanding $10 or more per acre of land, others still received less than $1 an acre for their land.[98]

Local elites also profited from the rapid increase in timber prices. In the early 1890s, buyers paid twenty cents (sometimes less) per hundred feet of poplar lumber, an average of less than $3 per tree. Just a few years later, 100 feet of poplar sold for 60 cents, whereas woods like black walnut fetched $1.50 per hundred feet. By the late 1890s, high-quality wood sold for as much as $9 per hundred feet, although poorer wood continued to sell for much less.[99]

In their dealings with ordinary people, local elites, whether independent entrepreneurs or corporate agents, could apply the same unscrupulous tactics they experienced from outside companies. H. L. White, for example, backed a $200 note for Samuel Buttry, a farmer, that allowed him to buy a piece of land. When White sued him for payment of the note, Buttry testified that he had partially repaid the debt by selling his oxen to Robert Potter to be applied against his debt. He also claimed that he was unable to "cipher" and asked for an "independent person" to compute his remaining debt. White blocked Buttry's request for an accounting of the debt and instead forced the sale of Buttry's land to repay his debt. In a similar vein, John D. and Laura White, children of Daughterty, gave D. R. Murray, a local farmer, a $125 note for transferring title to his land to NYK and then refused to honor the note until Murray took them to court. The Whites also refused to pay $1,750 of a $1,800 land purchase from Charles Scott, claiming that Scott had failed to obtain their signatures on the contract; moreover, the Whites sued Scott, claiming that the land had depreciated in value since the original sale and that they were entitled both to the land and to $380 in damages.[100]

The dealings of John D. and Laura R. White, extensively recorded in a series of civil suits, further illustrate the strategies used by local entrepreneurs to profit from the county's resource boom. John was then living in Louisville, where he had established a business buying and selling large tracts of coal, timber, and mineral lands along with Bluegrass farms and homes in central Kentucky and suburban lots in Louisville. His unmarried sister, Laura, one of the first female graduates of the University of Michigan (then Michigan University), had earned a degree in mathematics and was a founding member of the Association of Collegiate Alumnae, the predecessor of the American Association of University Women. Laura had returned to Clay County after her father's death to administer his extensive estate with her brother, before returning to school to study architecture at the Massachusetts Institute of Technology in Boston in 1878, and later at the Sorbonne in Paris. A vocal advocate of women's suffrage and an economic force in Clay County well into the twentieth century, she was active in negotiating loans and mortgages to local farmers as well as land and timber deals with local entrepreneurs and extralocal corporate interests.[101]

In partnership, John D. and Laura hired M. J. Treadway for their transactions in the mountains and provided him with large sums of money to buy land, timber, and mineral rights that they could then resell to large outside companies. Unfortunately for the Whites, Treadway entered Clay County just as the rush of buyers for NYK had made local citizens even more sensitive to the value of their land and what lay on and beneath it. As Treadway wrote to John D., the rush of outside buyers "have almost crazed these people."

Expecting to be able to buy at bargain prices, Treadway was frustrated to find mountaineers who refused to sell him land, timber, or mineral rights, hoping for better offers from other buyers. "Some ask fabulously high prices," he complained to the Whites, "and some will not sell at all." When confronted with a particularly irascible seller, Treadway warned the Whites, "I do not believe it would be best policy to *budge one inch*: for the others would expect to take the same advantage of us." Typical was Willis Garrard of Buffalo Creek who refused to provide a deed to his land until the Whites paid the entire sale amount. "I shook at him yesterday in the presence of witnesses after he had refused to extend time and [I] demanded a good deed conveying perfect title," Treadway wrote, "but he could not make it and said so. . . . [Yet] he is a sharp rascal and may go ahead and have the deeds made and come in and catch us napping."

The best strategy, Treadway counseled, was to stay ahead of other land companies. He urged the Whites to buy and pay off deeds quickly, before people realized the true value of their land. Hoping to pay no more than $5 an acre for well-timbered land ($6 if it had "extra fine" coal or timber) and no more than eighty cents an acre for mineral rights, John White was shocked when one landowner was able to sell his land for $10 an acre. White urged Treadway to "get everything," to "sweep the territory" before word of this sale reached up the creeks, and to "pick trusted men and go it on a big scale and don't let grass grow under your feet." To secure good timber buys before other local landowners became too wary, White ordered Treadway to use sub-agents in the field:

> I believe that if you had good, reliable sub-agents to buy all of the standing oak and poplar trees at reasonable price . . . that we could make good money out of it. Of course, we will have to buy them cheap. . . . In most cases you could buy them and pay only a nominal sum – cash, one dollar, or two dollars. Occasionally you would have to pay a man 5 or 10 or 20 dollars. But when you start out you ought to have 4 or 5 men – don't let either one of them know what the other is doing – and you bind each fellow to take a certain creek, or a certain territory, so that there would be no competition between your men; and also select men that would not talk too much, but rush right along and get options on 10,000 or 20,000 trees.[102]

Under White's orders, Treadway rushed up and down the county's creekbed communities, buying timber, mineral rights, and land with cash, through bonds, and by paying the back taxes of landowners, always careful to secure firm titles to land to protect the Whites against future legal challenges by syndicates who had been granted so-called "blanket patents" of Clay County land by the Kentucky legislature in the 1870s.[103]

Profits from Clay County's land and mineral-grab, however, ultimately depended on the construction of a railway line into the county. As late as the turn of the century, coal from most points in eastern Kentucky, including Clay County, "reached its markets only after a tortuous trip over crude mountain trails and down winding mountain streams." In Clay County, T. T. Garrard operated a coal mine in the 1880s, principally to supply fuel for his remaining saltworks. In the next decade, dozens of small coal mines opened, but these produced largely for home consumption and without hired employees. Interest in developing the commercial potential of coal by extending rail lines into the coalfields mounted in the early twentieth century as railroads, along with timber and coal companies, purchased considerable acreage across eastern Kentucky.[104]

Efforts to secure a railway line through Clay County began in earnest in 1907 with the establishment of the Manchester Traction Company, an enterprise backed by Edward G. Garrard, Robert Carnahan, and others from Clay County, Louisville, and Lexington, which issued stock to construct a railroad from Barbourville to Manchester, but the project collapsed. Two years later, the Cumberland Northern Railway Company issued stock for a proposed spur from the Knox County line, along Collins Fork, Goose Creek, and the South Fork and through the Beech Creek area to the Owsley County line. Such a line would have crossed the land of the county's most wealthy citizens, including the Whites and Garrards, and, in northern Clay County, the Combs, Hoggs, and Carnahans. However, despite acquiring "considerable acreage," making "careful surveys," locating a "feasible" line, securing rights of way, and issuing capital stock to a number of Knoxville businessmen and two from Manchester, including C. B. Lyttle, the boosters of this line were unsuccessful in interesting the Louisville and Nashville Railroad (L & N) and the proposal was abandoned. Three years later, the same railway company raised $60,000 for a proposed line up Horse Creek from Goose Creek but that, too, never materialized.[105]

In 1916, a newly formed entity, the Cumberland and Manchester Railway Company (C & M), again proposed a rail line along Collins Fork and Goose Creek to Manchester, crossing White and Garrard land. The C & M was organized by Charles Heidrich, a Pennsylvania railroad promoter. On its board of directors sat the earlier Clay County railroad investor, C. B. Lyttle, along with investors from across Pennsylvania. This branch was built in 1917, extending twenty-three miles from the L & N Cumberland Valley line at Barbourville to Manchester, with a three-mile branch line up Horse Creek to Herron; it served Knox and Clay Counties.[106] When the first train arrived in Manchester, grateful local citizens provided a "feast" to the train crew. But, again, it was those well positioned in the earlier economy who gained the most from the new railway. William T. Garrard and John C., Ellen, and C. R. White sold rights-of-way for the new rail line at substantial personal profit.[107]

The opening of Clay County to rail transportation permitted the first significant development of its coal resources, along with a small revival of its salt industry. By the early 1920s, some of the county's wealthiest families, among them the Whites, the Lyttles, and Nancy Potter, had begun mining its rich veins of coal.[108] Outside corporations also joined in. Champion Fiber Company of North Carolina leased the coal and salt on several hundred acres of Goose Creek. As with the 1890s timber boom, coal generated renewed ties between outside corporations and the local entrepreneurs, whose earlier investments in salt, land, and timber had positioned them well for the next wave of local resource extraction. The Garrards turned to coal mining and to banking, adding the Clay County Bank to their earlier investment in the Bank of Manchester, and the Whites invested in coal mines, lumber companies, and in newly established insurance and real estate companies.[109]

Resource exploitation in turn-of-the-century Clay County did little to reconfigure the vast gulf between its few economic giants, largely descendants of those entrepreneurs who established economic dynasties in the county a century earlier, and the vast majority of economically marginal households dependent on declining agriculture and poorly paid wage employment in timber and other resource extraction. Those who were well positioned in salt manufacturing profited from land speculation as salt declined and, later, from timber and mineral exploitation of the land. In the twentieth century, Clay County's economic fortunes became ever more tightly directed by the outside corporations and investors who owned its land and the rights to mine its subsurface minerals. Its local elites lost the ability to direct much of the county's economic development, but they retained enormous power over the small farmers, landless tenant farmers, and laborers of the county. The next chapter explores these continuing relations of coercion in the changing economic climate of the late nineteenth and early twentieth centuries.

8

FEUD VIOLENCE

with Pam Goldman, Sharon Hardesty, and Lee Hardesty

The traveling evangelist Reverend John Jay Dickey reached Clay County in October of 1897, eager to spread Christian education in the mountains. His message largely fell on deaf ears, however, as Dickey's arrival coincided with an explosion of violence in the county. In his diary, Dickey recorded the carnage: a deputy sheriff nearly murdered in front of his hotel, two men killed at a saloon on Horse Creek, a murder on Little Goose Creek, two men who "emptied their pistols at each other" on the streets of Manchester, a gun battle on Laurel Creek, an assault on Sexton's Creek, an unexplained death near Little Goose Creek, a murder by a band of "Ku Klux" on Bull Skin Creek, an ambush murder and arson on Teges Creek, and "quarrels, brawls and pistol drawings . . . too tedious to mention." "As I sat in my room in the second floor of the Lucas Hotel," Dickey wrote despairing, "I could hear the bullets whiz through the air . . . (v)iolence and blood mark the population."[1]

Dickey arrived in Manchester at the beginning of a series of incidents of interpersonal violence in Clay County and elsewhere in the southern mountains that outsiders were quick to label as "feuds" and that would earn Appalachia Kentucky a widespread reputation as the "Corsica of America." As he began to collect local history accounts, Dickey recognized that the county's violence was not random, but rather pitted against each other the longtime rival Garrard and White families and their allies. Indeed, tensions evident in the Abner Baker trial in antebellum times still structured county allegiances and animosities.

From the mid-1840s, until Dickey arrived in Clay County a half century later, the Garrards and Whites waged what political theorist Antonio Gramsci called "trench warfare" – "wars of position" in which both sides mobilized their supporters in civil society to compete for political office.[2] For the first decades after the Abner Baker conflict, these wars of position took place through local elections and the offices of congressman, clerk, treasurer, and state representative oscillated between the Garrards and Whites. After the political realignment of the Civil War, however, the Garrards – Democrats in a heavily Whig/Republican county – fared best in statewide and district-level elections (controlled by Democrats); the Whites generally dominated local elections.

Despite the trappings of democratic participation, Clay County's political institutions thus remained very fragile throughout the nineteenth century. Even well into the postbellum period, longstanding private conflicts, especially those between the Garrards and the Whites, intruded into public life. Private battles weakened and deformed local capacities for negotiation and mediated contestation, practices that political sociologist Margaret Somers argues are essential characteristics of a robust public political sphere.[3] A decade after the Abner Baker trial, for example, when John E. White, the nineteen-year-old son of Benjamin F. White, was accused of murdering a Garrard-supported jailor, his prosecution was led by T. T. Garrard. Tensions between the Garrards and the Whites similarly erupted in 1886 as A. J. Hacker, a Democrat and a Garrard friend, tried to get an African American man to vote Democrat. When John G. White objected, he and Hacker "drew their side arms and began to fire." Others joined in. In the fray, three men were killed, four or five wounded.[4]

The Reverend Dickey arrived in Clay County in time to witness the virtual collapse of civil order as lingering conflict between the Whites and Garrards escalated dramatically. In Gramsci's terms, such heightened violence represented a shift in the battle between the two families from the long-term "war of position" of earlier years to a violent and short-term "war of manoeuvre" aimed at the control of local government institutions. In this chapter, we explore the explosion of intense violence between Clay County's most prosperous and influential families at the turn of the twentieth century. Through the many stories of Clay County's famous feud as well as court records and other data, we examine the relationship between this violence and civil society in the county. We scrutinize how decades of deeply polarized and factionalized private interests eventually caused the local civil order to buckle at the turn of the twentieth century and how these political conflicts contributed to the county's long-term economic immiseration and political incapacity.

Chronology of the Feud

As in the 1840s, when county elites confronted one another over a single murder trial, contemporary observers traced the violent contestation of the late nineteenth century – Clay County's feud – to a series of seemingly mundane episodes. The first incident began in early 1898. George Hall, one of Sheriff William L. White's deputies, along with Frank Campbell, a store-keeper from the White-allied Howard family, tried to arrest Anse and John Baker, allies of the Garrards, for malicious shooting and wounding. According to a likely understated account, Bakers "rarely cooperated with the law very well under such circumstances" and a gun battle ensued. Anse Baker was wounded and John Baker's mule killed.

Hall and Campbell then rode into Manchester, boasting they had killed the Baker brothers. Members of the Baker family quickly assembled and set Hall's house and Campbell's store ablaze. Sheriff White arrested John and Anse Baker for arson, but the Bakers had little difficulty meeting bail with the help of T. T., Edward G., and Gilbert Garrard and S. H. Kash, a Garrard ally. Sheriff White refused to arrest either Hall or Campbell for the shooting of Anse Baker.[5]

As a half-century earlier, the Whites and Garrards again were lined up on opposite sides of a criminal case: Whites with Howards, Garrards with Bakers. Any hope for a mediated solution between the two families through Clay County's public institutions was dashed as others joined the fray and prepared for violence. A visitor arriving from Knoxville as local tensions increased commented that in Clay County, "more money was invested in shooting irons than in agricultural instruments." Well aware of the consequences of such widespread factionalism, presiding Judge A. H. Clark opened the 1898 term of court by declaring that "the lawlessness in this county should be put down if it required half the population to do it," but he faced a formidable challenge. Even a hearing on the arson charge against the Bakers was thwarted as fist fights broke out in court between followers of the Bakers and Howards. In frustration, Judge Clark sent the case to Knox County. There, all charges against the Bakers were dropped.[6]

At about the same time, a second incident set the White/Howard and Garrard/Baker factions on a collision course. Israel Howard was in business with Tom Baker, cutting timber along Crane Creek. According to the Bakers's version of events, trouble between the two partners began when Tom Baker bought an overdue $40 promissory note issued against Israel Howard's father, A. B. Howard, and insisted that Israel pay the note from his share of the timber business. The Howards's story was different. They claimed that A. B. Howard discovered that Tom Baker had been cheating his son in their timber business and that the $40 note had been satisfied earlier. Whatever the actual course of events, friction between the two partners grew intense. At first, both Howard and Baker apparently believed that a local court could adjudicate their contested debt and they jointly requested a hearing before a magistrate. But, again, confrontations between the contending parties undermined operations of the court. As "both parties always came to court with a heavily armed following," a magisterial solution was impossible and the parties continued to dispute ownership of the logs.[7]

When spring arrived, Israel Howard took advantage of seasonal rains to float the contested logs downstream to a lumber company in Frankfort, positioning his brothers and father on the riverbank to guard against any interference by the Bakers. After the logs were safely afloat, the Howard guards started for home. As they passed in front of the home of Gardner Baker, Gardner's wife (who is not named in any account) apparently saw the Howards "and running to the bell which always hangs over a mountain feudist's home, she rang it vigorously." A hail of bullets rained down on the Howard party. Israel's brother, Wilson, and a foster brother were killed and his father wounded.[8]

Seeing the massacre, a neighbor jumped on Wilson Howard's bloodstained horse and rode into Manchester to the home of another brother, James Howard, the county tax assessor. James responded initially, not with violence, but by petitioning local officials for help. Not surprisingly, given the ties between the Howards and the White-dominated county administration, James was given immediate assistance. In an interview with the New York *Herald* a decade later, he recalled that "I hurried to the county judge and sheriff and they promised they would do what they could."

"So great was the dread of the Bakers among the county people," Howard later recalled, that no one would approach the murder site to remove the bodies of the two slain Howards. In fact, such fear was justified. The following day, as the Howards prepared to bury their dead at the Laurel Creek cemetery, a "small army" of Baker partisans hidden in the adjacent woods opened fire on the mourners, forcing them to flee. The burial had to be moved to another cemetery.[9]

Incensed by these attacks from the Bakers, A. B. Howard – himself a former sheriff – marched to the county court. Drawing on the language of a state act passed to prevent lynching,[10] Howard swore that the Bakers and their allies had "banded and confederated themselves together for the purpose of injuring and destroying" his property and life. Again, local government officials were eager to cooperate with Howard. The county court ordered armed protection for Howard and the county fiscal court provided $84 to fund a posse for Howard's protection.[11]

These legal measures apparently did not satisfy the Howards. Soon thereafter, James Howard came upon George Baker – the county attorney and Tom Baker's father – and fired his gun, killing Baker. "The rage of the Bakers at the taking of their leader knew no bounds," James Howard later recalled. Mindful of their assault on the Howard internment, however, the

Bakers were unwilling to risk a retaliatory ambush by the Howards when Reverend Dickey presided at George Baker's open-air burial and few attended.[12]

The shootings of the leaders of both families – A. B. Howard and George Baker – caused violence in the county to spiral. James Howard recounts that "several times I was ambushed on my way between Manchester and father's." With their ties to Sheriff White, the Howards were granted special deputy sheriffs to surround and protect their homestead. Nonetheless, A. B. Howard's house was continually shot at and his children lived in terror that it would be burned. Similarly, the Bakers, and even the Garrards, feared for their lives and property as the Howards acted under the protection of the Whites. When Sidney Baker – a relative of the Howards, not related to the Bakers – killed another Baker, his bail was promptly posted by S. P. White and Baker was set free. T. T. Garrard installed an armed guard around his house and Reverend Dickey recorded the places on Garrard's farm where men had camped in the bushes for a chance to assassinate one of the Garrards.[13]

Violence in the early months of 1898 was intense, but largely confined to the families and allies of the combatants. Those who were not openly tied to the White or Garrards and who remained strictly nonpartisan felt little fear from the mounting violence. For example, an aspirant for a teaching position in Clay County visited Tom Baker (then a school trustee) just one day after Tom's father had been killed by James Howard. She recalled that Tom

> lived far out in the hills, up Crane Creek 15 miles or more from where I was staying. Taking a neighbor girl with me for company and guide, I rode it on horseback over typical mountain roads. . . . I approached Baker's home, a well-built and comparatively roomy log house, for he was by mountain standards a man of substance. . . . There were guns and guns – the deadly Winchesters and shotguns of the vendetta – on the wall and standing in the corners.

Despite Baker's sizeable firearm collection, the teacher expressed little apprehension about being interviewed by Tom Baker at his home in the middle of the feud.

> Of course, the feud was not discussed at length with me. I was an outsider. . . . The people I knew best deplored the war, but could not condemn the participants. You had to protect your honor, didn't you? . . . Having no connection with either faction, I knew that I was not in the slightest danger unless by accident.[14]

As Clay County's conflict continued, however, its reach extended. Over time, the violence of the feud nearly overwhelmed civil society and increasingly involved people far removed from the feuding families. Contemporary commentators bemoaned that "(e)ven the neutral families felt they were in danger . . . (and) began to go armed at all times. If men had to be away from home overnight they arranged for armed neighbors to protect their families. Both sides armed themselves for war." Fearful that "said trouble will cause great loss of life to the parties on both sides," the county judge ordered a posse of one hundred men to "arrest and disarm all persons who are armed on both sides," demanding that "when you get the jail full, chain them around the jail." The posse arrested eight Bakers and four Baker sympathizers, but claimed it could capture only two Howards. Each side was put in separate hotels under armed guard.[15]

The power of the Whites over local administration of justice continued into the courthouse. As Dickey wrote in his diary, "[t]he Whites have control of the courts and run things as they wish." Charges against the two Howards were quickly dropped, whereas the Bakers and their allies were charged with murder. (They later were acquitted.) But despite these partisan experiences, even those most actively battling the Whites would occasionally press local officials for protection against the Howards. Tom Baker, for example, appealed to the Clay County court to defend him against the Howards. Remarkably, the court responded and ordered a posse of two to ten men to protect Baker.[16]

Efforts at legal remedy, however, were not sufficient to end the conflict. Several months after the Baker roundup, Sheriff White ventured up Crane Creek – into Baker territory – to collect unpaid taxes. There he was ambushed and killed by Tom Baker and his brother Dee, both bitter over his role in the earlier prosecution of Anse and John Baker for arson. Shortly thereafter, the husband of a witness to the murder of Sheriff White was shot by an unknown assailant. Tom and Dee were charged with murder and mayhem, tried in Barbourville, and given life sentences, but their convictions were subsequently reversed by the Court of Appeals. As he presided at Sheriff Whites's burial, Reverend Dickey predicted that "[t]he Whites will now help the Howards to exterminate the Bakers."[17]

Dickey's words were prophetic. While Tom and Dee Baker were awaiting trial for assassinating Sheriff White, they, along with four other brothers and relatives, were indicted for the earlier murder of Wilson Howard and his foster brother, the assault on A. B. Howard, and the arson of several houses on Crane Creek. Fearful of the fate of Tom and Dee Baker in a White-dominated courtroom, the other four indicted Bakers refused to surrender. Instead, forty-two Baker family members set up an outdoor "fort" on the courthouse lawn to await trial. The Howard forces responded in kind. Each side summoned additional reinforcements until, according to the jailor, 75 to 100 men armed with Winchester rifles were arrayed on each side of the courthouse. Decrying "armed bands in this county who are threatening to come into court," Judge William Brown ordered a guard to prevent shooting in the courthouse. But he quickly saw the futility of assembling a guard of Clay County citizens. Like Dickey, who concluded that "there is not the respect for local authority necessary to enforce the law," Judge Brown concluded that he would need an outside force to keep the feud from spreading.[18]

In early June, Judge Brown traveled to Frankfort and petitioned Governor William O. Bradley to send state troops to protect the court. Governor Bradley acceded to the request and ordered the assistant state adjutant general to lead the troops, noting that "lives and persons of the citizens of Clay County are in danger and the civil power unaided by the military is wholly incapable of keeping the peace or enforcing the law." Fifty state troops arrived in Manchester, amidst rumors that the troops would be ambushed and shot and that ten barrels of whiskey, stolen from a warehouse near Manchester, were being distributed to armed fighters.[19]

Notwithstanding the presence of state troops at the courthouse, the four indicted Bakers continued to fear retaliation from the Howard forces gathered in Manchester. They sent a letter to Judge Brown declaring that they would surrender to the court only if granted a guarantee of protection. The judge concurred, noting that "if I should attempt to try the Bakers without being able to protect them there would be shooting, perhaps in the courthouse" and granted them protection. Despite widespread fear that "the Howards will try to shoot the Bakers, even though they are in custody of the troops," all four Baker men surrendered. To maintain peace in Manchester, the Baker trial was moved to London and the state militia withdrew from Clay County.[20]

Like other periods of peace, this, too, was short-lived. Within the month, renewed violence drew the Garrards and the Whites more deeply into the Baker/Howard conflict. In late July, a sniper ambushed and shot at Gilbert Garrard and his wife on their way to church. Shortly thereafter, John Baker and an African American man, Frank Clark, were killed from ambush as they rode toward T. T. Garrard's house. Now, even those far removed from the feuding parties felt unsafe. An examination of public school teachers was adjourned from Manchester to a distant part of the county to escape what one observer described as "continual shooting" in the county seat. News of the renewed discord in Clay County reached the state capital and Governor Bradley ordered the state adjutant general to mount a full-scale investigation into the civil conditions in the county. To no one's surprise, the report concluded that problems in the county were wholly the result of the feud and urged the deployment of state troops whenever necessary.[21]

In the fall of 1898, James Howard was escorted by Beverly P. White and nineteen guards dispatched by Clay County to stand trial in Laurel County Circuit Court for the murder of George Baker. According to the defendant, the change of venue was necessary "so great was the sentiment in my favor in Clay County." Even in Laurel County, though, tension in the courtroom ran high and the judge ordered a guard for the jail "owing to the feeling existing in the trial." After the first trial resulted in a hung jury, Howard was retried, found guilty, and sentenced to life imprisonment. Due to the "probable danger" that he "will be rescued," Howard was transferred to jail in Madison County. From there, with funds from the Louisville *Herald*, Howard appealed his conviction all the way to the Supreme Court, where it was eventually overturned.[22]

The following year, 1899, opened to even more bloodshed. A New Year's battle left several dead. It was followed by a series of ambush murders that killed more than twenty men. By June, the situation had escalated to the point that H. C. Eversole, a newly elected judge of the Clay County Circuit Court and a longtime supporter of John White, again pleaded with the governor to send state troops to restore order. The governor ordered a virtual army of state militia dispatched from Lexington: "100 good and reliable men with necessary cooks, surgeons and tentage and Gaitling gun."[23]

As they approached, the troops heard rumors that the feudists had declared war on the militia and many deserted as they reached the end of the railroad line and were being loaded on wagons for the final leg of the trip. On arriving in Clay County, the remaining militia proceeded up Crane Creek to arrest a number of Bakers who – except for Tom Baker – still had not been convicted in four full terms of court. Tom Baker, freed by the Court of Appeals on his conviction for the murder of William L. White and out on bail from his subsequent indictment for the Howard murders and arsons, also steadfastly refused to appear in court in Manchester. As the militia approached, the indicted Bakers did submit to arrest but refused to be put in the jail under guard of the Whites. Instead, the Bakers and their supporters pitched an encampment on the courthouse lawn in Manchester where they prepared for trial.

As the long-awaited retrial of the Bakers approached, supporters, opponents, and spectators poured into Manchester. The combination of the Baker prisoner encampment, the militia troops, and the expectant visitors created chaos in the county seat. "The town was so full of people that the military could not find quarters, so tents were pitched in the rear of the court house which [was] occupied by the soldiers with Tom Baker in their midst." It was a county spectacle, to which everyone brought their rifles and shotguns.[24]

Vainly, the state militia struggled to control a situation that local officials and the court could not or would not control. The state commander declared that "it was inconsistent for the defendants and the accusers, and the spectators to come to court heavily laden with shooting hardware" and ordered everyone to surrender their weapons at the courthouse door. Fearing that he would be assassinated for summoning the militia, Judge Eversole resigned his position – citing an ill mother in Perry County – and fled the county. He was replaced by a special judge brought from Pineville who also barred weapons from court proceedings. Anxious to reestablish order in Manchester, the new judge, too, granted Tom Baker's request for a change of venue from Clay County to Barbourville, away from the influence of the Howards and Whites.[25]

As he received news of the venue change, Tom Baker appeared at the entrance to his tent on the courthouse lawn, his wife at his side. A shot rang out, fired from the direction of the house of Sheriff Beverly White (who succeeded slain William L. White as sheriff). Tom Baker was hit in the heart and died. The militia reacted instantly. "Wiley and Jim Baker, crying for their arms and liberty, were locked up under a strong detachment. The body [of Baker] and that of the prostrate widow were also dragged into the Court House." Troops charged the home of Sheriff Beverly White, across the street from the courthouse, and found the gun and an empty shell, but no sniper. "With fixed bayonets," the militia then "charged the crowd that came swarming onto the Court House, perhaps to rescue the other Bakers, perhaps to kill them, or from curiosity." Bystanders to the shooting mounted horses and raced the news to the Howards and Whites camped outside Manchester and to the Bakers on Crane Creek.[26]

Tom Baker's assassination underscored the combined power of the Whites and Howards in Clay County. In his diary, Dickey wrote that "the Whites are in power and everything goes without opposition. Their friends are protected and their enemies keep quiet." When state troops attempted to escort the remaining Baker prisoners to Barbourville for trial, they were ambushed by twenty-five armed Whites and Howards. The militia was able to proceed only after threatening their attackers with the Gatling gun. The *Louisville Courier-Journal*'s assessment of the situation underscored the now-precarious position of the Bakers: "Time was when the Bakers would sally into Manchester and blaze away indiscriminately, but such a movement now would mean the wiping out of that faction. The Whites and Howards are well armed. They are disciplined, and own the only brick house in Manchester that could give protection." In Clay County, homes had become fortresses, the streets battlegrounds.[27]

Following the assassination of Tom Baker, the state militia retreated back to Frankfort. Armed confrontations spread across the county, reaching even to the remote northern Beech Creek area. Conditions were so fearful in Manchester that merchants bolted their doors and suspended operations. Witnesses to the Baker assassination were particularly apprehensive. Bob Baker, Tom's cousin, was one of those who claimed that he saw the shooting but was afraid to reveal the identity of the assassin after Daugherty White directed an African American man to shoot him. As the Berea *Citizen* remarked, "Things look more warlike now than ever in Clay County. Since the troops have left the feudists have the county to themselves."[28]

Escalation of the conflict was due in part to the entry of new families into the fray. Most significant among these was the large Philpot family, whose leader "Big John" had testified at Tom Baker's initial trial. The Berea *Citizen* claimed that the Philpots were "the strongest and most feared faction in this section," numbering 200 fighters armed with thirty-six Winchester rifles that they had shipped into the county to prepare for war. Perhaps the *Citizen*'s alarm about the Philpots was overstated, but others also cited the Philpot's fiercesome reputation: "It is a common saying in Clay that to kill a Philpot means that your own days are numbered. . . . They and their connections number over a hundred able to fight." Even Dickey, while insisting that the Philpots were "quiet law-abiding people and do not provoke attacks," conceded that they "boast they never let a man escape who injures one of their clan."[29]

Throughout the county, Philpots battled Griffins and Morrises (who sided with the Whites and Howard). One battle, in front of the schoolhouse on Little Goose Creek, was described by the London *Mountain Echo* as the "bloodiest and most deadly battle that was ever fought in all the bloody history of Clay County." Dickey recorded that "the ground where [the combatants] fell looks like a slaughter pen." This single incident left five men dead. Other encounters were narrowly avoided. When one of the Philpots met a farmer who offered his wagon to haul away the dead after a Griffin-Philpot battle, Philpot jokingly offered to finish off a load of Griffins for him. The farmer related the story to a Griffin and "there was a rush to arms, but through some agreement the matter was settled and no blood spilled."[30]

Fearing a complete collapse of civil order in Clay County, the commander of the Kentucky militia, Colonel Roger Williams, recommended to Governor Bradley that he declare martial law in Clay County immediately. Nonpartisan citizens made similar appeals, even petitioning state representative R. C. Ford (himself tied to the Garrards by marriage and business) to impose

marital law to end the "perfect reign of terror exist[ing] all over Clay County."
In response, Governor Bradley convened a group of attorneys and judges from
eastern Kentucky to consider the situation in Clay County. Although the
governor favored sending more troops to protect the county court, others
objected, noting that all county officers were allied with the Howards and
Whites against the Bakers and Garrards. Instead, they advised the governor
to abolish Clay County and divide it among adjacent counties. The governor
debated whether to convene the state legislature in special session to deal
with this matter, but the advent of the Spanish-American War interfered with
his plans.[31]

Murders and assaults continued at a high level in Clay County through
the autumn of 1899. Disproportionately, it was the allies of the Bakers and
Garrards who faced arrest and imprisonment. The consequences of White
control of the sheriff's office and the jail were strikingly evident when two
McCollum brothers and Jules Webb were arrested for the murders of two
men from the Howard/White side. None of those arrested was allowed bail,
and while in jail, Webb was shot through the window of his cell. In response,
the Clay County court ordered Sheriff Beverly White to summon sixteen men
to guard the jail and court due to "the prisoners now confined in the jail on
charges of murder on one side of a considerable feud."[32]

By the winter of 1899, the feud showed some signs of abating. In northern Clay County, J. A. Burns, a teacher, called together fifty of the most
prominent men of the area – including friends of the Bakers and the Howards
– to work out an agreement to end the feud. According to his biographer, it
was Burns's love for teaching that motivated his search for peace. The son of
a Baptist minister, Burns was born in Clay County, schooled in Ohio, and
returned to Clay County in 1892 at the age of twenty-seven. He taught and
established schools throughout the county, including on Crane Creek (at the
request of Tom Baker) and in Manchester. In 1899, Burns decided to start
an academy in Oneida, in the heart of the northern Clay County feud country.
His biographer wrote that Burns "wanted these parents [of Oneida] to vow
their sons to something better than the feudal blood atonement when they
got their first lisping education in their homes." Oneida Baptist College (later
the Oneida Baptist Institute, still in operation) was built on ten acres in
Oneida donated to Burns by Martha Coldiron Hogg. On the board of trustees
sat some of the most notable men of the northern Clay County feud.[33]

The truce of Oneida did not bring peace to the rest of Clay County. On
the contrary, one of Clay County's feudists became entangled in a wider political drama that brought even more outside attention to the county's feud.
In 1899, a hotly contested state gubernatorial contest pitted Republican
W. S. Taylor against Democrat William Goebel, an advocate of corporate

regulation. Taylor was declared the winner, but the election results were furiously contested by Democrats, who charged voting fraud in Louisville and in the eastern mountain counties. In 1900, the state election board agreed to reconsider the result. Allegedly with funding from the railroad interests, a thousand "well armed mountaineers" rode trains to the state capital to monitor the state election board. In the ensuing chaos, William Goebel was shot from the office window of the secretary of state as he stood in front of the state capitol building. He lived another three days, during which he was declared governor by the Kentucky General Assembly, and then died. Among those indicted for Goebel's murder was James Howard of Clay County. Rumors abounded that Howard had been convinced by Taylor or his supporters to kill Goebel in exchange for a pardon for his murder of George Baker. Howard was tried and convicted three times for Goebel's assassination, but two convictions were reversed on appeal and he was eventually pardoned by a later governor.[34]

It was not until 1901 that a peace treaty was signed between the Garrards and Whites, officially settling the feud of Clay County. The incident that precipitated the truce occurred in March of that year when T. T. Garrard and his son Edward G., together with twenty of their supporters, rode on horseback into Manchester, fully armed, to demand bail for Jules Webb, Taylor Spurlock, and William and Dennis McCollum, all Garrard allies charged with murder. As the Garrards entered the law office of their attorney, S. H. Kash, they were met with a hail of gunfire, reportedly 100 shots fired from the courthouse. The Garrards fled back up Goose Creek, with shots pursuing them. The sitting judge of Clay County, beholden to neither side of the feud, was incensed by the shooting and demanded an explanation from Sheriff Beverly White. White claimed that someone in the county clerk's office must have accidently shot a gun. Judge Tinsley then ordered all prisoners taken from the Manchester jail to London under the guard of twenty-five neutral men and announced that, hereafter, all visitors to the court would be searched for weapons.

Further, Tinsley pressed the Whites and Garrards to find a peaceful resolution of the feud violence. Aided by David L. Walker, a friend of both Whites and Garrards, Tinsley persuaded Beverly White to accede to the Garrards's demand to step down as sheriff and leave Clay County. He was replaced as sheriff by Walker. In turn, the Whites insisted that the Garrards agree not to provide bond for additional combatants. The Garrards refused, but Tinsley and Walker convinced the Whites to drop this demand. On March 13, 1901, articles of peace were drawn up and signed by John G. White of Winchester (representing the Whites) and J. R. Burchell (representing the Garrards). The "great truce of Clay" was in effect.[35]

Although the *Louisville Courier-Journal*'s report that until the truce, "there has been practically no law in Clay County for years" was exaggerated, the peace treaty did significantly dampen levels of violence, if not political contestation, in the county for a time. But the formulation of a truce between the private armies of the Whites and the Garrards underscored how incomplete was public control over private political and conflictual relations in the county. Law could be only reestablished by the agreement of competing elites. And even this negotiated peace was not long-lived. Violence flared against between the Philpots and Griffins in 1904, leaving one Philpot dead and several Griffins and their allies wounded.[36]

Three decades after the official truce, reports of feud violence again surfaced in Clay County. In an eery parallel with the 1890s, this outbreak of violence reached its apex when Frank Baker, a commonwealth attorney, was assassinated by an unknown sharpshooter at his uncle's house across from the Manchester courthouse – in much the same fashion as his uncle, Tom Baker, had been killed on the courthouse lawn by a sniper in 1899. Barn burnings and additional murders followed, with at least one murder witness – Police Judge C. P. Stivers – also killed in the conflict. After the Stivers killing, state militia were again deployed to Manchester to maintain control of the situation.[37]

The state investigation that followed the 1932 violence recommended that Clay County be abolished and divided as the only way to establish order and to end the "clan contests which have made the county notorious." "In no other county of the state," lamented the report, "has lawlessness prevailed for so long a time with such disastrous results to the people, nor has the character of crime reached the barbaric level in any other part of the State that has been in evidence in recent years in Clay."[38]

Causes of the Feud

What gave rise to the feud of Clay County? The sequence of events described earlier certainly indicates the continuing cleavages among local elites and their allies as well as the immediate precipitating actions that led to violence, but it reveals little about why the decades-long contestation for local power between Garrards and Whites intensified and became violent in the 1890s. For this, we need to probe beneath the events of the 1890s. We focus first on the economic relations that initially structured hostility between the Garrards and Whites. Following theorist Enzo Mingione's ideas of economic organization as embedded within a network of social relations, we then examine how economic changes in the late nineteenth century triggered a collapse of institutions of local governance and the intense interpersonal violence that came to be known as the feud of Clay County.[39]

Economic Relations

A major factor that precipitated violent conflict in the 1890s was the dramatic economic change taking place in Clay County and in the southern Appalachian mountains as a whole. Consistent with the sociological observation that social movements tend to occur at the "space-time edges" that arise "between different structural types of society," periods of intense interpersonal violence have commonly been understood as violent responses to the disruptive impact of modernization. This association is supported by Kentucky historian James Klotter who determined that the earliest feuds in the state occurred on the western fringe of the Kentucky mountains, where economic development was most advanced, and followed economic development into the more isolated sections to the east.[40]

In Clay County, however, economic change did not translate directly into violent conflict as might be expected if mountaineers were simply reacting with violence to the "shock of the new." The period of intense violence in the late 1890s did coincide with tremendous speculation in land, timber, and minerals by local entrepreneurs and outside corporations. But, as a half-century earlier, late nineteenth-century feud violence only peaked when a period of enormous economic expansion, here fueled by mass extraction of timber, coal, and other mineral resources, was followed by a sharp financial contraction in the 1893 national depression.

Moreover, contrary to studies that have traced litigiousness – a more institutionalized form of group conflict[41] – to processes of modernization, Clay County's economic change did not directly translate into increased conflict through the courts. In the years in which speculation caused land values to rise most quickly (1885–91), the rate of civil litigation in the county was unremarkable, an average annual rate of 4.1 lawsuits per 100 adult white men as compared with an overall annual average of 5.3 between 1845 and 1898. (To see this in perspective, the comparable figure for highly commercialized Bourbon County, Kentucky – for which we collected data over the same time period – was 16.8.) Even during the period of the most active feuding, from 1897 to 1898, the average litigation rate was only 5.0.[42]

Although it is thus too simplistic to posit that violent or legal conflict emerges simply as a result of economic change, there clearly was a connection between economic booms and crises and local conflict in Clay County. For one thing, as the Whites and Garrards knew well, political decision making was critical during times of economic expansion since political control provided the opportunity to safeguard investments and to profit from exploration and speculation. As a later commentator observed, "[when] the mountains were being opened for commercial exploitation, it occurred to both families that the quickest way to riches was through political power."[43]

In Kentucky, a state in which county offices were in many ways more important and strategic than offices at the state level, economic contestations quickly translated into county-level political conflict. As major actors and beneficiaries of resource development in Clay County, the Garrards and Whites profited handsomely from timber and coal mining. At the same time, their parallel economic success pushed them deeper into political conflict by raising the stakes of control over county offices, especially those of sheriff, treasurer, and assessor who were directly responsible for assessing and collecting taxes. Thus, economic change was associated with both legal and violent conflict in Clay County, but primarily through the intervening factor of local politics.[44]

Clay County's dual economy – based in subsistence agriculture and large-scale extraction – left the majority of the population dependent upon a few elite families. Especially as the viability of subsistence agriculture declined in postbellum decades, many people in the county relied on the Garrards, Whites, and a few other elite families, either directly as employees or indirectly as suppliers and consumers. In an economically bifurcated county, economic dependence assured political allegiance. Thus, although economic transformation exacerbated preexisting relations of antagonism among elites in the county, the form that violence took – the lines of allegiance and conflict in Clay County's feud – was conditioned by longstanding relations of dependency and clientelism between elites and non-elites.

Some of the most economically dependent allies of Clay County's elites were remarkably poor. Among the Philpots, a family tied to the Garrards and Bakers, for example, most members had been landless since antebellum times. In 1891, when the Garrards and Whites were busy buying and selling tens of thousands of acres of land and sending their children abroad to be educated, Issabella Philpot, the unmarried daughter of John Philpot, was accused of illegally squatting with her two sons on a small tract of land. Not a single family member who testified at her trial was literate. Most did not know their exact age.[45]

A decade before the peak of feud violence, in 1886, fully 65% of Philpot households listed in the tax rolls were landless as were 70% of Philpot heads of household in 1900. Even Philpots who owned land lived at the very margins, averaging a meager $274 in real estate in 1886. However, the Philpots's political loyalty to the Garrards apparently did not buy them protection from economic catastrophe. When Tim Philpot was presented with a $6.79 tax bill in 1894, he did not have enough property to cover the debt and was forced to have his land sold at auction. The same thing happened in 1876 over a $50 judgment against Tim Philpot. Throughout the early and mid-1890s, a number of Philpots lost their land or farm animals to creditors, or were evicted from illegally occupied lands.[46]

The Bakers were far more prosperous than the Philpots, although far less wealthy than the Whites and Garrards. Only 20% of Baker heads of household in 1900 did not own their residence (24% were landless in 1870) and the value of their land in 1886 averaged $528, nearly twice that of the Philpots. The Bakers had long been on "intimate terms" with the Garrards, "though far beneath them socially," a situation that Dickey attributed to common Democratic Party ties. Most Clay County offices were held by Whites, but George W. Baker and A. W. Baker had held positions as county attorney and prosecuting attorney throughout the latter decades of the nineteenth century, offices from which they were able to tyrannize adversaries. Moreover, George W. Baker earlier had served a term as sheriff, an office that gave him the opportunity to buy court-auctioned land at a substantial discount, as he did in a 1876 sale of Crane Creek land. Dickey summarized the Bakers's role in the county when he wrote, "[t]he Bakers have been running Manchester ever since I have been in it. It has been a reign of terror."[47]

The Howards were somewhat better off than the Bakers, but again far less wealthy than the county's financial elites. Only 12% of Howard household heads did not own their residences in 1900 and only 18% were propertyless in 1870. The sole Howard listed in the 1886 tax rolls was A. B. Howard, whose land was valued at $400 – substantially more than the Philpots, but a far cry from the $87,000 in land owned by a handful of Whites. His son, Wilson Howard, who later was killed in the feud, however, was substantially poorer and had to sell his land to pay a $9 debt.[48]

The Whites and Garrards occasionally provided financial opportunities for their allies, as John White did when he secured a mortgage for Israel Howard. But, as was the case with the Philpots, the Howards and Bakers were not always able to rely on their ties to the Whites and Garrards. Even at the height of feud violence, while the Bakers were solidly allied with the Garrards, A. W. Baker was forced to relinquish ownership of his home and the Center Store in Manchester to pay his Barbourville attorneys. Moreover, the Howards and Bakers commonly mortgaged or sold their land or other property to raise funds for their criminal defenses – sums that would have meant little financial hardship for the Whites or Garrards.[49]

More than economic assistance, elites provided political and legal protection for their allies. According to Dickey, "in this county, where the Whites and Garrards have been dividing the county for over fifty years it is hard to enforce the law. . . . They have been taking sides in these court proceedings all these years." Dickey denounced the abusive outcome of elite protection, noting that the Whites and Garrards have "corrupted the people of the county with their money, buying their votes, then shielding them from justice when they committed crimes." Not surprisingly, a descendant of the Garrards framed these relationships to us in much more benign terms, recalling T. T. Garrard handing out "clothes and bananas" and loaning his horse to fetch a doctor to deliver the babies of his employees.[50]

As the county's preeminent political elite, the Whites routinely used their political influence to shield the Howards from prosecution. In contrast, the Garrards used their economic clout to provide bail bonds for Bakers arrested on criminal charges, leading Dickey to comment that the Bakers "must be bad men, they have that name (but) they have always escaped punishment." When Tom Baker faced prosecution for arson, he turned to Gilbert Garrard for his bond. Likewise, it was T. T. Garrard who won John Baker's freedom from a Barboursville jail. According to Dickey, the Whites "interpret the actions of the Garrards in going on bond of the Bakers as an effort to destroy them. The Garrards deny the charge, saying that it only is to repay them for past favors." Nonetheless, in 1897, Dickey reported a persistent county rumor that Jim Garrard had assured the Bakers "kill who you please, we will stand by you."[51]

When conflict among elites turned to violence in the late 1890s, others who were bound by economic ties to the feud protagonists became footsoldiers in feud battles. Poor Clay Countians, especially, could be pressed into service by wealthy Garrards and Whites. Some served as intermediaries, as one boy who was put on a mule and sent as a messenger to a member of the opposing side. African Americans, the most vulnerable population in turn-of-the-century Clay County, often became involved in feud conflicts. Carlo Britton, an African American, was charged with killing one of the Garrards; his defense was funded by the Whites. Tom Watt, another African American, was said to have tried to kill the sole witness to Tom Baker's courtyard assassination, acting under the direction of Daughtery White.[52]

African Americans who were seen as allies of one side of the feud were vulnerable to attack by the other side. In a 1899 battle on Horse Creek, Frank Clark, an African American man, was shot from ambush alongside John Baker. In another episode, Dickey recorded the testimony of an eyewitness who recalls that he "saw William White, now deceased, jump onto Jim Tish

Philpot, a mulatto, and beat and cuff him about" because Philpot was an ally of the Bakers. James Collins, another African American, was killed in a feud battle in June 1898.[53]

Relations of domination and subordination in economic life commonly spilled over into public politics. As one writer noted, "with few exceptions the entire population depended upon [Whites or Garrards] for a livelihood. In this manner, the heads of the respective families became the leaders of the opposing political factions, ruling their supporters like ancient feudal chieftains." In 1901, John G. White of Winchester wrote to Andrew Baker of Manchester (a Republican maverick in a family of Democrats) urging him to vote against H. C. Faulkner, who "defended [Tom] Baker who fouly slew my brother," in the upcoming judicial race. "I assure you," White wrote, "that no one voting against Faulkner *and his* like, will ever regret it; as my vote and voice in the future will be subject to their will" and concluded by noting that his brother, Will, had saved Andy Baker's life. Such friendship and favors found easy recompense in politics. White concluded, "Please repay [Will] by doing all you can . . . and oblige your friend."[54]

Fighting for political advantage, the Whites and Garrards were dependent on non-elites to serve as jurors, sheriffs, and other state functionaries and as political allies in electoral battles. Clay County's most powerful families thus relied on stable ties to groups of non-elite families. As the stakes of local political power escalated with the increasing value of Clay County's land and natural resources, such networks of obligation and antagonism between elites and non-elites in the county hardened.[55]

Thus, although there clearly was a connection between economic booms and crises and the emergence of conflict in Clay County (in the 1840s as well as the 1890s), violence did not escalate simply because of the disruptive impact of economic change. Rather, speculation in county land and minerals during the 1880s heightened already existing tensions among the county's elite families, and the bonds of hierarchy and dependency between elites and non-elites made it possible for elites to engage in sustained violent conflict through intermediaries. These factors set the stage for the collapse of Clay County's fragile public political sphere and unrestrained violence between groups allied with the county's most powerful political and economic actors.

Institutional Collapse

When violence between those allied with the Garrards and Whites erupted at the turn of the century, local political institutions – county finances, elections, courts and legal systems – were paralyzed, although other public functions like schooling and the registering of deeds apparently continued. In capitalist societies, political institutions bolster existing economic and social relations by providing a forum for the peaceable (if not equitable) airing, negotiation, and resolution of conflicting private interests. But Clay County's institutions of local governance, born in the private battles of the cattle war a century before, were tightly bound to particular and conflicting interests and thus ill equipped to mediate private quarrels.

It is little wonder therefore that the immediate cause of the 1890s feud involved local politics. The first incident occurred in 1893 when Granville Philpot, an ally of the Garrards, won election to the state legislature as the representative from Clay, Jackson, and Owsley Counties. According to local legend, the Whites – long dominant in local and regional politics – feared that the election of Philpot signaled the beginning of a Garrard return to power in Clay County and pressed to strengthen their political grip on the county. Only three years later, they got their chance as the virtually unchallenged control of state offices by Democrats ended with the election of Republican Governor Bradley. In the past, the Democratic monopoly of state resources balanced the Republican hold on Clay County, resulting in a political stalemate and a measure of political moderation within the county. With Republican Governor Bradley's election, however, this changed. A White-controlled county could – and did – seek intervention by the state militia and pardons by the governor to increase its control on the local level. In the following year, the principals to the conflict came head to head as Beverly White defeated Gilbert Garrard in an election for sheriff and Whites swept most local offices, including the powerful position of tax assessor. Against this background of electoral contestation, the competing influences of Whites and Garrards began to incapacitate Clay County's institutions.[56]

The first crisis leading to the collapse of Clay County's political institutions involved county finances, specifically tax assessment and collection. Although state government relied on revenue from property taxes, assessment of property value and collection of taxes was left to often-resistant county officials. Counties received revenue from property tax collection, but county officials were beholden to powerful local elites and interests, not to state government. Thus, local officials often failed to list property on the tax rolls, deemed assessed value very low, or were unreliable about collecting taxes or turning tax receipts over to the state.[57]

The response of the state to tax mismanagement by the counties reflected its political weakness relative to county governments. Although the Kentucky legislature established a board of equalization to equalize assessments across the state, it also passed numerous acts that accorded individual county sheriffs an extension of time to pay collected taxes. Sheriffs of Clay County were frequent beneficiaries of these measures. In 1866, the general assembly passed an act to settle the delinquent revenue account of sheriff Daniel W. Murray. Thomas Cook, the next sheriff, apparently fared no better and the assembly granted him a one-year extension of time to pay his 1867 tax list, as they did Haywood Gilbert for the 1869 tax list. The following year, the state sued Wilson Morgan and his sureties for failure to pay 1870 taxes. Three years later, an Act of the Assembly declared its judgment that "there are no sheriffs in Clay and Breathitt Counties and that no person who is able to execute such bond as required by law can be procured to collect the revenue tax and county levy . . . for the year 1872 and the year 1873." In a pattern that was repeated throughout the 1880s in Clay and other counties, the state then appointed an outside tax collector who received up to 15% of the receipts.[58]

In this context, it was not highly unusual when Clay County sheriff, A. B. Howard, failed to submit tax receipts in 1890, 1891, and 1894, or even when D. K. Garrard, county treasurer, was accused in 1893 of embezzling tax receipts. But rapidly inflating land values both made these years particularly lucrative ones for tax collectors and heightened the consequences of tax forfeitures. At a time when demands on county services were at a unprecedented level due to rapid commercial and speculative development, the county's inability to garner tax receipts paralyzed county government.[59]

In its efforts to resolve this fiscal crisis, Clay County provoked a political crisis. To meet routine county expenditures – for road repair, payment of salaries of county officials, and other county services – county government borrowed loans from local (Garrard-owned) banks. As tax collection failed year after year, the county was unable to repay its former obligations and was forced to borrow additional amounts for continuing expenses. These fiscal practices set political and economic forces in the county on a collision course. Through their bank loans, the Garrards acquired a financial stranglehold over the county, but county political offices were virtually monopolized by the Whites, who controlled the numerically preponderant Republican Party. Thus, it was T. G. White, then a county clerk, who led the prosecution of former county treasurer D. K. Garrard's sureties for using county funds to make personal loans. And it was the Garrard-controlled Bank of London that sued A. B. Howard for failure to submit tax receipts and, later, for embezzlement.[60]

In the mid-1890s, as the county was unable to collect past tax levies from its former sheriff and treasurer, the fiscal crisis of the county grew more acute. Court actions from 1894, 1895, and 1896 show that claims against the county were being bought and sold by the Garrard-controlled Bank of Manchester and the merchant firm of Garrard and Murphy. In effect, these claims had become currency in the county. When tax collection was resumed in

1895, the Garrards insisted on submitting their claims against the county as payment of their tax bill, an action that both intensified the financial problems of the county and directly challenged the White-dominated political structure. Other court actions followed. Sheriff William L. White forced the sale at public auction of a $875 safe owned by the Bank of Manchester to pay the bank's $100 tax levy after the bank tried unsuccessfully to offset its tax liability with claims it held against the county treasury. Both the bank's efforts to win a restraining order to block the sale of its safe and suits by Garrards to force the county to honor tax claims were similarly unsuccessful. Such fiscal problems resulted from, and in turn intensified, the political conflict between the county's most powerful families.[61]

In the face of economic and fiscal crises in local government – and heightening tension between the county's most powerful families – why were local institutions of dispute resolution not able to prevent the escalation of conflict into violence? A commonplace assumption is that Appalachians turned to violent means to resolve disputes because they lacked institutions of conflict mediation.

Although legal practices clearly were established in Clay County from its creation, in the period of intense violence in the late nineteenth century – its so-called "feud" – the county's court and legal system did disintegrate for a period of time. However, the legal breakdown was a consequence, not a cause, of political conflict and the violence that accompanied it. The Circuit Court was near collapse in 1899 when feud-related violence convinced the judge to flee to another county and state militia were imported to protect the courthouse during trial proceedings. But, again, it was as much the case that violence undermined the court as that court malfunctioning gave rise to extralegal violence. Moreover, the turmoil in court proceedings does not appear to have affected other local institutions as severely. Even in the fall of 1899, at the peak of violence, for example, county deed books record an apparently peaceful sale and transfer of property between members of opposing feud factions, the sale of fifty acres on Crane Creek from G. W. Philpot to B. P. White.[62]

Evidence from the court docket also indicates the generally robust nature of Clay County's court system – even during much of the period of active feuding – although there are some important exceptions. We examined the outcomes of all civil cases from the 1890s involving a feud-neutral and a feudist. Typically, plaintiffs were much more likely than defendants to win cases. As plaintiffs, feudists won 92% of their cases against feud-neutrals (thirty-five of thirty-eight for Whites; forty-four of forty-eight for Garrards). When feud-neutrals sued those on the Garrard side, they won 83% of the time (forty-five of fifty-four). But feud-neutrals won only 74% of cases (twenty-three of thirty-one) against Whites (who controlled the county courts throughout most of this period). If we combine the outcomes in which plaintiffs won and in which the case was settled by agreement (likely to favor plaintiffs), we find no difference between the win rates of Whites or Garrards, but feud-neutrals were less than half as likely to win as defendants as were feudists (6% versus 14% and 13%). Thus, although case outcomes were not totally predictable by the allegiances of the parties involved, the courts did favor the wealthy and powerful feudist families over others, and somewhat favored Whites relative to Garrards.

Examination of civil cases in which defendants and plaintiffs were on opposing sides of the feud shows a similar, slight, partiality toward the Whites. For eleven cases with known outcomes in the 1890s in which those on the Garrard side were plaintiffs and those on the White side were defendants, Garrards won six and Whites won three; two were settled by agreement. In the twenty cases in which the Whites were plaintiffs against the Garrards, Whites won sixteen; as defendants, Garrards won none, and four were settled by agreement. Since settlements by agreement typically favored plaintiffs, Garrards won 73% of cases against Whites when they were plaintiffs; Whites won every case they brought against Garrards, again suggesting court partiality toward the White family.

It is the case, of course, as Little argues in a study of the nineteenth-century criminal court docket, that case files do not reveal "what actually happened" in disputed actions; they only tell us how these events and processes are codified and represented to the legal system.[63] The system of justice in class-stratified and capitalist societies effectively circumscribes or excludes a number of concerns from the reach of legal remedy. But within this framework, it is clear that legal and judicial systems continued to function fairly well throughout the nineteenth century in Clay County. Although court decisions reflect some partiality in favor of the White side of the feud, it was not the collapse of legal institutions that gave rise to violent disputing in Clay County. Rather, the courts and legal system became undermined by the same forces of political and economic conflict that spawned extralegal conflict and violent disputing.

It would be a mistake, however, to conclude that the collapse of Clay County's political institutions represented a more general failure of public civic life. The stereotyped image of Appalachia as a land of isolated individuals or families implies an absence of community life that a close scrutiny of historical evidence does not support. Clay County's nineteenth-century political institutions rested precariously on a base of historic private antagonisms, making them highly vulnerable during episodes of conflict, but these were by no means the only avenues of civic engagement or public life in the county. At the height of feud violence, for example, the Reverend Dickey chided the "revelers" of Manchester, a place where "dances occur every few nights. . . . Every event of any importance is celebrated with a dance. . . . God save this county." Earlier visitors to the county reached a similar, if less pejorative, conclusion. An antebellum candidate for U.S. Congress described his surprise to find a "crowd of nearly two thousand men, women and children, who had congregated from all parts of the County to see Court" in his visit to Manchester. After delivering a campaign speech, he noticed an "immense circle of men and women [surrounding] . . . a man dancing a solo to the fiddle of a small man, half Indian, named *Sisemore*, who had come from Lee county, in Virginia, to play for the occasion." Pressed by the crowd to join the fiddling, he complied lest his refusal "be ascribed by them to aristocratic pride and seal my destiny in the mountains."[64]

More institutionalized forms of public life, too, were present in nineteenth-century Clay County. In addition to institutions such as stores, taverns, and, by the early twentieth century, a hospital and eye clinic, Clay County had a number of churches and schools. As early as 1825, Clay County boasted a school near the salt furnaces, known as Clay County Seminary. By 1860, Clay County had seventy-eight schools, two Methodist-Episcopal churches, and eleven Baptist congregations, and by 1890, twenty churches and eighty schoolhouses. Church membership data were not available until 1906 when 27% of Clay Countians were reported to belong to a religious denomination, low in comparison to 40% for Kentucky as a whole, but a far cry from the image of mountaineers as resolute nonjoiners.[65] Too, such institutional life seemed relatively unaffected by the chaos of Clay County's political life and may have provided a least a modicum of civic life outside the factionalized structure of political and economic strife.

Consequences of the Feud

Clay County's recurrent episodes of deadly feuding were rooted in the political cleavages and institutional fragility of a society built on economic relations of hierarchy and dependency. But the violence that accompanied local state building in Appalachian Kentucky is more than an historical footnote. As we will discuss in the next chapter, the conflictual relations that characterized Clay County's economically and politically factionalized elite had enduring effects on the county's political and economic development. To a great extent, even the conditions of Clay County in the late twentieth century – its enduring political stagnation, political corruption, and chronic poverty

– are legacies of the institutionalization of county governance and the discursive understandings of Appalachia that accompanied violent feuding more than a century ago.

Institutional Legacies

An enduring aspect of Clay County's political life has been the inability of local government institutions to establish autonomy from factions of the county's contentious elite. This was particularly evident during the feud years when local courts were employed repeatedly to settle disputes between elite groups but collapsed during periods of severe and sustained intraelite conflict. Such partisan local institutions weakened the county's ability to promote a coherent set of elite interests at the same time as the extreme economic and political disenfranchisement of the majority of the population precluded effective non-elite representation. And such factors had long-term consequences, undermining the development of effective local political leadership and setting into motion the county's enduring political stagnation.

A second institutional legacy was the formation of a local governance structure in Clay County that was particularly vulnerable to corruption. Politics in Clay County were not institutionalized by eliminating earlier social relations of hierarchy and dependency; instead, these became embedded in the structure of local governance through the exchange of jobs for political and feud-based loyalty. Personal ties and connections became the foundation on which public politics was transacted and antagonisms from economic life easily spilled over into public policies and governance.

The expansion of local government in the twentieth century did not erode, but rather increased, the opportunities for political patronage. Nearly seventy years after Clay County's truce, for example, political corruption was still so pervasive that a judicial candidate was labeled reform-minded when he promised an end to Clay County's "rootin'-tootin', straight shootin'" days and declared hacksaws, whiskey, and pistols "off limits to prisoners in the county jail." And in 1986, a front page story in the *Wall Street Journal* reviewed another decade of bombings, sniper attacks, and unsolved murders and arsons in Clay County, citing the continuing paralysis of local courts to address these problems due to persistent jury tampering – which a local informant called "knowing the jury."[66] Sociologist Cynthia Duncan's analysis of Appalachian Kentucky underlines the pervasiveness of corruption and patronage relations into the late twentieth century:

> This patronage system extends well beyond the school system. The corruption that characterizes school-board races and school personnel

hiring extends into every aspect of community life. Whether it is access to free government food, access to slots in youth training programs, jobs in state government offices, or referrals to openings at a new fast-food restaurant or a good security job with a private firm, having an opportunity depends on whom you know or whom you supported in the last election.[67]

The overt use of public office for personal gain also shaped the relationship between local and state government. Just as Clay County's elites regarded the local public treasury as theirs for the taking, so, too, did they scheme to extract funds from the state coffers. One strategy involved Kentucky's fairly generous subsidies to local committees – which could be no more than a single local merchant – charged with overseeing the state's "feeble-minded poor." Anxious to benefit from the state's largess, counties across the state responded by naming increasing numbers of their populace as "pauper idiots." As the state auditor reported in 1881, "people go about hunting up children who do not manifest the ordinary degree of sprightliness, take them before the county court, obtain a verdict of idiocy with the understanding that the person be appointed the committee." By 1910, nearly one out of every one thousand state residents was designated a "pauper idiot" and placed on the state payroll, absorbing almost 4% of the state's entire budget. No accounting of the funds spent by the committees was required and, not surprisingly, payments did not always reach their intended targets. Even in a system of such widespread abuse, Clay County stood out in its ability to pry funds from the state. By 1910, the county claimed thirty-nine pauper idiots, a ratio of 1 for every 456 people in the county, more than twice the state average.

Even the violence of the feud presented an opportunity for local elites to make a claim on the state's purse. Feudists demanded that those in the other faction be arrested, and then petitioned the state for funds to be hired as jail guards. Indeed, open civil strife could be a particularly lucrative moneymaker since the state reimbursed feudists for their work in organizing local militias to stem the very violence in which they were involved. During the violence of the late 1890s, for example, Beverly P. White received $84.50 for summoning the guard to quell the conflict in which his family were key actors. Other feuding elites successfully billed the state for funds to provide housing, supplies, and meals to the civil guard during periods of civil unrest.[68]

Finally, the factionalism of local governance in Clay County subordinated economic development to political interests. In the nineteenth century, elite families' efforts to pursue strategic advantage through public institutions meant that Clay County's systems of taxation and assessment benefited and enriched particular sides of the feud, but paralyzed the local development of commerce and industry. In the long run, this established a system of governance in which partisan political considerations blocked any sustained public investment in local infrastructure or economic development, contributing directly to the lasting underdevelopment and impoverishment of the county.[69]

In a more general sense, Clay County's history of violent feuding suggests that the historical circumstances in which local politics develops can either help or hinder subsequent political and economic development. In Clay County, it was feuds among elites that formed the framework within which both economic development and local politics were organized. The contemporary corruption, political stagnation, and economic underdevelopment that mark Clay County today thus cannot be understood adequately without attention to the historical pathways through which its institutions of local political governance were forged.[70]

Discursive Legacies

In addition to institutional legacies, feuds left legacies of understanding, or misunderstanding, of life in the southern mountains. Feuding was the common term applied to sustained incidents of widespread violence throughout Appalachia, especially in Kentucky, at the turn of the twentieth century. This discursive description created a authoritative image of southern mountaineers in the minds of those who lived far outside the Appalachian region. Reports on Clay County's feud in the *New York Times* and other national media did much to persuade middle-class readers throughout the rest of the United States of the strange and peculiar nature of Appalachia and its apparently "benighted" population.[71] Typical was the image of the violent mountaineer from the pages of *Frank Leslie's Popular Monthly*:

> The Kentucky feudist is a man apart from his race; a type individual and distinct. By birth, tradition and environment, he is taught to regard the taking of human life with a little concern as he would feel in removing a stone from his path. His tall and uncouth figure stalks somberly across the page of history and his footsteps are marked with blood.[72]

Sensationalistic press coverage led to the identification of Kentucky in particular as "the land of feuds." Imagined to be "one of the most primitive regions of the United States," Appalachian Kentucky was depicted as a place where "bloodshed is a pastime," where "cruel and cowardly murder goes unpunished," and where "assassination is . . . its passion." Although feuds were widespread across the Kentucky mountains, Clay County was frequently singled out for the perceived ferocity of its populace. It was, one writer intoned, a place "tinged with the blood of the innocent and blackened by reasonless deeds of hate," where "death stalks abroad at noonday like a roaring lion seeking whom he may devour." By another account, "there [was] scarcely an acre within the county boundaries that d[id] not hold a spot where some member of the populace has been shot from ambush." According to a *New York Times* article, "Clay County knows that it has a bad name."[73]

In *Appalachia on Our Mind*, Henry Shapiro points out how naming functioned as explaining in the process of identifying and understanding social problems in the southern mountains. Newspaper reportage of violence in Clay County represents a good example of this phenomenon. Community conflicts were used by nonlocal writers to help define "Appalachia," and, once constructed, the idea of "Appalachia" was used to explain the forms of violence that erupted there. By attributing feud violence to the "ignorance" and "isolation" of southern mountaineers, writers underscored what they saw as the distinctive nature of the place and its people.

In the huge body of popular and scholarly commentary that the Clay County feud and others like it stimulated, writers developed a canonical set of explanations for Kentucky's violence. Feuds were seen to result from poverty, ignorance, and isolation, as having been triggered by the most trivial of incidents, prolonged by primitive clan loyalties, and tolerated because of the ineffectiveness of, or hostility toward, legal institutions in mountain society. In the words of a contemporary commentator, the feuds "have every earmark of the Scotch feuds among the clans . . . resort to violence requires little provocation. Altercations between friends suddenly angered or drinking, disputes over business settlements or family discords – of which the son-in-law is credited with many – may all lead to an outbreak." C. W. Watson and J. H. Wheelwright, presidents of Consolidated Coal Company, viewed the land whose resources they hungered after as "distant, detached, unknown. The feudists guarded every mountain path, outlawry mocked at order, a bloody mist overhung every valley and ignorance rested like a pall over the mountains." The feuding spirit, others contended, was rooted in direct lines of heredity from the Old World, "not a degenerate tendency, but the honest survival of the old Saxon and Celtic temper."[74]

Scholars, as well as journalists, helped shape public perception of mountain feuding and mountaineers. Particularly influential was a 1910 essay by Ellen Churchill Semple, a soon-to-be president of the American Association of Geography. In "The Anglo-Saxons of the Kentucky Mountains," Semple argued that "isolation and poverty" had "fostered the survival of the blood-feud among the Kentucky mountaineers," an institution that she believed could "be traced back to the idea of clan responsibility among their Anglo-Saxon forbearers." She dismissed the immediate causes of mountain conflict as "often of a trifling nature," resulting from "a misunderstanding in a horse trade, a gate left open and trespassing cattle, the shooting of a dog, political rivalry, or a difficulty over a boundary fence." Law could do little to remedy the situation, she reasoned, since "[w]hen the law invaded this remote region, it found the feud [already] established and the individual loath to subordinate himself to the body politic."[75]

Like other writers of the era, Semple's claim to authority derived not only from the so-called "scientific" premises of her discipline, but also from her claim to firsthand observation based on "a trip of 350 miles [on horseback] through the mountains." Nonetheless, her description of specific events in Clay County – the particular case on which her interpretation of feuds in general was based – appears, at least in part, to have been lifted without citation from a magazine article by J. Stoddard Johnson published two years earlier in *The Cosmopolitan*. For example, Johnson described an important episode in the Clay County trouble as follows:

> Now, Tom Baker did not relish the idea of giving himself up to the sheriff, Beverly T. White, brother of the man he had killed and kinsman to the clerk, jailer and judge. So he took to the hills until troops were sent to the county, when he surrendered himself to them.

Semple's account reads:

> In this same Howard and Baker feud, Tom Baker shot to death William White, an ally of the Howards and brother of the sheriff, as likewise kinsman of the county clerk, jailer, and judge. Naturally reluctant to give himself up to officials who were his personal enemies, Baker took to the hills until State troops were sent to the county, when he gave himself up to them.

Horace Kepart published a close variation of the Semple-Johnson description in 1913, adding an embellishment of his own that misnamed an additional Clay County combatant, and this version of the original, along with Kephart's misnaming, was published in 1942 by Alvin Harlow.[76]

These passages suggest that much of what appears to be commentary on Kentucky mountain feuds was really commentary on *writings* about feuds as popular and scholarly authors alike read and borrowed from one another freely. Their close and generally unacknowledged mutual reliance suggests that the locus of what has been taken to be the reality of feuding was as much on the printed page as in the hills of Kentucky. Since a scholar, Semple, relied on a popularizer, Johnson, who, it turns out, had originally cited an often quoted passage from John Fox, Jr.'s fiction as an authoritative description of the nature of feuds, it is reasonable to conclude that science, journalism, and fiction writing closely influenced one another in the creation of the popular imagination about feuding.[77]

To the journalists, essayists, and social scientists who flocked to Clay County at the end of the nineteenth century, mountain women were the most peculiar of this "peculiar people." A journalist who traveled to Manchester in the summer of 1901 seemed to take his readers on a human safari, directing attention to what he saw as the primitive state of women and children in this remote place:

> Now and again we would pass a small hut. . . . Wild and poorly clad forms would appear in the low doorways; faces almost expressionless would stare at us in a kind of apathetic wonder. Women's and children's faces for the most part; the men were away.[78]

Although women rarely appear in accounts of mountain politics, law, or business, they are featured in two oft-repeated tales from the Clay County feud. In both, women lurk in the background, spurring violence from the shadows. Feud women are seen as motivated by traditional maternal and wifely concerns, but in this "strange land," such allegiances become dangerous, menacing. The first story features the widow of Tom Baker, herself never named, in the classic role reserved for women in a vendetta: carrying the blood memory from father to son.[79] According to feud legend, as she grieved over the body of her dead husband, Tom's widow swore her twelve sons in a blood oath to avenge their father's assassination. "Each day," she is reported as saying, "I shall show my boys the handkerchief stained with his blood, and tell them who murdered him!" The second story features the wife of Gardner Baker, also unnamed, as the lookout who is said to have rung a dinner bell from her house on Crane Creek, signaling the arrival of the Howards and beginning a bloody ambush.[80]

The wives of Tom and Gardner Baker are the most prominent women in feud legend, but commentators insisted that many women acted as provocateurs behind the scenes of feud violence. The *Berea Quarterly* in 1909 concluded that women had "figured in all these feuds, sometimes as the precipitating cause, always in the capacity of an efficient and loyal retainer. She acted as spy and scout." Since women were protected by ethical standards from retaliatory feud violence, the magazine reasoned, they took "advantage of this unwritten law, crossing the lines of the enemy without personal danger beyond arrest." Others resolved that the Baker women were not unique, that "many of the women added fuel to the feud fires by gossip and by insults and by encouraging others to fight."[81]

These images of mountain women as afflicted but treacherous, as peripheral yet ominous, profoundly shaped the perception of women's role in nineteenth-century mountain life, riveting attention on women in family dramas and slighting them outside of that context. For those chronicling the Clay County feud, as well as for their readers far removed from the Appalachian mountains, such accounts served to validate the perception that it was the alliances, politics, and economic stakes of mountain men – not mountain women – that were key to understanding mountain violence, and mountain life as a whole. This perception persisted, notwithstanding the prominent roles played by such entrepreneurs and influential local actors as Laura White, the timber and coal investor, or Martha Coldiron Hogg, real estate magnate and benefactor of Oneida Baptist Institute, the location of the feud's first truce.

Popular accounts of feuding shaped many other public attitudes and policies toward Appalachia into the next century. For educators and reformers at work in the Kentucky mountains around the turn of the century, the occurrence of feuds there, and the vast amount of publicity they generated nationally, provided both an embarrassment and an opportunity. In order to secure charitable donations for projects aimed at uplifting mountain people, these workers had a profound interest in portraying the moral (and racial) worthiness of the local population they were attempting to serve.[82] The violence of feuds, however, threatened to call into question this very fact of worthiness. As Shapiro has said, "images of the mountaineer as pathetic and romantic gave way before a set of images of mountaineers as feudists and desperadoes, criminals and social deviants." At the same time, however, by placing mountain problems squarely at the center of public attention, feuds created opportunities to publicize the need for reform efforts. By interpreting feuds sympathetically as a regrettable but understandable consequence of ignorance and isolation, reformers could still justify their mission of uplift and make its urgency all the more apparent.

Contributors to this version of the feud story were at pains to discern traces of misplaced courage and honor in Kentucky bloodletting in order to justify the moral worthiness of their client populations. Thus, W. G. Frost, president of Berea College, proclaimed that "It gives us hope for their future that the frequent homicides [in Appalachian Kentucky] are not committed wantonly nor for purposes of robbery, but in the spirit of an

Homeric chieftain on some 'point of honor'." General O. O. Howard, former head of the Freedman's Bureau and founder of Lincoln Memorial College, likewise attempted to put a favorable spin on feuding by claiming that "[m]uch of [the feud] spirit comes from the present and past necessity of a head of a family protecting his family" and pointing out that "fortunately there is a reverence for women and children and they are spared" in feud confrontations.[83]

Subsequent writers followed the lead of Frost and Howard by describing feuds as the expression of the "great primal qualities" of "vigor and courage" in Appalachia's "Fighting Stock." Thus, an anonymous author in *The Berea Quarterly* concluded that mountain fighters' "impulses to avenge their own wrongs [was] not a degenerate tendency, but the honest survival of the Old Saxon and Celtic tempter" and further informed readers that "mountain homicides never occur as an accompaniment of robbery. They are performed invariably upon some 'point of honor,' and the ethical standard of the feudsman always protects women and children." Though decrying the conditions of isolation and ignorance and making a plea for the support of educational improvements in the mountains, Emerson Hough went even further in singing the praise of Cumberland feudists, calling them "a keen, bold breed of men . . . carrying on feuds as a religion . . . sweetly and graciously practicing the ancient laws of hospitality, sternly adhering to their ideas of personal honor, curiously unconventional, curiously unchanged."[84]

Once represented sympathetically, feuds could be used to justify charitable contributions in the region. In fact, agents of social reform and educational improvement in Appalachian Kentucky did much to keep a chastened image of feuds well before the public eye. At a meeting in Boston in 1900 to raise money for Berea College, President Frost opened his address to potential benefactors with a description of the Baker-Howard feud then raging in Clay County. He then told his audience that "[t]he mountain people are not so much a degraded population as a population not yet graded up" and asked them to contribute to Berea's educational efforts in the region. Three years later, while making what he called a "great plea for the educational uplift of Appalachian America" before a Chautauqua Assembly in New York on the topic of "Mob Spirit in America," Frost again recounted the Clay County feud and the number of lives it had taken. This time, he argued that "[t]he cure of the feud must lie in that moral progress which is called education," and he claimed that at Berea College, "[w]e are proposing not merely to prevent the mountain people from being a menace, but to bring the people of Appalachian America over from the ranks of the doubtful classes and range them with those who are to be the patriotic leaders and helpers of the new age."

Elsewhere, Frost publicized Berea's extension work in what he described as "the feud belt," including the value of a course offered on "How to Settle Family Feuds without Bloodshed." An anonymous article in *The Berea Quarterly* entitled "The College and the Feud" later claimed that "Berea eradicates the feud spirit," and described "the work of Berea College as a prime force in the destruction of the feud." The cover of this particular issue of the *Quarterly* featured a provocative photograph of two supposedly armed feudists entitled "Men Proud of Being Dangerous'" and other issues of the *Quarterly* ran photographs of Berea students described gratuitously in captions such as "A Daughter of the Feud-Country."[85] Significantly, these articles and photographs were published roughly a decade after the termination of most mountain feuds.

Berea College was not the only educational institution in Appalachia to publicize and benefit from stereotypes about Kentucky feuds. Cora Wilson Stewart, who witnessed feud violence firsthand as a young child in Rowan County, used feuds as a justification for her campaign against illiteracy; O. O. Howard linked Lincoln Memorial University's educational mission to feud eradication, claiming that "good roads and good education, will surely cure the feud spirit!"; and James Anderson Burns, founder of the Oneida Baptist Institute in Clay County, claimed that his private academy grew "out of an indomitable purpose to stop the feuds and, in doing so, to conserve the manhood and the womanhood of the mountaineers." Following the well-trod path of W. G. Frost to New York City, Burns spent three months there in 1908 lecturing on "Feud Conditions in the Cumberlands" in order to elicit financial support for his school, and in 1912, the popular writer Emerson Hough publicized Burns's success nationally in *The American Magazine*, claiming that "They say that feudism and moonshining is done in Clay County; and they date that back to 1899 and the [founding of the Oneida Baptist Institute]."[86]

Not all commentators, however, were confident about the ameliorative effects of education and social uplift. "Neither education, nor wealth, nor the refinements of civilization are as strong as the murder-lust in the Land of the Feuds," warned Hartley Davis and Clifford Smyth in an article in *Muncey's Magazine*. "Its regeneration will come only through the introduction of outside influences, or people who will dominate not only intellectually but numerically." According to this version of the story of mountain feuds, only with the domination of Appalachia and the displacement of its population by outsiders "will the Frankenstein of the Kentucky mountains receive its death thrust, and the Land of Feuds . . . cease to be a blot on the map of these United States." An article in *Frank Leslie's Popular Monthly* agreed: "So long as their mountain defiles remain uninvaded by the emigrant; so long as their mountain sides intimidate the prospective railroad line; and above all, so long as their wild, barbaric blood remains uncrossed by a gentler strain – just so long will their internecine wars prevail."[87]

With feuds in these accounts represented unsympathetically as "the spawn of ignorance, prejudice, and a free-giving way to man's worst passions," their eradication could be easily linked to the advance of capitalist economic development rather than social reform – this at the very moment that corporate railroad, timber, and mineral interests were scrambling to acquire Appalachian rights and properties.[88] Thus, the writer of an 1899 *New York Times* article entitled "Cause of Kentucky Feuds: Isolation, Ignorance, and Whiskey Said to be Responsible; Railroads Much Needed," concluded that "What Manchester [Clay County] needs most next to schools . . . is the civilizing railroad. It has been too much by itself." This particular writer did not say so but others (below) contended that if mountaineers resisted the so-called "civilizing" effects of corporate capitalist development, their recalcitrance – evidenced by the persistence of violence – might justify their being displaced from the rich treasure-house of natural wealth they inconveniently called "home." If commentators on the 1890s feud cited the lack of industrial development as a cause of the mountaineer's isolation, and the basis for proclivity to violent feuding, later the sense of what was *cause* and what was *effect* was reversed. An investigatory report on Clay County violence in the 1930s concluded that it was the feud itself that was preventing outside capital from developing local resources and reducing property values in the county. By virtue of their unchecked passions, mountaineers, the new thinking went, were responsible for the economic impasse in which they now found themselves.[89]

In describing the relationship between culture and imperialism in western writing, Edward Said points to "a structure of attitude and reference," which views "the outlying regions of the world [as] hav[ing] no life, history, or culture to speak of, no independence or integrity worth representing without the West." Alternatively, "when there is something to be described" in those regions, it is "unutterably corrupt, degenerate, irredeemable."[90] Both attitudes influenced how metropolitan writers in America viewed the Appalachian periphery before its industrialization.

In one account, Appalachia was a place where time stood still until its discovery and representation by social reformers who brought the region into the orbit of modern awareness, institutions, and progress. Thus, in a *Collier's Weekly* article entitled "Children of the Feudists," Bruce Barton described the exploratory tour that William G. Frost made through the hills of West

Virginia and Kentucky before assuming the presidency of Berea College as one of the "great voyages of discovery which have opened up unchartered continents and brought to light forgotten people." Much as if he had ventured to darkest Africa, Barton described Frost as having "uncovered the lost tribes of America: three million pure-blooded Americans who since the days when their ancestors first lost themselves in the mountains, have been as completely covered and forgotten as through the earth had opened to swallow them."[91]

If Appalachia at its best was viewed as latency and potentiality, a space where American middle-class culture could effect its alchemy, it was portrayed as a place and a people far less subject to redemption in accounts that called for the region's numerical domination by outsiders and for its "wild, barbaric blood" to be diluted by emigration. By portraying the Kentucky mountaineer as a person who "by birth, tradition, and environment" was "taught to regard the taking of human life with as little concern as he would feel in removing a stone from his path," writers spun an imperial tale about savagery in Appalachia that was the narrative equivalent of numerous other colonialist discourses throughout the West. For example, Patrick Brantlinger's analysis of the British myth of the "dark continent" of Africa as a center of barbarism and evil shows that "Africa grew 'dark' as Victorian explorers, missionaries, and scientists flooded it with light, because the light was refracted through an imperialist ideology that urged the abolition of 'savage customs' in the name of civilization." Paralleling America's fascination with Appalachian feuds, the extreme western fascination with cannibalism, according to Brantlinger, marked Africa as a degenerate place earmarked for the kind of correction that only western forms of cultural and economic penetration could provide.

Few people outside the Kentucky hills were watching, or cared, in the 1840s when the Garrards and the Whites began their struggle to dominate Clay County, Kentucky, but a half century later, when the control of such timber and mineral-rich counties became a matter of great importance, voices predictably arose proclaiming that the time had come for obstinate hillbillies to fade away as well. "The power to narrate," according to Said, "or to block other narratives from forming and emerging, is very important to culture and imperialism, and constitutes one of the main connections between them."[92] By creating an impression of Appalachians as a people in need either of uplift or dispersion, and the southern mountain region as a dark zone of chaos and violence in desperate need of what the *New York Times* called "the civilizing railroad," feud narratives gave American readers a framework through which to view the profound changes that were taking place at the turn of the century in Appalachian Kentucky and the spasm of violence that was accompanying its industrialization. That framework, however, obscured from vision the actual economic, political, and cultural strategies that we have described in this study as setting Appalachia on its road to poverty.

9

EPILOGUE

When James Brown first began his ethnographic study of Beech Creek in 1942, he found an already impoverished rural community. No traces were left of Clay County's once thriving nineteenth-century salt industry and very few descendants of its African American workforce remained in the area. The postbellum timber boom had ended several decades earlier. A railroad had penetrated Clay County only two decades before, and with it, coal mining expanded from the casual diggings that earlier had supplied fuel for salt-making to become a locally important industry, but not in the Beech Creek section of the county. The Beech Creek basin remained accessible only by foot or horseback up the narrow, winding creek bed as had been the case since the earliest days of settlement. Rural electrification was still a decade and a half or more away.[1]

Subsistence farming was the chief source of income in Beech Creek in 1942. Despite decreasing self-sufficiency, consumer expenditures among the families of the Beech Creek neighborhoods were dramatically low. But Beech Creek's farms were tiny. In contrast to the highly productive farms of eighty years earlier that had averaged 60 acres of improved land and 679 unimproved acres, Beech Creek farms averaged only 10 acres in crops in 1942; half were less than 50 total acres in size and one-third were less then 30. The population, however, had grown exponentially and was densely concentrated. In one of Beech Creek's three neighborhoods, 156 people lived in thirty-two impoverished households in a creek basin where only three households had lived in relative, if rustic, comfort in 1850.

After World War II, economic marginality in agriculture and decreasing employment opportunities in coal mining brought on by mechanization combined to force millions of people to leave Appalachia to look for employment elsewhere. The region lost two million people between 1950 and 1960 alone. In 1961, Harry K. Schwarzweller and J. J. Mangalam joined with James Brown to study the post–World War II migration from Beech Creek to the industrial centers of the Midwest by resurveying outmigrants who had resided in the Beech Creek neighborhoods at the time of Brown's initial 1942 study. The resulting study, published as *Mountain Families in Transition*, documented tremendous migration from the area in the years after Brown's study. Faced with the continuing impoverishment of Clay County – and, for some, drawn by economic opportunities in the wartime industries of the industrial Midwest – only 57% of those in Brown's initial survey still lived in Beech Creek in 1947. More left in the following decades. Most settled in southern Ohio or other cities of Midwest. A few remained in Clay County or adjacent counties, moving to towns or other rural neighborhoods. Less than 200 lived in the original Beech Creek neighborhoods in 1961. Perhaps ten people live there today.

Schwarzweller, Mangalam, and Brown found that the process of migration from Beech Creek was rooted in established resources of kinship and social class, including what we might today call the "social capital" of mutual aid and reciprocity. Those whose kin had access to jobs, land, or other financial resources left Beech Creek able to rely on family members both back home and in the area of destination for support and assistance. Kin in the area of destination could provide housing (or, rarely, employment), or networks of information and contacts to find these. Kin remaining in the Beech Creek neighborhoods could supply a cushion of safety. Only 17% of the migrants retained actual title to land in Clay County after their departure, but frequent visits by migrants to kin "back home" maintained relationships that ensured a place to which the migrant could return if necessary.

Importantly, social class positions structured how migrants left Beech Creek and how they fared in their area of destination. Despite only minimal class differences among those who ultimately left Beech Creek, the relative class positions of migrants nonetheless remained stable during the process of migration. In the nineteenth century, landless people had been the most likely to leave the area. In the twentieth century, however, the first to leave Beech Creek were families that Brown had identified as "high-class," whose educational, financial, and familial resources and connections allowed entire nuclear families to migrate together and to settle in established residential areas. These same resources provided access to well-paid, steady, working-class jobs in the area of destination. Ultimately, these families tended to resettle in neighborhoods with more expensive housing and few Appalachian migrants. Few maintained a homestead in Clay County.

In contrast, migrants from "intermediate-class" positions in Beech Creek tended to retain their Beech Creek land and to migrate in stages. They initially lived with kin, but, as the entire family migrated, eventually settled in semirural communities of Appalachian migrants.

Those from families Brown identified as "low-class" had more variable migratory patterns, depending in part on whether they had a base of landownership in Beech Creek. Some moved out of the Appalachian region. For these, kinship ties drew them into the impoverished ghettos of the industrial Midwest; a lack of familial economic support in either Beech Creek or the area of destination trapped them there. Some moved to farms or neighborhoods adjoining the original Beech Creek area in search of better farmland or closer proximity to roads; for the most part, these families remained poor. Those who remained in the largely depopulated Beech Creek neighborhoods lived on marginal farmlands. Nearly all were poor.

For many of those who stayed behind, life in Clay County has been difficult. One of central Appalachia's poorest counties, Clay County ranks among the poorest counties even in eastern Kentucky, where the poverty rate averages 42%, three times the national average. The Beech Creek neighborhoods are located in one of ten census tracts along the South Fork of the Kentucky River in Clay, Owsley, Perry, and Leslie Counties, where 54% of all children are living below the poverty level at the present time. Such poverty has been a persistent fact of life there for decades.[2]

Not all Appalachian subregions, however, are equally impoverished. In Southern Appalachia, the mountainous sections of Georgia, North Carolina, and South Carolina have experienced relative prosperity and growth, especially in metropolitan counties, but many rural counties in these Appalachian states as well as Tennessee and Mississippi continue to lag well behind the nation in per capita income. Some Northern Appalachia counties have experienced growth, but many more have experienced severe economic decline, especially those dependent on manufacturing, coal, and steel production where employment and per capita income have fallen because of deindustrialization.[3] Overall, poverty in the thirteen-state Appalachian region declined from 18% to 13% between 1970 and 1990, yet in Central Appalachia, one-fourth of the people were still poor in 1990, a rate of poverty greater than other low-income regions such as the Southeast and the Southwest.[4]

Although Clay County's road to rural poverty does not illuminate the economic pathways that each of Appalachia's diverse subregions are following, it does represent, in an extreme, the trajectory followed in much of Central Appalachia, especially the region's most persistently distressed communities. How can the poverty of Clay County and Central Appalachia be explained?

In Chapter 1, we outlined two theories that have dominated discussions of Appalachian poverty. The culture-of-poverty theory called attention to the traditional values and attitudes of mountain people and how these functioned as both a cause and consequence of Appalachian poverty. According to this approach, as traditional cultural patterns in the region became more and more out of synch with the dictates of modernity, many people, especially the poor, clung tenaciously to outmoded patterns such as familism and traditionalism. But doing so rendered them, and the children they raised, less and less able to adapt to the changing conditions of contemporary industrial and urban life. This theory has the merit of pointing to the importance of cultural legacies and the social institutions of family and community, but fails by viewing these not on their own terms, but as deficiencies, that is, as negative departures from hypothesized norms of capitalist rationality and individual achievement. It also fails to conceptualize the effects of economic exploitation and political domination on the mountain region.

The culture-of-poverty theory is countered by dependency theories that picture Appalachia as an internal colony. By calling attention to Appalachia as an exploited mineral colony, dependency theories help to clarify structural features of the Appalachian economy that are common to peripheral regions where extractive industries such as timbering and mining predominate. These patterns include economic growth with little real development or diversification, boom-and-bust economic cycles, endemic poverty and underemployment, population loss, environmental degradation, extralocal control, and local community incapacity.[5] By stressing economic exploitation over political domination, however, dependency theory conceptualizes the latter as simply a correlate of economics and fails to conceptualize the state as playing anything more than a passive role in the creation and perpetuation of regional poverty. Also, it tends to overlook the positive role of culture in economic regulation and in providing people with resources for economic survival and resistance to economic exploitation and political domination. Further, although rightly pointing to the historicity of corporate capitalist exploitation in the late nineteenth and twentieth centuries, it diverts attention from even earlier indigenous patterns of economic development and state making that laid the foundations for dependent development in "modern" Appalachia. By failing to probe the roots of Appalachia's road to rural poverty in the trajectory of its own developmental logic, dependency theory perpetuates the image of Appalachians as a people without history, that is, until Mr. Peabody's coal train pillaged their land and bodies and inscribed both with meaning.

In this study, we have tried to show how the transition to modern corporate capitalism in Appalachian Kentucky was embedded in prior agrarian social structures. First, we stressed the early origins of industry and commerce in Appalachian Kentucky that permitted the rise of local capitalist elites and its corollary, racial oppression. We then examined the cultural patterns of reciprocity associated with subsistence farming that we have conceptualized as Appalachia's "patriarchal moral economy," as well as the demographic contradictions that this farming system wrought. Finally, we have stressed the importance of clientelism and corruption in the making of the Appalachian local state. But our aim has not been simply to get the "story" of Central Appalachia "right," for such will always be an unfinished project as social change continues to pose new historical questions about the local and the global. Instead, we have tried to write an historical sociology of Appalachian Kentucky that suggests four lessons for public policymaking here and elsewhere in rural America. Central Appalachia's road to rural poverty, we believe, shows (1) that market-driven development is not a panacea for poor regions; (2) that even impoverished regions have rich social capital resources that must be preserved and enhanced; (3) that the local state is not simply a passive reflection of economic conditions, but a significant factor in its own right in shaping the course of rural social development; and, most generally, (4) that a long-term viewpoint on institutional legacies is crucial for understanding the challenge of persistent poverty.

Lesson 1: The Limits of Market-Driven Development

Appalachian scholars have begun to correct the impression, shared in different modalities by the culture-of-poverty theory and mainstream market-driven models of capitalist economic development that Appalachia, in the words of the Appalachian Regional Commission, was "a region apart" in its recent or more distant past.[6] By examining commerce and industry in antebellum Appalachia, scholars have recently begun to appreciate the extent of capitalist development that took place throughout Appalachia well before the growth of the modern coal and timber industries.

Clay County's salt industry was far from an isolated case of local antebellum capitalist industrial development. Appalachian salt production was second only to New York in 1860 and iron manufacturing in the northeastern counties of Appalachian Kentucky along the Ohio River made Kentucky the third largest iron producer in the nation that year as well. Saltmaking, as we have seen, linked Clay County to extraregional commodity chains, shaped the racial composition of the county, and laid the economic foundations for a local capitalist elite that, if not economically strong enough to exploit the region's rich natural resources on its own, was positioned to profit from handing over those natural and human resources to outside capitalists when the time was right. But market-driven capitalism in the antebellum era helped to sustain social inequality and exploitation, human enslavement, racial oppression, and political domination – not economic betterment. It resulted in the production of wealth for only a privileged few in Clay County, not prosperity for the majority. In the postbellum era of corporate capitalist expansion, a greater proportion of the county's population became integrated into capitalist market relations. Yet economic development did little to diminish the gulf between Clay County's small economic elite and the majority of its economically marginal households that depended on a declining agriculture and low-wage jobs in extractive industries.

The institutional legacies of capitalist economic relations in Central Appalachian counties like Clay County, Kentucky are evident today in the region's inability to sustain its population adequately and fairly. According to one of the most comprehensive regional studies to date, "Appalachia [in 1990] contains the new poor of economic restructuring and the old poor left over from the shortcomings of past forms of economic development."[7] Within Appalachia, Central Appalachia has experienced the widest swings in gaining and losing per capita income between 1969 and 1989 because of increased transfer payments and the energy boom of the 1970s that were followed by cutbacks in federally funded public programs and drops in energy-based employment. Richard Couto writes:

> Eastern Kentucky counties started with 55.5 percent of the nation's per capita income in 1969 and ended with 60 percent in 1989. This overall progress in two decades disguises the major gains made in the 1970s. Per capita personal income reached 66.7 percent of the national figure in the 1970s. In the 1980s, it fell to 60 percent. While Eastern Kentucky counties remain ahead of where they were in 1969, they fell far behind where the coal boom of the 1970s brought them.[8]

Although Clay County is not a major coal producer, mining accounts for a greater proportion of nonfarm jobs and income there than in the region as a whole. In 1989, mining contributed 19% of all nonfarm jobs and 35% of nonfarm income in the county compared with only 7.3% of employment and 14.4% of income for Appalachian Kentucky. Dependency on mining subjects even marginally productive localities like Clay County to the characteristic boom-and-bust cycles of that industry. Such dependency is reflected in the fact that only seven years earlier, mining had accounted for almost twice as many (36%) of Clay County's nonfarm jobs and 57% of its nonfarm income. In this seven-year period, the number of mining operations fell from 179 to only 24, indicating both the small scale and ephemeral quality of much of the county's mining. Although the official unemployment rate in 1989 was greater than 9%, the "real" rate of unemployment (including people not looking for work who would reenter the labor force if jobs were available) was estimated to be at least 54%.[9]

Despite the widespread faith in the efficacy of market-driven economic development that exists today, "the current Appalachian economy is in serious trouble because the industrial economy of America and the globe is changing." Richard Couto writes: "In 1981 and 1982, the Appalachian region lost *two and one-half* manufacturing jobs for every *one* it had gained from 1970 to 1980. Job loss continued throughout the 1980s [so that by] . . . 1990, serious economic decline reminiscent of the 1960s was evident in Central Appalachia."[10] Two recent studies have tried to explain why the region has faired so badly.

Andrew Isserman claims that "[m]uch of the Appalachian condition relative to the rest of the nation [including poverty, low income, and deficits in jobs and education] can be understood in terms of its urbanization relative to the nation." He asserts that this is especially true in Central Appalachia, where only 15% of the population resides in metropolitan areas compared to 60% and 65% of the populations in Northern and Southern Appalachia, respectively, and where metropolitan poverty rates are not substantially greater than for the nation as a whole.[11] But focusing on the lack of urbanization treats a symptom as a cause and begs the question of why persistent rurality has been a central feature of Central Appalachia's capitalist development.[12] It fails to question why Appalachia has experienced economic growth but little real, sustainable development and why investments in public goods such as education, housing, and healthcare are so inadequate in rural and Central Appalachia.

A more compelling study points to the failure of American public policy in the region, by showing that market-driven investments, both public and private, shortchange areas of economic marginality and decline, that is, the very communities that require such investments in the long run to move populations from poverty to economic security. It contends that the "human problems of the Appalachian region, and other areas of economic and social need, are, at root, problems of social capital: the investments a political body makes to produce and reproduce human beings in community." Especially problematic is the linkage between employment, markets, and the investments in healthcare, education, housing, culture, and the environment that are biased against poor people and poor communities.

> In general, investment in social capital [i.e., public goods] comes from private sources, follows upon the needs of private capital, and has as its central purpose the production, reproduction, and distribution of a labor force for private capital. When groups of people have subordinate roles in the economy, the social capital invested in them is modest. When people have no role in the economy, even less social capital is invested in them.[13]

The author, Richard Couto, demonstrates that as the need for a labor force in the mining, steelmaking, and textile towns of the Appalachians diminished, investments in public goods "dried up."[14] Couto's perspective is valuable for addressing a national policy failure of tragic proportions in both urban and rural America that goes a long way toward explaining why Appalachian problems have not been meaningfully addressed by federal efforts. However, he does not attempt to explain the *social origins* of the problems in Central Appalachia that public policy must confront including a local political environment that stifles democratic participation in policymaking. Nor, in this study, does he discuss the social and cultural resources still lodged in local Appalachian communities that enable individuals both to cope with poverty and to challenge the status quo.[15]

Lesson 2: The Need to Preserve Cultural Strategies That Sustain Social Capital

Our study has stressed the role of capitalist market relations in early Appalachia far more than most other historical studies. A recognition of early capitalist development and greater social inequality in Appalachia than previously imagined errs, however, when it totalizes market capitalism. Such is the case of one recent writer who claims that landownership concentration and agrarian capitalism deterred subsistence farming in Appalachia by severing the population from the means of production and leading to its gradual proletarianization.[16] James Brown found a poor but not proletarianized population in Beech Creek when he first conducted research there in the 1940s. Our research documents how a once thriving, subsistence farming system helped to set Appalachian Kentucky on its route to poverty by limiting capital accumulation and economic diversification, encouraging population growth, and destabilizing the balance of land and population.[17] Further, by gradually lowering the rural standard of living, subsistence farming depressed the level of wages necessary to recruit workforces to industry in the region while helping to subsidize the costs of their reproduction.[18]

Besides helping to pave a distinctive road to impoverishment, however, Beech Creek's patriarchal moral economy – although premised on age and gender inequality – also encouraged patterns of reciprocity among kin and neighbors that have provided rural Appalachians there and across the region with durable reservoirs of social capital. Appalachians have drawn on these cultural resources in times of scarcity, in periods of transition such as migration to coal camps or Midwest cities, in struggles for unionization and reform in the coal fields, and, most recently, in contemporary struggles to protect jobs, health, communities, and the environment. The patterns of reciprocity Brown observed in Beech Creek have been described by subsequent researchers as enduring features of Appalachian rural community life many years after people left the farm-based, hollow communities where such bonds were first nurtured.

Thirty-three years after Brown first observed Beech Creek, Allen Batteau studied hundreds of households located along main roads in another Appalachian Kentucky county in 1975. He found that the residential distribution of population there was remarkably isomorphic with kinship proximity despite the fact that people were no longer clustered in the creek beds and hollow communities of an earlier era. He concluded that to a large extent, the rural community was still constituted by an array of familial groupings that clustered kinfolk together and that the patterns of kin-based reciprocity described by Brown a generation earlier were still viable. Batteau also found that the local population, like the nineteenth-century Beech Creekers described in Chapter 5, still viewed land not as a commodity, but as "family land," that is, "as a status resource, a tie between neighbors, and a homeplace." This definition pitted them against commercial and government interests in the county that defined land as "a factor in cost-benefit calculation and profit maximization"[19]

Stable ties to land and kin are also seen as key to the survival and self-reliance of an even more widely dispersed, low-income population in eastern Kentucky described in the 1990s by Rhoda Halperin. "Multiple livelihood strategies" of subsistence gardening, temporary wage labor, and informal (flea) marketing, she finds, allow economically marginal Appalachians to sustain a livelihood despite very low incomes. But these practices depend on "long-lasting and highly reliable relationships with other people, especially relatives but also neighbors and friends" that provide a reservoir of social capital that Halperin found to stretch across three generations of interdependent kin in ten mountain counties. According to Halperin, such cultural practices, described in folk idiom as "making ends meet 'the Kentucky way'," can be understood as "forms of resistance to capitalism [i.e., wage labor] and dependency upon the state."[20] The public policy implication is clear. Cultural strategies that sustain social capital in impoverished communities should be strengthened, not weakened.

Lesson 3: The Importance of the Local State

The culture-of-poverty theory views the "social capital" Appalachian poor people have invested in kinship and locality as a cultural deficit rather than a resource but other scholars understand its productivity. One important arena for its deployment is local politics where social capital is invested for both progressive and conservative causes.

Despite stereotypes of fatalism and passivity, Central Appalachia may well lead the nation today in the proliferation of vigorous citizens' movements for social, economic, and environmental justice.[21] Although critical of the political limits of "neo-populism," a recent study of citizen activism in Appalachia by Stephen Fisher shows that "[h]istorical memory and a reliance on and defense of traditional values – a strong commitment to land and family, an emphasis on self-rule and social equality, and patriotism – have fueled many of the resistance efforts in the region" to "the devastating impact of modernization, trickle-down economics, an unresponsive government, and concentrated corporate ownership and power on people's lives, jobs, and communities in Appalachia."[22] The author of a study of an environmental struggle in Appalachian Virginia concludes similarly:

A reverence for tradition, culture, family, heritage, and religion spurred on those involved in the Brumley Gap struggle. People did not want to give up land that had been in their families for centuries. They refused to walk quietly away from the close-knit community which they had built up over the years. Many of the younger people fought more to protect the community's elderly from heartbreak than they did for themselves. Others wanted to be able to pass on their land – and their values – to their children.[23]

Allen Batteau, on the other hand, has shown that relationships among neighbors and kin also form a "core resource for network formation" in the routine county-level politics in eastern Kentucky that often serve to promote the status quo.

Political knowledge in this community consists of knowing these networks, knowing how to do somebody a favor, and knowing how to get a favor done. . . . Such favors, or "accommodations," include help in getting jobs, introductions to politicians, help in getting aid from government programs, or transportation to the hospital.[24]

Elsewhere, he describes the structure of the local polity as

a lattice-work of patron/client ties, extending down from state and national capitals, to county politicians, to magistrates and neighborhood politicians, to family patriarchs, to household heads, to individual voters. This lattice-work is a hierarchy of personal relationships involving considerable reciprocity and accountability, encompassing most of the politically active – voting – population.[25]

The trust and solidarity stored in kinship and friendship networks thus can be mobilized to link individuals to larger social structures and interests but their deployment depends on politics. That "[s]trong bonds among neighbors [and kin] may bind dependent, private individuals to partial and private interests" as Richard Couto notes,[26] is well illustrated by the mobilization of supporters and opponents of Dr. Abner Baker, Jr.'s hanging in the nineteenth century and the political feuds that ensued from that event in Clay County.

No scholar has been more persuasive in linking social capital to government performance and efforts to revitalize U.S. democracy than Robert Putnam in *Making Democracy Work*.[27] Through a study of differential civic participation in Italy, Putnam has argued that social capital, defined as trust, networks, and norms of reciprocity, underlies successful community and regional development including both effective governance and economic development. But Putnam's is a beguiling theory. Like Habermas, whose work we discussed in Chapter 4, Putnam stresses the role of civic participation in making for a healthy democracy. Unlike Habermas, who recognizes the domination ("colonization") of civic life ("the lifeworld") by markets and the state ("systemic steering mechanisms"),[28] Putnam treats social capital as the independent variable and the state, viewed uncritically as a benign institution, as the dependent variable. Critics have argued that this view of the state, however, leads Putnam to misread Italian history. He is criticized for overlooking state actions in Italy's "uncivil" southern region that were, in fact, implemented to erode counterhegemonic institutions of trust and participation because these were important sources of resistance to state domination and the economic interests it supported.[29]

Despite its liberal intent, by viewing civic participation as a primal cause rather a component of political order, Putnam's approach ends up resembling a politically acceptable version of the culture-of-poverty theory, which may help to explain its popularity. Uncivil regions, as Edward Banfield argued earlier in his theory of "amoral familism" in Italy, have bad governments and lack community mindedness because they are culturally bereft of trust and cooperation.[30] Jack Weller made a similar argument about Appalachia when he claimed that frontier "independence-turned-individualism" had become a great "stumbling block for the [the mountaineer] finding a place in our complex and cooperative society."[31]

Although Brown noted that "the Beech Creek neighborhood was not a strongly integrated group in which people felt great loyalty to the neighborhood itself, were individually immersed in it, and had strong cooperative ties with everyone else in the group" and that "there was little neighborhood pride, little cooperation in common tasks for the good of the whole group, and considerable conflict and bitterness among the people," he attributed this state of affairs to a family conflict that had arisen within the Beech Creek basin, not to Appalachian culture. Further, he contrasted the lack of cooperation in the Beech Creek basin to the greater solidarity of the other two Beech Creek neighborhoods.[32]

In this book, we have examined factionalism and constraints on the development of the public sphere in Clay County as the results of the elite mobilization of clients for political ends. And, we have interpreted bad governance, that is, the corruption and clientelism that political rivals fostered in Clay County as they mobilized social capital on behalf of narrow factional interests, as an important determinant in its own right of Appalachia's road to rural poverty and therefore a practice that any public policy seriously aimed at the eradication of poverty must confront. As important as it is, however, the Appalachian local state has not received sufficient attention among scholars.

To understand the contribution of the local state to persistent poverty in Appalachia, it is important to distinguish conceptually the characteristic mode of political domination in the region (clientelism) from its historically contingent expression (feuding). The patterns of state domination we described in Chapters 4 and 8 resemble those of many Third World governments and the states of European societies such as Italy, Greece, and the Balkans, where clientelism structures the dominant form of political order. Here, trust, solidary networks, and norms of reciprocity, that is, social capital resources, are strategically mobilized as networks of patronage to link subalterns to elites, often to the exclusion of policies that might engender democracy and more equitable and sustainable forms of economic development.[33]

In such political orders, governance and state capacity are further weakened by the historically contingent conflicts that often arise among elite factions. Studies of political leadership show that fragmented leadership limits state and local community capacity. "Communities which appear best able to act on matters of local concern are graced with a leadership that is skilled in involving a diverse set of actors in local decision-making activities, who operate on the basis of democratic principles, and who place the welfare of the total community above the needs of any given special interest."[34] Feuding occurred in twenty eastern Kentucky counties near the end of the nineteenth century and undoubtedly constrained the already limited capacity of the clientelist county governments of Appalachian Kentucky to confront the host of problems they faced in improving the well-being of their populations.[35]

Lesson 4: The Need for Long-Term Viewpoints

Bloody and long-lasting as it was, Clay County's feud and the patterns of clientelism and corruption that fueled and were intensified by it, happened a long time ago. Can they, like the county's early nineteenth-century salt industry and the developmental dynamic of subsistence farming, still matter in understanding the persistence of poverty in Clay County today? Events from the 1960s, and those in the present, suggest that the answer is yes.

Comparative studies of clientelist states show that clientelism and corruption often endure despite bureaucratic growth and centralization as the expansion of state programs and resources provide further opportunities for patronage and personal gain.[36] An excellent study of two reform movements in Clay County bears out this pattern while illustrating the limits of civic participation when political domination is not altered.[37]

Douglas Arnett studied a program spearheaded by Manchester's business community from 1960 to 1965 to improve Clay County's physical infrastructure in order to attract outside industry as well as the Community Action Programs (CAP) initiated during the War on Poverty from 1964 to 1967. A participant in both movements, he described the political structure of Clay County in the 1960s as typical of many eastern Kentucky counties. Locally dominant Republicans controlled county offices but worked closely with local Democrats whose party dominated Kentucky state government, sometimes even fusing to back the same candidates for office.[38] Clay County Republicans controlled county-level patronage, the most important reward being jobs in the school system, the county's largest employer, and Democrats controlled programs funded by the state such as local highway maintenance, also a major employer. In the context of Clay County's perpetually dismal economy, the leaders of both parties used public employment and threats of job dismissal as potent rewards and sanctions to maintain their political control.

Finally, the personalistic and violent factionalism that divided the Garrards and the Whites for so many decades had been transcended by an enduring political machine in Clay County. Unchallenged since the 1930s, it was headed by a Republican husband-and-wife team who had been superintendents of the county school system, one following the other, since 1927 and by the president of the Bank of Manchester who was long-term chair of the Clay County Democratic Party. No Garrards were left in Clay County by the 1960s, but descendants of once antagonistic families, the Whites and

Bakers, were cooperating members of this local regime, suggesting that clientelism was the determinant mode of political domination in Clay County while feuding and factionalism were historically important but contingent elements of local state development. After serving for a number of years as sheriff, Charles H. White, a direct descendant of Hugh White, was county judge executive from 1954-1969. His son, John E. White, represented Clay County in the state legislature during the 1960s. Once again, a Baker served as county clerk (as did his daughter when we were conducting this research.)

It was in the context of this political environment, according to Arnett, that Clay County's small business leaders formed the Clay County Development Association in 1961. Led by a used-car salesman who was then president of the local Kiwanis Club and mayor of Manchester, this organization aimed to make civic and infrastructural improvements that might attract outside industry to Clay County in response to the high level of unemployment brought about by mechanization and declining demand in the county's coal industry. The Development Association benefited from a strong reservoir of social capital within its middle-class constituency and much hard work for more than a decade. It wrote grants and leveraged funding for a number of significant projects: a water and sewer system for Manchester (but not its low-income outskirts); a flood control project, including a dam and recreational reservoir; a land fill; road improvements; placement of a district highway office and service garage in the county; an airport; a hospital; a low-income housing project; and an industrial park. Except for the low-income housing, none of these projects directly targeted the needs of the county's many poor people. Nor did they involve them in their planning and implementation. It was generally assumed, however, that poor people would benefit from whatever economic growth might trickle down to them from jobs that were attracted to Clay County by such infrastructural improvements.

While a few key supporters of the development association, such as John E. White, son of the county judge, reportedly kept the local political regime appraised of its efforts and courted its favor, the dominant power holders in the Clay County political machine tolerated but stayed largely aloof from such efforts. Arnett writes:

> Those businessmen involved in the export of coal and timber in Clay County by and large did not participate in the efforts to build a physical infrastructure and attract industry and jobs to the area [being primarily interested in keeping taxes low] . . . the major figures in the political power structure [who routinely protected the economic inter-

ests of these businessmen] also held themselves apart from the work of the county development association. This may be explained in part by the fact that the projects carried out by the association offered little or no opportunity for them to increase their control over patronage; their power would not be increased.

He adds that "the local elite was willing to tolerate the work of the development association as long as the innovations involved were merely 'functioning innovations' and not 're-structuring innovations' which would threaten the social structure."[39]

Tolerance and benign neglect, however, were not the local machine's response to the federal programs of the War on Poverty, which called for "maximum feasible participation" of the poor in projects designed to improve their well-being and encourage their involvement in community affairs. The infusion of more than $1,500,000 in new federal poverty funds to Clay County during the first year and a half of the War on Poverty, and the intent of allowing poor people a significant role in its allocation, were direct challenges to the local political machine and its control over patronage.

Arnett's account of the struggles to control "community action" in Clay County is remarkably similar to that chronicled by Huey Perry in *"They'll Cut Off Your Project,"* a saga of the cooptation and defeat of antipoverty programs in Mingo County, West Virginia, feud-torn site of the Hatfield and McCoy feud and, like Clay County, one of Appalachia's most persistently poor counties.[40] According to Arnett, the Clay County school superintendent first attempted to coopt initiatives of the Office of Economic Opportunity (OEO) by incorporating an agency that would be the recipient of federal funds for the county. She handpicked cronies to staff it with no involvement by the poor and had herself appointed as chair of its board of directors. When that strategy failed, county officials attempted to intimidate welfare recipients, county employees, and the relatives of both to vote for the machine's representatives on the board of the Community Action Program.

Reportedly the first antipoverty program in the nation to be defunded for failing to allow genuine representation of poor people in its planning and implementation, Clay County's CAP was eventually merged with a multi-county program that OEO officials hoped would be able to function autonomously from control by county political machines. Considerable tension soon arose, however, between Clay County officials and VISTA workers and Appalachian Volunteers assigned to the multicounty CAP program and the latter were denied access to Clay County school buildings for Head Start and other youth programs. State representative John E. White complained to the Louisville *Courier-Journal* that "Peaceful citizens all at once are spouting hate. . . . The organizers are teaching class hatred. The business people are 'big shots.' The county officials are 'power structure bosses.' Let a man find a job making $800 a month and he becomes an 'enemy.' "[41] Like its Mingo County, West Virginia, counterpart, the multicounty program soon came under attack by the district's Democratic representative in the U.S. Congress and was eventually abolished. Arnett writes:

> It should be emphasized that political leaders . . . were generally not opposed to receiving federal money for the antipoverty programs, just as they had not opposed receiving New Deal funds decades earlier. They had no objections to giving more money or services to poor people, so long as the federal government was paying for it. Their position, however, was that all federal resources should be channeled through existing institutions and organizations controlled by local power structures. This would allow them to maintain control of patronage coming into the counties and to strengthen their already secure positions.[42]

News stories from Clay County in 1997 show further why public programs that fail to challenge corrupt and nondemocratic local governments and agencies are unlikely to bring about meaningful change or best serve the populations they target. The Daniel Boone Development Council, serving Clay, Jackson, Laurel, Rockcastle Counties and headquartered in Manchester, is an antipoverty program with a $5,000,000 annual budget to provide transportation, job training, child care, home winterization, help with heating bills, and other services for low-income people. In 1997, state auditors found "credible" allegations of "fraud, abuse, and criminal acts" in the program's administration. They discovered, for instance, that the agency, which owns seventy vehicles, routinely "rented its vehicles to better-off vacationers for trips to places such as Disney World, and the customers were given agency credit cards to pay for gasoline and toll-road fees with no accounting of how the cards were used." Reportedly, staff workers were told to give rental receipts directly to the agency director or one associate, but not to the finance officer as was the normal procedure for other receipts. Further allegations included the disappearance of several thousand dollars worth of building materials donated by a religious charity for home improvements for low-income residents and the transfer of a property in Clay County purchased by the agency with a federal grant and bank loans to a private business owned by the director and several relatives.[43] In follow-up articles, the *Lexington Herald-Leader* questioned the priorities of several other community action agencies in Appalachian Kentucky and reported that some operated with virtually no input from the low-income populations they served despite a requirement that one-third of their board members "represent" the poor.[44]

Corruption, conflicts of interest, and the use of public resources for private gain are not new public problems in Clay County. In 1994, it was revealed that Daugh White, Manchester's mayor for twenty-four years, had "sold at least 10 Chevrolets to the city and received thousands of dollars in taxpayers' money for maintenance work on the vehicles" even though doing so was in violation of a state conflict of interest law that had been in effect since 1942. When challenged by a member of the city council for refusing to accept the lowest bid for a police car that came from a Ford dealership, White reportedly stated, "I'll not accept the lowest bid, and I'm the one that signs the checks. So, that's just the way it is." The unsalaried mayor told a reporter, "I would at least like to see them get a Chevrolet, because I can service it."[45]

Reporters discovered that White was not the only official in Clay County to have done business with the city improperly. Some years before, a former city council member had sold oil to the city through his private company. In 1991, the city sold a small piece of land to a council member for one dollar.[46] In 1994, a Manchester councilwoman transferred a dilapidated building she owned to her daughter four days before a contract was signed to spend $45,000 in grant money to renovate it for a homeless shelter. The councilwoman's daughter agreed to charge no rent during the first three years of occupancy, but eventually the renovated property would revert back to her.[47]

Such transgressions might have gone unnoticed had one of Kentucky's two statewide newspapers not begun to publish a long series of articles in 1994 on corruption in Kentucky counties. These reports were spurred by the indictment of eighteen members of the state legislature for fraud and by the impetus this scandal gave to the demand for stronger government ethics laws in Kentucky. Although Appalachian counties were not the only ones in Kentucky reported to engage in ethically unsound or illegal practices, they predominated among the list of abusers. Perhaps most corrupt were a number of Letcher County officials. Indictments were brought against the circuit judge on charges of taking money and marijuana as bribes for protecting criminal suspects; the prosecuting attorney for federal charges of forgery, conspiracy, and obstruction of justice; a former jailer for jury tampering; and the former county judge executive for a kickback scheme that took $20,000 from a county government that was $750,000 in debt. Additionally, the Kentucky Education Commissioner charged Letcher County school board members with "gross mismanagement" of local schools.[48]

The newspaper reported many other instances of corruption in Appalachian Kentucky including vote buying and vote fraud in Clay and Magoffin Counties and the arrest for jury-rigging of a Magoffin ex-sheriff who years before had been imprisoned for vote buying. A Leslie County judge-executive awarded $450,000 in county business to his brother without seeking competitive bids. The Knox County attorney pled guilty to trying to sell his office for $50,000. Allegedly, a Powell County clerk had backdated deposits to cover $100,000 in missing funds, the Leslie County sheriff was responsible for $74,000 of missing public funds, and the McCreary County waste management secretary/treasurer had written checks to herself for nearly $8,000. (More recently, sheriffs have been arrested in Lee and Breathitt Counties for drug trafficking and drug coverups, respectively.[49])

Nepotism is not illegal in Kentucky, but the newspaper pointed out the potential conflicts of interest in numerous mountain counties where top officials hire spouses, children, and siblings to work in their offices. In Floyd County, for instance, the judge-executive, jailer, circuit clerk, sheriff, county attorney, commonwealth's attorney, and the property valuation administrator had each employed spouses or children as assistants. In Martin County, when officials debated passing an ethics codes that would have rationed nepotism to only one immediate family member per official, a magistrate stated: "I'm not voting for a thing unless we can make sure my people can get hired if the state closes our jail. I may not be in this for long, but I think you should be able to hire who we please. We've been doing it for as long as anyone can remember." His mother, the Martin County jailer, was employing three sons, a daughter, and a daughter-in-law at the jail; her family took home nearly $120,000 in yearly income and benefits from their employment by the county.[50]

Road projects were another source of patronage and corruption in mountain counties to which the newspaper called attention. In Pike County, Kentucky's largest county and a major coal producer with a budget of $22 million, 331 employees and at least 1,549 county-maintained roads, citizens complained that magistrates pave what amounts to private driveways for county favorites while other roads are neglected.[51]

Finally, the newspaper charged that "secret, slapdash" public meetings were "obstacles to democracy" throughout the state, but especially in Appalachian Kentucky. A staff writer reported, for instance, that Leslie County citizens' efforts to propose environmental regulations on oil drilling had been frustrated by the changing and unannounced meeting times of their county court, then headed by an oil distributor. Breathitt County officials had conducted a public hearing on a controversial school closing when heavy rains had flooded the neighborhood in question and few residents were able to attend. The reporter wrote: "Meeting times get changed at the last minute. Agendas are unavailable. Public forums take place during snowstorms and floods. Controversial topics are left until the end of the meeting, forcing speakers to wait for hours. Then there's the biggie: secret sessions." Despite an open-meetings law, a Letcher County citizen-activist, for instance, reported regularly seeing county magistrates meet in the county judge-executive's office for an hour or so before beginning public meetings.[52]

More recently, the confusion between private interests and the public good and the resistance by officials to sharing power with citizens, and especially poor people, was evident from news stories reporting problems in Appalachia's first federally designated "empowerment zone." Empowerment zones, along with "economic communities" funded at lower levels, were the principal antipoverty initiatives of the Clinton-Gore presidential administration. Along with six urban zones, three rural empowerment zones were created in the nation's most impoverished rural regions, Appalachia, the Southwest, and the Southeast, each with promise of $40 million in grants and tax breaks over the next decade for economic development purposes. The Appalachian empowerment zone is comprised of three noncontiguous eastern Kentucky counties, Clinton, Jackson, and Wayne.

Despite the fact that a criterion for designation as an empowerment zone was evidence of substantial involvement of an economically and socially diverse citizenry during the planning and proposal stages, early activities in the Appalachian zone appear to have been compromised by elitism and possible conflicts of interest. In Clinton County, activists protested a plan to lure a low-wage, chicken processing plant to the county with subsidies including a $4 million water-plant project that environmentalists feared would harm two area lakes. Earlier, activists were dismayed by disclosure of the county's purchase for $300,000 of an eighty-acre site for the chicken plant that had been assessed at only $50,000. According to reports, the county purchased the property without "advertising for bids or considering other options" from a relative of the Clinton County judge-executive. Similar controversy arose in Wayne County over the proposed purchase of land for an industrial park from the business partner of that county's judge-executive despite an asking price that was higher than any other sites offered. Finally, according to a newspaper summary, a citizen's review team in Jackson County complained that "A small group of insiders holds the reins of power. People at the grassroots struggle to be heard. Meetings are held behind closed doors or with members' backs to the audience."[53] Like the allegations of corruption in 1997 in Clay County's antipoverty agency and the cooptation of its OEO programs thirty years earlier, events from Appalachia's empowerment zone programs suggest that even model programs in Appalachia are jeopardized by deeply entrenched political practices that must be challenged directly before meaningful policies can be effected.

We have emphasized the patterns of clientelism and corruption that characterize county governments in Appalachian Kentucky because antipoverty efforts must first begin with political transformation. Institutionalized patterns of hierarchy and dependence must be challenged because local states can do things to improve living standards and economic opportunities. Despite the difficulties inherent in overcoming economic dependency and poverty, studies of economic development efforts in Third World nations show that state policies can improve incomes and lower poverty rates.[54] A comparative study of the development efforts of southern states in the United States likewise concludes: "what states, cities, and counties do matters. A lot."[55] Historically, however, local governments in Appalachian Kentucky have subordinated economic development to political interests. And, with the exception of some locally initiated but short-lived OEO programs, federal programs have not challenged such practices.

A generation ago in deference to private economic interests, the Appalachian Regional Commission side-stepped economic development strategies such as public ownership of coal mining or publicly owned electrical power generation that might have contributed to sustainable development in the coal fields. Rather than attacking root causes of poverty in the capitalist economy and the local state, the agency focused only on such infrastructural improvements as highways that, in the words of a critic, were "conceptually and politically limited to those conventional consensus approaches capable of emerging from existing federal agencies and state politics."[56] Our reading of reported shortcomings in the Clinton Administration's empowerment and enterprise zone programs in Appalachia suggests that the will to confront long-term institutional practices that create and sustain poverty are as absent at the federal level today as thirty years ago.

Nonetheless, there is much to be encouraged by in the vigorous struggles for social and economic justice that citizens are waging throughout Appalachia. In Clay and Jackson Counties, for instance, a grassroots organization initiated by parents in the mid-1970s to advocate for educational improvements, Appalachian Communities for Children, has expanded to provide adult education, teen counseling, life skills training, youth services, and long-term community development. Recently, it was selected as one of five programs nationally to receive major funding for its work from the Points of Light Foundation.[57] In neighboring Owsley County, Kentucky's poorest county, "elected officials have joined regular citizens in encouraging home-grown businesses, not just factories lured by tax breaks and low wages" as part of a commitment to "sustainable development." The local bank "gives bonus pay to employees who attend community meetings in their free time" and a local "Action Team," formed in 1992, "includes citizens, elected leaders and business people, has snagged government and private grants to hire staff; to launch a vegetable cooperative and a goat producers' association for local farmers; to start a savings-incentive program for seventh graders; and to offer workshops to would-be entrepreneurs." Its job creation program netted 150 new jobs – not all that many but a significant accomplishment nonetheless in a poor county with only sixteen manufacturing jobs.[58]

Scores of such programs exist throughout Central Appalachia, prompting one regional activist to assert that "One thing we need to recognize in Appalachia is the strength that is there because we have the community networking and the support groups. The hope is not from the outside but from what we can give to the rest of the world."[59] But Appalachia's poverty cannot be overcome by local effort alone, important as that is. Federal investments by the Appalachian Regional Commission have helped to create jobs and opportunities in some Appalachian counties, but ARC funds have been cut back dramatically and, because of the ARC's "growth center" investment strategy that dictated federal funding for many years, they have rarely reached the most economically distressed rural counties in the region.[60] Struggles in the region to reform the local state and politics, to preserve the cultural strategies that bolster social capital in poor communities, and to channel market-driven economics toward more equitable and sustainable forms of economic development must be supported and strengthened by linkages to similar efforts throughout the nation. Only then, perhaps, can Appalachia's long road to rural poverty begin to be reversed.

APPENDIXES

Appendix 1

Data and Methodology

In this appendix, we detail the data and methodology of this study, including units of analysis, the time period for which data were examined, and decision rules used to define the study population and to link data records over time and across individuals. This appendix describes only our major sources of longitudinal and quantifiable data. Most of these data have been entered into computerized files, organized as linked individual and household records. Specifics of other data, for example, data gathered from state records, Governor's papers, newspaper accounts, contemporary observers' accounts, oral histories, and secondary works are included in chapter endnotes.

Census of Population

Beech Creek

For individuals living in the Beech Creek area, we coded all information from the U.S. Census of Population for the years 1850, 1860, 1870, 1880, 1900, and 1910. (The 1890 manuscript federal census was destroyed by fire.) These records are in manuscript form, as the handwritten manuscript schedules completed by individual census enumerators. These records include only free African Americans; slaves were enumerated separately. We begin with 1850 because this is the first census that includes names of household members other than the head of household. Because of the generally accorded unreliability of the 1870 census for southern states, we include reliability checks whenever possible when using these data.

For our study years, we coded all information from the manuscript U.S. Census of Population records of every ancestor (and their neighbors) of James S. Brown's original (1942) Beech Creek population. We used Brown's extensive genealogical data to identify ancestors of the 1942 study population in 1880, a base year chosen for its detailed census information on household relationships. Using a methodology developed by Kenzer[1] and Hahn[2] that uses consecutive enumeration as an indicator of neighborhood proximity, we then coded information on all individuals in households on census pages in which the ancestral households were clustered in 1880. Genealogical data from 1942 and data from the 1880 census were used to trace individuals and their *ancestors* through the 1870, 1860, and 1850 manuscript censuses and their *descendants* in the 1900 and 1910 manuscript censuses. This allowed us to approximate the entire population of the rural (unbounded) geographic area of Beech Creek and to establish kinship relationships over time. These census data were organized in individual and household files. Individuals are linked to other household members through household codes and to other family members, ancestors, and descendants through relationship codes.

Clay County

Countywide, we coded all information for individuals selected in a random one-in-four sample from the 1860 manuscript U.S. Census of Population. This census includes only free (non-enslaved) residents of Clay County.

Census of Agriculture

Beech Creek

For all household heads identified in the Beech Creek population census as farmers (the vast majority of the population), we coded all information about their property and agricultural production from the manuscript U.S. Censuses of Agriculture for 1850, 1860, 1870, and 1880, the only available years. Data on individuals from the U.S. Census of Population and data on farms from the U.S. Census of Agriculture are linked across census records and over time. By using household and relationship codes, individual records are linked both to records of household members and to records of nonresident family members.

Clay County

We coded all information from the manuscript U.S. Census of Agriculture for 1860 for the farm of every individual selected in the one-in-four sample of the 1860 U.S. Census of Population for Clay County who was also listed in the U.S. Census of Agriculture. These were linked to the corresponding records on individuals and households from the 1860 U.S. Census of Population.

Tax Records

Beech Creek

We coded all information on taxable property from the Clay County tax roll records for individuals whom we identified as Beech Creek residents in the manuscript U.S. Census of Population for the years 1850, 1860, 1870, 1879, and 1892. For 1850, 1860, and 1870, we use individuals identified in the corresponding U.S. Census of Population. For 1879, we use individuals iden-

Appendix 1. Data and Methodology

tified in the 1880 U.S. Census of Population. For 1892, we use individuals identified in either the 1880 or the 1900 U.S. Census of Population. We use the years 1879 and 1892 to extend our data on property holdings and property values after the time period in which these data were collected in the U.S. Census of Agricultural census.

Clay County

From the 1850 Clay County tax rolls, we coded all data on every taxpayer in Clay County in that year. For 1892, we coded tax roll data from a one-in-five sample of Clay County taxpayers.

Deeds

Beech Creek

In order to examine patterns of land acquisition, inheritance, and retention, we coded data on buyer, seller, price, and parcel size for 275 land transactions recorded in Clay County deed books from the early 1800s to 1910 for two principal family groups.

Court Records

As part of our analysis of Clay County's long-enduring feud, we made use of court records from the Clay County Circuit Court. In addition to their value for recording the use of litigation as a strategic technique of disputation, the civil and criminal case files contained numerous documents and depositions that provided information on local politics, economic production, consumption and pricing, family genealogies, relationships between local residents and extralocal corporations, relationships between local government and state government, gender relations, race relations, and social change.

Court case records are an invaluable source of sociohistorical data, particularly for regions like early rural Appalachia with few newspapers or surviving public, commercial, or industrial records. However, these records are difficult to use in sociohistorical research for several reasons. During most of the period under study, all documents in the case records were handwritten. Most cases were not indexed. Documents from a single case often were spread across several case files. Simply compiling and organizing case documents in chronological sequence was extremely time-consuming. Although many cases had fewer than a dozen documents, some cases were very large with hundreds of separate documents. For example, one case involving a dispute between a local elite family and an outside corporation took 133 single-spaced type-written pages simply to summarize. Moreover, without legal training, it is difficult to untangle substantive and procedural issues in the case records. Names of parties can be actual names or standard judicial pseudonyms; amounts of judgments can be literal or not. These issues are more difficult in the archaic language of nineteenth-century law.

In this project, all civil and criminal court cases were compiled, coded, summarized into chronological case files, linked to related antecedent or descendant cases, and evaluated for adequacy and fairness of legal and judicial proceedings by one of three attorneys: Pam Goldman, Sharon Hardesty, and Lee Hardesty, each of whom has both a law degree and background in sociohistorical research. The attorneys worked more than 2,000 hours on these cases, compiling and evaluating more than 1,000 feud-relevant civil and criminal cases in their entirety as well as providing decennial summaries for nearly 400 cases.

Clay County

The following case records were read, summarized, evaluated, and coded:
From the civil court docket:

(i) all case files for civil cases adjudicated in Clay County Circuit Court in which a member of a feuding family was party as plaintiff(s) or defendant(s) from 1807 to 1849 (411 cases) and from 1890 to 1901 (361 cases);
(ii) all chancery and common law case files from Clay County and, for comparative purposes, the same files from Bourbon County, a more commercial, market-embedded county of the Kentucky Bluegrass, from 1844 to 1901;
(iii) summary data only (case type; method of resolution; disposition) for 395 cases unrelated to the feud in 1810, 1830, 1840, 1860, 1880, and 1900; these data were used to provide baseline information on court processes in the Clay County Circuit Court.

From the criminal court docket:

(i) records and court order book entries for criminal cases filed in Clay County Circuit Court from 1893–1902 (300 cases; earlier records are lost);
(ii) Clay County Fiscal Court records of payments to sheriffs, deputy sheriffs, jailers, prosecuting attorneys and witnesses for criminal arrests, prosecutions, and incarcerations from 1890 to 1900.

Appendix 1. Data and Methodology

Beech Creek

For comparative purposes, we analyzed all court records involving one large family group in Beech Creek from 1806 to 1900.

Special Subgroups

Slaveholders

We coded all information on slaveholders in the separately enumerated slave listing in the U.S. Censuses of 1850 and 1860 for Clay County. The slave census reports only names of slaveholders, along with the age, sex, and color of each individual slave owned by that owner. In 1860, there is also information on number of slave houses. For all slaveholders, we link data from the slave census to individual, household, and (when available) farm data from the 1850 and 1860 U.S. Censuses of Population and Agriculture and to all data on these individuals in the 1850 and 1860 Clay County tax rolls.

African Americans

We coded all data from the U.S. Census of Population for every non-enslaved African American in Clay County in the years 1850, 1860, 1870, 1880, 1900, and 1910, including all individuals living in mixed-race households and households headed by whites. For all African Americans, we also coded all information from the U.S. Censuses of Agriculture for 1850, 1860, 1870, and 1880, all land transactions recorded in Clay County deed books between 1850 and 1910, and all tax records for 1850, 1860, 1870, 1879, and 1892. Since the racial categorization of persons as "black" versus as "mulatto" was unstable over time (i.e., individuals are listed as "black" in one census year and "mulatto" the following decade), we coded both as "African American." The racial categorization of "white," in contrast, was stable over census years.

Merchants

We coded all information from the U.S. Census of Population for every individual identified in the census as a merchant in the years 1850, 1860, 1870, 1880, 1900, and 1910. These are linked to the corresponding records on farms from the U.S. Census of Agriculture for 1850, 1860, 1870, and 1880, and, in a few cases, to individual and household records on slaveholding. These are also linked to information on each merchant operating in Clay

County between 1840 and 1890 collected from the credit reports of the R. G. Dun and Company.

Manufacturing Establishments

We coded all data from the U.S. Census of Manufacturing for all establishments operating in Clay County in 1850, 1860, 1870, or 1880. Also, we collected data on every major salt, timbering, minerals and mining, railroad, and land company that operated in Clay County at any time during the nineteenth or early twentieth centuries.

Feudists

We coded all data from the manuscript records of the U.S. Censuses of Population of 1850, 1860, 1870, 1880, 1900, and 1910, and the U.S. Censuses of Agriculture of 1850, 1860, 1870, and 1880 for all immediate members of feuding families and other major feud actors. These data are linked to records from state tax rolls from 1850, 1860, 1870, 1879, and 1892, to court records for 1807–49 and 1890–1902 for cases in which any member of the feuding family was a party, as principal or surety (see earlier), and to deeds, mortgages, bonds, wills, records of apprenticeship, slave contracting, commercial development and patent rights, and other county records.

Appendix 2

Genealogies

Selective Genealogy of Whites in this Volume

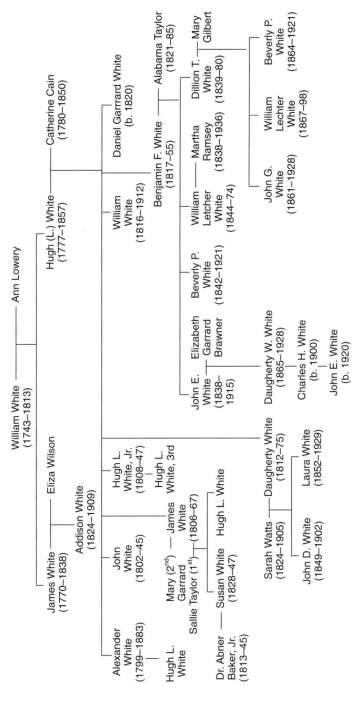

Source: Charles H. White, Jr., *White Family Genealogy* (unpublished manuscript, n.d.).

Selective Genealogy of Garrards in this Volume

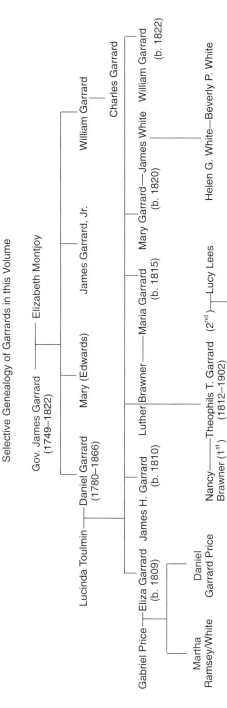

Source: Anna Russell des Cognets, *Governor Garrard of Kentucky: His Descendants and Relatives* (privately printed, 1962).

NOTES

Chapter 1

1. President's National Advisory Commission on Rural Poverty, *The People Left Behind* (Washington, D.C.: U.S. Government Printing Office, 1967).
2. Cynthia Duncan, ed., *Rural Poverty in America* (New York: Auburn House, 1992); Thomas Lyson and William Falk, eds., *Forgotten Places: Uneven Development in Rural America* (Lawrence: University Press of Kansas, 1993); Rural Sociological Society Task Force on Persistent Rural Poverty, *Persistent Poverty in Rural America* (Boulder, CO: Westview Press, 1993).
3. William P. O'Hare, *The Rise of Poverty in Rural America* (Washington, D.C.: Population Reference Bureau, 1988).
4. For recent overviews of poverty and economic distress in Appalachia, see Dwight Billings and Ann Tickamyer, "Uneven Development in Appalachia," in Lyson and Falk, *Forgotten Places*, 7-29; Richard Couto, *An American Challenge: A Report on Social Trends and Social Issues in Appalachia* (Dubuque, IA: Kendall/Hunt, 1994); Cynthia Duncan, "Persistent Poverty in Appalachia," in Duncan, *Rural Poverty*, 111-32; Andrew M. Isserman, "Appalachia, Then and Now: An Update of 'The Realities of Deprivation' Report to the President in 1964," *Journal of Appalachian Studies* 3 (1997): 43-70.
5. Ann Tickamyer and Cecil Tickamyer, "Poverty in Appalachia," *Appalachian Center Data Bank*, Report #5 (Lexington: University of Kentucky Appalachian Center, 1987), 1-39.
6. It is especially disappointing to compare recent journalistic discussions of Appalachian poverty with those published a generation ago since this comparison reveals how little popular understandings of Appalachia, and rural poverty in general, have advanced. A recent report on "Enduring Poverty in Appalachia" that appeared in the *Washington Post* in 1994 was almost identical to reports on "The Strange Case of West Virginia" and "The Tragedy of Appalachia" that appeared in *The Saturday Evening Post* in 1960 and 1964. Compare Guy Gugliotta, "The Persistence of Poverty: In Eastern Kentucky,

347

Evidence of a War That Has Not Been Won," *The Washington Post* (National Weekly Edition), January 3-9, 1994, pp. 6-8, with Roul Tunley, "The Strange Case of West Virginia," *The Saturday Evening Post*, January 6, 1960, pp. 19-21, 64-6, and Richard Armstrong, "The Tragedy of Appalachia," *The Saturday Evening Post*, August 22-29, 1964, pp. 34-43.

7. See Cynthia Duncan and Ann Tickamyer, "Poverty Research and Policy for Rural America," *The American Sociologist* 19 (1988): 243-59, for a discussion of this agenda.

8. For economic comparisons of North, Central, and Southern Appalachia, see Billings and Tickamyer, "Uneven Development," and Couto, *An American Challenge*.

9. Couto, *An American Challenge*, 144.

10. "Seven Kentucky Counties Among the Nation's Poorest," *Lexington Herald-Leader*, September 6, 1994, p. B-3.

11. John Fox, Jr., *Blue-Grass and Rhododendron: Outdoors in Old Kentucky*, 28 (New York: Scribner's, [1901] 1920), Ellen Churchill Semple, "The Anglo-Saxons of the Kentucky Mountains: A Study in Anthropogeography," *Bulletin of the American Geographical Society* XLII ([1901] 1910): 561-95.

12. Henry D. Shapiro, *Appalachia on Our Mind: The Southern Mountains and Mountaineers in the American Consciousness, 1870-1920*, 106 (Chapel Hill: University of North Carolina Press, 1978).

13. E. Carl Litsey, "Kentucky Feuds and Their Causes," *Frank Leslie's Popular Monthly* LIII (January 1902): 283.

14. See articles in the *Lexington* (Kentucky) *Herald-Leader* on "Little Kingdoms: Local Government at Your Expense" dated January 30, 31; February 2, 4, 6, 7, 9, 11, and 13, 1994.

15. See Huey Perry, *"They'll Cut Off Your Project"; A Mingo County Chronicle* (New York: Praeger, 1972).

16. Robert Munn, "The Latest Rediscovery of Appalachia," in Bruce Ergood and Bruce Kuhre, eds., *Appalachia: Social Context Past and Present* (Dubuque, IA: Kendall/Hunt, 1976 [1st ed.]), 8-10.

17. Our effort to place these traditions of writing about Appalachia relies heavily on Dwight Billings, Mary Beth Pudup, and Altina Waller, "Taking Exception with Exceptionalism: New Approaches to the Social History of Early Appalachia," in Mary Beth Pudup, Dwight Billings, and Altina Waller, eds., *Appalachia in the Making: The Mountain South in the Nineteenth Century* (Chapel Hill: University of North Carolina Press, 1995), 1-24, which includes a more comprehensive bibliography than here. The most important intellectual history of the "myth of Appalachia" is Shapiro's *Appalachia*, but for a review of later discursive practices, see Allen W. Batteau, *The Invention of Appalachia* (Tucson: University of Arizona Press, 1990).

18. See W. G. Frost, "Appalachian America," *Woman's Home Companion* 23 (1896): 3-4, 21; and "Our Contemporary Ancestors in the Southern Mountains," *Atlantic Monthly* 83 (1899): 311-19.

19. George E. Vincent, "A Retarded Frontier," *The American Journal of Sociology* 4 (1898): 1-20.

20. Shapiro, *Appalachia*, ix.

21. David Whisnant, *Modernizing the Mountaineer* (New York: Burt Franklin, 1980).

22. David Whisnant, *All That Is Native and Fine: The Politics of Culture in an American Region* (Chapel Hill: University of North Carolina Press, 1983).

23. J. W. Williamson, *Southern Mountaineers in Silent Films: Plot Synopses of Movies about Moonshining, Feuding, and Other Mountain Topics* (Jefferson, NC: McFarland, 1994).

24. Among the most highly regarded ethnographic community studies are James S. Brown, *Beech Creek: The Social Organization of an Isolated Kentucky Mountain Neighborhood* (Berea, KY: Berea College Press, [1950] 1988); Marion Pearsall, *Little Smoky Ridge* (Birmingham: University of Alabama Press, 1959); and John B. Stephenson, *Shiloh: A Mountain Community* (Lexington: University Press of Kentucky, 1968). Important recent studies include Allen Batteau, "Mosbys and Broomsedge: The Semantics of Class in Appalachian Kinship Systems," *American Ethnologist* 9 (1982): 445-66; Patricia D. Beaver, *Rural Community in the Appalachian South* (Lexington: University Press of Kentucky, 1986); and F. C. Bryant, *We're All Kin: A Cultural Study of a Mountain Neighborhood* (Knoxville: University of Tennessee Press, 1981).

25. See Kathleen Blee and Dwight Billings, "Reconstructing Daily Life in the Past: An Hermeneutical Approach to Ethnographic Data," *Sociological Quarterly* 27 (1986): 443-62, for a discussion of how historical insights can be recovered from ethnographic studies where standard sources of historical information are unreliable, fragmented, or nonexistent.

26. William Elsey Connelley and E. M. Coulter, *History of Kentucky*, 2 vols. (Chicago: American Historical Society, 1922).

27. Jack E. Weller, *Yesterday's People: Life in Contemporary Appalachia*, 13 (Lexington: University of Kentucky Press, 1966).

28. An example of scholarly work of that era is Richard Ball, "A Poverty Case: The Analgesic Subculture of the Southern Appalachians," *American Sociological Review* 33 (1968): 885-95.

29. Weller, *Yesterday's People*, pp. 32, 33, 37, 7. Weller's list of cultural traits was derived from an influential survey by Thomas Ford, "The Passing of Provincialism," in Thomas Ford, ed., *The Southern Appalachian Region: A Survey*, 9-34 (Lexington: University of Kentucky Press, 1962). For an empirical critique of Ford's research, see Dwight Billings, "Culture and Poverty in Appalachia: A Theoretical Discussion and Empirical Analysis," *Social Forces* 53 (1974): 315-23.

30. See Richard Couto, *Appalachia: An American Tomorrow* (Knoxville: Report to the Commission on Religion in Appalachia, 1984).

31. For a scholarly and popular example, respectively, see Ball, "Poverty Case," 885-95, and Rena Gazaway, *The Longest Mile: A Vivid Chronicle of Life in an Appalachian Hollow* (Baltimore: Penguin, 1969).

32. Rupert Vance, "An Introductory Note," in Weller, *Yesterday's People*, p. vii.

33. Vance, "Introductory Note," ix.

34. Quoted by Whisnant, *Modernizing the Mountaineer*, 129, in a chapter that provides an excellent critique of the assumptions that guided the early programs of the Appalachian Regional Commission and, more generally, the economic thinking prevalent during the 1960s.

35. David S. Walls, "Central Appalachia: A Peripheral Region within an Advanced Capitalist Society," *Journal of Sociology and Social Welfare* 4 (1976): 233.

36. See Perry, *"They'll Cut Off."*

37. Surprisingly little historical research has been done on this important period, but see J. Glen, "The War on Poverty in Appalachia: A Preliminary Report," *Register of the Kentucky Historical Society* 87 (1989): 40-57.

38. For a collection of representative writings from that era, see Helen Lewis, Linda Johnson, and Don Askins, eds., *Colonialism in Modern America: The Appalachian Case* (Boone, NC: Appalachian Consortium Press, 1978).

39. Quoted in Helen Lewis, "Fatalism or the Coal Industry?" originally published in *Mountain Life and Work* (December 1970) and reprinted in Ergood and Kuhre, *Appalachia*, 155.

40. One of the best examples is Helen Lewis, Sue Kobak, and Linda Johnson, "Family, Religion, and Colonialism in Central Appalachia: Or, Bury My Rifle at Big Stone Gap," in Jim Axelrod, ed., *Growing up Country* (Clintwood, VA: Council of the Southern Mountains, 1973), 131-156.

41. Lewis, "Fatalism or the Coal Industry," 153.

42. Among the most important studies are John Gaventa, *Power and Powerlessness: Quiescence and Rebellion in an Appalachian Valley* (Urbana: University of Illinois Press, 1980); Appalachian Land Ownership Task Force, *Who Owns Appalachia? Landownership and Its Impact* (Lexington: University Press of Kentucky, 1983); and Rodger Cunningham, *Apples on the Flood: The Southern Mountain Experience* (Knoxville: University of Tennessee Press, 1987).

43. A recent example of the application of culture of poverty theory to the region is David Cattell-Gordon, "The Appalachian Inheritance: A Culturally Transmitted Traumatic Stress Syndrome," *Journal of Progressive Human Services* 1 (1990): 41-57; for a critique of this article, see Karen Tice and Dwight Billings, "Appalachian Culture and Resistance," *Journal of Progressive Human Services* 2 (1991): 1-18.

44. See Alan Banks, Dwight Billings, and Karen Tice, "Appalachian Studies,

Resistance, and Postmodernism," in Stephen L. Fisher, ed., *Fighting Back in Appalachia: Traditions of Resistance and Change* (Philadelphia: Temple University Press, 1993), 283-301.

45. M. Maloney and B. Huelsman, "Humanism, Scientism, and Southern Mountaineers," *People's Appalachia* 2 (1972): 24-7; Stephen Fisher, "Victim-Blaming in Appalachia: Cultural Theories and the Southern Mountaineer," in Ergood and Kuhre, *Appalachia*, 139-48.

46. Ann R. Tickamyer and Cynthia M. Duncan, "Poverty and Occupational Structure in Rural America," *Annual Review of Sociology* 16 (1990): 67-86.

47. Kathleen M. Blee and Dwight B. Billings, "Reconstructing Daily Life in the Past: A Hermeneutical Approach to Ethnographic Data," *Sociological Quarterly* 27 (1986): 443-62.

48. The most systematic analysis of the impact of landownership patterns on the region was the eighty-county survey of Appalachian Land Ownership Task Force, *Who Owns Appalachia?*

49. Marxist scholars in the region were quick to point out that "the idea that the primary or formative social conflict in the Appalachian region [was] one between geographical regions (*Appalachia v the United States* or the 'outside') or between people who live in those different regions" was "especially unsatisfactory." See Alan Banks, Stephen Fisher, Jim Foster, and Doug Gamble, eds., "Essays in Political Economy: Towards a Class Analysis of Appalachia," *Appalachian Journal* 11 (1984): 19.

50. Curtis Seltzer, *Fire in the Hole: Miners and Managers in the American Coal Industry* (Lexington: University Press of Kentucky, 1985).

51. Janet Smith, David Ostendorf, and Mike Schechtman, *Who's Mining the Farm?* (Rochester: Illinois South Project, 1978).

52. Harry Caudill, *Night Comes to the Cumberlands: A Biography of a Depressed Area* (Boston: Little, Brown, 1962).

53. Ronald D Eller, *Miners, Millhands, and Mountaineers: Industrialization of the Appalachian South, 1880-1930* (Knoxville: University of Tennessee Press, 1982).

54. John Prine and the theorists of internal colonialism were correct about their central premise. "Mr. Peabody" ruined whatever was available.

55. Ann Markusen, *Regions: The Economics and Politics of Territory* (Totowa, NJ: Rowman and Littlefield, 1987), 29, 28.

56. Fisher, ed., *Fighting Back.*

57. Our understanding of the processes of incorporation and peripheralization is influenced by Immanuel Wallerstein, *The Modern World-System III: The Second Era of Great Expansion of the Capitalist World-Economy, 1730-1840s* (San Diego: Academic Press, 1989). Also helpful are Christopher Chase-Dunn, *Global Formation: Structures of the World-Economy* (Cambridge, MA: Blackwell, 1989), and

Thomas D. Hall, "Incorporation in the World-System: Toward A Critique," *American Sociological Review* 45 (1986): 390-402.

58. Barrington Moore, Jr., *Social Origins of Dictatorship and Democracy: Lord and Peasant in the Making of the Modern World* (Boston: Beacon Press, 1966).

59. Peter Evans and John D. Stephens, "Development and the World Economy," in Neil Smelser, ed., *Handbook of Sociology* (Newbury Park, CA: Sage, 1988), 764.

60. Ibid., 756.

61. For examples of sociologists who apply Moore's approach to American regional development, see Dwight B. Billings, *Planters and the Making of a "New South"* (Chapel Hill: University of North Carolina Press, 1979); Max Pfeffer, "Social Origins of Three Systems of Farm Production in the United States," *Rural Sociology* 48 (1983): 540-62; Charles Post, "The American Road to Capitalism," *New Left Review* 133 (1982): 30-51.

62. Jay R. Mandle, *The Roots of Black Poverty: The Southern Plantation Economy after the Civil War* (Durham, NC: Duke University Press, 1978); also Billings, *Planters.*

63. Unless otherwise indicated, data on Clay County and the surrounding ten-county poverty area are taken from Ronald D Eller with Phil Jenks, Chris Jasparro, and Jerry Napier, *Kentucky's Distressed Communities: A Report on Poverty in Appalachian Kentucky*, Report of the Appalachian Center (Lexington: University of Kentucky, 1994).

64. According to ibid., the economic disparity between Appalachian Kentucky and the rest of the state increased markedly during the 1980s as measured by a number of indicators such as proportion of poverty.

65. "Seven Kentucky Counties among Nation's Poorest," *Lexington {Kentucky} Herald-Leader*, September 6, 1994, p. B-6.

66. C. Theodore Koebel and Michael Puie, *Annual Estimates of Poverty for Counties in Kentucky, 1979-1986* (Louisville: University of Louisville Urban Studies Center, 1988).

67. 1990 data for Clay County are based on the U.S. Census of Population as reported in Eller et al., *Kentucky's Distressed Communities.*

68. Brown, *Beech Creek*, 24.

69. We use "head of household" to refer to the main economic actor in the household.

70. Harry K. Schwarzweller, James S. Brown, and J. J. Mangalam, *Mountain Families in Transition: A Case Study of Appalachian Migration* (University Park: Pennsylvania State University Press, 1971), 40.

71. Schwarzweller et al., *Mountain Families*, 49, 54.

72. In an ethnographic study of another Appalachian community observed at a later point in time, John Stephenson observed confusion in the local stratification

system as "the bases of social ranking [were] shifting away" from land ownership and family name toward occupation, education, and income. One informant, who felt that "people were more nearly the same" in the past, expressed
confusion saying, "I'm not sure what would be today that counts. It's not too
clear." See Stephenson, *Shiloh*, 38, 36.

Chapter 2

1. "A Letter from Kentucky" (G. Hubert Smith, ed.), *The Mississippi Valley Historical Review* xix (1932): 95, 91.
2. Quoted in Mary Verhoeff, *The Kentucky Mountains: Transportation and Commerce, 1750 to 1911* (Louisville: John P. Morton, 1911), 96.
3. A natural pass at Cumberland Gap on the borders of Kentucky, Virginia, and Tennessee channeled population through the Cumberland Plateau and up into Kentucky along the western edge of the mountains. Only later did population from central Kentucky double back into the rugged hills of eastern Kentucky.
4. Virginia Clay McClure, "The Settlement of the Kentucky Appalachian High-lands," Ph.D. diss., University of Kentucky, 1933, 166.
5. James and Hugh White, *Book of Accounts, Goose Creek Salt Works, 1806-1810* Louisville, KY: The Filson Club Library.
6. In *The End of Capitalism (as we knew it): A Feminist Critique of Political Economy* (Cambridge, MA: Blackwell, 1996), The economists who write as J. K. Gibson-Graham warn against the neglect of varied forms of production that has occurred with exclusive attention to capitalist relations of economic life in political economy theory.
7. James Lane Allen, "Through the Cumberland Gap on Horseback," in *The Blue-Grass Region of Kentucky and Other Kentucky Articles*, (New York: Harper & Bros., 1899): 232, 235, 231. See also John Fox, Jr., "The Southern Mountaineer," *Blue-Grass and Rhododendron: Out-doors in Old Kentucky* (New York: Scribner's, [1901] 1920).
8. Allen, "Through the Cumberland Gap," 231, 245.
9. Horace Kephart, *Our Southern Highlanders: A Narrative of Adventure in the Southern Appalachians and a Study of Life among the Mountaineers.* (New York: Outing, 1922), 446.
10. Quoted in McClure, "Settlement,"138; Arnold Toynbee, *A Study of History* (New York: Oxford University Press, 1947), 149.
11. McClure, "Settlement," 138; Weller, *Yesterday's People,* 10; Caudill, *Night Comes,* 18, 6; Harry Caudill, *Darkness at Dawn: Appalachian Kentucky and the Future* (Lexington: University Press of Kentucky, 1976), 13, 6, 13.
12. Unthinking Appalachia is difficult. According to Shapiro, *Appalachia,* 263,

"Since the 1920s, as a result [of the discourse on Appalachia], no one has been able to ask whether the mountaineers do in fact compose a distinct group in the American population with distinct cultural and genetic traits, any more than anyone has been able to ask whether Appalachia – originally the mountainous portions of eight southern states – does in fact compose a discrete region of the nation. Indeed, these assumptions lie at the heart of the myth of Appalachia."

13. The data describing the Kentucky River are taken from Mary Verhoeff, *The Kentucky River Navigation* (Louisville, KY: John P. Morton, 1917). This fine scholarly work describes the history of the Kentucky River and its territory as a whole without distinguishing between Appalachian and Bluegrass Kentucky and is one of the most important sources for the economic history of the mountains before coal and railroads. Thomas Clark's *The Kentucky* (Lexington: University Press of Kentucky, [1942] 1992) is more anecdotal but also narrates the history of the Kentucky River country as a whole. On the wilderness road, see Robert L. Kincaid, *The Wilderness Road* (Indianapolis: Bobbs-Merrill, 1947).

14. Christopher Chase-Dunn, *Global Formation: Structures of the World Economy* (New York: Blackwell, 1989), offers a good discussion of this concept as does Michael Hector, *Internal Colonialism: The Celtic Fringe in British National Development, 1536-1966.* (Berkeley: University of California Press, 1975).

15. The distinction between "market" and "social historians" is made by Allen Kullikoff, "The Transition to Capitalism in Rural America" (*William and Mary Quarterly*, 3rd Series, XLVI [1989]), which provides an excellent critical overview and bibliography of this debate. For an early effort to relate this debate to studies of Appalachia, see Dwight Billings, Kathleen Blee, and Louis Swanson, "Culture, Family, and Community in Preindustrial Appalachia," *Appalachian Journal* 13 (1986): 154-70.

16. Christopher Clark, "Household Economy, Market Exchange, and the Rise of Capitalism in the Connecticut Valley, 1800-1860," *Journal of Social History* 13 (1979): 175.

17. John Mack Faragher, *Sugar Creek: Life on the Illinois Prairie* (New Haven: Yale University Press, 1986): 98-9; Steven Hahn, "The 'Unmaking' of the Southern Yeomanry: The Transformation of the Georgia Upcounty, 1860-1890," in Steven Hahn and Jonathan Prude, eds., *The Countryside in the Age of Capitalist Transformation* (Chapel Hill: University of North Carolina Press, 1985): 181.

18. Charles Sellers, *The Market Revolution: Jacksonian America, 1815-1846* (New York: Oxford University Press, 1991), 5, 6 (note).

19. Frederick Bode and Donald Ginter, *Farm Tenancy and the Census in Antebellum Georgia* (Athens: University of Georgia Press, 1986), 5; Kullikoff, "Transition to Capitalism," 128.

20. Mark Granovetter, "Economic Action and Social Structure: The Problem of Embeddedness," *American Journal of Sociology* 91 (1985): 481-510.

21. See Karl Polanyi, *The Great Transformation: The Political and Economic Origins of Our Time* (Boston: Beacon Press, 1944), esp. 68-76; Karl Polanyi, *The Livelihood of Man* (New York: Academic Press, 1977), esp. 35-43; and Jürgen Habermas, *The Theory of Communicative Action 2: Lifeworld and System* (Boston: Beacon Press, 1987), 113-97. Eric Wolf's taxonomy of world systems is likewise based on the same three modes of integration (culture, coercion, and commerce) that he connotes as "kin-based," "tributary," and "market" modes of production/reproduction. See his *Europe and the People without History* (Berkeley: University of California Press, 1982).

22. Enzo Mingione, *Fragmented Societies: A Sociology of Economic Life beyond the Market Paradigm* (Cambridge, MA: Blackwell, 1991), 4.

23. Sellers, *Market Revolution*, 63.

24. On the transformation of North America from an external arena to an incorporated periphery, see Immanuel Wallerstein, *The Modern World System III* (New York: Academic Press, 1989). For an excellent discussion of the transformation of Kentucky from the era of Boone to Clay, see Stephen Anthony Aron, "How the West Was Lost: The Transformation of Kentucky from Daniel Boone to Henry Clay," Ph.D. diss., University of California at Berkeley, 1990.

25. For a general discussion of the North American fur trade in relation to European capitalism and its impact on native peoples, see Eric Wolf, *Europe and the People*; for an overview of the history of the Cherokee nation in relation to Appalachia's settlement and development by whites, see John Finger, "Cherokee Accommodation and Persistence in Southern Appalachia," in Pudup et al., *Appalachia*, 25-49. According to Dag Ryen, "Cherokee" in *Kentucky Encyclopedia* (Lexington: University Press of Kentucky, 1992), 181, the Cherokee population had declined from 250,000 to 25,000 by 1650 because of exposure to European diseases. On the connection between salt licks, buffalo traces, hunting trails, and modern road building in Kentucky, see Verhoeff, *Kentucky Mountains*, and John A. Jakle, "Salt on the Ohio Valley Frontier, 1770-1820," *Annals of the American Association of American Geographers* 59 (1969): esp. 687-95.

26. Edward C. O'Rear, "Eastern Kentucky," *Filson Club History Quarterly* 28 (1954): 115. On early settlement and explorations, see Connelley and Coulter, *History of Kentucky*, Vol 1., George Chinn, *Kentucky: Settlement and Statehood, 1750-1800* (Frankfort: Kentucky Historical Society, 1975) and Lowell H. Harrison and James C. Klotter, *A New History of Kentucky* (Lexington: University Press of Kentucky, 1977), 10-33. Also, on the rapidity of settlement, see Steven A. Channing, *Kentucky: A Bicentennial History* (New York: Oxford University Press, 1977), and for an important discussion of the demographic pressures in the

Upper South, see John Otto, *The Southern Frontiers, 1607-1860* (Westport, CT: Greenwood Press, 1989).

27. For Wallerstein's discussion of the processes of incorporation and peripheralization and the role of commodity chains, see *World System III*, esp. 130-1 and 189. For a discussion of slave labor in relation to the twin processes of commodification and coercion in peripheral zones of the capitalist world system and a comparison of the views of Marx and Wallerstein, see Chase-Dunn, *Global Formation*.

28. James Oakes, *Slavery and Freedom: An Interpretation of the Old South* (New York: Knopf, 1990), 97, as quoted in Robert Tracy McKenzie, *One South or Many? Plantation Belt and Upcountry in Civil War Era Tennessee* (Cambridge: Cambridge University Press, 1994), 32.

29. Good discussions of land laws in colonial Virginia and early Kentucky and their impacts on patterns of ownership and settlement are found in Paul Gates, "Tenants of the Log Cabin," *The Mississippi Valley Historical Review* 49 (1962): 3-31; Neal O. Hammon, "Land Acquisition on the Kentucky Frontier," *Register of the Kentucky Historical Society* 78 (1980): 297-321; and Neal O. Hammon, "Settlers, Land Jobbers, and Outlyers: A Quantitative Analysis of Land Acquisition on the Kentucky Frontier," *Register of the Kentucky Historical Society* 84 (1986): 241-62.

30. Wilma Dunaway, "Speculators and Settler Capitalists: Unthinking the Mythology about Appalachian Landholding, 1790-1860," in Pudup et al., eds., *Appalachia*.

31. For contrasting emphases, compare Dunaway, "Speculators and Settler Capitalists," who stresses how speculation promoted inequality and inhibited settlement, with Otto, *Southern Frontiers*, 50, 66, who claims that land was "readily available" in the southern backcountry and that "colonial and metropolitan governments usually encouraged settlement by generously distributing headright and other land grants."

32. For a general discussions of these forms of distributing land, see Gates, "Tenants," and Otto, *Southern Frontiers*; for a quantitative analysis of their comparative impacts on ownership in various sections of Kentucky, see Hammon, "Settlers."

33. Early land companies and the explorations they sponsored in Kentucky territory are described in Connelly and Coulter, *History of Kentucky I*.

34. George Washington, who possessed considerable lands himself on the Appalachian frontier, warned other speculators that "any person, therefore, who neglects the present opportunity of hunting out good lands, and in some measure marking and distinguishing them for his own (in order to keep others from settling them), will never regain them." Quoted in Dunaway, "Speculators," and in Aron, "How the West Was Lost," 180.

35. Narratives of these two first efforts at settlement abound in published histories of Kentucky, but a definitive history of the Transylvania Company has not been written.
36. Gates, "Tenants," 3; Thomas D. Clark, *Historic Maps of Kentucky* (Lexington: University Press of Kentucky, 1979), 45; Channing, *Kentucky*, 42.
37. Gates, "Tenants," 3.
38. Clay is quoted in "Patterns," 45; Channing, *Kentucky*, 43; Gates, "Tenants," 6.
39. Hammon, "Settlers," 250. Dunaway, "Speculators," suggests reasons for why her figures may underestimate absentee ownership in Kentucky.
40. Channing, *Kentucky*, 43.
41. Douglas C. North, *The Economic Growth of the United States, 1790-1860* (Englewood Cliffs, NJ: Prentice Hall, 1961), 64; Elizabeth Perkins, "The Consumer Frontier: Household Consumption in Early Kentucky," *Journal of American History* 78 (1991): 499.
42. Mary Beth Pudup, "The Limits of Subsistence: Agriculture and Industry in Central Appalachia," *Agricultural History* 64 (1990): 74; Altina Waller, *Feud: Hatfields, McCoys, and Social Change in Appalachia, 1860-1900* (Chapel Hill: University of North Carolina Press, 1988); Durwood Dunn, *Cades Cove: The Life and Death of a Southern Appalachian Community, 1818-1937* (Knoxville: University of Tennessee Press, 1988); John Inscoe, *Mountain Masters: Slavery and the Sectional Crisis in Western North Carolina* (Knoxville: University of Tennessee Press, 1989):12, 11. For Virginia, see Robert D. Mitchell, *Commercialism and Frontier: Perspectives on the Early Shenandoah Valley* (Charlottesville: University Press of Virginia, 1977); R. Mann, "Mountains, Land, and Kin Networks: Burkes Garden, Virginia, in the 1840s and 1850s," *Journal of Southern History* LVIII (1992): 411-34; and Kenneth W. Noe. *Southwest Virginia's Railroad: Modernization and the Sectional Crisis* (Urbana: University of Illinois Press, 1994). In an especially well-executed study, McKenzie, *One South*, finds significant differences in the extent of commercial farming in eastern Tennessee counties depending on their distance from the Great Valley. On the general question of isolation in Appalachian Tennessee, see David C. Hsiung, *Two Worlds in the Tennessee Mountains: Exploring the Origins of Appalachian Stereotypes* (Lexington: University Press of Kentucky, 1997). For overviews of these debates, see H. Tyler Blethen and Curtis W. Wood, "The Appalachian Frontier and the Southern Frontier: A Comparative Perspective," *Journal of the Appalachian Studies Association* 3 (1991): 36-47; and Ron L. Lewis and Dwight B. Billings, "Appalachian Culture and Economic Development: A Retrospective View on the Theory and Literature," *Journal of Appalachian Studies* 3 (1997): 3-42.
43. Perkins, "Consumer Frontier," 489.
44. French explorations of Kentucky lands predated the earliest English explorations by more than a half century. On early fur trading and the Louisville

merchants banking activities, see Connelly and Coulter, *History of Kentucky I*, esp. 299; also Jakle, "Salt," 692. For the role of hunting on the Kentucky frontier, see Aron, "How the West Was Lost."

45. These early trading ventures are described in Connelley and Coulter, *History of Kentucky I*; Verhoeff, *Kentucky River*; and Thomas Clark, *A History of Kentucky* (Lexington: University Press of Kentucky, 1960), esp. 156-73. The latter discusses Wilkinson's controversial exploits, including his possibly treasonous negotiations with Spain (pp. 85-90).

46. North, *Economic Growth*, 53; Aron, "How the West Was Lost," 340. On Kentucky's early exports, see Clark, *A History*, 156-73. The definitive history of the rise and decline of Lexington relative to the other urban centers of the early western frontier is Richard Wade, *The Urban Frontier: Pioneer Life in Early Pittsburgh, Cincinnati, Lexington, Louisville, and St. Louis* (Cambridge, MA: Harvard University Press, 1959).

47. Wade, *Urban Frontier*, 20; Perkins, "Consumer Frontier," 490. In 1802, Michaux wrote: "The majority of the inhabitants of Kentucky trade with Lexington merchants; they receive their merchandise from Philadelphia and Baltimore in thirty-five or forty days including the journey of two days and a half from Limestone where they land all the goods destined for Kentucky. . . . All the specie collected in the course of trade is sent by land to Philadelphia; I have seen convoys of this kind that consisted of fifteen or twenty horses." (Quoted in Verhoeff, *Kentucky River*, 89.) Another observation by Michaux, however, stating that much of the business of Kentucky merchants was "done by way of barter" because of the "extreme lack of specie" in the state, suggests that his claim about the convoys may have indeed leaned toward the apocryphal. (Quoted in Elizabeth Parr, "Kentucky's Overland Trade with the Antebellum South," *Filson Club Historical Quarterly* 2 [1928]: 80.)

48. Aron, "How the West Was Lost," 370; see also James Ramage, *John Wesley Hunt: Pioneer Merchant, Manufacturer, and Financier* (Lexington: University Press of Kentucky, 1974).

49. Wade, *Urban Frontier*, 49-53; Aron, "How the West Was Lost," 340-416; Clark, *History*, 165-73.

50. James F. Hopkins, *A History of the Hemp Industry in Kentucky* (Lexington: University Press of Kentucky, 1951).

51. List of factories from Verhoeff, *Kentucky River*, 92.

52. Wade, *Urban Frontier*, 21, 210-11.

53. Ibid., 110, 109, 125; Aron, "How the West Was Lost," 370, 392.

54. North, *Economic Growth*, 66; see also Wallerstein, *World System III*.

55. Verhoeff, *Kentucky River*, 101.

56. Parr, "Kentucky's Overland Trade," 71.

57. Connelly and Coulter, *History of Kentucky I*, 708; Parr, "Kentucky's Overland

Trade"; Paul Henlein, *Cattle Kingdom in the Ohio Valley, 1783-1860* (Lexington: University Press of Kentucky, 1959). The huge volume of hogs driven from Kentucky via the Wilderness Road led to that route being called the "Kaintuck Hog Road" in the early nineteenth century according to Channing, *Kentucky*, 54.

58. Margaret Walsh, "The Spatial Evolution of the Mid-Western Pork Industry, 1835-75," *Journal of Historical Geography* 4 (1978): 1-22; see also Verhoeff, *Kentucky River*, 101.

59. Wade, *Urban History*, 71, 177.

60. The best accounts of Kentucky's internal improvements in regard to transportation are found in Verhoeff's two studies, *Kentucky River* and *Kentucky Mountains*. For a discussion of economic accumulation strategies as the "hegemonic projects" of states that interprets the latter as both a site and object of struggle, see Bob Jessop, *State Theory: Putting the Capitalist State in Its Place* (University Park: Pennsylvania State University Press,1990), esp. chap. 7.

61. See case of *Andrew Craig v Conley Findley and Company* (1808) for an early dispute over livestock contracts in the records of the Clay County Circuit Court. All Clay County Circuit Court records are available in manuscript form at the Kentucky Department for Libraries and Archives in Frankfort, Kentucky.

62. Thomas Clark, "Salt, A Factor in the Settlement of Kentucky," *Filson Club History Quarterly* 12 (1938): 42; North, *Economic Growth*, 66; Jakle, "Salt," 701, 702.

63. Clark, "Salt," 46. The summary of data from the *Kentucky Gazette* is also taken from Clark, "Salt," 45, who also reports that the Kentucky butchering meatpacking industry yielded $6,462,598 in 1850.

64. Jakle, "Salt," 701.

65. Clark, "Salt," 50; Verhoeff, *Kentucky River*, 154.

66. Verhoeff, *Kentucky River*, 82.

67. Verhoeff, *Mountain Transportation*, 126, 168, 169, 170.

68. Primarily because of manufacturing in the Hanging Rock region, Kentucky was the third largest iron-producing state in 1860. Michael Hudson and Charles D. Howes, "Iron Industry," in *Kentucky Encyclopedia*, 455-7. See also Tyrel Moore, "Economic Development in Appalachian Kentucky, 1800-1860," in R. D. Mitchell, ed., *Appalachian Frontiers: Settlement, Society, and Development in the Preindustrial Era* (Lexington: University Press of Kentucky, 1990).

69. Wilma Dunaway, *The First American Frontier: Transition to Capitalism in Southern Appalachia, 1700-1860* (Chapel Hill: University of North Carolina Press, 1996), 164.

70. Standardizing aggregate wealth in 1839 by the number of voters, Clay County averaged 38% of the state average, or only $958 as compared to the Kentucky average of $2,529 per voter. In Fayette County that year, the average per voter

was $7,157 and in Kentucky's richest county, Bourbon, the average was $8,169. See *House of Representatives Journal* (Frankfort: State of Kentucky, 1839), Appendix, 207.

71. 1815 property valuations, reported by the state board of assessors in the *Kentucky Gazette*, Monday, November 27, 1815, are averaged by an extrapolation of the populations for 1810 and 1820. Property valuations for 1850 are from the Auditor's Report, *Kentucky Legislative Documents* #10, (Frankfort: State of Kentucky, 1850), 156, 157, 306, 307.

Chapter 3

1. These figures were calculated from a list of Clay County households published in William C. Kozee, *Pioneer Families of Eastern and Southeastern Kentucky* (Baltimore: Genealogical Publishing, 1973).

2. Lee Soltow, "Kentucky Wealth at the End of the Eighteenth Century," *The Journal of Economic History* XLIII (1983): 617. The same article describes Kentucky's tax rolls as "far superior to tax lists in other states" (p. 619) because counties were legally required to report all males over 21 in residence regardless of land or possessions and because the state required citizens to report all lands held, regardless of county location, on the tax rolls of the counties of their principal residence.

3. Calculated from the Clay County tax roll for 1816. Since the process of land acquisition often required a considerable amount of time in early Kentucky, it seems certain that many of those listed as landless on the tax roll were still in the process of establishing ownership. Some evidence of this is suggested by the fact that during the three final monthly sessions of the Clay County Court in 1815, twenty-one individuals claimed that by this date they had "improved" tracts of "vacant" land ranging from 150 to 200 acres in the county, but only three of these persons appeared as landowners on the 1816 tax lists. In each case, they reported small tracts of land (generally about fifty acres) that may have been acquired previously.

4. Soltow, "Kentucky Wealth."

5. For a comprehensive survey of inequality across the region that challenges convention wisdom that early Appalachia was egalitarian, see Dunaway, *First American Frontier*.

6. Calculated from the 1840 Clay County Tax Roll and a one-in-four sample of individuals from the 1860 federal population census.

7. Mitchell, *Commercialism and Frontier*, 52.

8. See deeds dated August 8, 1816, and November 15, 1816, in Clay County Deed Book "A." Also see the April 12, 1813, agreement by Elisha Brown grant-

ing James Clinton power of attorney "to transact his business in North Carolina and to receive of the administrator of his deceased father George Brown his share of estate that he may be entitled to."

9. For a more accurate view of early settlers and frontier society, see the excellent collection of articles in Mitchell, *Appalachian Frontiers*.

10. See two transactions between Egbert Fort and Elias Fort dated February 25, in 1812 in Clay County Deed Book "A."

11. A typescript copy of "A Brief Narrative of the Life of Abner Baker," written in 1826, is available in the Kentucky Historical Society, Frankfort. Baker's wealth is reported on the 1825 Clay County Tax Roll.

12. The name "Adoniram Andrews" is a pseudonym, as are all the names by which we refer to individuals and families in Beech Creek in order to preserve the anonymity that James Brown promised them when he began his study many years ago. Where possible, we have used the same pseudonyms for individuals Brown discusses in his own publications. All other Clay County names that we report throughout this book have been collected from manuscripts and public records and are not pseudonyms.

13. Biographical information on Andrews (pseudonym) has been published in various newsletters of the Clay County Historical Society that we do not cite in order to protect anonymity. We have also obtained information on Andrews from James Brown's research materials in Special Collections of the University of Kentucky Library and from personal conversations with Dr. Brown.

14. Brown, *Beech Creek*, esp. 122-47.

15. Gail S. Terry, "Family Empires: A Frontier Elite in Virginia and Kentucky, 1740-1815," Ph.D. diss., College of William and Mary, 1992, 5, 23, 4, 4. For an analysis and quantitative assessment of how land speculation influenced settlement and early patterns of inequality in the Appalachian South as a whole, see Wilma Dunaway, "Speculators and Settler Capitalists: Unthinking the Mythology about Appalachian Landholding, 1790-1860," in Pudup et al., *Appalachia*, 50-75.

16. On the concept of "hegemony," which is derived from the political sociology of Antonio Gramsci, see T. Jackson Lears, "The Concept of Cultural Hegemony: Problems and Possibilities," *American Historical Review* 90 (1985): 567-93.

17. William C. Kozee, *Pioneer Families of Eastern and Southeastern Kentucky* (Baltimore: Genealogical Publishing, 1973), 831. Biographical information on the Whites is taken from Kozee, *Pioneer Families*, 831-8 ("White Family of Clay County"), and an extensive but unpublished White family history by Charles H. White, Jr. (*White Family History*, n.p., n.d.).

18. White, *White Family History*, 13.

19. See Clay County Tax Assessment Book, 1840.

20. Kozee, *Pioneer Families*, 100.

21. John White represented the Congressional district that included Madison County out of which Clay County was formed. His cousin, Addison White, a son of James White, represented an Appalachian Virginia district in the U.S. House of Representatives from 1851 to 1853.
22. H. E. Everman, *Governor James Garrard* (Bourbon County, KY: Cooper's Run Press, 1981), 4.
23. Everman, *Governor*, 1, 2.
24. Calculated from lists of patents in Willard R. Jillson, *The Kentucky Land Grants: A Systematic Index to All of the Land Grants Recorded in the State Land Office at Frankfort, Kentucky, 1782-1924* (Baltimore: Genealogical Publishing, 1971).
25. Everman, *Governor*, 3, 4. Biographical information on James Garrard is primarily from this source. Information on the Clay County Garrards is taken from Kozee, *Pioneer Families*, esp. 245-7; and from Anna R. DesCognets, *Governor Garrard of Kentucky: A Genealogical Study* (Lexington, KY: James M. Byrnes, 1898).
26. The choice of a name for Bourbon County, immortalized by the whiskey first made there by farmers like James Garrard, as well as the name of its county seat, Paris, was influenced by the Garrards, both to recognize the role of France in the Revolution as well as their own French heritage.
27. Everman, *Governor*, 21, ii.
28. Ibid., 21.
29. On the Garrards' leadership in importing fine cattle into Kentucky, see the "Diary of Charles T. Garrard," *Register of the Kentucky State Historical Society* 29, 30 (1931, 1932): 400-15; 37-60.
30. John J. Dickey attributes this statement to the wife of Judge S. N. Dickerson in *Diary*, Roll 3, p. 2173. Unless otherwise indicated, our references to the John Jay Dickey *Diary* refer to Microfilm Roll 3 (1898), a copy of which is available in the Margaret I. King Library Special Collections and Archives of the University of Kentucky. Page references refer to a nondated typescript by Ruth B. Carr, a copy of which is in our possession.
31. Channing, *Kentucky*, 92.
32. Mary Beth Pudup, "Beyond the 'Traditional Mountain Subculture': A New Look at Pre-Industrial Appalachia," in Jim Lloyd and Anne G. Campbell, eds., *The Impact of Institutions in Appalachia: Proceedings of the 8th Annual Appalachian Studies Conference* (Boone, NC: Appalachian Consortium Press, 1986), 114-27. As its title suggests, even this insightful article stresses the importance of understanding the region's early commercial economy rather than the even more neglected topic of antebellum industry. For a comprehensive survey of early industry in the entire region, see Dunaway, *The First American Frontier*, esp. chap. 6.
33. On iron making in Appalachian Kentucky, see Tyrel G. Moore, "Economic

Development in Appalachian Kentucky, 1800-1860," in Mitchell, *Appalachian Frontiers*, 222-34.

34. Limited anecdotal information is contained in articles written by descendants of the White family: Roy R. White, "The Salt Industry of Clay County, Kentucky," *The Register of the Kentucky Historical Society* 50 (1952): 238-41; and Bessie White Hager, "The Whites of Clay County as Salt Makers," *The Register of the Kentucky Historical Society* 50 (1952): 242-8. See also John F. Smith, "The Salt-Making Industry of Clay County, Kentucky," *Filson Club History Quarterly* 1 (1927): 134-41. The Kanawha, (West) Virginia salt industry, however, is well documented in John E. Stealey III, *The Antebellum Kanawha Salt Business and Western Markets* (Lexington: University Press of Kentucky, 1993).

35. Lewis and Collins, *History of Kentucky II* (1874), gave 1798 as the date of first settlement in Clay County. However, in a deposition to the Clay County Court from Gallatin County, Illinois, William Sweeten stated that he lived there in order to claim land for Governor James Garrard in 1796 or 1797, suggesting that the rush to control the Goose Creek salt sources was well underway in the late eighteenth century (*Wm. Garrard et. al. v Moses Martin and John Bates {Richard Roe}*, Clay County Circuit Court, 1822). White, "Salt Industry," 238, claims that Collins settled in future-Clay County "somewhere between 1778 and 1790," even though the earliest date precedes commonly accepted dates of settlement in Appalachian Kentucky.

36. For the earliest information on technology, costs, and profitability of making salt in Clay County, see the Clay County Court cases of *John White* [no kin to the Clay County Whites] *v John Crooke (Adm. for John Amis)* (1809) and *Andrew Craig and Joseph Craig v Hugh White and George Baugh* (1810).

37. Verhoeff, *Kentucky Mountains*, 127-8.

38. Verhoeff, *Kentucky River*, 150; also U.S. Census of Manufacturing for 1810, Clay County, Kentucky, manuscripts.

39. See *John Bates v John Crooke (Adm. of the estate of John Amis, Dec.)*, Clay County Circuit Court, 1808.

40. Census of Manufacturing, 1820, manuscript.

41. See Dickey, *Diary*, Reel 4, esp. p. 2717, for T. T. Garrard's account of the history of his family's saltmaking firm.

42. Compare manuscripts of the U.S. Census of Manufacturing (Clay County) for the years 1820 and 1850.

43. See the agreement between John and Edith Ballenger and James White in Clay County Deed Book "A" dated February 6, 1804.

44. See *Garrard v Pace*, Clay County Circuit Court, 1835, for evidence of early salt-making in Kentucky's Northfork valley.

45. See the agreement between Hugh White and James White dated July 7, 1824, in Clay County Deed Book "A."

46. According to the U.S. Census of Manufacturing for 1850, the largest firm in the county belonged to James and Daugherty White, who employed twenty-five slaves to produce 70,000 bushels of salt with $40,000 in capital.

47. On the economic competition between the Whites and the Garrards, see Hager, "Salt Industry," 23.

48. The names of these early proprietors are gleaned from Clay County's earliest deed and court order books. Additionally, the appearance of men such as William Dees, Mathias Cain, John Wilson, Gustavis Quarrier, and Hezekiah Hall in civil court cases filed between census years suggests that the list of firms in the federal manuscript censuses of manufacturing operated by members of the White and Garrard families identifies industrial survivors but does not adequately represent all entrepreneurs who were active at one time or another during the history of the Clay County salt industry. For the interesting case of Rhoda Taylor, who attempted, but failed, to develop salt wells on her own land, see the testimony in *Hugh White v Heirs of Thomas Smith, Clay County Circuit Court,* Clay County Circuit Court, 1834.

49. See properties conveyed to Daniel Garrard and John Bates, respectively, by sheriff auctions on June 10, 1816, and July 12, 1817, resulting from executions in favor of central Kentucky firms such as Tillford, Scott, and Trotter (Lexington), Fields and Barnum (Richmond), and others.

50. See the *Kentucky Gazette* 19 (September 3, 1805).

51. Both cases appear as identified in the text in the Clay County Circuit Court for the years 1810 and 1814, respectively.

52. See Dickey, *Diary*, Reel 3, p. 2073, for the deposition of "Capt. Byron" (son-in-law of saltmaker Alexander White).

53. See interview with Anderson Philpot (March 21, 1898) in Dickey, *Diary*, Reel 3, p. 2197. For additional information on the use of coal, see Hager, "Whites as Salt Makers," 246, and Verhoeff, *Kentucky River*, 154, who reports that the principal mine [in the Goose Creek area] was owned by General [T. T.] Garrard.

54. Roy White, "Salt Industry," claims that members of the White family made salt until 1884.

55. According to the "Report on the Kentucky River Navigation" by the Kentucky Engineer's Office (*Journal of the House of Representatives, State of Kentucky,* 1836): 93, ten active salt wells (among fifteen) were producing between 200,000 and 250,000 bushels per year during the 1830s, suggesting that the level of production for the census year 1840 may have been lower than normal because of the national economic depression that was occurring at that time.

56. See Daniel Garrard, "Jack's Creek to Goose Creek Salt-works," *Journal of the Kentucky House of Representative, 1818-1819* (January 6, 1819): 130-2 for a description of the effects of drought and a fall in demand in the two years before 1820.

57. Fred Bateman and Thomas Weiss, "Comparative Regional Development in Antebellum Manufacturing," *Journal of Economic History* 35 (1975): 182-208. According to Dunaway, *First Frontier*, 90% of the region's manufacturing establishments in 1860 employed less than five full-time laborers.

58. The extent to which capital was invested in slave labor can be seen in Table 3.1 by comparing the amount of capital invested in nine firms before emancipation ($162,000) with the amount invested in the four firms that were in operation in 1870 ($16,600). In the latter year, one-fourth of the output of the earlier period was achieved with only one-tenth the capital although no technological changes are in evidence.

59. A mortgage agreement between James H. Garrard and Daniel Garrard dated November 3, 1841 (Clay County Deed Book "C"), mentions each of these locations in the Bluegrass where Goose Creek salt was then being sold.

60. On the markets for Clay County salt, see Verhoeff, *Kentucky River*, esp. 152-7; Roy White, "Salt Industry"; and Dickey, *Diary* (Reel 3), esp. interviews with J. W. Culton (p. 2072), Capt. Byron (p. 2069), and Judge Dickerson (p. 2160). For additional information on Tennessee markets, see Harriet Simpson Arnow, *The Flowering of the Cumberland* (Lexington: University Press of Kentucky, 1984): 293; and Thomas Clark, "Salt, A Factor in the Settlement of Kentucky," *Filson Club History Quarterly* 12 (January, 1938): 42-52.

61. Jakle, "Salt," 709.

62. Stealey, *Antebellum Kanawha*.

63. "West Virginia's Pioneer Industry: Salt Making in the Kanawha Valley," *Newsletter of the West Virginia and Regional History Collection* 7 (1991): 1-4; Stealey, *Antebellum Kanawha*.

64. According to Jakle, "Salt," 700, several of central Kentucky's saltworks required 1,000 gallons of brine to make one bushel of salt compared with only 100 gallons of brine from the Kanawha Valley. Verhoeff, *Kentucky River*, reports a ratio of 80 gallons of brine to one bushel for the Goose Creek industry. Price information for price is from Jakle, "Salt"; see also Verhoeff, *Kentucky River*, 104.

65. William Talley, "Salt Lick Creek and Its Salt Works," *The Register of the Kentucky Historical Society*, 64 (1966): 85-109.

66. See *Richard Deering v Hugh White*, Clay County Circuit Court, 1821, which charges that the latter used an apparatus without consent that the plaintiff had patented in 1814 for the improved boring and pumping of water.

67. See road enactment dated January 2, 1818, *Acts of the General Assembly of Kentucky, 1817-1818* (Frankfort: Kendall and Russells, 1818).

68. Mary Verhoeff, *Kentucky Mountains*, 127-33. See also *Acts of the General Assembly for the Commonwealth of Kentucky*, 1832: 78; 1823: 267; 1825: 180.

69. Verhoeff, *The Kentucky Mountains*, 127, 168.

70. Verhoeff, *The Kentucky Mountains*, 176.

71. Antes Snyder, "Report of the Survey of Goose Creek & the South Fork of Kentucky, and of a Connection between Goose Creek and Cumberland River," *Journal of the House of Representatives of the Commonwealth of Kentucky* (1837): 137-41.

72. Ibid.

73. According to Stealey, *Antebellum Kanawha*, 171, the sales agency of Ruffner, Donnally, and Co. owned four steamboats and as many as 400 flatboats around 1850.

74. Garrard, "Jack's Creek."

75. Kentucky Engineer's Office, "Report on the Kentucky River Navigation," *Journal of the House of Representatives of the Commonwealth of Kentucky* (1836): 93.

76. Snyder, "Survey of Goose Creek & South Fork," 138.

77. A vivid description of these trips is given in "Down the Kentucky on a Raft," in John Fox, Jr., *Blue-Grass and Rhododendron: Out-doors in Old Kentucky* (New York: Scribner's, [1901], 1920): 55-76.

78. Snyder, "Survey of Goose Creek and the South Fork."

79. Daniel Garrard, "Jack's Creek to Goose Creek;" Verhoeff, *Kentucky River Navigation*, 22. For the appointment of two saltmakers, John Gilbert and John Murphey, as commissioners on the Red Bird River, see *Acts of the Twenty-third General Assembly of the Commonwealth of Kentucky* (Louisville, KY: Gerard and Burry, 1815). For a general discussion of the clash of interests in early American river clearances, see Gary Kulik, "Dams, Fish, and Farmers: Defense of Public Rights in Eighteenth-Century Rhode Island," in Hahn and Prude, *The Countryside*, 25-50.

80. Verhoeff, *Kentucky River Navigation*, 25.

81. Report of the Board of Internal Improvements, *Appendix to the House of Representative Journal* (January 22, 1836): 6-7. Advocating improvements on the Kentucky River, the same report lamented the fact that the city of Louisville was then importing annually more than two million dollars worth of salt, iron, coal, and lumber (including $115,000 worth of salt) from Ohio, Pennsylvania, and Virginia, even though all of this could have been supplied by sources upriver in the Kentucky River highlands where sufficient improvements had been made.

82. *Report of the Board of Internal Improvement to the General Assembly* (Frankfort: State of Kentucky, 1855): 13-15; "Report of the Board of Internal Improvement, 1835," in *Kentucky Collected Documents, Appendix to the H. R. Journal*, 4; "Annual Report of the Board of Internal Improvement of the State of Kentucky, January, 1840," in *Kentucky Collected Documents* 1 (1939-40): 199.

83. Robert Kincaid, *The Wilderness Road* (Indianapolis: Bobbs-Merrill, 1947), esp. 208-15. The Cincinnati Southern railroad eventually traversed the Kentucky

and Tennessee portions of this route, but it was not built until the 1870s and did not reach into Clay County. See Lowell Harrison and James C. Klotter, *A New History of Kentucky* (Lexington: University Press of Kentucky, 1997), 246-7.

84. Compare the "Annual Report[s] of the Board of Internal Improvements to the General Assembly" for 1848 and 1855.

85. See the section of Dickey's, *Diary,* entitled "Biography of T. T. Garrard – March 20, 1899," Reel 4, pp. 2713-33.

86. Stealey, *Antelbellum Kanawha*, esp. 184-90. See also Margaret Walsh, *The Rise of the Midwestern Meat Packing Industry* (Lexington: University Press of Kentucky, 1982).

87. Stealey, *Antebellum Kanawha*, 184. The business failures of Alexander White and William White in the early 1850s were described to John Dickey in an interview with "Judge" Dickenson (*Diary*, Reel 3, p. 2170) and confirmed by the record of mortgages and conveyances of property by the both Whites in Clay County Deed Book "D." (See September 6, 14, and 15, 1852, for transactions of Alexander White; September 17 and 18, 1852, for William White.)

88. Perhaps compensating for rumors that her father-in-law Daniel Garrard was a Confederate sympathizer, T. T. Garrard's wife reportedly told the federal officer in charge of the destruction of the saltworks that "not only the valuable property, but all else that she and her husband (a colonel in our service) owned, might be destroyed if such destruction would help to restore the Union." Ella Lonn, *Salt as a Factor in the Confederacy* (University: University of Alabama Press, 1965): 290.

89. Lonn, *Salt*, 188-90. Also *Official War Records* (Washington, D.C.: Archives of the War Department, Series I, Vol. xvi): 1150-3. Several Goose Creek saltmakers, including T. T. Garrard, filed Civil War Claims for compensation for damages but were never repaid according to a reference service report dated December 2, 1959, from the National Archives and Records Service (copy in our possession).

90. For evidence on salt prices see testimony regarding salt prices in the cases of *Montgomery v White and Baugh*, Clay County Circuit Court, 1810, and *Moses Foley v Hugh White*, Clay County Circuit Court, 1828; Captain Byron interview (on Alabama markets) in Dickey, *Diary,* Reel 3, p. 2068. For 1844, compare Benjamin F. White's *Merchant Day Book* with Stealey *Antebellum Kanawha*. For more systematic information on salt prices in Cincinnati, see Thomas Senior Berry, *Western Prices before 1861: A Study of the Cincinnati Market* (Cambridge, MA: Harvard University Press, 1943): 286-317.

91. Compare price information reported in Stealey, *Antebellum Kanawha*, esp. 170-83, with entries on wholesale salt sales in Manchester by Benjamin F. White from October 1845 through 1853 as reported in White's daybook.

92. For identification of Quarrier as a Kanawha saltmaker, see Stealey, *Antebellum Kanawha*, 164.
93. For a White family remembrance of the White-Garrard price wars, see Hager, "White Family," 246. The continuing effort by Kanawha manufacturers to control prices is a central topic of Stealey, *Antebellum Kanawha*, which claims that despite ultimate ineffectiveness, these Appalachian saltmakers pioneered in creating the first trust in American industrial history.
94. Compare testimony on evaporation technology in the case of *Daniel G. and Hugh L. White v Jesse Lincoln and Robert Cravens*, Clay County Circuit Court, 1850, with Stealey, *Antebellum Kanawha*. Also, according to the latter, nearly all brine pumps were powered by steam in the Kanawha Valley by the 1830s, but horse and mule power remained prevalent in Clay County as shown by the county's 1850 manuscript census of manufacturing.
95. For a list of typical properties in a salt firm, see mortgages between Wilson and Quarrier and Blackburn and Kincaid & Co. (January 14, 1841) and Robert Wickliff & Co. (February 27, 1841), both in Clay County Deed Book "C."
96. Stealey, *Antebellum Kanawha*, 141.
97. Case of *W. H. (Wade) Walker v Daniel Bates*, Clay County Circuit Court, 1843.
98. See Chapter 5 for a discussion of how these estimates were arrived at.
99. Dickey, *Diary*, Reel 3, interview with "Judge" Dickerson, 2172.
100. See, for example, Daniel Garrard's testimony on hiring slaves in the case of *Mary Dickerson (Adm. for Archer Dickerson) v John Bates*, Clay County Circuit Court, 1821.
101. For an informative picture of subsequent economic development in a former saltmaking community in the Kanawha Valley, see Todd Hanson, *Campbell's Creek: A Portrait of a Coal Mining Community* (Charleston, WV: Pictorial Histories Publishing, 1989).
102. Christopher Chase-Dunn, *Global Formation: Structures of the World Economy* (Cambridge: Blackwell, 1989): 220. The empirical support for Chase-Dunn's argument comes from Andre Gunder Frank, *Mexican Agriculture 1521-1630: Transformation of the Mode of Production* (Cambridge: Cambridge University Press, 1979).
103. These data were calculated for all members of the White and Garrard families with information from the 1850 and 1860 Clay County manuscript censuses of agriculture, manufacturing, and slaveholding. It is likely, as well, that the proceeds from tenant-operated farms increased for both families during this period, but such information cannot be obtained from the census manuscripts.
104. Dunaway, *First American Frontier*, 193.
105. Ibid., 229.
106. For example, James White's business associate Claiborne White (no kin) supplied local merchants with goods on credit from eastern merchants (*C. W. White*

& *Co. v Stephen Gibson*, Clay County Circuit Court, 1822), and Daniel Garrard sometimes acted as the local subagent of such merchants (see the agreement between J. C. Wilson and Gustavius Quarrier and George Wilson, July 26, 1839, Clay County Deed Book "C." For an example of borrowing cash to pay off debts to other creditors, see *C. and J. White & Co. v John Woods*, Clay County Circuit Court, 1838.

107. Dickey, *Diary*, Reel 3, pp. 2194, 2130, 2072-3, 2170.

108. Ibid., pp. 2373, 2367-8, 2117, 2197, 2128, 2073.

109. See depositions from the above named persons in the case of *W. H. (Wade) Walker v Daniel Bates*," Clay County Circuit Court, 1843; also Clay County Circuit Court cases of *George Frazer v Daniel Bates' Executors* (1847) and *Samuel Lucas v Bates' Executors* (1846). Jones's deposition is found in the case of *Bledsoe, Deceased v Bates' Executors*" (1849).

110. See the following cases in Clay County Circuit Court: *George Hooker v Daniel Bates' Executors* (1848); *John Woods v Daniel Bates' Executors* (1845); *Calvin Handy v Bates, Dec.* (1849); *Jesse Colton v Bates' Executors* (1850); *Frank Ballinger v Daniel Bates Executors* (1849).

111. Daybook of James and Hugh White, Upper Goose Creek Saltworks (1806-14), Filson Club Historical Society, Louisville, Kentucky.

112. Based on the 1810 federal census. We located a few other customers with reasonably certainty in central Kentucky localities such as Madison County, but the fact that a good many others were not enumerated in the federal census as Kentucky residents suggests that by this date, White had already established a considerable volume of business outside Kentucky – probably in Tennessee where he had previously traded.

113. Elizabeth A. Perkins, "The Consumer Frontier: Household Consumption in Early Kentucky," *The Journal of American History* 78 (1991): 486-510, esp. Table 1.

114. See also August 1807 deed between Patrick Riley Sr. and Zaccariah Riley conveying pewter dishes and plates in Clay County Deed Book "A" and the deed between Samuel and Richard Smith also conveying pewter plates and dishes, knives, and forks.

115. Merchants in Shenandoah valley towns like Winchester, Virginia, settled most transactions in cash and almost none in agricultural commodities as early as 1790, yet Kentucky merchants in non-Appalachian, cash-poor towns such as the important Ohio River community of Maysville still traded on primarily a credit basis throughout the first decade of the nineteenth century. Compare Warren Hofstra and Robert Mitchell, "Town and Country in Backcountry Virginia: Winchester and the Shenandoah Valley, 1730-1800," *Journal of Southern History* LIX (1993): 619-46; and Craig Friend, "Inheriting Eden: The Creation of Society and Community in Early Kentucky, 1792-1812," Ph.D. diss., University of Kentucky, 1995.

116. Wage rates varied between three shillings for days spent "working at the well," "pitching wood," or "driving wagon" to six shillings for "tending kettles" or "drawing water." Slaves received 1/6 shilling for each night they worked at the furnaces. In comparison, White credited farmers with six shillings for providing one gallon of honey or two bushels of corn or sweet potatoes. A razor cost six shillings as did a pair of overalls, a hoe cost ten shillings/six pence, and yard of calico cost nine shillings.

117. Ledger of Benjamin F. White, 1843-1855, in Kentucky Department for Libraries and Archives, Frankfort.

118. Apparently, in Marxist terms, participating in the commodification of one's own labor necessitated the reliance on further commodities for household reproduction. See Harriet Friedmann, "World Market, State and Family Farm: Social Bases of Household Production in the Era of Wage Labor," *Comparative Studies in Society and History* 20 (1978): 546-86.

119. See U.S. Census of Population (manuscripts) for Clay County, 1850.

120. Whether Gregory owned or rented this farm is unclear from the records. The census taker in 1850 reported Gregory's unimproved acres as well as the monetary value of his farm – categories of information usually omitted for tenants – yet he did not appear on the 1850 tax roll as a property owner. In either case, owning or renting a farm presented a different mix of options than selling his labor to White, which apparently drew him away from the company store.

121. Karl Marx, *Capital*, Vol. I (Moscow: Progress Publishers, 1954): 76-87; George Lukacs, *History and Class Consciousness* (Cambridge; MA: The MIT Press, 1968): 83-222.

122. Granovetter, "Economic Activity and Social Structure: The Problem of Embeddedness," *American Journal of Sociology* 91 (1985): 495; John Lie, "The Concept of Exchange," *American Sociological Review* 57 (1992): 508.

123. Lawrence M. Freidman, *A History of American Law*, 2nd ed. (New York: Touchstone, 1985), 267.

124. Ellen Semple Churchill, "The Anglo-Saxons of the Kentucky Mountains [1901]," *Bulletin of the American Geographical Society* XLII (1910): 581, 589.

125. They also reveal the existence of many business firms otherwise not visible from sources such as the manuscript censuses of manufacturing.

126. See the following cases, respectively, that were heard before the Clay County Circuit Court: *Hugh L. White v Randolph Smith*, (1808), *Jacob and Henry Baker v Hezekiah Hall*, (1809), *Andrew Craig v Conley Findley*, (1809), *Hugh White v Alexander Bales*, (1809), and *Hugh White v William Pearl, Sr. & Jr*, (1808).

127. In the case of *James Montgomery v Hugh White and George Baugh* (1810), the plaintiff charged that the defendants failed to deliver salt to Lincoln County as promised; for similar cases, see *John Freeman v James and Hugh White* (1811);

William Anderson v Hugh White (1811); and *William Newton v Hugh White* (1810).

128. On the legal meaning of such inscriptions, see Connelley and Coulter, *History of Kentucky II*, 608. For more recent scholarship on Kentucky's debt crisis of 1818-20, see Sandra F. VanBurkleo, " 'The Paws of Banks': The Origins and Significance of Kentucky's Decision to Tax Federal Bankers, 1818-1820," *Journal of the Early Republic* 9 (Winter 1989): 457-87.

129. See *Aldridge & Abner v Claiborne & James White & Co.*, Clay County Circuit Court, 1834, in which the plaintiffs sought to enforce nine such notes issued by the defendants.

130. See, for example, the following cases in 1830: *White & Russell v Enoch Abner & Others; Claiborne White & Co. v John Root*; and *Jeremiah Combs v Hugh White*. The first case in our sample of a promissory note written for silver or gold was *Trustees of the Clay County Seminary v William Reid & James White* (1936).

131. Friedmann, *American Law*, 267.

132. Each of these cases was heard before the Clay County Circuit Courts on the dates listed.

133. See Clay County Book of Wills.

134. See "Settlement with the Executions of Daniel Bates, Dec'd.," Clay County Book of Wills and Probates (October 30, 1847): 198-205.

135. See "Daniel Bates, Dec'd.'s Combined Appraisement," Clay County Book of Wills and Probates, 177-9.

136. See "Adoniram Andrews" (pseudonym) "Appraisement and Sale Bill," Clay County Book of Wills and Probates.

137. See the following cases heard by the Clay County Circuit Court: *E. Garrard & Sons v Mathias Cain* (1839) and *White and Russell v Muncey and Murphey* (1841).

138. Deposition of Elhanan Murphey in the case of *Wade Walker v Daniel Bates*, Clay County Circuit Court, 1843.

139. The effects of the national depression were felt even in geographically remote Harlan County in extreme southeastern Kentucky as noted in the autobiography of Thomas W. Parsons. Parsons wrote that his father "had traded a good deal and owed considerable money, but had a great deal of stock on hand, hogs, cattle, and horses, and was running along evenly when the great panic of 1839-40 struck him and he went down with a crash." See Frank F. Mathias, *Incidents and Experiences in the Life of Thomas W. Parsons from 1826 to 1900* (Lexington: University Press of Kentucky, 1975), 18. We are grateful to Lee Hardesty for this reference.

140. See agreement between Hugh L. White and Hugh White dated March 14, 1839, in Clay County Deed Book "D".

141. See the following agreements in Clay County Deed Book "C": James H. Garrard and Lyne Kinningham (April 27, 1841); James H. Garrard and Daniel Garrard

(November 3, 1841); T. T. Garrard and Daniel Garrard (November 3, 1841); J. H. Garrard and Daniel Garrard (April 6, 1842).

142. See the deeds regarding the bankruptcy and economic restructuring of the firm of Wilson and Quarrier in Clay County Deed Book "B" dated September 25, 1837, and March 5, 1838; in Order Book "C," see the deeds entered October 2, 1838; May 20, 1840; January 14, 1841; February 27, 1841; April 20, 1842; and February 15, 1843.

143. See agreement between Stephen Gibson and Daniel Bates dated May 2, 1843, and the conveyance of property (owned jointly with William Reid) by Wiley Hibbard and E. W. Murphey, deputy sheriffs, to Daniel Bates on July 11, 1843. Gibson was also forced to mortgage 1,900 acres of land to Leander Miller and Barton Potter on July 5, 1943. All three transactions are recorded in Clay County Deed Book "C."

144. See *David Walker (Adm. for D. Bates, Dec.) v John House*, Clay County Court, 1850.

145. See *Stivers and Walker (Adms. of Daniel Bates, Dec.) v Daniel Garrard and Others*, Clay County Circuit Court, 1846.

146. See agreements between Julius Hacker and John Gilbert, Jr., dated May 29, 1841, and between Hacker and Daniel Garrard dated April 29, 1841, both in Deed Book "C."

147. See *Barton Potter v Thomas Philpot*, Clay County Circuit Court, 1839.

148. See 1841 agreements recorded in Clay County Deed Book "C" between Potter and each of these individuals dated, respectively, January 22, March 26, April 24, December 17, March 3, and August 24.

149. See Clay County tax rolls, 1837 and 1843. In contrast to Potter's good fortune, Kentucky as a whole experienced a decrease in the valuation of taxable property of $77,854,369 from 1839 to 1843. See Annual Report of Auditor, Public Accounts, Doc. No. 1, "Auditor's Report," Kentucky Documents, 1859-60.

150. A recent study of antebellum North Carolina, however, found that nearly all affluent mountaineers were slaveholders. Moreover, whereas the overall rate of slaveholding in the North Carolina mountains was low, some mountain counties had very substantial numbers of slaves. John Inscoe, *Mountain Masters, Slavery, and the Sectional Crisis in Western North Carolina* (Knoxville: University of Tennessee Press, 1989). See also J. Winston Coleman, "Lexington's Slave Dealers and Their Southern Trade," *The Filson Club History Quarterly* 12 (1938): 1-23; Carter G. Woodson, "Freedom and Slavery in Appalachian America," *Journal of Negro History* 1 (1916): 132-50.

151. The correlation between improved acres and number of slaves for slaveholding farmers in Clay County is 0.54 in 1850 and 0.75 in 1860. See also Inscoe, *Mountain Masters*.

152. James B. Murphey, "Slavery and Freedom in Appalachia: Kentucky as a

Demographic Case Study," *Register of the Kentucky Historical Society* 80 (1982): 151-69.

153. The proximity of Clay County to Lexington, a major slave market until the Civil War, may have facilitated the hiring of slaves. See Frederic Bancroft, *Slave-Trading in the Old South*, 130, 145-64 (Baltimore: J. H. Furst, 1931); see also Coleman, "Lexington's Slave Dealers"; and Murphy, "Slavery and Freedom."

154. *Harriet (of color) v William White*, Clay County Circuit Court, 1849.

155. *William Newton v Hugh White*, Clay County Circuit Court, 1810; *Arthur Rankin v Hugh White*, Clay County Circuit Court, 1822; *Alexander White v Daniel Bates*, Clay County Circuit Court, 1832; *Luther Browner v Alexander White and Co.*, Clay County Circuit Court, 1838; *Walter Taylor v Elizabeth Garrard & Sons*, Clay County Circuit Court, 1838; *Alexander Hooker, administrator for estate of Matilda O. Flack v Elizabeth, Daniel, James & William Garrard*, Clay County Circuit Court, 1838; "*Harriet (of Color) v William White*," Clay County Circuit Court, 1849.

156. *Alfred Hooker, administrator of Matilda O. Flack v Elizabeth, Daniel, James, & William Garrard*, 1838; *James H. Letcher, administrator for estate of Stephen G. Letcher v Hugh White & Granville Love*, Clay County Circuit Court, 1847.

157. *John White v John Crooke, estate administrator of John Amis*, Clay County Circuit Court, 1809; *Arthur Rankin v Hugh White*, Clay County Circuit Court, 1822; *Mary Dickerson, administrator of the estate of Archer Dickerson v John Bates*, Clay County Circuit Court, 1822.

158. *William Newton v Hugh White*, Clay County Circuit Court, 1810.

159. *Daniel Walker & George Stivers, administrators for Daniel Bates' estate v Stephen Gibson, Sr.*, Clay County Circuit Court, 1848; *Margaret Bledsoe, administrator for Joseph Bledsoe's estate v executors for Daniel Bates*, Clay County Circuit Court, 1849.

160. *George Stivers and Daniel Walker, administrators for Daniel Bates' estate v Daniel Garrard, J. H. Garrard, T. T. Garrard, & Luther Browner*, Clay County Circuit Court, 1846.

161. Calculated from Clay County Tax Roll, 1850.

162. *Thomas Roberts v John Bates*, Clay County Circuit Court, 1811; *Alexander White v Daniel Bates*, Clay County Circuit Court, 1832.

163. *Alexander White v Thomas Lockard, Sheriff*, Clay County Circuit Court, 1834.

164. *Mary Dickerson, administrator of Arthur Dickerson's estate v John Bates*, Clay County Circuit Court, 1822.

165. *Jacob Oxford, guardian for infant heirs of William Rogers v George Rogers, John Rogers, and others*, Clay County Circuit Court, 1829. According to Bancroft, *Slave-Trading*, 133, estate sales throughout Kentucky frequently included slave auctions.

166. *Claiborne White & Co. v Paul Pigg*, Clay County Circuit Court, 1830.

167. *Alexander White v Daniel Bates*, Clay County Circuit Court, 1832; *Alexander White v Thomas Lockard, Sheriff*, Clay County Circuit Court, 1834.

168. Clay County Court Order Book "D," 1840, p. 465.

169. This more closely resembled the pattern of slaveholding in South as a whole. John Boles, *Black Southerners, 1619-1869* (Lexington: University Press of Kentucky, 1984).

170. Forty-four percent owned between five and ten slaves, another 12% owned between eleven and twenty, and 6% owned more than twenty slaves.

171. Inscoe, *Mountain Masters*, 76.

172. Ibid.

173. See Ibid. for a discussion of slave purchases for investments in Appalachian North Carolina.

174. Boles, *Black Southerners.*

175. Elizabeth Fox-Genovese, *Within the Plantation Household: Black and White Women of the Old South* (Chapel Hill: University of North Carolina Press, 1988).

Chapter 4

1. See Clay County Order Book "B" (1815-32), court sessions of March 9, 1818, and February 29, 1831.

2. See, for example, the court session of November 9, 1819 (Order Book "B") that allotted $86 for six aged and infirm persons. At its session of November 12, 1821, the court ordered the auction of 100 acres of land for the benefit of Lucy Bowling, "a widow and destitute of any estate whatever except for her wearing apparel [*sic*]."

3. Robert M. Ireland, *The County in Kentucky History* (Lexington: University Press of Kentucky, 1976), vii.

4. Robert M. Ireland, *The County Courts in Antebellum Kentucky* (Lexington: University Press of Kentucky, 1972), 6.

5. See Ireland's discussion of the judicial and financial business of county courts in ibid., 18-61.

6. Quoted in Frank Mathias, "The Turbulent Years of Kentucky Politics, 1820-1850," *The Register of the Kentucky Historical Society* 72 (1974): 309.

7. Mathias, "Turbulent Years," esp. 314; and Jaspar Shannon, "The Political Process in Kentucky," *Kentucky Law Journal* 45 (1957): esp. 402-10; Ireland, *County Courts.* Kentucky, in 1885, was the last state in the nation still adhering to voice voting.

8. According to James Oakes, *The Ruling Race: A History of American Slaveholders* (New York: Knopf, 1982): 144, "nearly three out of four . . . judges were slaveholders in Kentucky counties where only one out of three heads of families had slaves." See also Ireland, *County Courts*, 7-17.

9. Information on early court officers is taken from William C. Kozee, *Pioneer*

Families of Eastern and Southeastern Kentucky (Baltimore: Genealogical Publishing, 1973), 100-4. Unfortunately, the earliest surviving court order book dates only from 1815.

10. Slaveowning and wealth information is calculated from Clay County tax assessment records for 1840; we examine the 1841 court rather than that of 1840 because the surviving order book for the former year allows a more complete reconstruction of court membership.

11. Kozee, *Pioneer Families*, 100-4.

12. The "cattle war" was still very much alive in the memories of older Clay Countians when John J. Dickey interviewed them ninety years later. Several told Dickey versions of the story and two persons quoted poems or songs about the conflict, suggesting how strongly the "war" was anchored in oral tradition. One version in particular described militia commander Hugh White's response to John Amis's call for military support as follows: "You have got yourselves in trouble \ get out if you can. \ I'll neither come to your assistance, \ nor send a single man." See especially Dickey's interviews with Melville Johnson, John Eversole, and T. T. Garrard as well as his own reconstruction of the event on Reel 3.

13. Jess Wilson, "The Old Cattle War," in his *The Sugar Pond and the Fritter Tree*. (Berea: Kentucky Imprints, 1981), 44-51. Perhaps the most direct fallout from the cattle war was the Strong-Amis feud in Breathitt County, Kentucky, that pitted children and grandchildren of the original combatants against one another after the Civil War. Judge Edward Callahan Strong, who presided over a key criminal trial relating to this feud, told J. J. Dickey in 1898 that "The effects of the [Cattle] war have never ceased to this day." See Dickey, *Diary*, Reel 3. Those journalists who covered Kentucky feuds in the national press and insisted, as had novelist John Fox, Jr., that all feuds were the outgrowth of an unnamed earlier conflict may have been influenced by such stories of the cattle war and the presumed effects on its descendants. See, for example, Emerson Hough, "Burns of the Mountains," *The American Magazine* (1913): 13-20.

14. Clive Y. Thomas, *The Rise of the Authoritarian State in Peripheral Societies* (New York: Monthly Review Press, 1984), 16.

15. Wilson, "Old Cattle War," 48.

16. Roy White, "History of Clay County, IV," *The [Clay County] Manchester Guardian*, Friday, June 10, 1932, (typescript copy, courtesy of Jesse Wilson).

17. Wilson, "Old Cattle War," 48.

18. Kozee, *Pioneer Families*; White, "History, IV."

19. Compare Martin Crawford, "Political Society in a Southern Mountain Community: Ashe County, North Carolina, 1850-1861," *Journal of Southern History* LX (1989): 373-90; and Van Beck Hall, "The Politics of Appalachian Virginia, 1790-1830," in Mitchell, *Appalachian Frontiers*, 166-86. Hall stresses policy

differences between Appalachian counties with towns and commerce and those without. Crawford stresses the interests and authority of slaveholders in Appalachia for understanding why geographically isolated mountain counties were more closely integrated into the politics of the wider antebellum South than has commonly been imagined. We interpret both sets of factors – urban and commercial development and slaveholding – as indicators of the extent of capitalist development in antebellum Appalachia previously downplayed in earlier accounts of the region.

20. Frank F. Mathias and Jasper B. Shannon, "Gubernatorial Politics in Kentucky, 1820-1851," *The Register of the Kentucky Historical Society* 88 (1990): 245-77.

21. The earliest county court order book ("A") was destroyed by fire, but Roy White's sketches of early Clay County history, published in the local newspaper during the 1930s, were based in part on it. We are grateful to Jess Wilson for sharing his "scrap book" of these newspaper stories with us. The oldest surviving record of court actions is Order Book "B," 1815-32.

22. White, "Clay County History"; Clay County Order Book "B", sessions of June 9, 1817, December 14, 1818, and November 27, 1826.

23. In Court Order Book "B," see appointment of Daniel Garrard and Daniel Bates as turnpike commissioners (September 11, 1815); appropriation to Daniel Garrard, river commissioner (December 14, 1818); and appointment of Alexander White, John Bates, James H. Garrard, and Hugh White as slave patrollers on Goose Creek (January 26, 1829); White, "County History"; see court orders for apprenticeship of four children of George Freeman, "a man of color" in Clay County Deed Book "B" dated December 19, 1836. On the role of apprenticeships in the social control and economic exploitation of poor women and their children, especially African Americans, see Victoria Bynum, *Unruly Women: The Politics of Social and Sexual Control in the Old South* (Chapel Hill: University of North Carolina Press, 1992).

24. Peter Schneider, Jane Schneider, and Edward Hansen, "Modernization and Development: The Role of Regional Elites and Noncorporate Groups in the European Mediterranean," in Steffen W. Schmidt et al., eds., *Friends, Followers, and Factions: A Reader in Political Clientelism* (Berkeley: University of California Press, 1977).

25. Ireland, *County Courts*, reports that a committee of the Kentucky House of Representatives concluded in 1846 that the sheriffalty was probably sold in every Kentucky county, but Ireland doubts that the practice was truly universal.

26. See *Samuel Todd v Abner Baker & John Bates*, Clay County Circuit Court, 1811; also *John Bates v Samuel Todd*, Clay County Circuit Court, 1811.

27. Based on Clay County Tax Roll for 1825.

28. Joel B. Grossman and Austin Sarat, "Litigation in the Federal Courts: A Comparative Perspective," *Law and Society Review* 9 (Winter 1975): 325.

29. Austin Sarat and Susan Silbey, "The Pull of the Policy Audience," *Law and Policy* 10 (April/July 1988): 138; Frank Munger, "Afterward: Studying Litigation and Social Change," *Law and Society Review* 24 (May 1990): 615. See also Eric Monkkonen, "The American State from the Bottom Up: Of Homicides and Courts," *Law and Society Review* 24 (May 1990): 521-31.

30. For a more complete analysis of these data, see Kathleen M. Blee and Dwight B. Billings, "Violence and Local State Formation: A Longitudinal Case Study of Appalachian Feuding," *Law & Society Review* 30(4) (1996): 671-705.

31. Clark, *A History*, 413-14.

32. See, for example, attorneys listed in "*H. and J. White v. Bates*, and *H. and J. White v. Bates, Garrard &c*," Case 162-Chancery-October, 1832, in *J. J. Marshall's Reports*, 1832, pp. 538-54.

33. These jurists include Thomas Montgomery, Samuel McKee, George Walker, Robert Letcher, William Logan, Tungston Quarles, and Martin Hardin. See Roy White, "An Historical Scrap Book of Clay County," unpublished, copy in the authors' possession: chap. VII.

34. Ellen Churchill Semple, "The Anglo-Saxons of the Kentucky Mountains [1901]," *Bulletin of the American Geographical Society* XLII(8) (August 1910): 581, 589.

35. Semple, "Anglo-Saxons," 587; Hartley Davis and Clifford Smith, "The Land of Feuds," *Munsey's Magazine* XXX (November 1903): 170; S. S. MacClintock, "The Kentucky Mountains and their Feuds (Part II)," *American Journal of Sociology* 7 (1901): 171; Weller, *Yesterday's People*, 11.

36. Jeanette Keith, *Country People of the New South: Tennessee's Upper Cumberland* (Chapel Hill: University of North Carolina Press, 1995): 72.

37. Waller, *Feud*, 86.

38. For interesting examples of each, see, respectively: *Nicholas Brown v Moses Foley v Hugh White*, Clay County Circuit Court, 1828; *Andrew & Joseph Craig v Hugh White & George Baugh*, Clay County Circuit Court, 1810; and *Mary Dickerson, Administrator for Archer Dickerson v John Bates*, Clay County Circuit Court, 1822.

39. See the record of George Stivers to establish lines for two surveys patented in the name of James Kincaid dated February 18, 1836, in Clay County Deed Book "C."

40. See the case of *John Doe (William Garrard, James Garrard, and Daniel Garrard) v Richard Roe (Moses Martin and John Bates)*, Clay County Court, 1822.

41. See the following cases in the Clay County Circuit Court: *J. Bates v J. Crooke, adm. for J. Amis* (1808); *J. White v J. Crooke, adm. for J. Amis* (1809); *S. Todd v J. Bates* (1811) and *J. Bates v S. Todd* (1811); *S. Todd v Abner Baker & John Bates* (1811); *S. Todd v J. Bates* (1813); *J. White v J. Crooke & L. Amis* (1813); *S. and J. Todd v J. Bates* (1814); *J. Bates v John Craig, adm. for S. Todd* (1814); and

W. Smith & W. Carson, adm. for Stephen Langford v J. & H. White (1814). See also agreement between J. Bates and J. & H. White dated October 17, 1811, in Clay County Deed Book "A."

42. The latter survey, along with another 96,000 acres in Estill and Montgomery counties also patented by Franklin, were exposed to sale by the state auditor of public accounts for delinquent taxes in 1819. See "Non-Residents' Lands-Continued," *Argus of Western America-Extra* (Frankfort, Kentucky), July 25, 1819: 8. See also the deed between Edmond Randolph, Governor of Virginia and Thomas Franklin, January 26, 1787, Clay County Deed Book "A," p. 107. For reference to Ballard Smith and Monroe tracts, see the deed of John Sampson of Allegheny County, Pennsylvania, and Daniel Garrard, November 6, 1834, Book "B," p. 240; and for reference to Wyncoop's survey, see the 1837 report of surveyor and commissioners on a 61,758 survey in the name of James Reynolds, Book "B," p. 403.

43. See Clay County Circuit Court case of *John Doe (John Savory) v Richard Roe (Hugh White, Daniel Garrard and others)* (1810) and the case of *John Savory v Hugh White & Co., John Bates, Daniel Garrard, and others* (1811).

44. *William Bledsoe v Hugh White & George Baugh*, Clay County Circuit Court, 1809; *John Doe (Robert Alexander & Others) v Richard Roe (James Garrard, James Garrard, Jr., William Garrard, and Daniel Garrard)*, Clay County Circuit Court, 1817.

45. Quoted in Connelley and Coulter, *History*, II: 718.

46. Bessie White Hager, "The Whites of Clay County as Salt Makers," *The Register of the Kentucky Historical Society* 50 (1952): 244.

47. Charles H. White, Jr., "White Family Genealogy" (unpublished, no date). We are grateful to Jess Wilson for providing us a copy.

48. See John Jay Dickey's interview with T. T. Garrard (March 20, 1899), *Diary*, Reel 2, p. 2716; see also Charles White, "White Family."

49. Hager, "Whites of Clay County," 246.

50. See John Jay Dickey's interview with T. T. Garrard (March 20, 1899), *Diary*, Reel 2, p. 2718.

51. Gordon McKinney, *Mountain Republicanism* (Chapel Hill: University of North Carolina Press, 1978), 96.

52. See the agreement between Hugh L. White, Jr., and Hugh White dated March 14, 1839, Clay County Deed Book "D"; agreements between Daniel Garrard and James H. Garrard and T. T. Garrard, both dated November 3, 1841, Clay County Deed Book "C"; and Wilson and Quarrier restructuring dated September 25, 1838, Clay County Deed Book "B."

53. See magistrate's orders from December, 1839, through June, 1840, Clay County Court Order Book "C."

54. *Simeon Stivers v William White, Franklin White, Daugherty White, Hugh L. White & Others*, Clay County Circuit Court, 1839.

55. See interview with Henry Lucas dated December 22, 1898, in James J. Dickey, "Diary," Reel 3, p. 2117.

56. Deposition of Joseph Eve in *Daniel Bates v James H. Garrard, T. T. Brawner, Julius Hacker, William White, James White, Sydney Williams, Daugherty White, Franklin White, Daniel White, and William Garrard*, Clay County Circuit Court, 1840. Eve was undoubtedly acquainted with all the parties involved since he had been president of the Second Bank of Kentucky in nearby Barbourville as early as 1818 and owned land in Clay County. See "Joseph Eve," in *Kentucky Encyclopedia*, 391.

57. See eight separate cases filed in Clay County Circuit Court by Daniel Bates on October 9, 1840; see also *Daniel Bates v James H. and T. T. Garrard, Luther Brawner, Julius Hacker & Others*, filed in Clay County Circuit Court on October 13, 1840.

58. See the following cases in Clay County Circuit Court (1841): *Ezekeil Fields, assignee for William Walker v Daniel & Theophilus Garrard*; *William Walker v Daniel Garrard & Julius Hacker*; *George Stivers v James H. & T. T. Garrard*; *Jeremiah Combs v Jeremiah Smith & Daniel Garrard*; *David V. and Wade Walker v Joseph Cooke & T. T. Garrard*. In 1842, see *David V. Walker v Bethel Ely & Daniel Garrard*. See also the mortgage between Julius Hacker and Daniel Garrard in Clay County Deed Book "O," dated April 27, 1841.

59. *Leander Miller v James H. & T. T. Garrard*, Clay County Circuit Court, 1841; *Curtis Field v Daniel, James H., & T. T. Garrard*, Clay County Circuit Court, 1841; Garrard mortgages to Lyne Kinningham and Daniel Garrard in Clay County Deed Book "C" (1841); *Daniel Bates v Luther Brawner, James H. Garrard, Theophilus Garrard, & Daniel Garrard*, Clay County Circuit Court, October 25, 1841; Garrards and Brawner mortgage to Daniel Bates in Clay County Deed Book "C" (May 2, 1843); *Stivers & Walkers, administrators for Daniel Bates' estate, v Daniel, James H., Theophilus Garrard & Luther Brawner*, Clay County Circuit Court, 1846.

60. See depositions in *Issac Jones v Hugh White, Sr. & Daugherty White*, Clay County Circuit Court (1842) and Circuit Court Order Book "D," dated April 14, 1842; affidavit from William Williams, Clay County Clerk, April 15, 1843, in Gov. Letcher papers, box 6, folder 111 in Kentucky Department for Libraries and Archives, Frankfort; Auditors Office to Gov. Letcher, April 22, 1843, Gov. Letcher papers, box 6, folder 111; George Stivers to Gov. Letcher, April 20, 1843, Gov. Letcher papers, box 6, folder 111.

61. Samuel Ensworth to Gov. Robert Letcher, July 6, 1843, Gov. Letcher papers, box 6, folder 113.

62. Theophilus T. Garrard to Gov. Robert Letcher, July 7, 1843, Gov. Letcher papers, box 6, folder 113.

63. Office of Attorney General to Gov. Robert Letcher, July 26, 1843, Gov. Letcher

papers, box 6, folder 113; Gov. Robert Letcher, Executive Journal (Reel 993673), July 25, 1843, and December 23, 1843.

64. C. W. Crozier, *Life and Trial of Dr. Abner Baker, Jr. (a Monomaniac) who was Executed October 3, 1845* (Louisville, KY: Prentice and Wessinger, 1846).

65. Testimony of Theophilus Garrard, "Transcript of Abner Baker, Jr. Trial," Gov. William Owsley papers, box 15, folder 296, Kentucky Department for Libraries and Archives, Frankfort; John Davis testimony, "Trial;" Frank White testimony, James T. Woodward testimony, Mr. Payne testimony, Hiram Hibbard testimony, "Trial."

66. Testimony of Dr. Harvey Baker (brother), Miss Almira Baker (sister), and Mrs. Elizabeth McKee (sister); also Abner Baker, Sr., to Gov. Owsley, July 20, 1845, in Crozier, *Life and Trial*, 115; James Garrard and Theophilus Garrard testimony in "Trial"; testimony of Hiram Hibbard, Jonah Davis, and Harvey Baker in "Trial."

67. Testimony of Theophilus Garrard and James T. Woodward, "Trial"; "Judge Robertson Address," in Crozier, *Life and Trial*, 49.

68. William Garrard to Col. A. R. McKee, October 23, 1845, and Abner Baker, Sr., to Dr. C. W. Crozier, December 3, 1845, in Crozier, *Life and Trial*, 147, 142.

69. Testimony of Daniel Garrard, Theophilus Garrard, and James H. Garrard, "Trial." See letters from attorneys J. A. Moore, October 7, 1845, and J. Kincaid, October 8, 1845, to Gov. Owsley praising the quality of proceedings in Baker's original court of inquiry including interrogation on behalf of the Commonwealth of Kentucky that was done with "considerable ability . . . [and] fidelity to the Commonwealth" despite the regrettable absence of prosecuting counsel, published in Crozier, *Life and Trial*, 3. On Baker's trip to Cuba, see Dr. William Baker to Gov. Owsley, July 18, 1845, Gov. Owsley papers, box 15, folder 300. James White testified ("Trial") that he drove Daniel Bates' slave Pompey away from Baker after he shot Bates, suggesting that Bakers' fears of Bates' slaves may have had some basis in reality.

70. Testimony of Theophilus Garrard, "Trial"; Crozier, *Life and Trial*, 4, 5.

71. Crozier, *Life and Trial*, v, vi; "Trial" records; Abner Baker, Sr., to Dr. C. W. Crozier, December 3, 1845, in Crozier, *Life and Trial*, esp. 142. For prosecutors' denial of contingent fees, see A. F. Caldwell and Silas Woodson to Gov. Owsley, August 18, 1845, in Gov. Owsley papers, box 15, folder 304 in Kentucky Department for Libraries and Archives, Frankfort.

72. Crozier, *Life and Trial*, 3; "Trial" records, July 7, 1845; Commonwealth of Kentucky, 15th Judicial District, Order Book 4 (E), July 7 and July 8, 1845, pp. 259, 260, Kentucky Department for Libraries and Archives, Frankfort.

73. Crozier, *Life and Trial*, 50.

74. James H. Garrard testimony, "Trial." Dr. William Baker to Mary Bates, October 15, 1844, Gov. Oswley papers, box 15, folder 294.

75. Testimony of Jonah Davis and James A. Beasley, "Trial"; see also testimony of Barton Potter.

76. Crozier, *Life and Trial*, 50; "Judge Robertson Address," esp. 54-9 in Crozier, *Life and Trial*. For an excellent analysis of the application of antebellum criminal law in this case and the absence of felony appeals in Kentucky at that time, see Robert M. Ireland, "The Judicial Murder of Abner Baker, 1844-1845," *The Register of the Kentucky Historical Society* 88 (1990): 1-23.

77. "John White," in *Kentucky Encyclopedia*, 947; Abner Baker, Sr., to Dr. C. W. Crozier, December 3, 1845, in Crozier, *Life and Trial*, 142-6.

78. See the numerous petitions to Governor William Owsley supporting or opposing pardon in Owsley papers, box 15, folders 295-310. Abner Baker, Sr., to Gov. Owsley, July 23, 1845, folder 301. William Moore to Gov. Owsley, folder 301. Samuel Ensworth to Gov. Owsley, July 18, 1845, folder 299. William Garrard to Col. A. McKee, October 23, 1845, in Crozier, *Life and Trial*, 147.

79. A. Caldwell to Gov. Owsley, August 4, 1845, and Green Adams to Gov. Owsley, August 7, 1845, both in Gov. Owsley papers, box 15, folder 303.

80. Abner Baker, Sr., to Gov. Owsley, July 23, 1845, Gov. Owsley papers, box 15, folder 301; petition from Samuel Hibbard et al., July 18, 1845, folder 299. See also John Hibbard to Owsley, July 22, 1845, folder 301.

81. Letters in Gov. Owsley papers, box 15, folder 305 (September 1844), document these conflicting claims. Judge T. Quarles ordered the Clay County jailor to increase the number of guards at the jail, stating that "an armed force has been concentrated not far from Manchester to rescue Abner Baker" (September 1, 1845); W. H. Caperton et al. to Gov. Owsley, September 8, 1845, also claimed that an armed force had been seen gathering. See also Thomas Robert's claim, dated September 6, 1845, to have intercepted a letter from Abner Baker, Jr., to William Garrard asking him to raise a rescue force of 300 men. Governor Owsley dispatched Peter Dudley, Adjutant General, to Clay County with as many militia as needed, September 7, 1845.

Once in Clay County, however, Dudley reported that an attack was "not imminent" (September 9, 1845). However a letter from J. Caldwell to Gov. Owsley, September 20, 1845, was still reporting rumors that "the Bakers had threatened to rescue Abner or burn the town to ashes." See Dr. Harvey Baker's letter to Gov. Owsley (September 11, 1845, in folder 305) denying rumors of a rescue plan and as well as William and Caleb Baker to Gov. Owsley, September 16, 1845, in Gov. Owsley papers, folder 306. See also William Garrard's denial of same to Col A. McKee, October 23, 1845, in Crozier, *Life and Trial*, 148. On Dudley's kinship to Daniel Garrard, see DesCognets, *Governor Garrard*. For Dudley's probable involvement with the Garrards in salt commerce prior to the Baker crisis, see mortgage between J. H. Garrard and Daniel Garrard, November 3, 1841, Clay County Deed Book "C."

82. "Dr. A. Baker's Address under the gallows at Manchester, Ky.," October 3, 1845, from the *Knoxville Register*, reprinted in Cozier, *Life and Trial*, 149, 150.

83. Dr. Issac Ray, quoted in Ireland, "Judicial Murder," p. 22; *Knoxville Register*, reprinted in Crozier, *Life and Trial*, 148; Ireland, "Judicial Murder," p. 22. The term "judicial murder" appears to have been used first by Baker's attorney, J. Hays, in correspondence to the governor, September 24, 1845, Gov. Owsley papers, box 15, folder 307.

84. When Manchester was incorporated by the state legislature in 1844, Barton Potter, Leander Miller, William Woodcock, and John and George Cole – all Bates' allies – were authorized to organize the town according to White, "History Scrapbook," September 30, 1932.

    On the Mexican War, see John J. Dickey's interview with Theophilus Garrard, March 20, 1899, in *Diary*, Reel 4, pp. 2713-2731, and "Mexican War and Peace," in Federal Writers' Project, *Military History of Kentucky* (Frankfort: State Journal, 1939), esp. 121-3. In the election of 1851, Elhanon Murphey, nephew of John Bates, who was elected to the highest ranking office in the new local government system, county judge, owned two slaves but no land. Considerably wealthier were John Gilbert, sheriff, who owned $8,045 worth of property including eight slaves, and Felix Gilbert, surveyor, who owned $7,545 in property including nine slaves. Among elected magistrates, however, one owned a single slave, four owned no land, and only one owned property worth more than $1,000 according to Clay County tax rolls for 1850 or 1851. Court officers are listed in White, "History Scrapbook," November 11, 1932.

85. James C. Scott, "Patron-Client Politics and Political Change in Southeast Asia," in Steffen Schmidt, Laura Guasti, Carl Lande, and James C. Scott, eds., *Friends, Followers, and Factions: A Reader in Political Clientelism* (Berkeley: University of California Press, 1977): 123-46.

86. Eric Wolf, "Kinship, Friendship, and Patron-Client Relations in Complex Societies," in Schmidt et al., eds., *Friends, Followers*, 167-77.

87. See grants of powers of attorney to William Phelps and Thomas McGitton in Clay County Deed Book "A" (1815), pp. 127-38.

88. On Andrew Hacker's role in the 1886 clash, see J. W. Carnahan to Berea College President William G. Frost, September 3, 1903, in "Appalachian Feud Collection," Special Collections, Berea College Library.

89. "Ladies of Clay County" to Gov. Owsley, July 17, 1845, Gov. Owsley papers, box 15, folder 299.

90. Kozee, *Pioneer Families*; Connelley and Coulter, *History of Kentucky*, Vol. II, 849.

91. Letter from Peter Dudley to Gov. Owsley, September 11, 1845, Gov. Owsley papers.

92. Before signing a petition favoring Baker's pardon, Mrs. Barton Potter had already contradicted her husband's testimony in the Baker trial by testifying

to her belief in Baker's insanity. See "Trial" testimony. On the role of families in the clientelist politics of Appalachian Kentucky, see Allen Batteau, "Legitimacy in the Appalachian Local Polity," paper presented at Southern Anthropological Society, April 14, 1978.

93. Scott, "Patron-Client Politics," 124.

94. Peter Evans, *Embedded Autonomy: States and Industrial Transformation* (Princeton: Princeton University Press, 1995). See also Eric Olin Wright's informative review essay in *Contemporary Sociology* 25 (1996): 176-9.

95. For a record of payments to named guards, see "Commonwealth of Kentucky to Eli Bowling," Commonwealth of Kentucky 15th Judicial District, Order Book 4 (E), November 1845, Kentucky Department for Libraries and Archives, Frankfort.

96. Jürgen Habermas, *The Structural Transformation of the Public Sphere* (Cambridge, MA: The MIT Press, 1989). See also Craig Calhoun, ed., *Habermas and the Public Sphere* (Cambridge, MA: The MIT Press, 1993).

97. Habermas, *Structural Transformation*, 24.

98. William Morris to Gov. Owsley, August 4, 1845, box 15, folder 303, Gov. Owsley papers; Thomas Cook to Gov. Owsley, August 7, 1845, in Gov. Owsley papers, box 15, folder 303; William Andrews and William Johnson (pseudonyms) to Gov. Owsley, no date, folder 309. For an example of change in the other direction, see letter to Gov. Owsley from Thomas Gates, John Boyd, John Elledge, D. Maupin, S. Roberts, and J. Williams stating that they had earlier signed a remonstrance against pardon but were not in favor of one, October 28, 1845, folder 309.

On the general presence of intimidation, forty of the most prominent but highly partisan citizens of Clay County including several Walkers, Whites, and other allies of the late Daniel Bates wrote that "threats have been made a different periods against not only those who have engaged actively in the prosecution of the prisoner but upon those who are peaceable citizens anxious for the preservation of law and order and in obedience to the summons of the jailor have assembled at this place to watch over to prevent the escape of Baker." See John Hibbard et al. to Gov. Owsley, September 13, 1845, Gov. Owsley papers, box 15, folder 306.

99. Richard C. Brown, "Danville Political Club," in *Kentucky Encyclopedia*, 252-3.

100. Actually, Garrard, a captain in the War of 1812, wrote principally about Harrison's "bungling imbecility" in war to challenge that candidate's image as a military "hero." He closed by regretting that "fatigue" and the already great length of his essay prevented him from discussing such other important matters as "abolition, the currency and the condition of the state." See Daniel Garrard, *An Address to the Young Men of Kentucky Comprising a Brief Review of the Military Services of General William Henry Harrison during the War between*

Great Britain and the United States (Frankfort, KY: Robinson and Adams, 1840), esp. 29.

101. According to Habermas, *Structural Transformation*, newspapers and commerce were two principal factors that helped give birth to the European bourgeois public sphere in the eighteenth century. See also David Zaret, "Petitions and the 'Invention' of Public Opinion in the English Revolution," *American Journal of Sociology* 101 (1996): 1497-1555.

Chapter 5

1. See the 1869 travel story of Will Wallace Harney in W. K. McNeil, ed., *Appalachian Images in Folk and Popular Culture*, 2nd ed. (Knoxville: University of Tennessee Press, 1995).
2. Weller, *Yesterday's People*.
3. Brown, *Beech Creek*, 385; James S. Brown, "The Family Group in a Kentucky Mountain Farming Community," *Kentucky Agricultural Experiment Station Bulletin* 588 (1952): 28-9; Brown, *Beech Creek*, 162.
4. Pearsall, *Little Smoky*, 92, 100; emphasis in original.
5. Stephenson, *Shiloh*, 73, 128.
6. Mary K. Anglin, "Lives on the Margin: Rediscovering the Women of Antebellum Western North Carolina," in Pudup et al., *Appalachia*, 185-209.
7. Later sociologists used the concept of "familism" as an attitudinal measure, losing even the ethnographer's attention to actual social practices and relations. See, for example, James K. Crissman, "Family Type and Familism in Contemporary Appalachia," *Southern Rural Sociology* 6 (1989): 29-44.
8. Pearsall, *Little Smoky*, 99-100.
9. Stephenson, *Shiloh*, 105.
10. Kathleen M. Blee and Dwight B. Billings, "Reconstructing Daily Life in the Past: A Hermeneutic Approach to Ethnographic Data," *Sociological Quarterly* 27 (1986): 443-62.
11. We draw on the conceptual work of family historians who have described family strategies as life trajectories formulated within the family sphere that have as their primary concern the survival of the family and its household, while recognizing the heterogeneity of interests and actions within households. See Kathleen M. Blee, "Family Ties and Class Conflict: Politics of Immigrant Communities in the Great Lakes region, 1890-1920," *Social Problems* 31 (1984): 311-21; Tamara Hareven, *Family Time and Industrial Time* (New York: Cambridge University Press, 1982); Tamara Hareven, "Family History at the Crossroads," *Journal of Family History* 12 (1987): ix-xxiii; Graham Crow, "The Concept of 'Strategy' in Recent Sociological Literature," *Sociology* 23 (1989): 1-24.

12. James S. Brown, "The Conjugal Family and the Extended Family Group," *American Sociological Review* 17 (1952): 301.

13. In 1860, for example, the sole married woman employed for wages was a nineteen-year-old African American seamstress (Clay County Census of Population, 1860).

14. Clay County Circuit Court records (see discussion of case sampling in Appendix 1).

15. Brown, "Conjugal Family"; idem, "Family Group."

16. Brown, "Family Group;" 28-9.

17. Allen Batteau, "'Mosbys and Broomsedge: The Semantics of Class in an Appalachian Kinship System," *American Ethnologist* (1982): 445-66. See also Rhoda Halperin, *The Livelihood of Kin: Making Ends Meet "The Kentucky Way"* (Austin: University of Texas Press, 1990).

18. Pearsall, *Little Smoky*, 49, 50, 51, 83, 82, 88; Stephenson, *Shiloh*, 95.

19. Mary Beth Pudup, "Town and Country in the Transformation of Appalachian Kentucky," in Pudup et al., *Appalachia*, 270-96.

20. Pearsall, *Little Smoky*, 168, 169.

21. This critique of the "culture of poverty" is distinct from previous criticisms of this theory. For example, whereas Carol Stack attacks the idea of a culture of poverty by showing the hidden rationality in *consumption* cooperation among the urban poor, our critique of ethnographic data recovers the inherent rationality in production activities and cooperation among "self-sufficient producers." See Michael Merrill, "Cash Is Good to Eat: Self-Sufficiency and Exchange in the Rural Economy of the United States," *Radical History Review* (1977): 42-71; Kevin Kelly, "The Independent Mode of Production," *Review of Radical Political Economics* 11 (1979): 38-48.

22. Pearsall, *Little Smoky*, 55, 56.

23. Stephenson, *Shiloh*, 26-7; emphasis in original.

24. See David Alan Corbin, *Life, Work and Rebellion in the Coal Fields: The Southern West Virginia Miners, 1880-1922* (Urbana: University of Illinois, 1981).

25. The most useful of the northeastern studies include Kelly, "Independent"; Merrill, "Cash"; James A. Henretta, "Families and Farms: Mentalité in Preindustrial America," *William and Mary Quarterly* 35 (1978): 3-32; Christopher Clark, "Household Economy, Market Exchange and the Rise of Capitalism in the Connecticut Valley, 1800-1860," *Journal of Social History* 13 (1979): 169-90. On the south, see Steven Hahn, *The Roots of Southern Populism: Yeoman Farmers and the Transformation of the Georgia Upcountry, 1850-1890* (New York: Oxford University Press, 1983). A good bibliography of such works can be found in A. Kulikoff, "The Transition to Capitalism in Rural America" *William and Mary Quarterly* 46 (1989): 120-44; For a preliminary comparison of findings from these studies and Appalachian

ethnography, see Billings et al., "Culture." See also Billings et al., "Taking Exception."

26. For example, some social historians argue that family roles and household structures were altered in subsistence-based agrarian communities in order to maximize the entrepreneurial possibilities of an emerging market economy (Phillip J. Greven, Jr., *Four Generations: Population, Land and Family in Colonial Andover, Massachusetts* (Ithaca, NY: Cornell University Press, 1970); Robert A. Gross, *The Minutemen and Their World* (New York: Hill and Wang, 1976): 180-5, whereas others argue that household shifts represent continuing strategies of mutual aid rather than gambits meant to maximize market opportunity (Henretta, "Families"; Clark, "Households").

27. See David Weiman, "Farmers and the Market in Antebellum America: A View from the Georgia Upcountry," *Journal of Economic History* 47 (1987): 627-47; see also Hahn, *Roots*. On the north, see Clark, "Households."

28. Nancy Folbre, "The Logic of Patriarchal Capitalism: Some Preliminary Propositions," paper presented to the Social Science History Association Annual Meetings (1987): 6; Linda Kerber, *Women of the Republic* (Chapel Hill: University of North Carolina Press, 1980).

29. Dunaway, *First Frontier*.

30. Articles in Joan Smith, Immanuel Wallerstein, Hans-Dieter Evers, eds., *Households and the World Economy* (Beverly Hills: Sage, 1984), 8, usefully reconceptualize households as "basic units of an emerging world-system," away from traditional views of households as directly reflecting the mode of production or as homogeneous and cooperative systems. On the reproduction of households under conditions of subsistence versus commodity production, see Harriet Friedman, "Household Production and the Natural Economy: Concepts for the Analysis of Agrarian Formations," *Journal of Peasant Studies* 6 (1978): 71-100. See also Robert Brenner, "The Origins of Capitalist Development: A Critique of Neo-Smithian Marxism," *New Left Review* 104 (1977): 25-92.

31. E. P. Thompson, "The Moral Economy of the English Crowd in the Eighteenth Century," *Past and Present* 50: 79; Folbre, "The Logic," 3.

32. Describing agriculture in Clay County at the time of the Civil War, John Smith wrote that "some of the substantial people of the section had very fine horses and other stock." See John F. Smith, "Salt Making Industry of Clay County, Kentucky," *Filson Club History Quarterly* 1 (1927): 140.

33. "Kentucky: Its Resources and Present Condition," First Annual Report of the Commissioner of the State Bureau of Agriculture, Horticulture and Statistics," *Kentucky Documents* (1878): 317; Ninth Biennial Report of the Bureau of Agriculture, Labor, and Statistics," *Kentucky Documents* (1891): 119.

34. Rolla Tryon as quoted in J. Atack and F. Bateman, *To Their Own Soil: Agriculture in the Antebellum North* (Ames: Iowa State University Press, 1987): 205.

35. "Kentucky: Its Resources and Present Condition."

36. See Anglin, "Lives on the Margins."

37. Brown, *Beech Creek*, 6.

38. Mitchell, *Commercialism and Frontier*, 4.

39. See also Batteau, "Mosby and Broomsedge."

40. The study was reported more fully in Dwight B. Billings and Kathleen M. Blee, "Causes and Consequences of Persistent Rural Poverty: A Longitudinal Case Study of an Appalachian Community," Final Report to the Rural Economic Policy Program of the Aspen Institute and the Ford Foundation (1991): 104-7, and Appendixes one and two to Chapter five.

41. Brown, *Beech Creek*, 10.

42. A theoretically rich study of land as a cultural symbol of family independence, security, achievement, and identity is Robert C. Ostergren, "Land and Family in Rural Immigrant Communities," *Annals of the Association of American Geographers* 71 (1981): 400-11.

43. Sonya Salamon and Ann Mackay Keim, "Land Ownership and Women's Power in a Midwestern Farming Community," *Journal of Marriage and Family* (1979): 109-19; Susan Grigg, "Women and Family Property: A Review of U.S. Inheritance Practices," *Historical Methods* 22 (1989): 116-22.

44. Deed Book R, 475 (March 27, 1896) and *G. W. Baker v Robert McCollum, Nancy McCollum, Daniel McCollum, Mary Webb and John Webb (husband), James McCollum, Luther McCollum, Blevens McCollum, Jane McCollum*, Clay County Circuit Court, 1892.

45. *Ester White v Joseph Hacker and George Burns*, Clay County Circuit Court, 1900; *Kentucky Mineral and Timber Company v Silas Hoskins, J.B. Bowlin, John Collins, Archibald Collins, John Wages*, Clay County Circuit Court, 1894.

46. *James Baker v Laura Baker*, Clay County Circuit Court, 1890; *Joseph Philpot v Olly Philpot*, Clay County Circuit Court, 1895; *Abner Baker v Emily Baker*, Clay County Circuit Court, 1895; *John C. White v Ellen White*, Clay County Circuit Court, 1893; *James McCollum v Ellen McCollum*, Clay County Circuit Court, 1892.

47. Our stress on the geographical differentiation of Clay County's neighborhoods as expressed in variable quantities of slaveholding, tenancy, and farm ownership is consistent with Ralph Mann's analysis of the diversity among farm communities in Appalachian Virginia during the antebellum period. See his "Diversity in the Antebellum South: Four Farm Communities in Tazewell County, Virginia," in Pudup et al., *Appalachia*, 137-62.

48. Dunaway, *First American Frontier*, 90.

49. Ibid., 385, n. 4, claims to control for the landless kin of landowners by aggregating landless households into propinquitous households of landowning kin, but her method does not account for nonpropinquitous households of sons who will eventually inherit the land of their fathers.

50. Folbre, "Logic," 6.
51. On the determination of "life chances" in a capitalist economy by positionality in property, labor, and credit markets, see S. N. Eisenstadt, ed., *Max Weber, On Charisma and Institutions Building* (Chicago: University of Chicago Press, 1968): 170-2.
52. See Appendix 1 on our dispute samples.
53. David M. Engle, "The Oven Bird's Song: Insiders, Outsiders, and Personal Injuries in an American Community," *Law and Society Review* 18 (1984): 555-82.
54. Kephart, *Our Southern Highlanders*, 37. For a discussion of the stereotyping of Appalachian agriculture, see Jack Temple Kirby, *Rural Worlds Lost* (Baton Rouge: Louisiana State University Press, 1987): esp. 80-111.
55. For an example of such attributions made without the systematic investigation of farm practices, see Pearsall, *Little Smoky*.
56. Ronald Eller, *Miners, Millhands, and Mountaineers: Industrialization of the Appalachian South, 1880-1930* (Knoxville: University of Tennessee Press, 1982), 6; Appalachian Land Ownership Task Force, *Who Owns Appalachia?* (Lexington: University Press of Kentucky, 1983), 81. See also Dan Pierce, "The Low-Income Farmer: A Reassessment," *Social Work in Appalachia* 3 (1971): 8.
57. See F. McDonald and G. McWhiney, "The Antebellum Southern Herdsman," *Journal of Southern History* 41 (1975): 147-66. On the impact of the closing of the range, see J. C. King, "The Closing of the Southern Range: An Exploratory Study," *Journal of Southern History* 48 (1982), and on early livestock droves in Appalachia, see P. Salstrom, "The Agricultural Origins of Economic Dependency, 1840-1880," in Mitchell, *Appalachian Frontiers*, 261-83.
58. J. S. Otto, "The Decline of Forest Farming in Southern Appalachia," *Journal of Forest History* 49 (1983): 18-26; J. S. Otto, "The Migration of the Southern Plain Folk: An Interdisciplinary Synthesis," *Journal of Southern History* 51 (1985): 183-200; J. S. Otto and N. E. Anderson, "Slash-and-Burn Cultivation in the Highlands South: A Problem in Comparative Agricultural History," *Comparative Studies in Society and History* (1982): 131-47. For evidence that forest farming was recently practiced in some parts of Appalachia, see J. F. Hart, "Land Rotation in Appalachia," *Geographical Review* 67 (1977): 148-66.
59. Waller, *Feud*; U.S. Department of Agriculture, *Economic and Social Problems and Conditions of the Southern Appalachians* (Washington, DC, 1935). See also M. B. Pudup, "Social Class and Economic Development in Southeastern Kentucky," in Mitchell, *Appalachian Frontiers*, 235-60. On the difference in extent of commercialization in the Tennessee mountains between valley and ridge counties, see McKenzie, *One South*.
60. Data on Clay County are based on a population sample of every fourth household listed in the 1860 manuscript census of Clay County (approximately 250

households). We matched as many as possible of these households with individuals listed as operating farms in the 1860 manuscript census of agriculture ($n = 122$) and we matched individuals identified in the 1860 manuscript schedules of slaveholding with farm operators in the agricultural census ($n = 37$).

61. Case studies report antebellum tenancy levels ranging from as high as 55% in one eastern Tennessee county (Dunn, *Cades Cove*) to as low as 3.6% in a southeastern Kentucky county (Pudup, "Limits of Subsistence") whereas the author of a regionwide study of manuscript farm census records concludes that 25% of all farmers in Appalachia were landless in 1860 (W. Dunaway, "Southern Appalachia's People without History: The Role of Unfree Laborers in the Region's Antebellum Economy," paper presented to Social Science History Association, 1989). Researchers also dispute how to interpret the social relations of farm tenancy in Appalachia. Pudup, in "Limits," suggests that tenant status largely reflected age, gender, and family status rather than social class, but Dunaway, in "People without History," p. 4, argues that tenants "comprised a sizeable sector of the farm population and provided a coerced labor supply for the region's agricultural production." Since Brown found that between 50 and 75% of all the possible relationships within the three Beech Creek neighborhoods in the 1940s were kin relationships to some degree, it is likely that tenancy within Beech Creek was shaped more by family rather than social class relations but it is also true, as county court records reveal, that elite landowners in Clay County rented lands to tenant farmers. In the latter situation, social class relations were predominant. For oral history accounts of the harshness of such arrangements in Clay County and elsewhere in eastern Kentucky, see Jim Garland (Julia Ardery, ed.), *Welcome the Traveler Home* (Lexington: University Press of Kentucky, 1983): 27, 31; and Schackelford and B. Weinberg, *Our Appalachia: An Oral History* (Lexington: University Press of Kentucky, 1977).

62. Frederick Bode and Donald Ginter, *Farm Tenancy and the Agricultural Census in Antebellum Georgia* (Athens: University of Georgia Press, 1986).

63. T. Arcury, "Agricultural Change in the Mountain South at the Turn of the Century" Center for Developmental Change Report 8 (Lexington: University of Kentucky, 1989).

64. Northern rather than southern farms provide the most appropriate comparison for Clay County and Beech Creek farms since both groups of farmers (including Clay County's slave owning farmers) practiced general (diversified) farming rather than the production of staple crops such as cotton, tobacco, and – in other parts of Kentucky – hemp that characterized much of southern agriculture. Data on northern farms are from Atack and Bateman, *To Their Own Soil*.

65. Sally Maggard, "From Farmers to Miners: The Decline of Agriculture in

Eastern Kentucky," in L. Busch, ed., *Science and Agricultural Development* (Totowa, NJ: Allanheld, 1981).

66. Because inclusion in the county tax rolls was based on less stringent criteria than inclusion in the federal census of agriculture – in 1860, for instance, we could locate seventy Beech Creek farmers in the tax rolls but only fifty-nine in the census that year – caution must be exercised in comparing data from tax lists with census data from earlier years. Also, the absence of 1890 census manuscript data prevents us from assessing the reliability of the 1892 tax reports.

67. Elsewhere we have reported that household declined in size from a mean of 6.87 members in 1850 to 5.18 members in 1910. See Dwight Billings and Kathleen Blee, "Family Strategies in a Subsistence Economy: Beech Creek, Kentucky, 1850-1942," *Sociological Perspectives* 33 (1990): 63-88.

68. Our analysis utilizes methods reported in J. Atack and F. Bateman, "Self-Sufficiency and the Marketable Surplus in the Rural North, 1860," *Agricultural History* 58 (1984): 296-313; and in J. Atack and F. Bateman, *To Their Own Soil*. The equations are based on calculations of the nutritional needs of each farm household, adjusting for age and gender of its members, as well as feed requirements of livestock and variable proportions of crops assumed to have been held back for the next year's seed. Caloric needs as well as crop and livestock production are each translated in "corn equivalent units." A surplus is defined as any production of corn equivalent units (in bushels) over and beyond the consumption (and seed) requirements of the farm and its livestock. We modified the Atack and Bateman equations in one important respect, however, by not including the feed requirement for hogs in our calculations since the feeding of hogs on forest masts is assumed to have been universal among mountain farmers, an option not available in many areas of the North. The continuing importance of open-range grazing in Clay County is indicated by a *New York Times* article dated December 14, 1899, which noted that hogs were doing well there because it was "a good mast year."

69. Atack and Bateman, *To Their Own Soil*, 220.

70. In his published autobiography, labor organizer and folk singer Jim Garland (*Traveler*, 31) recalls that during his boyhood in Clay County around the turn of the century, "My mother said that during the years my father sharecropped, the family literally became naked. When someone had to go to the store, all the family's garments were pooled so this one person would have enough to wear."

71. Adding hog feeding to the 1860 equations would have increased the proportion of farmers failing to produce surpluses from 9 to 30% for that year.

72. See McDonald and McWhiney, "Antebellum Southern Herdsmen."

73. Kelly Morgan and Mrs. Kelly Morgan, *History of Clay County, Kentucky*, Bicentennial Ed. (Manchester, KY: Morgan Book, 1976). 168.

74. From *War of the Rebellion: Official Records of the Union and Confederate Armies*, Series I, Vol. XVI, Part I, published under the direction of the Hon. Elihu Root, Secretary of War (Washington, DC: U.S. Government Printing Office, 1902), 1145-53. We are grateful to Jess Wilson of Clay County for this information.

75. By 1910 only three counties – Harlan, Leslie, and Rowan – all in eastern Kentucky, had lower yields of corn per acre than Clay. *Nineteenth Biennial Report of Agriculture, Labor, and Statistics for 1910-1911* (Frankfort: Kentucky State Journal Printing, 1912).

76. As late as 1930, only 10 of 190 Appalachian counties are estimated to have had higher general fertility rates than Clay County according to G. DeJong, *Appalachian Fertility Decline* (Lexington: University Press of Kentucky, 1968).

77. Richard Easterlin, "Factors in the Decline of Farm Family Fertility in the United States: Some Preliminary Research Results," *Journal of American History* 63 (1976): 600-14.

78. Folbre, "The Logic"; see also Gerda Lerner, *The Creation of Patriarchy* (New York: Oxford University Press, 1986); and Caldwell, "A Theory of Fertility," 553-77. Gail Terry notes the utility of family empires for the elite families of the region also in "Family Empires: A Frontier Elite in Virginia and Kentucky." Ph.D. diss., College of William and Mary, 1992, 65.

79. Dickey, *Diary,* June 1898.

80. "The 1891 Report of the Kentucky Bureau of Agriculture, Labor and Statistics, Ninth Biennial Report," in *Kentucky Documents*, 1891, made special note that "farm laborers are scarce" in Clay County.

81. Schwarzweller et al., *Mountain Families*, 4.

82. Brown, *Beech Creek*, 12, 229.

83. Waller (*Feud*) found a similar pattern in her study of the Tug Valley.

84. The family names are pseudonyms used by Brown in *Beech Creek.*

85. Full data are presented in Billings and Blee, "Causes and Consequences."

86. We have shown elsewhere that cooperation among households within the larger "family groups" first described by Brown was crucial for the survival of units not producing sufficient quantities of food. See Billings and Blee, "Family Strategies."

87. Brown, *Beech Creek*, 266.

88. Ibid., 267; italics added.

89. Ibid., 268.

90. Caudill, *Darkness at Dawn*, 23.

91. See Billings and Blee, "Causes and Consequences," for demographic evidence on nineteenth-century outmigration.

92. Otto, "Migration of Southern Plain Folk," 195.

93. Ibid., 196.

94. According to the *Eighteenth Biennial Report of the Bureau of Agriculture, Labor, and Statistics* (1908-9), virtually all available farmland in Clay County had been "rigorously farmed," including "precipitous hillside and narrow crest."

95. On the extent, timing, and impact of timbering in Appalachian Kentucky, see Eller, *Miners*, 28-127.

96. Otto, "Decline of Forest Farming," 24.

97. Brown, *Beech Creek*, 28.

98. Ibid.

99. Quoted in Michael McDonald and John Muldowny, *TVA and the Dispossessed: The Resettlement of Population in the Norris Dam Area* (Knoxville: University of Tennessee Press, 1982), 121.

100. According to McDonald and Muldowny, *TVA,* many farmers in the Norris Basin of eastern Tennessee were impoverished by 1930, when their farms averaged only 23.7 in crops and gross farm incomes (including in-kind home consumption) averaged less than $10,000 per capita.

101. If one were to compare household arrangements only at the beginning and end points of the period under investigation, 1850 or 1860 and 1910, and also compare these points in time with the pattern observed by Brown in 1942, one might erroneously conclude that household composition in this Appalachian community reflected a history of long-term stability. The great variability in household composition between 1870 and 1900, however, illustrates the importance of observing household arrangements at many points in time.

102. We follow Barbara Laslett's ("Household Structure on an American Frontier: Los Angeles, California, in 1850," *American Journal of Sociology* 81, 1975: 122) work and define the burden of dependency as the ratio of persons below fifteen years or over sixty-four years in a household to all household members. For simple (nuclear) families, the dependency score is 0.59. For simple-with-other, extended families and multiple families, it is 0.56, 0.57, and 0.42, respectively.

103. We use methods developed by Roger Ransom and Richard Sutch, *One Kind of Freedom: The Economic Consequences of Emancipation* (New York: Cambridge University Press, 1977), to assess the productivity of farm households based on data collected in the comprehensive agricultural census of 1880 to take advantage of data collected then, not available in early years.

104. Bettye Hobbs Pruitt, "Self-Sufficiency and the Agricultural Economy of Eighteenth-Century Massachusetts," *William and Mary Quarterly*, Series 3, 41 (1984): 349.

105. Interview by Anne Shelby.

106. Terry, "Family Empires"; Hugh White account book, 1843; Letter to Hugh White from L. Kinningham, December, 14, 1843.

107. Schwarzweller et al., *Mountain Families*, 3.

108. Pearsall, *Little Smoky*, 48.

109. Ibid., 49; italics added.
110. K. Lockridge, "Land, Population, and the Evolution of New England Society, 1630-1790," *Past and Present* 39 (1968): 69.
111. Ibid.
112. Quoted in ibid.
113. We computed kinship proximity in Clay County, using measures developed in Daniel Scott Smith, "'All in Some Degree Related to Each Other'; A Demographic and Comparative Resolution of the Anomaly of New England Kinship," *American Historical Review* 94 (1989): 44-79. For 1810, we find same surname (isonymic) proximity next door (adjacent to sampled household) for 18.6% of households and isonymic proximity within five households for 13.9%. For 1910, we find isonymic proximity next door for 20.6% of households and within five households for 34.9% of all households in Clay County. (In the Beech Creek area, the 1910 figures are 30.4% next door and 34.8% within five households.) Smith finds next-door proximity for 26.4% and within five household proximity for 36% in a 1790 study of New England, comparable to the Clay County figures for 1910. He comments (p. 45) that "Americans in 1900 were considerably less likely to live near kin than they were in 1790." On the impact of outmigration on kinship, see Allan Bogue, "Social Theory and the Pioneer," *Agricultural History Review* 74 (1960): 30-1; and Mitchell, *Commercialism and Frontier*. On historical comparison, see Dwight B. Billings and Kathleen M. Blee, "Bringing History Back In: The Historicity of Social Relations," *Current Perspectives in Social Theory* 7 (1986): 51-68.
114. Migration scholars find that community integration serves as a constraint on outmigration. See Peter Uhlenberg, "Noneconomic Determinants of Nonmigration: Sociological Considerations for Migration Theory," *Rural Sociology* 38 (1973): 296-311; Neal Ritchey, "Explanations of Migration," *Annual Review of Sociology* 2 (1976): 363-404. In this case, however, integration into kinship networks ultimately made successful migration possible. Schwarzweller et al., *Mountain Families*.
115. Dwight Billings, "Religion as Opposition: A Gramscian Analysis," *American Journal of Sociology* 96 (1990): 1-31.
116. See Paul Salstrom, *Appalachia's Path to Dependency: Rethinking a Region's Economic History, 1730-1940* (Lexington: University Press of Kentucky, 1994).

Chapter 6

1. The term "white" in fact obscures the considerable ethnic diversity in nineteenth-century Clay Clounty. When John J. Dickey, a prominent Methodist evangelist, school builder, and diarist in Appalachian Kentucky, interviewed

descendants of these early settlers at the end of the century, he found them reporting ethnic ancestries that recalled a diverse European and African heritage. The Allen, Lyttle, House, Spivey, Wooton, Angell, and Philpot families traced their ancestors to England, whereas the Eversoles, Hamptons, Lynxes, Treadways, Houndshells, Coldirons, Hignites, and Raders were descendants of German (sometimes "Dutch") settlers. The Davidsons, McCollums, Faulkners, Pattersons, and Robertsons claimed to be from Scotland, but some of the "Irish" – the Carnahans, Begleys, Creeches, Blacks, Ponders, McDaniels, Roats, and Hayres – may actually have been descendants of Ulster Scots as well. The Garrards and Amises were French. By some accounts, the Whites were either English or Scottish and the Gilberts English or French. Two Nicholson cousins described a same grandfather as being from "Wales" and "the North of Ireland." Significantly, almost none of the families Dickey interviewed remembered anything concretely about Old World ways (Dickey, *Diary*). The fact that many were confused about their origins or showed little interest in the topic suggests that European ethnocultural differences had already been blended in the melting pot of Appalachian settlement long before their ancestors had ventured into early Kentucky. Clay County's considerable African American population (only a few of whom Dickey interviewed), however, was set apart and highly stigmatized from the earliest times. For a study of how commercial exchange helped to forge a common culture among early European immigrants in eastern Appalachia, see James D. Rice, "Old Appalachia's Path to Interdependency: Economic Development and the Creation of Community in Western Maryland, 1730-1850," *Appalachian Journal* 22 (1995): 348-75.

2. There are very few persons categorized in the census as other than white or African American in Clay County. For an interesting parallel between the common stereotypes of African Americans and Appalachian whites, see James Klotter, "The Black South and White Appalachia," *Journal of American History* 66 (1980): 832-49.

3. This is similar to Douglas Massey and Nancy Denton's discussion of the creation of chronic African American poverty in northern inner cities in their *American Apartheid* (Cambridge, MA: Harvard University Press, 1993).

4. In Rowan and Powell Counties, 6 and 5.5% of the populations, respectively, were enslaved in 1860.

5. Robert P. Stuckert, "Black Populations of the Southern Appalachian Mountains," *Phylon* 48 (1987): 141-51; James B. Murphy, "Slavery and Freedom in Appalachia: Kentucky as a Demographic Case Study," *Register of the Kentucky Historical Society* 80 (1982): 151-69.

6. Murphy, "Slavery and Freedom;" Stuckert, "Black Populations."

7. *Mary Dickerson, administrator of Archer Dickerson's estate v John Bates*, Clay County Circuit Court, 1822. On the mechanisms of slave hiring, see Clement Eaton,

"Slave-Hiring in the Upper South: A Step Toward Freedom," *Mississippi Valley Historical Review* 46 (1963): 663-78.

8. John Inscoe's study of western North Carolina, *Mountain Masters, Slavery, and the Sectional Crisis in Western North Carolina* (Knoxville: University of Tennessee Press, 1989), also found that local courts were willing to convict masters for maltreatment of their slaves.

9. *Harriet of color v William White*, Clay County Circuit Court, 1847.

10. From interviews in Laurel County and Clay County, Kentucky, in Federal Writers' Project, 1936-8 (preparers), *Slave Narratives, a Folk History of Slavery in the United States from Interviews with Former Slaves* (Washington, DC: Library of Congress, 1941), Reel 7.

11. From interviews in Laurel County and Clay County, Kentucky, in Federal Writers' Project, *Slave Narratives*, Reel 7.

12. Clay County Will Book "A": 127-30.

13. *Margaret Bledsoe, administrator of Joseph Bledsoe v Daniel Bates' executors*, Clay County Circuit Court, 1849; *Allison (of color) v Stephen W. Bates*, Clay County Circuit Court, 1844.

14. *David V. Walker and George Stivers v Stephen Gibson, Sr.*, Clay County Circuit Court, 1848; *George Stivers and David V. Walker, administrators of Daniel Bates v Daniel Garrard, James H. Garrard, T. T. Garrard and Luther Browner*, Clay County Circuit Court, 1846.

15. From interview in Laurel County, Kentucky, in Federal Writers' Project, *Slave Narratives*, Reel 7.

16. Auctions were a common way that slaves were sold in Kentucky, according to J. Winston Coleman, Jr., "Lexington's Slave Dealers and Their Southern Trade," *The Filson Club History Quarterly* 12 (1938): 1-23; see also *John White v John Crooke, adm. of estate of John Amis, deceased*, Clay County Circuit Court, 1809.

17. From interview in Clay County, in Federal Writers' Project, *Slave Narratives*, Reel 7.

18. Ibid.

19. Criminal cases 453, 454, 460, and 465, all heard in the October 1830 terms of Clay County Circuit Court; also *Owen (of color), a slave of Mrs. Hannon*, Clay County Court, Criminal Case, 1847; see also Bertram Wyatt-Brown, "Community, Class, and Snopesian Crime: Local Justice in the Old South," in Orville Vernon Burton and Robert C. McMath, Jr., eds., *Class, Conflict and Consensus: Antebellum Southern Community Studies* (Westport, CT: Greenwood Press, 1982), 173-206.

20. Case heard in April 1841 in Clay County Circuit Court. See also George C. Wright, *Racial Violence in Kentucky, 1865-1940: Lynchings, Mob Rule and "Legal Lynchings"* (Baton Rouge: Louisiana State University Press, 1990).

21. *Allison and others (of color) v Stephen W. Bates*, Clay County Circuit Court,

1855; *Allison (of color) v Stephen W. Bates*, Clay County Circuit Court, 1844.

22. *Theophilus (of color) v Stephen W. Bates*, Clay County Circuit Court, 1844; *Cuffie (of color) v Stephen W. Bates*, Clay County Circuit Court, 1844; *Berry (of color) v Stephen W. Bates*, Clay County Circuit Court, 1844; *Berry Jr. (of color) v Stephen W. Bates*, Clay County Circuit Court, 1844; *Claiborne (of color) v Stephen W. Bates*, Clay County Circuit Court, 1844; *Alssysa (of color) v Stephen W. Bates*, Clay County Circuit Court, 1844; *Jane (of color) v Stephen W. Bates*, Clay County Circuit Court, 1844.

23. *Claiborn (of color) Theophilus v Stephen W. Bates*, Clay County Circuit Court, 1847.

24. *Harriet (of color) v William White*, Clay County Circuit Court, 1847.

25. Our data include marriages of white men to African American women, not the reverse. However, in the one-in-four sample from the 1860 Clay County population census, there is a case of a mulatto landowning farmer living with a white wife and their children.

26. *Margaret Bledsoe v Bates Executors*, Clay County Circuit Court, 1849.

27. Merchant records of Hugh White; see also Elizabeth A. Perkins, "The Consumer Frontier: Household Consumption in Early Kentucky," *Journal of American History* 78 (1991): 485-510.

28. Juliet E. K. Walker, "The Legal Status of Free Blacks in Early Kentucky," *The Filson Club Historical Quarterly* 57 (1983): 382.

29. Ronald L. Lewis, "From Peasant to Proletarian: The Migration of Southern Blacks to the Central Appalachian Coalfields," *Journal of Southern History* 55 (1989); Stuckert, "Black Populations"; George C. Wright, *The Forced Removal of Afro-Americans from Rural Kentucky* (Frankfort: Friends of Kentucky Public Archives, 1990); Wright, *Racial Violence*.

30. There are problems interpreting the absence of persistence over time in census data. People disappear from census pages when they die as well as when they move. Moving can be across country or simply over the county line. The lack of persistence in the census also may be an artifact of poor enumeration, particularly of African Americans. To assess this, we checked whether any African American missing in one census reappeared in Clay County in a subsequent census, but found none.

31. Clay County Will Book "A", pp. 117, 74.

32. We restrict this analysis to household heads for three reasons. First, census data on ownership in 1900 and 1910 are only unambiguous for household heads. Second, using household heads reduced the number of women who might be misclassified as nonpersisters due to changing surnames. Third, we are interested in migration decisions based in household economic considerations (more so than, say, migration for marriage); these usually reflect decisions about employment for the household head.

33. Orville Vernon Burton, *In My Father's House are Many Mansions* (Chapel Hill: University of North Carolina Press, 1985).

34. On nineteenth-century residential mobility, see Stephan Thernstrom, *The Other Bostonians: Poverty and Progress in the American Metropolis, 1880-1970* (Cambridge, MA: Harvard University Press, 1973); Laurence Glasco, "Migration and Adjustment in the Nineteenth-Century City: Occupation, Property, and Household Structure of Native-born Whites, Buffalo, New York, 1855," in Tamara K. Hareven and Maris A. Vinovskis, eds., *Family and Population in Nineteenth-Century America.* (Princeton: Princeton University Press, 1978): 154-78; Stephan Thernstrom and Peter Knights, "Men in Motion: Some Data and Speculations about Urban Population Mobility in Nineteenth-Century America," *Journal of Interdisciplinary History* 1 (1970): 17-49; and David Gagan and Herbert Mays, "Historical Demography and Canadian Social History: Families and Land in Peel County, Ontario," *Canadian Historical Review* 54 (1973): 27-47.

35. In contrast, Burton (*In My Father's*) found landownership associated with higher rates of persistence among African Americans in Edgefield, South Carolina.

36. James C. Bonner finds a similar pattern in Hancock County, Georgia, reported in his "Profile of a Late Antebellum Community," *American Historical Review* 49 (1944): 666.

37. Burton, *In My Father's.*

38. U.S. Census of Population, Clay County, 1850 and 1860, in manuscript; Loren Schweninger, *Black Property Owners in the South, 1790-1915* (Urbana: University of Illinois Press, 1990); Burton, *In My Father's.*

39. Walker ("The Legal Status," 382) suggests that natural increase accounted for a large segment of the state's free African American population. Birth and death records, which would provide more definitive insights into the reasons for African American population decline, are highly unreliable for rural Appalachia.

40. Walker, "The Legal Status," 389.

41. See also Nancy S. Landale and Stewart E. Tolnay, "Group Differences in Economic Opportunity and the Timing of Marriage: Blacks and Whites in the Rural South, 1910," *American Sociological Review* 56 (1991): 33-45.

42. Luther P. Jackson, "Free Negroes of Petersburg, Virginia," *Journal of Negro History* 12 (1927): 365-88; Schweninger, *Black Property Owners*; Stuckert, "Black Populations."

43. Clay County Will Book "A"; Clay County tax rolls, 1840-79; U.S. Census of Population and U.S. Census of Agriculture, 1850, 1860, 1870, in manuscript.

44. Loren Schweninger, "Property Owning Free African-American Women in the South, 1800-1870," *Journal of Women's History* 1 (1990): 13-44; Schweninger, *Black Property Owners.*

45. Jacqueline Jones, *The Dispossessed: America's Underclass from the Civil War to the Present* (New York: Basic Books, 1992).

46. Clay County Deed Books.

47. Ibid., 1847-57, 1866, 1870.

48. *Griffin v. Griffin*, Clay County Circuit Court, 1853; Clay County Deed Book "D," p. 241, 1852.

49. *Griffin v Griffin*, Clay County Circuit Court, 1853; Elijah was also listed in the tax rolls as owning slaves – initially two slaves in 1848 and seven slaves by 1858 – but these may have been family members who he was not able to legally emancipate.

50. John T. Houdek and Charles F. Heller, Jr., "Searching for Nineteenth-Century Farm Tenants: An Evaluation of Methods," *Historical Methods* 19 (1986), 55, point out that before 1880, tenancy was not necessarily associated with impoverishment.

51. Sharon Ann Holt, "Making Freedom Pay: Freedpeople Working For Themselves, North Carolina, 1865-1900," *Journal of Southern History* 60 (1994): 229-62, cautions that some African Americans listed in the census as servants were simultaneously working as small proprietors, generating income and resources through gardening and other forms of household economies, but we do not have data on such secondary occupations.

52. See also Landale and Tolnay, "Group Differences."

53. Clay County tax rolls of 1870 and 1879. This rate of tenancy is only slightly lower than Lewis's ("From Peasants") estimate that 85% of southern rural blacks in 1890 were tenant farmers or sharecroppers.

54. Holt, "Making Freedom," 267.

55. U.S. Census of Population and U.S. Census of Agriculture, 1850 and 1860, in manuscript.

56. Ibid., 1870, in manuscript.

57. Baker had $200 in 1860 and $60 in 1870, and Parker owned livestock worth $240 in 1860 and $100 in 1870.

58. In 1860, for example, stable African American tenants averaged $357 in livestock; the average in that year for all African American tenants was $285; owners averaged $309. In 1870, one African American farmer, William Walker, who had been a tenant in every census year from 1850 to 1870, had an astonishing $800 in livestock, including thirty cattle, four milk cows, eight oxen, and forty-five pigs, a figure far above the average holdings of either tenants or owners of either race.

59. See also Schweninger, *Black Property Owners*.

60. Jones, *The Dispossessed*.

61. Schweninger, "Property Owning."

62. The 1870 U.S. Census of Population specifically distinguishes paid domestic

wage workers (recorded as "housekeepers") from unpaid family members who do housework (listed as "keeping house").

63. U.S. Census of Population and U.S. Census of Agriculture, 1850, 1860, 1870, in manuscript.

64. Clay County Will Book "A"; see also U.S. Census of Population and U.S. Census of Agriculture, 1870 and 1880, in manuscript; 1870, 1879, and 1892 Clay County tax rolls; Clay County Deed Books.

65. Clay County Deed Books "E," p. 360; "D," p. 241; "B," pp. 156-7; see also U.S. Census of Population and U.S. Census of Agriculture, 1850 and 1860, in manuscript; Clay County tax rolls.

66. A large body of literature addresses these and related issues about African American household and family structure. See Steven Ruggles, "The Origins of African-American Family Structure," *American Sociological Review* 59 (1994): 136-51; Steven Ruggles, "The Transformation of American Family Structure," *American Historical Review* 99 (1994): 103-28; Joyce Aschenbrenner, "Extended Families Among Black Americans," *Journal of Comparative Family Studies* 4 (1973): 257-68; Barbara Finlay Agresti, "The First Decades of Freedom: Black Families in a Southern County, 1870 and 1885," *Journal of Marriage and the Family* 40 (1978): 697-706; Sara McLanahan, "Family Structure and the Reproduction of Poverty," *American Journal of Sociology* 90 (1985): 873-901; S. Philip Morgan et al., "Racial Differences in Household and Family Structure at the Turn of the Century," *American Journal of Sociology* 98 (1993): 798-828; and Steven Ruggles and Ron Goeken, "Race and Multigenerational Family Structure, 1900-1980," in Scott J. South and Stewart E. Tolnay, eds., *The Changing American Family: Sociological and Demographic Perspectives* (Boulder, CO: Westview Press, 1992): 15-42.

67. U.S. Census of Population, Slave Census, 1850 and 1860, in manuscript. This is almost identical to the percentage of slaves who lived in units of ten or more across the South, as reported in John B. Boles, *Black Southerners, 1619-1869* (Lexington: University Press of Kentucky, 1984).

68. It is unlikely that manumission played any significant role in the declining number of slaves in Clay County. There were only thirty-one manumissions from all of Appalachian Kentucky between 1850 and 1860 (Murphy, "Slavery and Freedom") and Clay County records show few manumissions during this period.

69. U.S. Census of Population, 1860, in manuscript; interview in Laurel County, in Federal Writers' Project, *Slave Narratives*, Reel 7.

70. See Agresti, "The First Decades." For a later period, see Linda Gordon and Sara McLanahan, "Single Parenthood in 1900," *Journal of Family History* 16 (1991): 97-116. The demography of household composition is also a function of demographic conditions, that is, the availability of certain types of persons (the

elderly, males, etc.) in a population. See Steven Ruggles, "Availability of Kin and the Demography of Historical Family Structure," *Historical Methods* 19 (1986): 93-102; see also Steven Ruggles, "The Demography of the Unrelated Individual, 1900-1950," *Demography* 25 (1988): 521-36.

71. This is the reverse of what Agresti ("The First Decades") found in a study of a nonplantation farming community in early postbellum Florida.

72. Ruggles, "The Transformation"; see also Miriam King, "All in the Family? The Incompatibility and Reconciliation of Family Demography and Family History," *Historical Methods* 23 (1990): 32-40; Steven Ruggles, "Family Demography and Family History: Problems and Prospects," *Historical Methods* 23 (1990): 22-30; and idem, "Availability of Kin."

73. See Ruggles, "The Transformation."

74. Daniel Scott Smith, Machel Dahlin, and Mark Friedberger, "The Family Structure of the Older Black Population in the American South in 1880 and 1900," *Sociology and Social Research* 63 (1979): 544-65; see also Burton, *In My Father's*.

75. This contrasts sharply with the ability of white-headed households to expand or contract in the face of economic hardship, discussed below.

76. See also Smith et al., "The Family Structure."

77. This rate is higher for white women than Smith et al., "The Family Structure," found overall for the South in 1880 and 1900.

78. See Phillippe Aries, *Centuries of Childhood: A Social History of Family Life* (New York: Vintage, 1962); Lloyd deMause, ed., *The History of Childhood* (New York: Harper, 1975); see also Glen H. Elder, Jr., *Children of the Great Depression* (Chicago: University of Chicago Press, 1974).

79. Walker, "The Legal Status," 392; Holt," Making Freedom Pay."

80. The 1839 Clay County Circuit Court; U.S. Census of Population and U.S. Census of Agriculture, 1850 and 1860, in manuscript.

81. Schwartzweller et al., *Mountain Families*.

Chapter 7

1. Verhoeff, *Kentucky Mountains*, 8. Other factors also served to increase the political and social marginality of Clay County at this time, including the death of a number of the county's pioneer elites – among them Hugh White, John Gilbert, Jr., and Felix Gilbert – and considerable migration from Clay County to the West. See White, *Historical Scrapbook*.

2. Clay County figures are based on a one-in-four sample of all non-enslaved Clay County households drawn from the 1860 U.S. Census of Population. For studies suggesting that Clay County was not out of line with the extent of inequality elsewhere in 1860, see Lee Soltow, *Men and Wealth in the United*

States, 1850-1870 (New Haven: Yale University Press, 1975); Gavin Wright, *The Political Economy of the Cotton South* (New York: Norton, 1978); Dong Hyu Yang, "Notes on the Wealth Distribution of Farm Households in the U.S., 1860," *Explorations in Economic History* 21 (1984): 88-102; Hahn, *The Roots*; Burton, *In My Father's House*; Atack and Bateman, "Self-Sufficiency."

3. Eller, *Miners*, 10, 11.

4. Clay County was more egalitarian in 1860 than the more highly commercialized communities on the eastern edge of the Appalachians had been in an earlier era. Thus, Robert Mitchell (*Commercialism and Frontier*) found that the richest 10% of the population owned 48% of the land in the lower valley in 1800. In the less commercialized upper valley, however, the richest 10% of the population owned 35% of the land in 1800, a level almost equivalent to Clay County at a comparable stage of development at a later period of time.

5. Land values held steady around $2.00/acre in the postbellum period, tiny in comparison with the $45.00/acre that land in the Bluegrass county of Bourbon averaged, but nearly double the value of land in Pike County, in the far eastern part of the state. By the twentieth century, Clay County's farms produced substantially below the state average. In 1901, Clay County farms generated 18.8 bushels of corn per acre, compared to Kentucky's average of 20.9 bushels per acre. In 1913, they generated 12.5 bushels an acre, compared to the state average of 15.2 bushels an acre. See Legislative document 1, "Proceedings of the State Board of Session, 1901" (Louisville: George G. Fetter, 1901), and "Proceedings of the State Board of Equalization, 1913" (Louisville: George G. Fetter, 1913). Manufacturing statistics are from the 1860 U.S. Census. Excepting saltworks, Clay County's establishments (a boot and shoe manufacturer, one leather works, a liquor distillery, one sawmill and a wool carding plant) had a total of $12,125 in capital and generated a total annual product of only $14,350 and an annual payroll of $2,400. For comparative data, see Atack and Bateman, "Self-Sufficiency."

6. Data from the 1870 U.S. Census and from "Kentucky: Its Resources and Present Condition," in The First Annual Report of the Commissioner of State Bureau of Agriculture, Horticulture and Statistics, 1878, found in 1877-8 *Kentucky Documents*.

7. From manuscript archival records of the R. G. Dun and Company, in the Baker Library, Harvard University, and Library of Congress, Washington, D.C. For data on the northeast, see Atack and Bateman, "Self-Sufficiency." Data on Clay County are from 1860 U.S. Census of Population.

8. We estimate tenancy by combining data from the U.S. Censuses of Population and Agriculture according to methods developed by Frederick Bode and Donald Ginter in *Farm Tenancy and the Agricultural Census in Antebellum Georgia* (Athens: University of Georgia Press, 1986). Using this method, we estimate

that no less than 25% and more likely 35 to 41% of Clay County farmers operated rented farms in 1860. This level of tenancy is quite similar to levels in 1860 estimated by Hahn (*Roots*) and Burton (*In My Father's*) for the piedmont regions of Georgia and South Carolina and by Waller (*Feud*) for the Tug River Valley of Appalachia. The finding for Beech Creek, however, stands in sharp contrast to Altina Waller's finding in *Feud* that tenancy increased in the Tug Valley from 37% in 1860 to 62% by 1900 and to Alan Banks's documentation of increasing landlessness in the industrializing counties of Eastern Kentucky ("Land and Capital in Eastern Kentucky, 1890-1965," *Appalachian Journal* 8 (1980): 8-18).

9. Clay County manuscript tax rolls, 1892; U.S. Census of Population, 1860 and 1870.

10. The 1880 and 1900 U.S. Census of Population and 1880 U.S. Census of Agriculture.

11. Kenneth Lockridge, "Land, Population, and the Evolution of New England Society, 1630-1790," *Past and Present* 39 (1968): 70.

12. Data from Clay County Deeds.

13. Brown, *Beech Creek.*

14. Findings are from a series of statistical models based on the work of Atack and Bateman ("Self-Sufficiency") that estimate wealth holding in Clay County in 1860 and in Beech Creek in 1850, 1860, 1870, 1879, and 1892 as a function of age, sex, occupation, and literacy. With the exception of 1879, the model itself accounts for progressively smaller amounts of the variation in wealth holding over time. See Billings and Blee, "Causes and Consequences." See also Folbre, "The Logic."

15. "Kentucky: Its Resources and Present Condition."

16. The rate of accumulation of real property declined from 16 to 9% between 1850 and 1870, whereas the rate of accumulation of taxable property dropped from 14 to 5% between 1860 and 1892. Clay County figures are from U.S. Census of Population, 1850, 1860, and 1870, and Clay County tax rolls, 1892. Comparative figures from Soltow, *Men and Wealth*; Richard Lowe and Randolph Campbell, "Slave Property and the Distribution of Wealth in Texas, 1860," *Journal of American History* 63 (1976): 316-24; Atack and Bateman, "Self-Sufficiency."

17. Edward L. Ayers, *The Promise of the New South: Life After Reconstruction* (New York: Oxford University Press, 1992), 86.

18. Information on the careers of antebellum and early postbellum merchants combines data from the U.S. Census of Population with records of the Robert G. Dun credit rating company (later Dun and Bradstreet). The U.S. Census of Population no longer reported information on individuals' personal property and real estate holdings after 1870, so the census tells us very little about Clay

County's turn-of-the-century merchants. Pudup ("Town and Country") argues that before the 1880s, being a merchant was not a lifelong occupation; rather, men (and sometimes women) alternated between farming and merchandising.

19. Kelly Morgan and Mrs. Kelly Morgan, *History of Clay County, Kentucky*, Bicentennial Ed. (Manchester, KY: Morgan Book, 1976).

20. Mary Beth Pudup, "Social Class and Economic Development in Southeastern Kentucky, 1820-1880," in Mitchell, *Appalachian Frontiers*, 251. See also Eugene A. Conti, Jr., "The Cultural Role of Local Elites in the Kentucky Mountains: A Retrospective Analysis." *Appalachian Journal* 7 (1979-80): 51-68.

21. Barton Potter also owned a large number of slaves and substantial tracts of real estate, both town lots and farms. He leased his farmland to tenants; Clay County tax rolls, 1860; U.S. Census of Population, 1860 and 1870; U.S. Census of Agriculture, 1860 and 1870.

22. In the authors' possession, on loan from Bart and Kaye Smith, Manchester.

23. Edward Akers, *The Promise of the New South: Life After Reconstruction* (New York: Oxford University Press, 1994), 84.

24. See *S. A. and A. W. McMurray v Maxline Baker*, Clay County Circuit Court, 1895; *Isabell Campbell v William Bishop and A. W. Baker*, Clay County Circuit Court, 1896; and *Bank of Manchester v Andrew Baker*, Clay County Circuit Court, 1897.

25. As late as 1877, jeans, linens, socks, shoes, and other clothing were produced at home using locally grown flax, wool, and cotton according to "Kentucky: Its Resources and Present Condition."

26. The 1870 U.S. Census of Population; Potter's merchant and account books, in the authors' possession.

27. In the 1870 U.S. Census of Population, Levi Andrews is shown as owning $1,200 in real estate and $695 in personal property.

28. The 1870 Census of Population; 1870 Census of Agriculture; Potter merchant books, 1886.

29. Deed Book "F," p. 156, from E. A. and James G. Potter to R. G. Potter, November 22, 1867.

30. *Annual Report of the Kentucky Bureau of Agriculture, Horticulture and Statistics, 1880*: 221; Kentucky State Auditor, *Reports*, 1872-80; Deed Book "H," p. 522 (June 4, 1878); Deed Book "H," p. 565 (October 24, 1878).

31. *R. G. Potter, adm. for Barton Potter v William Begley*, Clay County Circuit Court, 1878; *N. C. Potter v R. H. Grimes*, Clay County Circuit Court, 1891; *R. G. Potter v Edmond Philpot and Frederick Benge*, Clay County Circuit Court, 1877.

32. From an annual average of one or two lawsuits through the 1860s, Potter's litigation increased to four a year in the mid-1870s and then to an annual average of seven during the mid-1890s. See *R. G. Potter, administrator for Barton Potter v Samuel Buttry*, Clay County Circuit Court, 1877; *R. G. Potter v James Clark*,

Clay County Circuit Court, n.d. [ca. 1877]; *R. G. Potter v G. W. Cottrell*, Clay County Circuit Court, 1877; *R. G. Potter's receivers v Jacob Hornsby*, Clay County Court, 1891; *R. G. Potter's receivers v Lyttleton Mizey*, Clay County Circuit Court, 1887; *Susan Benge v N. C. Potter*, Clay County Circuit Court, 1897; U.S. Census of Population, 1860.

33. *E. A. Potter's devisees v N. C. Potter*, Clay County Circuit Court, 1886; *R. G. Potter v A. M. Combs*, Clay County Circuit Court, 1879.

34. R. G. Potter, along with B. P. White, was sued by Laura and John D. White in 1877 over a promissory note and sued by B. F. White in 1878 in a land dispute. See *Laura and John D. White v Robert G. Potter and B. P. White*, Clay County Court, 1877; *B. F. White v James G. Potter, trustee of R. G. Potter*, Clay County Circuit Court, 1878; *R. G. Potter's receivers v A. M. Combs*, Clay County Circuit Court, 1881; *R. G. Potter v A. M. Combs*, Clay County Circuit Court, 1888; *R. G. Potter v A. M. Combs*, Clay County Circuit Court, 1892; *R. G. Potter's receivers v A. M. Combs*, Clay County Circuit Court, 1898.

35. The 1879 tax rolls list Potter as owning $20,000 real estate. *R. G. Potter v A. M. Combs*, Clay County Court, 1879.

36. Bart Smith has in his possession copies of deeds of land transactions by N. C. Potter in 1884, 1889, 1890, 1892, 1893, 1894, 1897, 1898, 1899, 1901, 1904, and 1908 – many by commissioner sale.

37. *N. C. Potter, assignee of L. A. Byron v James L. Barrett and B. P. White*, Clay County Circuit Court, 1893; *Vincent Boreing v R. G. and N. C. Potter*, Clay County Circuit Court, 1893. The 1890 Clay County tax rolls list Boreing as owning 4,891 acres.

38. *N. C. Potter, assignee of L. A. Byron v James L. Barrett and B. P. White*, Clay County Circuit Court, 1893; *J. G. and J. H. White v N. C. Potter*, Clay County Circuit Court, 1893; *J. G. and D. W. White v N. C. Potter*, Clay County Circuit Court, 1893; *N. C. Potter v Caleb Dezare and B. P. White*, Clay County Circuit Court, 1897; *N. C. Potter v William Treadway and A. W. Baker*, Clay County Circuit Court, 1897; *N. C. Potter v H. B. Illonium and Timothy Philpot*, Clay County Circuit Court, 1899; *N. C. Potter v A. W. Baker, Alfred Wilson, J. H. Tinsley and H. C. Faulkner*, Clay County Circuit Court, 1899; Deed Book "T": 330-1.

39. Deed Books "J," May 31, 1886; "L," 37 (April 5, 1887); "I," 542 (May 31, 1886), and "L," 37 (April 5, 1887). In both contracts with the Philpots, R. G. Potter signed as N. C. Potter's agent, as married women were not allowed to control their own property. In 1897, N. C. Potter went to court to correct an earlier deed to show that she, and not R. G., bought land at a sheriff's sale; *N. C. Potter v Green White*, Clay County Circuit Court, 1895; *A. W. Baker v Morgan Iniart*, Clay County Circuit Court, 1897; interview with Bart Smith, Manchester.

40. As soon as women gained legal rights, they became actors in court, acting as administratrix of their husbands' estates. See *Sam South v John C. White*, Clay County Circuit Court, 1890.

41. Clay County Circuit Court order book, January 29, 1879.

42. *J. R. Burchell v Ellen C. Lyttle's heirs*, Clay County Circuit Court, 1890; see also *J. R. Burchell v B. P. White and David Hobbs*, Clay County Circuit Court, 1890.

43. Prenuptial agreement is in Deed Book "R," 262 (March 2, 1894). See also Darrell C. Richardson, *Mountain Rising* (Oneida, KY: Oneida Mountain Press, 1986), and a private communication from Jess Wilson, Clay County.

44. Deed book "R," 262 (March 2, 1894).

45. *William L. White, then Katie White, Adm. v H. G. Coldiron, J. W. Wright, Martha Hogg*, Clay County Circuit Court, 1898.

46. Deed Books for 1896 and 1895.

47. *Delaney Combs, adm. of Samuel Combs v G. W. Baker*, Clay County Circuit Court, 1896.

48. *Madison Steuart v Daniel Philpot and Pleasant Philpot*, Clay County Circuit Court, 1896. Martha Hogg was not the only woman to rent land to tenants. In a court dispute over land ownership with Bates Shackleford in 1893, Martha Ramsey White testified that she bought the land when she was 18 years old for $200 cash and that she had rented the land to tenants since that time (*Bates Schackelford by Janus R. Schackelford v Martha C. White*, Clay County Circuit Court, 1893.)

49. Deed Book "U," 440 (August 1, 1899, and July 25, 1899).

50. Mary Beth Pudup "Social Class," 240.

51. Articles of incorporation, Bank of Manchester, Clay County Corporation Record, Vol. 1; *The Bank of Manchester v William L. White, sheriff*, Clay County Circuit Court, 1895; Ayers, *The Promise*; U.S. Census of Population, 1900; Records of the R. G. Dun Company.

52. R. G. Dun and Company Reference Book, Vol. 127.

53. William Roscoe Thomas, *Life among the Hills and Mountains of Kentucky* (Louisville: Standard Printing Company, 1930). Natural gas was bubbling up from the surface at Burning Springs, nine miles from Manchester, in the 1870s. Lewis Collins, *History of Kentucky* (Berea: Kentucke Imprints, 1976 [1874]); U.S. Census of Population, 1870; "Kentucky: Its Resources and Present Condition."

54. Richardson, *Mountain*, 39; Eller, *Miners*, 89.

55. U.S. Census of Manufacturing, 1870; U.S. Census of Agriculture, 1870; R. G. Dun records; Thomas D. Clark, *The Greening of the South: The Recovery of Land and Forest* (Lexington: University Press of Kentucky, 1984).

56. U.S. Census of Agriculture, 1880; U.S. Census of Manufacturing, 1880; U.S. Census, "Forests," 1880, 545; Ninth Biennial Report of the Bureau of

Agriculture, Labor and Statistics, 1891, "Clay County," in *Kentucky Documents*, 1891.

57. Richardson, *Mountain*, 41-2; R. C. Ballard Thruston, *Report on the Timbers on Lines Proposed for the Extension of the Cumberland Valley Branch of the Louisville and Nashville Railroad*, 23 (Louisville: Courier-Journal Printing, 1887); Eller, *Miners*, 86-127.

58. Clark, *Greening*, 10, 18, 24.

59. Richardson, *Mountain*, 40, 45, 43; Clark, *Kentucky*, 331; John Fox, Jr., *Blue-Grass and Rhododendron* (New York: Scribner's, 1920), 60.

60. Richardson, *Mountain*, 40, 44, 52-3; Clark, *Kentucky*, 328-9; F. F. Roberts, "The Old Reliable."

61. Richardson, *Mountain*, 43.

62. Ibid., 43, 44; Thomas D. Clark, *The Kentucky*, 10, 325 (Lexington: University Press of Kentucky, 1992 {1942}); see also Clark, cited in Richardson, *Mountain*, 47-8.

63. Richardson, *Mountain*, 41; Eller, *Miners*, 89, 90, 91.

64. Richardson, *Mountain*, 41; Thruston, "Report," 23; *Elijah Gregory, administrator for W. T. Gregory v Nimrod Cotton, Allen Moberly, T. J. Cotton and J. G. White*, Clay County Circuit Court, 1891; *G. W. Baker v G. W. Daniel, William Allen and J. G. Judd*, Clay County Circuit Court, 1896.

65. Eller, *Miners*, 92.

66. Float contract with R. M. Wilson and J. C. Napier, July 1909, in Burt and Brabb Lumber Company files, University of Kentucky Library; Eller, *Miners*, 94.

67. Clark, *Greening*, 10, 24; Eller, *Miners*, 104.

68. Quoted in Eller, *Miners*, 110-11.

69. Eller, *Miners*, 92, 93, 94. For a comprehensive study of the impacts of the timber industry in one Appalachian state, see Ronald L. Lewis, *Transforming the Appalachian Countryside: Railroads, Deforestation and Social Change in West Virginia, 1880-1920* (Chapel Hill: University of North Carolina Press, 1998).

70. Horsley also bought some tracts of land, e.g., 2,000 acres on Buffalo Creek from G. W. Baker and other tracts on Laurel Creek and Crane Creek in 1887 (Clay County Deeds, Grantee Index). Many of these deeds were written as "broad form" deeds, giving the owner of subsurface minerals the right to remove mineral wealth by any means necessary. Horsley was not the only agent of corporate interests to come to Clay County in search of rights. In 1887, Clay Countians were also selling land to New York and Kentucky Land Company. See 1887 deed from Joseph Schackleford et al. (Deed Book "O," p. 73); Anderson Baker sale to New York and Kentucky Land Company at $4.50/acre on August 26, 1890 (Deed Book "O," p. 43), and land and timber sales to Asher Brothers (later A. B. Asher Lumber) on Red Bird Creek in 1889 and 1890).

Asher Lumber Company was founded by Thomas Jefferson Asher, a Clay County native, and acquired thousands of acres before being bought out by the Michigan-based Burt and Brabb Lumber Company in 1896; Eller, *Miners*, 94.

71. See the many deeds in 1891 and 1887 from Philpots and Howards and in 1889 and 1890 from Andersons and Bakers in Clay County deed books; Deed Book "X," 421 from Horsley to Kenton Coal.

72. Alan Banks, "Labor and the Development of Industrial Capitalism in Eastern Kentucky." Ph.D. diss., McMaster University, 1979. See also his "Class Formation in the Southeastern Kentucky Coalfields, 1890-1920," in Pudup et al., *Appalachia*, 321-46.

73. See John Gaventa, *Power and Powerlessness: Quiescence and Rebellion in an Appalachian Valley* (Urbana: University of Illinois Press, 1980).

74. Slick-talking corporate agents and naive locals play major roles in the Appalachian land grab as portrayed by Robert Schenkkan in his 1992 Pulitzer Prize–winning play, "The Kentucky Cycle." For critical responses to the historical assumptions of this play, see Dwight Billings, Gurney Norman, and Katherine Ledford (eds.), *Confronting Appalachian Stereotypes: Back Talk from an American Region* (Lexington: University Press of Kentucky, 1999).

75. Harry Caudill, *Theirs Be The Power: The Moguls of Eastern Kentucky* (Urbana: University of Illinois Press, 1985), 12, 13. Elsewhere, noting that "a childish trust in others has long been a characteristic of the Appalachian mind," Caudill claimed that mountain people understood nothing about the value of their land. "As they had never learned to farm it effectively, they now failed to comprehend the value of its mineral deposits and, in effect, practically donated these riches to the rest of the world." See Caudill, *Darkness at Dawn*, 15, 13. See also Jack Weller, *Yesterday's People*, 15.

76. Quoted in Laurel Schackelford and Bill Weinberg, *Our Appalachia: An Oral History* (Lexington: University Press of Kentucky, 1977), 153; insert in original.

77. Quoted in Schackelford and Weinberg, *Our Appalachia*, 154.

78. Brown, *Beech*, 266.

79. *Leava Hibbard v Henry Hibbard and Anderson Baker*, Clay County Circuit Court, 1894, and Deed Book "Q," 275, January 12, 1894, deed from Leanna Hibbard to Henry Hibbard.

80. *Pleasant Walker v Wiley Carpenter and B. P. White*, Clay County Circuit Court, 1890.

81. Clay County Will Book 2, December 26, 1888.

82. *Commonwealth of Kentucky v T. J. Henderson et al.*, Clay County Circuit Court, 1890; Deed Books "L," 615; "N," 69; "N," 71; "O," 108; "K," 200; Commissioner Deed Book 2, 517.

83. Deed Book "P," 76 (August 1, 1887), and "O," 160 (January 17, 1891).

84. Eller, *Miners*, 54-5. For a similar conclusion to ours, see Robert S. Weise, "Selling Mineral Rights in Floyd County, Kentucky," paper presented at the Appalachian Studies Association annual conference, 1993.

85. Land values computed from the *Biennial Reports of the Auditor of Public Accounts of Kentucky* (Frankfort: State of Kentucky, 1883-6), 287; Kentucky State Auditor, *Report, 1889; J. C. Napier v John G. White*, Clay County Circuit Court, 1891.

86. Banks, "Land and Capital."

87. Clay County tax rolls, 1892; *The Kentucky Mineral and Timber Company v James Hoskins et al.*, Clay County Circuit Court, 1894.

88. "Governor's Message," *Kentucky House Journal, 1869-70*, quoted in Eller, *Miners*, 49.

89. Deed Book 2, 395.

90. *The International Development Company v A. B. Howard*, Clay County Circuit Court, 1896, and, on appeal, 113 *Kentucky Reports* (April 1902 term), 450-5. Land was owned by H. Anna Jones, then H. Haynes, then George Baird, and then E. Patterson.

91. *Annual Report of the Kentucky Bureau of Agriculture, Horticulture and Statistics*, 1880, 221; also Kentucky State Auditor, *Reports*, 1889-95; "Ninth Biennial Report of the Bureau of Agriculture, Labor and Statistics," 1891; *Bell County Investment Company v Edward Uhl et al.*, Clay County Circuit Court, 1894; Deed Book "P," 337 (August 28, 1890) from Mansfield Machine Works of Mansfield, Ohio; Deed Book "P," 339 (November 24, 1891) from Hibbards in Ark; "P," 340 (November 21, 1891) from Nantz in Texas.

92. Deed Book "P," 126 (October 21, 1890); "O," 43 (September 26, 1890) from Anderson Baker to Joseph Churchill; *Jesse Allen v Joseph Churchill et al.*, Clay County Circuit Court, 1895.

93. *John G. White v New York and Kentucky Land Company et al.*, Clay County Circuit Court, 1893.

94. The same court ordered sale of White timber bought by these two corporations in 1893; *B. P. and John C. White v New York and Kentucky Land Company*, Clay County Circuit Court, 1895; *John G. White v New York Kentucky Land Company*, Clay County Circuit Court, 1893. In the case *David Davidson et al. v New York and Kentucky Land Company*, Clay County Circuit Court, 1897, the land was sold seven times between 1890 and 1895, largely between out-of-state corporations.

95. See, for example, *A. W. Baker and James D. Black v D. T. Jones et al.* (Clay County Circuit Court, 1896) in which A. Baker and James D. Black, attorneys, sue eleven former clients for unpaid fees from when they were hired to defend against land disputes. In each case, the original land was sold to pay judgment. Commissioner Deed Book 2, June 12, 1895. Also *Central Appalachian*

Corporation, Ltd. v Henry Hensley, Clay County Circuit Court, 1900; *New York and Kentucky Land Company v A. B. Howard*, Clay County Circuit Court, 1891.

96. Pudup, "Boundaries of Class," 159; Miscellaneous Clay County Deed Book, September 20, 1912.

97. *R. G. Potter and L. A. Byron, receiver v Winnie Runion et al.*, Clay County Circuit Court, 1892; *Campbell Smith (for New York and Kentucky Land Company) v B. P. White and John C. White*, Clay County Circuit Court, 1890; and *John D. White v New York and Kentucky Land Company*, Clay County Circuit Court, 1891.

98. Kentucky State Auditor, *Report, 1891; John G. White v New York and Kentucky Land Company*, Clay County Circuit Court, 1893; Deed Books "O," 393 (May 9, 1891); "P," 191 (April 18, 1891); "U," 369 (February 18, 1901); "Q," 637 (February 2, 1894); *John E. White v A. B. Asher and Henry Hensley*, Clay County Circuit Court, 1899; *Edward Uhl v Kentucky Mineral and Timber Company*, Clay County Circuit Court, 1894; Deed Book "O," 424 (April 29, 1891); Deed Book "Y," 172; Deed Book "Z," 195; Deed Book 71, 544 (September 16, 1939); *John E. and Thomas White v T. T. Garrard*, Clay County Circuit Court, 1894; interview with Evelyn Garrard Strode in Winchester, Kentucky, November 14, 1891. See sale of Abner Baker's land on Goose Creek to B. F. White for seventy-one cents an acre on April 7, 1891, in Deed Book "P," 463.

99. Compare prices in *P. B. Reynolds v B. P. White and John C. White*, Clay County Circuit Court, 1892, with *Elijah Gregory, administrator for W. T. Gregory v Nimrod Cotton, Allen Moberly, T. J. Cotton and J. G. White*, Clay County Circuit Court, 1891; also *G. W. Baker v G. W. Daniel, William Allen and J. G. Judd*, Clay County Circuit Court, 1896; *Pleasant Philpot and Daniel Philpot v Robert Baker*, Clay County Circuit Court, 1895; *H. B. Marcum and Timothy Philpot d.b.a. Marcus & Philpot v G. W. Philpot*, Clay County Circuit Court, 1899; *John E. White v A. B. Asher and Henry Hensley, partners*, Clay County Circuit Court, 1899; *Hiram Hoskins, R. C. Ford and J. H. Garrard, late partners d.b.a. Hiram Hoskins & Co. v J. B. Hoskins*, Clay County Circuit Court, 1900; and *D. Lloyd Walker v W. J. Roberts, R. M. Jackson and Vincent Boreing*, Clay County Circuit Court, 1900.

100. *Stephen B. White, adm. of Hugh L. White, dec. v Samuel Buttry*, Clay County Circuit Court, 1892; *D. R. Murray v John D. and Laura White*, Clay County Circuit Court, 1891; *Charles Scott v John D. and Laura White*, Clay County Circuit Court, 1897.

101. Private communication from Louise P. Hoy, Ashland, Kentucky. See *John E. White and Thomas White v T. T. Garrard*, Clay County Circuit Court, 1894; *John C. Morgan v Laura R. and J. D. White*, Clay County Circuit Court, 1893; *Charles Scott v John D. White and Laura R. White*, Clay County Circuit Court, 1897. In 1920, at the age of 67, Laura wrote to the University of Michigan Alumni

Office from her home in Clay County that she was "living on my farm (which I rent out shares, that is, for half of crops) and watch after my mineral and timber interests." On Laura White, see *Ashland {Kentucky} Independent* (March 19, 1990); Louisville *Courier Journal* (January 27, 1929); *Woman's Who's Who of America, 1914-1915*; Alumni Records Office, University of Michigan; Clay County Mortgage Book 2, 628 (September 1899). We thank Nancy Blazer of Ashland, Kentucky, for providing some of these sources.

102. *M. J. Treadway v John D. White*, Clay County Circuit Court, 1893.

103. Roy White, *Historical Scrapbook*; Hugh White's 1826 patent was found in 1894 to conflict with T. T. Garrard's patent, leaving the court to resolve which was the junior patent in *John E. White and Thomas White v T. T. Garrard*, Clay County Circuit Court, 1894.

104. Kincaid A. Herr, *The Louisville and Nashville Railroad, 1850-1940, 1941-1959* (Louisville: L & N Magazine Publisher, 1959), 115-16; Fourth Annual Report of the Inspector of Mines of Kentucky, 1887; Fifth Annual Report of the Inspector of Mines of Kentucky, 1888; Seventh Annual Report of Inspector of Mines, 1890; Ninth Biennial Report of the Kentucky Bureau of Labor, Agriculture, and Statistics, 1891; *The L & N Today – Division by Division* (Louisville: L & N RR, 1966).

105. *Corporation Record*, August 23, 1907, entry for "Manchester Traction Company" and March 6, 1909, entry for Cumberland Northern Railway Company.

106. In 1927, the C & M line was leased by L & N Railroad.

107. Clay County Court, *Corporation Record*, May 12, 1909; August 20, 1912; February 12, 1916; letter from Milton H. Smith, president, Louisville and Nashville (L & N) Railroad Company to H. Walters, February 24, 1916, and letter from Milton Smith to John S. Williams, January 23, 1919, both in Chairman's File – correspondence 1669, box 49, 77-11; minutes of the Cumberland and Manchester Railroad Company, Reels 7 and 8, "predecessors and subsidiaries," articles of incorporation (1916); H Corporation Record, May 10, 1915, entry for Cumberland and Manchester Railroad; "Articles of Incorporation" in minutes of the Cumberland and Manchester Railroad Company, 1915, Reels 7 and 8 of the L & N Collection, *Louisville and Nashville*, 149, 150; Richard E. Prince, *L & N Steam Locomotives* (Louisville: L & N Railroad, 1968); F. F. Roberts, *The Old Reliable Enters New Territory* (L & N Employees Magazine, January, 1928, 13-14). All available at L & N Archives, Louisville, Kentucky.

108. Although Clay County was underlain with deep coal veins, its superficial veins were much thinner, around twelve inches, with a layer of bituminous coal around thirty inches and a six-foot vein about 20-100 feet below the water courses. This configuration ultimately hampered large-scale underground coal mining in the county.

109. Thomas, *Life Among the Hills*, 370-2; *Annual Report of the State Department of Mines of Kentucky, 1922* (Frankfort: State Journal Company, 1922); articles of incorporation of the Bank of Manchester, in *Bank of Manchester v William L. White, sheriff*, Clay County Circuit Court, 1895. On White investments, see Corporation Record entries for January 19, 1918 (John E. White Coal Company), March 5, 1919 (Inter-Mountain Insurance and Real Estate Exchange), August 28, 1920 (King Blue Gem Coal Company), and October 2, 1935 (New McCreary Lumber Company). For Garrards, see Corporation Record entries for March 26, 1903 (Clay County Bank), October 17, 1917 (Horse Creek Coal Company), September 17, 1918 (Horse Creek Coal Company), and June 3, 1920 (Paw Paw Coal Company).

Chapter 8

1. Dickey, *Diary*, roll 3, entries February 21, 23, 28, 1898.
2. Antonio Gramsci, *Selections from Prison Notebooks* (New York: International Publishers, 1971).
3. Margaret Somers defines a political public sphere as "a contested participatory site in which actors with overlapping identities as legal subjects, citizens, economic actors, and family and community members, form a public body and engage in negotiations and contestations over political and social life" in her "Citizenship and the Place of the Public Sphere: Law, Community, and Political Culture in the Transition to Democracy," *American Sociological Review* 58 (1993): 589.
4. E. Carl Litsey, "Kentucky Feuds & Their Causes," *Frank Leslie's Popular Monthly* 53 (1902): 283-91. John White was acquitted and then, ironically, married into the Garrard family before pursuing a successful career in timber, commerce, and public office. Letter from J. W. Carnahan of Toledo to President Frost of Berea, August 3, 1903, in Appalachian Feud Collection, Berea College, Special Collections. Another version of the 1886 story claims that a sixteen-year-old boy fired a shot into the ground when he saw the man who had killed his father, and then others drew weapons and three were killed. Both accounts agree that no one was ever convicted for the shooting.
5. Darrell C. Richardson, *Mountain Rising* (Oneida, KY: Oneida Mountain Press, 1986); Alvin F. Harlow, *Weep No More My Lady* (New York: Whittlesey House and McGraw-Hill, 1942); Litsey, "Kentucky Feuds"; Clay County Circuit Court, Criminal Case Order Book, 1898.
6. Dickey, *Diary*, February 8 and 21, 1898; *Louisville Courier-Journal*, June 11, 1899, p. 1; Richardson, *Mountain*; Clay County Circuit Court, Criminal Order Books, 1898.

7. *Louisville Courier-Journal*, June 11, 1899, p. 1; *New York Herald*, February 5, 1905, p. 3; *New York Times*, December 3, 1899, p. 17; Harlow, *Weep*; Dickey, *Diary*, April 13, 1898.

8. James M. Ross, "The Great Feuds of Kentucky," *The Wide World Magazine* 24 (1909): 191-5.

9. Richardson, *Mountain*; Harlow, *Weep*; *New York Herald*, February 2, 1905, p. 3.

10. George C. Wright, *Racial Violence in Kentucky, 1865-1940: Lynchings, Mob Rule and "Legal Lynchings"* (Baton Rouge: Louisiana State University Press, 1990).

11. Orders of the Clay County Court, September 25, 1897; April 7, 9, and 14, 1898.

12. Dickey, *Diary*, April 13, 1898; *New York Herald*, February 5, 1905, p. 3; *New York Times*, December 3, 1899, p. 17; Richardson, *Mountain*.

13. Orders of the Clay County Court, April 12, 1898; Litsey, "Kentucky Feuds"; Clay County Circuit Court, Criminal Order Book, 1898; Richardson, *Mountain*; Dickey, *Diary*, August 8, 1898.

14. Harlow, "Weep"; Richardson, *Mountain*; *New York Herald*, February 5, 1905, p. 3.

15. Orders of the Clay County Court, April 9, 1898; Dickey, *Diary*, April 13, 1898; Richardson, *Mountain;* Harlow, "Weep."

16. Dickey, *Diary*, October 3, 1898; Clay County Circuit Court, Orders, April 12, 1898.

17. Dickey, *Diary*, June 4, 1898, and August 14, 1898; *New York Times*, December 3, 1899, p. 17.

18. Ellen Churchill Semple, "The Anglo-Saxons of the Kentucky Mountains," *Bulletin of the American Geographical Society* XLII (1910 [1901]): 561-94; *London Mountain Echo*, June 14, 1898; Clay County Circuit Court, Criminal Order Book, June 17, 1898; Richardson, *Mountain*; Dickey, *Diary*, June 11, 1898.

19. Letter of June 8, 1898, from Gov. Bradley to Walter S. Forrester, Assistant Adjutant General, in *Reports of the Adjutant General, 1893-1898*; Gov. Bradley Executive Journal 2, entries of June 8, July 22, and July 26, 1898; *London Mountain Echo*, June 14, 1898; *Louisville Courier-Journal*, June 10, 1898.

20. Gov. Bradley's Executive Journal 2, entries for June, 1898; letter of June 8, 1898, from Gov. W. O. Bradley to Walter Forrester, Assistant Adjutant General in Kentucky State Adjutant General, *Reports* (1898); Federal Writer's Project, *Military History of Kentucky* (Frankfort: State Journal, 1939); *Louisville Courier-Journal*, June 1, 10, 11, 13, and 14, 1898; *London Mountain Echo*, June 14, 1898.

21. "Berea College, Kentucky." Untitled June 25, 1898 clipping in the Berea College Collection, Berea College; Kentucky State Adjutant General, *Report*, June–July 1898; Gov. Bradley Executive Journal 2, entry for July 26, 1898;

Federal Writers Project, *Military*; Litsey, "Kentucky Feuds"; Dickey, *Diary*, July 24, 1898; Harlow, "Weep."

22. Clay County Fiscal Court, fall session, 1898; Clay County Circuit Court Criminal Order Book, 1898; *New York Herald*, February 5, 1905, p. 3; *London Mountain Echo*, October 21, 1898; Laurel County Circuit Court records, August 8, 17, and 18, 1898; Litsey, "Kentucky Feuds"; Richardson, *Mountain*.

23. *London Mountain Echo*, December 1898; Gov. W. O. Bradley Executive Journal 2, entry for June 1, 1899; Federal Writers Project, *Military*; *New York Times*, December 3, 1899, p. 17; "Face to Face," untitled December 25, 1898 clipping in the Berea Collection, Berea College.

24. Litsey, "Kentucky Feuds"; Harlow, *Weep*; Richardson, *Mountain*; Ross, "Great Feuds"; *Louisville Courier Journal*, June 14, 1898.

25. Richardson, *Mountain*; Harlow, *Weep*.

26. *New York Times*, June 12 and December 3, 1899; Harlow, *Weep*.

27. Dickey, *Diary*, June (unspecified date) 1899; *Louisville Courier-Journal*, June 13, 1899.

28. *New York Times*, June 12, 1899, p. 1; *Louisville Courier Journal*, June 13, 1899; *Berea Citizen*, July 21, 1899.

29. *Berea Citizen*, July 21, 1899; Dickey, *Diary*, July 18, 1899; Litsey, "Kentucky Feuds"; Richardson, *Mountain*; Harlow, *Weep*.

30. Dickey, *Diary*, July 16, 1899; *New York Times*, October 26, July 18, and December 3, 1899; *London Mountain Echo*, July 21, 1899.

31. Bradley Executive Journal 2, June 1, 1899; Harold Coats, *Stories of Kentucky Feuds* (Knoxville, TN: Holmes-Darst Coal Company, 1942); *Louisville Courier-Journal*, June 17, 1899, p. 1.

32. *Louisville Dispatch*, November 18, 1899; Clay County Fiscal Court, Records, November 18, 1899; Richardson, *Mountain*.

33. Emerson Hough, "Burns of the Mountains," *American Magazine* (1913): 13-20; Richardson, *Mountain*; Clay County Corporation Records, December 20, 1899.

34. James C. Klotter, *William Goebel: The Politics of Wrath* (Lexington: University Press of Kentucky, 1977); Lewis F. Johnson, *Famous Kentucky Tragedies and Trials* (Cleveland: Banks-Baldwin Law Publishing, 1916).

35. *Louisville Courier-Journal*, March 9 and 14, 1901; Richardson, *Mountain*; Report of the Adjutant General, Legislative Document 9 (Louisvilles, KY: George G. Fetter, Dec. 31, 1901); Coats, *Stories*.

36. *Louisville Courier-Journal*, March 14, 1901; *New York Times*, September 3, 1904; Coates, *Stories*.

37. *Louisville Courier-Journal*, September 19 and December 16, 1932, and February 4, 1933; see also J. Edgar Hoover, "The Meanest Man I Ever Knew," *American Magazine* (April 1937): 5, 8-9.

38. *Louisville Courier-Journal*, February 2, 1933, and December 5, 1943; Harlow, *Weep*.

39. A more colorful, descriptive view of Clay County's feud can be found in John Ed Pearce, *Days of Darkness: The Feuds of Eastern Kentucky* (Lexington: University Press of Kentucky, 1994). Larry Griffin, "Narrative, Event-structure Analysis, and Causal Interpretation in Historical Sociology," *American Journal of Sociology* 98 (1993): 1094. As Ronald Aminzade, *Ballots & Barricades: Class Formation & Republican Politics in France, 1830-1871* (Princeton: Princeton University Press, 1993; 244) argues, there may be continuity between the conditions that lead to violent and nonviolent outcomes; E. Mingione, *Fragmented Societies: A Sociology of Economic Life Beyond the Market Paradigm* (Cambridge: Blackwell, 1991). This analysis is based in part on an examination of case files of cases adjudicated in Clay County Circuit Court.

40. Anthony Giddens, *A Contemporary Critique of Historical Materialism* (Berkeley: University of California Press, 1981), 23; James C. Klotter, "Feuds in Appalachia: An Overview," *Filson Club Historical Quarterly* 56 (1982): 290-37; Richard E. Miller and Austin Sarat, "Grievances, Claims and Disputes: Assessing the Adversary Culture," *Law and Society Review* 15 ([1975] 1989): 10.

41. See Stephen B. Goldberg, E. D. Green, and F. E. A. Sander, *Dispute Resolutions* (Boston: Little, Brown, 1985): 4; Joel B. Grossman and Austin Sarat, "Litigation in the Federal Courts: A Comparative Perspective," *Law and Society* 9 (1975): 321-46.

42. All cases are from the Clay County Circuit Court.

43. A. L. Lloyd, "Background to Feuding," *History Today* 2 (1952): 451-7.

44. Robert M. Ireland, *The County Courts in Antebellum Kentucky* (Lexington: University Press of Kentucky, 1972): 13; Robert M. Ireland, *The Court in Kentucky History* (Lexington: University Press of Kentucky, 1976): vii. County level offices were appointed rather than elected until 1851, according to Roy White, *Historical Scrap Book*. As an example of the power of the sheriff, in 1898, Sheriff B. P. White put up for auction fifty acres of land belonging to Sidney M. Baker who owed $100 on a bond. The land was purchased by G. W. Philpot for $60 (or $1.20 an acre) who immediately resold it to Sheriff White. Deed Book "T," 493, November 17, 1899.

45. *Ely Philpot v William Hayne*, Clay County Circuit Court, 1891.

46. Deed Books "Q," 417, June 15, 1894; "T," 493, January 4, 1897; "H," 59, August 23, 1876; *Ely Philpot v William Hayne*, Clay County Circuit Court, 1891; *Ed Gibson, administrator v heirs of Joe Philpot*, Clay County Circuit Court, 1896; *B. P. White, Sr. v Daniel Philpot and Pleasant Philpot*, Clay County Circuit Court, 1896; *The Commonwealth of Kentucky and Clay County v Livingston Philpot*, Clay County Circuit Court, 1898; U.S. Census of Population, 1900; Clay

County tax rolls, 1886; Clay County Mortgage Book 3, 2 (July 1899); Clay County Mortgage Book 2, 626 (July 1899).

47. Dickey, *Diary*, July 3 and June 4, 1898; Deed Book "G," 586, March 10, 1876; U.S. Census of Population, 1870, 1900; Clay County tax rolls, 1886.

48. U.S. Census of Population, 1870, 1900; Clay County tax rolls, 1886; *Stephen Barrett v Wilson Howard*, Clay County Circuit Court, 1899.

49. Deed Books "Q," 202 (July 12, 1893), "L," 594 (November 17, 1888), and "T," 330; *N. C. Potter v A. W. Baker, Alfred Wilson, J. H. Tinsley and H. C. Faulkner*, Clay County Circuit Court, 1899; Clay County Mortgage Books 2, 638 (September 1899); 3, 79 (March 1900); and 3, 153 (February 1901).

50. Dickey, *Diary*, June 4 and 8, 1898; undated, ca. early 1899, 2687; authors' interview with Evelyn Garrard Strode, November 14, 1891, Winchester, Kentucky.

51. Dickey, *Diary*, June 4 and 8, July 3, 6, 11, and 24, 1898.

52. Letter to the authors from Wilma Napier Howell, Salem, Indiana, April 1, 1991; *Louisville Courier-Journal*, June 20, 1899, p. 2; *Berea Citizen*, July 21, 1899.

53. Dickey, *Diary*, July 24, June 4 and 18, 1898; also Litsey, "Kentucky Feuds;" Richardson, *Mountain*.

54. Letter from John G. White of Winchester, Kentucky, to Andy Baker of Manchester, Kentucky, August 31, 1901. Thanks to Jess Wilson of Clay County for this reference.

55. Ross, "The Great Feuds." On issues of state functionaries, see Wolfram Fischer and Peter Lundgreen, "The Recruitment and Training of Administrative and Technical Personnel," in Charles Tilly, ed., *The Formation of National States in Western Europe* (Princeton: Princeton University Press, 1975): 456-561; see also Bertram Wyatt-Brown, "Community, Class, and Snopesian Crime: Local Justice in the Old South," in Orville V. Burton and Robert C. McMath, Jr., eds., *Class, Conflict, and Consensus: Antebellum Southern Community Studies* (Westport, CT: Greenwood Press, 1982): 173-206.

56. It is not coincidental that contested elections for sheriff and county assessor touched off the 1890s phase of feuding. As social historians note, offices of tax assessment and collection often become economically pivotal in a period of economic change and speculative fervor. See Gabriel Ardant, "Financial Policy and Economic Infrastructure of Modern States and Nations," in Tilly, *Formation*, 164-242; Richardson, *Mountain*; Johnson, *Famous Kentucky*; Lloyd "Background"; Governor Bradley Executive Journal, 1897-9, various entries; Adjutant General, *Reports, 1896-1901*, various entries; also see *New York Herald* interview of Jim Howard (1905), quoted in Richardson, *Mountain Rising*, 95-101.

57. This is covered extensively in Hambleton Tapp and James Klotter, *Kentucky:*

Decades of Discord, 1865-1900 (Frankfort: Kentucky Historical Society, 1977).

58. State of Kentucky, *Acts of the Assembly*, 1866-1873 and 1880-1890.

59. A number of civil actions were filed by the county against Sheriff Howard, but none was successful. The main case against Howard eventually was reversed on appeal (18 *Kentucky Law Reporter*, filed June 23, 1896, 412-15).

60. *Clay County Clerk v T. T. Garrard*, Clay County Circuit Court, 1891; *First National Bank of London and others v A. B. Howard and sureties*, Clay County Circuit Court, 1892; *Clay County Court v A. B. Howard*, Clay County Circuit Court, 1893; *First National Bank of London and others v A. B. Howard and sureties*, Clay County Circuit Court, 1893.

61. *The Bank of Manchester v William L. White*, Clay County Court, 1895.

62. Deed Book "T," 496.

63. Craig B. Little, "The Criminal Courts in 'Young America': Bucks County, Pennsylvania, 1820-1860, with Some Comparisons to Massachusetts and South Carolina," *Social Science History* 15 (1991): 457-78.

64. See Robert D. Putnam, *Making Democracy Work: Civic Traditions in Modern Italy* (Princeton: Princeton University Press, 1994); Dickey, *Diary*, December 4, 1898 and August 5, 1899; George Robertson, *An Outline of the Life of George Robertson, Written by Himself* (Lexington, KY: Transylvania Printing and Publishing Company, 1876), 45-6.

65. F. F. Roberts, "The Old Reliable"; Lewis Collins, *History of Kentucky*, Vol. 2, 2nd ed. (Berea: Kentucke Inprints, 1976); Ninth Annual Report of the Bureau of Labor and Statistics, 1891; U.S. Census of Population, 1860, 1870; U.S. Census "Religious Bodies: 1906;" U.S. Census "Religious Bodies: 1916;" Mortgage Book 3: 127-8, 133; Deed Book "G," 145; Samuel W. Thomas and George Rogers Clark Press, eds., *Dawn Comes to the Mountains* (Louisville, KY: George Rogers Clark Press, 1981).

66. *Louisville Courier Journal*, January 26, 1970; *Wall Street Journal*, February 28, 1986, pp. 1, 23.

67. Cynthia Duncan, "Persistent Poverty in Appalachia: Scarce Work and Rigid Stratification," in Duncan, *Rural Poverty*, 125.

68. Arthur H. Estabrook, "The Pauper Idiot in Kentucky," *Social Forces* 7 (1928): 68-72; Orders of the Clay County Court, November 1, 1897, and April 18, 1898.

69. See also Giovanni Arrighi and Fortunata Piselli, "Capitalist Development in Hostile Environments: Feuds, Class Struggles, and Migrations in a Peripheral Region of Southern Italy," *Review* 10 (1987): 702-11; and Putnam, *Making Democracy Work*, for similar developments in the peripheral regions of Italy.

70. Sociologists have begun to appreciate the importance of regionally specific articulations of civil society, governance, and public spheres with the formation of local state structures. See Margaret Somers, "Citizenship and the Place

of the Public Sphere: Law, Community, and Political Culture in the Transition to Democracy," *American Sociological Review* 58 (1993): 587-620; George Steinmetz, *Regulating the Social: The Welfare State and Local Politics in Imperial Germany* (Princeton: Princeton University Press, 1993); and John Walton, *Western Times and Water Wars: State, Culture and Rebellion in California* (Berkeley: University of California Press, 1992). Important earlier contributions to a theory of the local state are Nicos P. Mouzelis, *Politics in the Semi-Periphery: Early Parlimentarism and Late Industrialization in the Balkans and Latin America* (New York: St. Martin's Press, 1986); Peter Evans and John D. Stephens, "Development and the World Economy," in Neil Smelser (ed.), *Handbook of Sociology* (Newbury Park, CA: Sage, 1988): 739-73; and S. S. Duncan and M. Goodwin, "The Local State and Local Economic Policy: Why the Fuss?," *Policy and Politics* 13 (1985): 227-54.

71. The early film industry exploited and heightened America's fascination with violent hillbillies. According to Jerry Williamson, between 1904 and 1927, at least 476 silent films depicted life in the southern Appalachians. Of these, 92 featured feuds and 145 featured moonshining along with countless assaults and homicides. See J. W. Williamson, *Southern Mountaineers in Silent Films: Plot Synopses of Movies About Moonshining, Feuding, and Other Mountain Topics* (Jefferson, NC: McFarland, 1994).

72. Litsey, "Kentucky."

73. To locals, however, Clay County's violence was simply a "war." See Richardson, *Mountain;* Klotter, "Feuds"; *New York Times,* June 19, 1899, p. 6; Klotter and Tapp, *Decades.* Mountain violence was of great concern to state officials in Kentucky. It is the topic of a number of gubernatorial inaugural messages, including in 1884 (a section entitled "Lawlessness"), in 1889 (a section entitled "Enforcing the Law"), and in 1898 (a section entitled "Mobs"). All are found in the *Kentucky Senate Journal.* Hartley Davis and Clifford Smyth, "The Land of Feuds," *Munsey's Magazine* XXX (1903): 161, 162; Litsey, "Kentucky Feuds," 287; Ross, "Great Feuds:" 191; *New York Times,* December 3, 1899, p. 17.

74. J. Stoddard Johnston, "Romance and Tragedy of Kentucky Feuds," *The Cosmopolitan* 27 (1899): 551-8. Watson and Wheelwright are cited in Carolyn Clay Turner and Carolyn Hay Traum, *John C. C. Mayo: Cumberland Capitalist* (Pikeville, KY: Pikeville College Press, 1983); "How to Make Something of This Fighting Stock," *Berea Quarterly* 16 (113): 9-16.

75. Semple, "Anglo-Saxons," 586, 580, 566.

76. Semple, "Anglo-Saxons," 564, 588; Johnson, "Romance," 557; compare Kephart, *Our Southern,* 405 with Harlow, *Weep,* 235.

77. Johnson, "Romance," 553, quoted a long passage from John Fox, Jr.'s short story, "The Kentuckians," which he described as "perhaps the best explanation of the feud."

78. Litsey, "Kentucky Feuds," 283-91.

79. This is analyzed skillfully in Renate Siebert, *Secrets of Life and Death: Women and the Mafia*, 39-40 (London: Verso, 1996).

80. Lloyd, "Background"; *New York Times*, June 12, 1899, p. 1.

81. Elijah Dinzey, "Mountain Feud – By a Mountain Man," *Berea Quarterly* 13 (1909): 13; see also "How to Make," *Berea Quarterly* 16 (1913): 9-16; Richardson, *Mountain*.

82. Popular writers of that era had begun to fix on the idea that the majority of Appalachians were Scotch-Irish, an erroneous notion that seemed to account for many of the peculiarities attributed to the "Southern Highlanders," especially clannishness and blood feuding. For a typical account stressing the preponderance of Scotch-Irish numbers and cultural influence on Appalachia, see James Watt Raine, *The Land of Saddle-bags* (New York: Council of Women for Home Missions and Missionary Education Movement of the United States and Canada, 1924), esp. 33-62. In *The Southern Highlander and His Homeland* (New York: Russell Sage Foundation, 1921), John C. Campbell viewed the English as the largest settlement population, but claimed that the Ulster migrants strongly influenced the exaggerated individualism he attributed to the mountaineers. For a discussion of how racism, ethnocentrism, and stereotypes of a WASP or Celtic Appalachia were used to justify Appalachian uplift efforts, see Shapiro, *Appalachia on Our Mind*. David Hackett Fischer's *Albion's Seed* (New York: Oxford University Press, 1989) and Rodger Cunningham's *Apples on the Flood* (Knoxville: University of Tennessee Press, 1987) stand out in modern scholarship for attempting to explain Appalachian culture and regional development in terms of ethnicity. For a critique of Fischer's work by Appalachian scholars, see the text of a 1991 Appalachian Studies Association symposium in *Appalachian Journal* 19 (1992): 161-200. For a more balanced assessment of the Scotch-Irish in Appalachia, see Kenneth W. Keller, "What Is Distinctive about the Scotch-Irish," in Mitchell, *Appalachian Frontiers*, 69-86. Some of these explanations are not too dissimilar from the assumptions that continue to frame contemporary understandings of nineteenth-century mountain feuding. In 1922, Horace Kephart, *Our Southern Highlanders* (Knoxville: University of Tennessee, 1922 [1984]), 422) traced mountain feuds to traditions of violence brought to the region by its "warlike" Scotch-Irish settlers and perpetuated by decades of cultural and geographical isolation and by a social organization that places a high value on kinship loyalty. Despite recent scholarship that documents the ethnic diversity of settlement patterns in the southern mountains, the prominent historian David H. Fischer (*Albion's Seed*, 668) continues to maintain that "strong continuities in family feuding can be traced from the borders of North Britain to the Appalachian backcountry."

83. Davis and Smyth, "Land of Feuds," 162; Frost is quoted in Shapiro, *Appalachia*,

111; General O. O. Howard, "The Feuds in the Cumberland Mountains," *The Independent*, April 7, 1904, pp. 787, 788.

84. "How to Make Something Out of this Fighting Stock," *Berea Quarterly* XVI: (1913): 9; Hough, "Burns of the Mountains," 2.

85. "Kentucky Feuds," *Berea Quarterly* 4 (1899): 17-18. William G. Frost's statements include "The American Mountaineers," *Berea Quarterly* 4 (1900): 12; "The Mountain Feud," *The Chautauqua Assembly* XXVII (August 11, 1903): 5; "University Extension in Kentucky," *The Outlook* (September 1898): 79; and "The College and the Feud," *Berea Quarterly* XVI (1913): 7.

86. James McConkey, *Rowan's Progress* (New York: Pantheon, 1992); O. O. Howard, "Feuds," 786; James Anderson Burns, *The Crucible: A Tale of Kentucky Feuds* (Oneida, KY: Oneida Baptist Institute, 1938): 105; Hough, "Burns of the Mountains," 16.

87. Davis and Smyth, "Land of Feuds," 172; Litsey, "Kentucky Feuds," 287.

88. See *Louisville Courier Journal*, February 2, 1933, p. 1; December 5, 1943, pp. 3, 2.

89. Shapiro, *Appalachia*, 102; Eller, *Miners*; "Cause of Kentucky Feuds . . . Railroads Much Needed," *New York Times*, December 3, 1899, p. 17.

90. Edward W. Said, *Culture and Imperialism* (New York: Vintage, 1994): xxiii, xxii.

91. Bruce Barton, "Children of the Feudists," *Collier's Weekly* 51 (August 23, 1913): 8.

92. Said, *Culture*, xiii. For further discussion of Clay County feud narratives as cultural imperialism, see Dwight Billings and Kathleen Blee, " 'Where the Sun Set Crimson and the Moon Rose Red': Writing Appalachia and the Kentucky Mountain Feuds," *Southern Cultures* 21 (1996): 329-52.

Epilogue

1. Brown, *Beech Creek*.

2. Ronald D. Eller with Phil Jenks, Chris Jasparro, and Jerry Napier, *Kentucky's Distressed Communities: A Report on Poverty in Appalachian Kentucky*. Report of the Appalachian Center (Lexington: University of Kentucky, 1994); Richard A. Couto, *An American Challenge: A Report on Economic Trends and Social Issues in Appalachia* (Dubuque, IA: Kendall/Hunt, 1994).

3. Couto, *American Challenge*.

4. Andrew M. Isserman, "Appalachia Then and Now: An Update of 'The Realities of Deprivation' Report to the President in 1964," *Journal of Appalachian Studies* 3 (1977): 43-70.

5. Remarkable agreement on the descriptive characteristics of extractive peripheries in the United States and the world system exists among researchers of diverse theoretical orientations. Compare Stephen Bunker, "Modes of Extrac-

tion, Unequal Exchange, and the Progressive Underdevelopment of an Extreme Periphery: The Brazilian Amazon, 1600-1980," *American Journal of Sociology* 89 (1984): 1017-64; Candice Howes and Ann R. Markuson, "Poverty: A Regional Political Economy Perspective," in A. Hawley and S. Mills, eds., *Nonmetropolitan America in Transition* (Chapel Hill: University of North Carolina Press, 1981), 437-63; Richard Krannich and A. E. Luloff, "Problems of Resource Dependency in U.S. Rural Communities," in Andrew W. Gilg, David Briggs, Robert Dilley, Owen Furuseth, and Geoff McDonald, eds., *Progress in Rural Policy and Planning 1* (London and New York: Belhaven Press, 1991), 5-18; Jeffrey D. Sachs and Andrew M. Warner, "Natural Resource Abundance and Economic Growth," Development Discussion Paper 517a, Harvard Institute for International Development, Harvard University, 1995; and Working Group on Natural Resources, "Theories in the Study of Natural Resource-Dependent Communities and Persistent Rural Poverty in the United States," in Rural Sociological Society Task on Persistent Rural Poverty, *Persistent Poverty in Rural America* (Boulder, Co: Westview Press, 1993), 136-72.

6. The opening words of the Appalachian Regional Commission's Report to the President in 1963 are quoted in Isserman, "Appalachia Then and Now," 43.

7. Couto, *American Challenge*, 88.

8. Ibid., 89.

9. Reflecting the lack of economic diversification, manufacturing and service sector employment in Clay County is much lower than in Appalachian Kentucky as a whole. Manufacturing in the county accounts for only 6.3% of jobs and an even lower percent of nonfarm income (4.6%) compared to 15.3 and 17.3%, respectively, throughout the mountain counties of Kentucky. Although service sector jobs increased by 40% in eastern Kentucky during the 1980s as jobs in manufacturing and mining disappeared, Clay County's service sector was one of two in the region that increased by less than 10% during the same period, despite declining employment in the other sectors. Transfer payments play a great role in the local economy, yet despite a poverty rate of almost 46%, only 24% of the population in the South Fork district, which includes Clay County, receives public income assistance (Eller et al., *Distressed Communities*). This disparity between income and assistance suggests the importance of a local "informal" economy for survival outside the official contours of public and private provisioning. According to Couto, *American Challenge*, 97, 18.4% of Appalachian per capita income in 1989 resulted from transfer payments in comparison with a national level of 14.6%. For a graphic description of the dependence of business activity upon transfer payments in Clay County during the late 1960s, see Bill Peterson's description of "check day" in Manchester in *Coaltown Revisited: An Appalachian Notebook* (Chicago: Regnery, 1972). Although growing illegal drugs may have little direct impact on the region's

poor, Clay County, along with neighbor counties Leslie and Owsley, was one of the top three marijuana producing counties in Kentucky for the period 1988-92 according to police eradication reports. See Bill Estep, "Fields of green: Kentucky's changing marijuana economy," a three-part series in the *Lexington Herald-Leader*, December 13, 1992, pp. A1, A8, A9; December 14, 1992, pp. A1, A8, A9; and December 15, 1992, pp. A1, A8. A regression analysis of variations among Appalachian Kentucky counties in marijuana eradication found that among twenty-one economic predictor variables, only county poverty rates explained any variance (16.5%). See Richard Clayton and William Estep, *Marijuana Cultivation and Production in the United States, Appalachia, and Kentucky: The Context and Consequences* (Geneva: United Nations Research Institute on Social Development, Switzerland, 1993).

10. Couto, *American Challenge*, 44, 46 41.
11. Isserman, "Appalachia Then and Now," 45.
12. See Mary Beth Pudup, "Town and Country in the Transformation of Appalachian Kentucky," in Pudup et al., *Appalachia*, 270-96, for an analysis of early settlement patterns and town development as features of changing patterns of agriculture and industrialization.
13. Couto, *American Challenge*, 9.
14. Ibid., 10.
15. Couto does, however, address Appalachian community resources and struggles for social justice in a book entitled *Which Side Are You On? Mediating Structures, Social Capital, and the Democratic Prospect* (Chapel Hill: University of North Carolina Press, forthcoming).
16. Wilma Dunaway interprets her work on antebellum capitalist development as "debunking the subsistence homesteader myth" (*First American Frontier*, 123). Paul Salstrom makes different assumptions, however, in another quantitative analysis of nineteenth-century agriculture that stresses the prevalence of subsistence farming throughout the Cumberland-Allegheny plateau as we do here. See Paul Salstrom, *Appalachia's Path to Dependency: Rethinking a Region's Economic History, 1730-1940* (Lexington: University Press of Kentucky, 1994).
17. The applicability of Brown's description of Beech Creek to many of the farming communities of the Allegheny-Cumberland plateau can been affirmed by comparing data on Beech Creek to farming patterns described in U.S. Department of Agriculture, *Economic and Social Problems and Conditions of the Southern Appalachians*, Miscellaneous Publication No. 205 (Washington, DC: U.S. Government Printing Office, 1935), which documents the predominance of subsistence farming in Appalachia. See also P. G. Beck and M. C. Forster, *Six Rural Problem Areas Relief-Resources-Rehabilitation*, Research Monograph I (Washington, DC: Federal Emergency Relief Administration, 1935).
18. See Salstrom, *Appalachia's Path*, 60-82.

19. Allen Batteau, "Mosbys and Broomsedge: The Semantics of Class in an Appalachian Kinship System," *American Ethnologist* 9 (1982): 463.

20. Rhoda H. Halperin, *The Livelihood of Kin: Making Ends Meet "The Kentucky Way."* (Austin: University of Texas Press, 1990), 2, 146.

21. For a sense of the extent and range of these movements, compare Stephen L. Fisher, ed., *Fighting Back in Appalachia: Traditions of Resistance and Change* (Philadelphia: Temple University Press, 1993), to Mary Ann Hinsdale, Helen M. Lewis, and S. Maxine Waller, *It Comes from the People: Community Development and Local Theology* (Philadelphia: Temple University Press, 1995), and Couto, *Which Side.*

22. Stephen L. Fisher, "New Populist Theory and the Study of Dissent in Appalachia," in Fisher, *Fighting Back*, 320, 319.

23. Quoted in Couto, *Which Side.*

24. Batteau, "Mosbys and Broomsedge," 450, 451. See also Cynthia Duncan, "Persistent Poverty in Appalachia: Scarce Work and Rigid Stratification," in Cynthia Duncan, ed., *Rural Poverty in America* (New York: Auburn House, 1992): 111-34.

25. Allen Batteau, "Legitimacy in the Appalachian Local Polity," paper presented at Southern Anthropological Society annual meeting, 1978, p. 9; quoted by permission of the author.

26. Couto, *Which Side.*

27. Robert D. Putnam, *Making Democracy Work: Civic Traditions in Modern Italy* (Princeton: Princeton University Press, 1993). For an empirical test of the relationship between social capital and economic development efforts in the United States, see Jan Flora, Jeff Sharp, Cornelia Flora, Bonnie Newlon, and Tom Bailey, "Entrepreneurial Social Infrastructure and Locally-Initiated Economic Development," *The Sociological Quarterly* 38 (1997): 623-46.

28. Habermas's theory of the colonization of the lifeworld by bureaucratic and market steering mechanisms is presented in *The Theory of Communicative Action*, 2 vols. (Boston: Beacon Press, 1995).

29. Filippo Sabetti, "Path Dependency and Civic Culture: Some Lessons from Italy about Interpreting Social Experiments," *Politics and Society* 24 (1996): 19-44. See also in the same issue other cogent critiques by Ellis Goldberg and Margaret Levi.

30. Edward C. Banfield, *The Moral Basis of a Backward Society* (Glencoe, IL: The Free Press, 1968).

31. Weller, *Yesterday's People*, 32.

32. James S. Brown, "The Social Organization of an Isolated Kentucky Mountain Neighborhood," Ph.D. diss., Harvard University, 1950, 162. Brown told us that he did not probe Beech Creekers about the Clay County feuds because he discerned considerable tension among them whenever he brought up the topic.

Our research shows that at least one person in Beech Creek was killed by feud-related violence.

33. Nicos P. Mouzelis, *Politics in the Semi-Periphery: Early Parlimentarism and Late Industrialization in the Balkans and Latin America* (London: Macmillan, 1986).

34. The quotation is from G. Isreal and L. Beaulieu, "Community Leadership," in A. E. Luloff and L. E. Swanson, eds., *American Rural Communities* (Boulder, Co: Westview Press, 1990), as quoted in Louis E. Swanson, "Social Infrastructure and Economic Development," in Tom Rowley, David Sears, Glenn Nelson, Norman Reid, and Marvin Yetley, eds., *Rural Development Research* (Westport, CT: Greenwood Press, 1996): 113.

35. Altina L. Waller, "Feuding in Appalachia: Evolution of a Cultural Stereotype," in Pudup et al., *Appalachia*, 347-76.

36. Compare Mouzelis, *Politics in the Semi-Periphery*; James C. Scott, "Patron-Client Politics and Political Change in Southeast Asia," in Steffen W. Schmidt et al., eds., *Friends, Followers, and Factions: A Reader in Political Clientelism* (Berkeley: University of California Press, 1977): 123-46; Susan Purcell, "Mexico: Clientelism, Corporatism, and Political Stability," in S. N. Eisenstadt and Rene Lemarchand, eds., *Political Clientelism, Patronage and Development* (Beverly Hills: Sage, 1981): 191-216; and Mario Caciagli and Frank Belloni, "The 'New' Clientelism in Southern Italy: The Christian Democratic Party in Catania," in Eisenstadt and Lemarchand, *Political Clientelism*, 35-55.

37. Douglas O'Neil Arnett, "Eastern Kentucky: The Politics of Dependency and Underdevelopment," Ph.D. diss., Duke University, 1978.

38. Arnett was in an excellent position to report on both movements since he was active in both, first as president of the Clay County Development Association and later as executive director of the Clay County Community Action Agency. For additional background on political parties and patronage in Kentucky, see Malcolm Jewell and Everett Cunningham, *Kentucky Politics* (Lexington: University Press of Kentucky, 1968).

39. Arnett, "Eastern Kentucky," 137-8.

40. Huey Perry, *"They'll Cut Off Your Project": A Mingo County Chronicle* (New York: Praeger, 1972). For another graphic description of Mingo County's local government, see Bill Peterson, "The Courthouse Gang," in *Coaltown Revisited* (Chicago: Regnery, 1972): 204-22.

41. Quoted in Arnett, "Eastern Kentucky:" 204.

42. Ibid., 172. Although the New Deal falls outside the temporal focus of our study, Jerry Bruce Thomas's study of *An Appalachian New Deal: West Virginia in the Great Depression* (Lexington: University Press of Kentucky, 1998), 3, supports our stress on the importance of the local state by showing how in West Virginia "local issues and powerful interest groups stood in the way" of national reform initiatives.

43. Associated Press, "Anti-poverty agency rented vans to wealthy, report says," *Lexington Herald-Leader*, January 26, 1997, p. B3. See also Karen Samples, "Material didn't all go to poor, poverty agency workers say," *Lexington Herald-Leader*, January 30, 1997, p. A9; idem, "Attorney: Let poverty agency chief give his side," *Lexington Herald-Leader*, January 17, 1997, pp. B1, B5.

44. Karen Samples, "Anti-poverty groups face questions over priorities," *Lexington Herald-Leader*, February 16, 1997, pp. A1, A14; and idem, "Some who represent poor are well-off," *Lexington Herald-Leader*, February 16, 1997, p. A14.

45. Karen Samples, "Manchester mayor sold cars to city, broke law," *Lexington Herald-Leader*, April 17, 1994, pp. A1, A12. See also Lee Mueller, "Manchester official upset that new law didn't close loophole," *Lexington Herald-Leader*, October 11, 1994, pp. A1, A4; and (unsigned), "No cure in sight: Business as usual in Manchester," *Lexington Herald-Leader,* April 19, 1994, p. A10.

46. Samples, "Mayor sold cars."

47. Karen Samples, "Grant fixed up house owned by councilwoman's daughter," *Lexington Herald-Leader*, April 17, 1994, p. A12. Profiteering from public office and services for the poor may both go back very far in the county's history. As we noted in the previous chapter, an investigation of relief for the "feeble-minded poor" in Kentucky in the late 1920s, for instance, revealed that the state-funded rates of relief for "pauper idiots" in a number of mountain counties were unimaginably high. Under this system of relief, financial support for these poor was awarded by county courts directly to "committees," generally local merchants who were not required to account for their expenditures of the funds and who, according to the report, found the "pauper idiot" to be "the lever wherewith to secure public funds." Clay County's rate of support for these poor was the highest among all Kentucky counties surveyed. See Arthur Estabrook, "The Pauper Idiot in Kentucky," *Social Forces* 7 (1928), 68-72.

48. Karen Samples, "Scandal might affect Letcher murder cases," *Lexington Herald-Leader*, November 16, 1993, pp. A1, A9; "Justice embarrassed: Letcher court scandal grows and grows," *Lexington Herald-Leader*, November 17, 1993, p. A12; Bill Bishop, "In Letcher, the corny truth leads to better government," *Lexington Herald-Leader*, October 5, 1994, p. A11; Associated Press, "Letcher schools chief responds to charges," *Lexington Herald-Leader*, May 6, 1994; see also Jay Grelen, "Letcher County optimistic inquiry making difference," *Lexington Herald-Leader*, November 29, 1992, pp. A1, A10.

49. See the following articles in the *Lexington Herald-Leader*: "Clay men indicted in

vote-buying," October 15, 1993, p. B3; Lee Mueller, "11 more in Magoffin face vote-fraud charges," November 16, 1993, pp. A1, A8; Lee Mueller and Robert Campbell, "Ex-sheriff accused of jury-rigging," September 21, 1994, pp. A1, A7; Karen Samples, "Leslie judge-executive criticized over handling of fuel bids," September 6, 1994, pp. B1, B4; "Timeline," Special Reprint, March 3, 1994, pp. 4, 5; Lee Mueller, "Lee sheriff, 24 others indicted on drug charges," February 19, 1994, pp. A1, A6; "Breathitt Sheriff hit with second indictment," December 19, 1996, p. C3.

50. Bill Estep, "Hiring of family members widespread, survey shows," *Lexington Herald-Leader* (Special Reprint), March 3, 1994, pp. 3, 5; Lee Mueller, "Martin jailer keeps mom, pop tradition," *Lexington Herald-Leader* (Special Reprint), March 3, 1994, pp. 3, 4; Lee Mueller, "Martin ethics code draft allows hiring of one relative," *Lexington Herald-Leader*, September 23, 1994, p. A6.

51. Lee Mueller, "Pike officials strike blacktop gold," *Lexington Herald-Leader* (Special Reprint), March 3, 1994, pp. 16, 19.

52. Karen Samples, "Secret, slapdash meetings obstacles to democracy, some Kentuckians say," *Lexington Herald-Leader*, Otober 4, 1993, p. A1. This report was prompted in part by efforts of an important grassroots organization, the Kentucky Local Governance Project, which is dedicated to local-level democratic reform.

53. See the following articles and editorials in the *Lexington Herald-Leader*: Gail Gibson, "Federal economic zone unrest continuing," December 19, 1996, pp. A1, A10; Gail Gibson, "Building of Cagle's plant may be delayed, " December 19, 1996, p. C1; Bob Geiger, "Gore plays down empowerment zone problems," February 23, 1996, p. B3; "Weak local oversight," November 21, 1995, p. A18; Gail Gibson, "Jackson report criticizes empowerment zone officials," February 8, 1997, pp. A1, A10; "Ill at ease with EZ," February 11, 1997, p. A8.

54. See Peter Evans and John D. Stephens, "Development and the World Economy," in Smelser, *Handbook of Sociology*.

55. MDC, *The State of the South: A Report to the Region and its Leadership* (Chapel Hill, NC: 1996), 17.

56. Whisnant, *Modernizing the Mountaineer*, 146.

57. Ernest Jasmin, "Families are focus of E. Ky. program," *Lexington Herald-Leader*, March 23, 1994, Community p. 9. This exemplary program is also described in Couto, *Which Side*.

58. Karen Samples, "Owsley unites for its future: Activists struggling to bring growth, jobs," *Lexington Herald-Leader*, January 20, 1997, pp. C1, C3.

59. Quoted in Couto, *Which Side*.

60. Eller et al., *Kentucky's Distressed Communities*.

Appendix 1

1. Robert C. Kenzer, *Kinship and Neighborhood in a Southern Community: Orange County, North Carolina, 1849-1881* (Knoxville: University of Tennessee Press, 1987).
2. Steven Hahn, "The Unmaking of the Southern Yeomanry: The Transformation of the Georgia Upcountry, 1860-1890," in Jonathan Prude, ed., *The Country-side in the Age of Capitalist Transformation* (Chapel Hill: University of North Carolina, 1985), 79-203.

INDEX

427

Index

Index

White, Daniel Garrard, 117, 122
White, Daugh, 332
White, Daugherty, 80, 97, 277; agriculture, 76, 97, 190; Garrard-White feud, 119–20, 122, 125, 130, 290, 297; politics, 97, 118; salt manufacturing, 64, 67, 75; slave ownership, 211, 231
White, Eliza, 64
White, Ellen, 279
White, Hugh, 72, 80, 115–17, 205, 253, 329; commerce, 81–4, 89, 91–2, 95, 255; Garrard-White feud, 119–20; politics, 106–7, 109; salt manufacturing, 57, 64, 204, 250–1; slave ownership, 28, 211, 213
White, Hugh L. (son of Hugh) (d.1848), 89, 91
White, Hugh L. (grandson of Hugh), 253, 254, 276–7
White, J. H., 253
White, James (brother of Hugh), 56–7, 64, 69, 81–2, 84, 115
White, James (son of Hugh), 80, 118; agriculture, 76, 97, 190; Garrard-White feud, 122, 124–5, 127, 258; salt manufacturing, 64, 67; slave ownership, 95, 231
White, John (unrelated to Clay County Whites) 109, 115
White, John (1802–45) (Hugh's son), 57, 112, 127–8, 274, 277–8, 362 n.21
White, John C. 274–6, 279
White, John D., 57, 112, 118, 288, 296
White, John E., 282
White, John E. (1960s), 276, 329–30
White, John G., 276, 282, 292, 298
White, Laura R., 276–7, 310
White, S. P., 285

White, Susan, 119, 126–7; see also Abner Baker, Jr.
White, T. G., 300
White, Thomas, J., 275–6
White, William, 74, 119–20, 122, 211, 214
White, William Letcher, 253
White, William L.(sheriff), 301; Garrard-White feud, 283, 285–6, 288–9, 297–8, 308
White family, 176–8, 259; salt manufacturing, history of, 57, 64
Wilderness Road, 30, 44, 47, 67, 70, 243
Wilkinson, James, 41–2
Williams, Roger, 290
Williams, Sarah Johnson, see Johnson, Sarah
Williams, Sydney, 122
Wilson, George, 122
Wilson, John C., 107
Wilson, Samuel, 9
Wilson family, 132
Wolf, Eric, 131
women: business and commerce, 64, 260–2, 276–7, 405 n. 48; "femme sole," 261; and feuds, 309–10; and home manufacturing, 142, 169; living with nonkin, 233–6; occupations, 227–8; portrayal in print, 309–10; property ownership, 173, 229–30, 271; see also slavery
Woods, Elizabeth, 100
Woodward, James T., 64, 74, 92, 98, 125
Word, Sophia, 212–13
World War II, 316
Wright, Warren, 270
Wyncoop, Benjamin, 116

Yesterday's People: Life in Contemporary Appalachia, 10, 29, 113